D0114528

OVITZ

OVITZ

*The Inside Story of Hollywood's
Most Controversial Power Broker*

ROBERT SLATER

McGRAW-HILL

New York   San Francisco   Washington, D.C.   Auckland   Bogotá
Caracas   Lisbon   London   Madrid   Mexico City   Milan
Montreal   New Delhi   San Juan   Singapore
Sydney   Tokyo   Toronto

Library of Congress Cataloging-in-Publication Data

Slater, Robert, date.
    Ovitz / Robert Slater.
        p.   cm.
    ISBN 0-07-058103-7
    1. Ovitz, Michael.   2. Theatrical agents—United States—
Biography.   3. Executives—United States—Biography.   I. Title.
PN2287.078S62   1997
659.2'9781'092—dc21
[B]   97-13046
                                                                       CIP

McGraw-Hill   &

A Division of The McGraw·Hill Companies

1 2 3 4 5 6 7 8 9 0   DOC/DOC   9 0 2 1 0 9 8 7

ISBN 0-07-058103-7

Credits for Photo Insert: (*page 1, wedding photo*): Courtesy of Michael and
Judy Ovitz and Wachsman-Staley Photography; (*page 2, top, CAA founders*):
© Berliner Studios; (*page 3, top, Robert Redford and Michael Ovitz*): © Lee
Salem; (*page 3, bottom, Paul Newman and Michael Ovitz*): Courtesy of Chris
Hunter; (*page 4, top, CAA atrium*): © Groskinsky; (*page 4, bottom, Tom Hanks
with Michael and Judy Ovitz*): © Berliner Studios; (*page 5, top, Arne Glimcher,
Julian Schnabel, and Michael Ovitz*): © Berliner Studios; (*page 6, top, President
Clinton and Michael Ovitz*): © Berliner Studios; (*page 6, bottom, Martin Scorsese
and Michael Ovitz*): Courtesy of Michael Ovitz and Martin Scorsese; (*page 8,
Michael Eisner and Michael Ovitz*): © Alan Berliner/Gamma Liaison. All other
photos courtesy of Michael and Judy Ovitz.

This book is dedicated to my wife Elinor,
For her love and support throughout the years.

Contents

The Search for Ovitz

WHILE I WAS writing this book, hundreds of people asked me why I had decided to write about Michael Ovitz. It's really pretty simple.

Over the past few years I've written a number of books on American business personalities. I began with a book on Jack Welch, the chairman of General Electric; then I turned to Wall Street investor George Soros; on to Jack Bogle, chairman of the Vanguard mutual fund group. Ovitz seemed like a natural follow-up: the single most powerful business figure in Hollywood, an enigmatic man whose full story had yet to be told.

Welch and Bogle cooperated with me, Soros did not. Two out of three wasn't bad. Anyway, I had gotten pretty spoiled. I had assumed, perhaps naively, that I was likely to get the cooperation of anyone I chose to write about. Yet the more I learned about Michael Ovitz, the less likely it seemed that I would get his cooperation. Sure, he had given a few newspaper and magazine interviews, but to him people like me simply were poison. He didn't even want to hear of us, much less *from* us. Yet I had to try.

December, 1995. I write Ovitz a letter, mostly as a courtesy to inform him that I am under contract to write a book about him and his career. I have little expectation that he will follow in the footsteps of Jack Welch and Jack Bogle and meet with me. I ask if I can interview him and his acquaintances. As it happens, my letter arrives on his desk just two months after Ovitz has become president of The Walt Disney Company, after resigning as chairman of Creative Artists Agency, which he had co-founded in 1975.

January 19, 1996. I follow up my letter with a phone call to Disney's Vice President for Corporate Communications, John Dreyer. Dreyer mentions that Ovitz has asked him to get copies of my previous business biographies.

Monday, January 29: 6 p.m. Michael Ovitz phones. *Interesting . . .* Getting a phone call from Ovitz is always an experience. First there comes a phone call in advance from his secretary, asking if you're going to be available for a phone call from Mr. Ovitz in forty-five minutes or whenever. *Will I be ready for a phone call from Michael Ovitz in forty-five minutes! Ah, yeah, I'll do my best to adjust my schedule. . . .*

I put myself on Red Alert, order a cup of coffee, and keep my cell phone at the ready. The phone rings at 6:00 p.m. sharp. "Mr. Ovitz is on the line." He is brief and to the point. He has looked over some books I have authored, found them to be fair and straightforward, and would like to meet with me to discuss my project. We agree to meet in mid-March.

Wednesday, March 13: 4:15 p.m. The meeting takes place at Ovitz's office in Disney headquarters in Burbank, California. He asks right off the bat, "Why me?" He talks about himself for a while, saying that he finds it amusing that others think him so powerful. He has never thought of himself as the dominant force in Hollywood. I suppose that this is his way of saying he isn't worth writing about. He says that he has never cooperated with anyone on a book project about himself, though he has been approached a number of times; he has "mixed emotions" about the whole thing. He promises to phone me the next day, to let me know whether he will be able to cooperate with me.

Thursday, March 14: 4:30 p.m. Ovitz calls to say that he still isn't ready to say yes. But he adds that he has reread my book *The New GE: How Jack Welch Revived an American Institution,* and is now "leaning" toward cooperating. He promises to have a final answer for me within the next twenty-four hours.

Friday, March 15: 4:25 p.m. True to his word, he calls me in the afternoon to say that he has decided "to do this." He is warmer, friendlier than he was in the phone conversation of the day before. He says he plans to spend the weekend putting together a list of 25 names of people he feels I should interview, plus their phone numbers. I can get the list from his office on Monday. He says he has no objection to my talking to others not on the list, if I choose to do so.

Monday, March 18: 12:30 p.m. I call Ovitz's office and ask if the list is ready. I'm told that it will be soon. When an Ovitz aide hands me the list, I am flabbergasted. For what I find there are the names not of 25 Ovitz friends, but 70 of the most famous stars in Hollywood. What a list! It includes

Sean Connery
Paul Newman
Tom Cruise
Robin Williams
Magic Johnson
Jerry Seinfeld
David Letterman
Sydney Pollack
Barry Levinson

2:00 p.m. I'm eager to get started with the research for the book, not knowing how long it may take me to see all the people on Ovitz's list. I'm reasonably sure that most will insist on obtaining Ovitz's approval before they consent to speak to me. So that afternoon, in order to get the ball rolling, I place 20 phone calls.

5:20 p.m. The phone rings. Sean Connery? David Letterman? I can't wait to find out. A woman's voice. So far, so good. "Mr. Ovitz is on the line." *Mr. Ovitz? Why is he calling?* I can't imagine. I listen to the voice, not at all the same voice I had heard just three days before. This time I hear anger and fury and pain. I don't have to be a genius to know that something is wrong. *Very* wrong. The barrage of words stuns me. I have trouble focusing on what he is actually saying. The last thing I have expected is an angry phone call from Ovitz, certainly not this early on.

Listening to him carefully, I slowly begin to reconstruct what has happened. He was away from his office all day. Returning in the afternoon, he found phone messages from most of the people I had just called. They wanted to know if Ovitz wanted them to speak to me. He was furious that I had phoned so many of those on the list so quickly. *Why is he so steamed? Didn't he expect me to call these people? He's the one who gave me the list. What was I supposed to do, sit on it?*

Never letting up, never giving me a chance to get a word in, he sputters that I have done something terrible, that these people will talk to each other and leak to the media the fact that he is cooperating on a book about himself. He tells me that such "instant publicity" will upset him very much, because it will look like he's trying to promote himself through my book. You might say I was "confused," but that would be an understatement. I was dumbfounded. What kind of a person *was* he?

Here I am trying to write a book about him, and within hours of the project getting under way, he's lacing into me as if I have committed some terrible crime.

He keeps saying to me, "Take ten. Take ten." Meaning what? Take ten minutes off, as a breather? Call only ten people on the list? There was no way to know, and I was afraid to ask. He said he would meet with me next week. Next week seemed *very* far off. I felt that we needed to talk right away, and in a calmer atmosphere. But how could I calm him down? Was it even my business to try? All I could think was: *I'm trying to write a book about what Michael Ovitz is really like, and here he is providing me with the most insightful read-out of his personality imaginable. He has just explained himself very, very candidly to me by means of all these stinging remarks.* I have an ominous feeling that I haven't heard the last from the very perturbed Mr. Ovitz.

7:00 p.m. Michael Crichton is on the line. Author of *Jurassic Park* and *Disclosure* and *The Lost World. That* Michael Crichton. He had been in that first batch of 20 phone calls. He said he would be happy to meet with me. *Now* what was I supposed to do? Ovitz was telling me to "Take ten," and yet the most successful novelist in America was expressing an interest in talking to me. Was I supposed to tell Crichton that, despite my earlier request for an interview, *I* couldn't see *him?* I decided to let Crichton be one of the "ten" whom Ovitz had admonished me to "take." We agreed to meet the next day at 3:00 p.m.

Tuesday, March 18: 12:30 p.m. Lunching with a friend, I hear the phone ring again. This time it's an Ovitz aide, sounding a lot friendlier than Ovitz had the day before and passing on a message. "Mr. Ovitz wants you to stop phoning anyone else on the list until he has a chance to talk to you." Now I was *really* upset. I quickly became the world's worst luncheon companion. My friend went chirping along with all the juiciest Hollywood gossip, and all I could think was: *I'm supposed to meet Michael Crichton in a few hours, and Ovitz has just asked me to steer clear of his list.* What a predicament!

3:00 p.m. I interview Michael Crichton for two hours. What a treat! As he moves his six-foot-nine-inch frame around his home in Santa Monica, ducking beneath the arches, I wonder, *why didn't he choose a house with higher arches?* More to the point, why hadn't I chosen a subject for a book who wouldn't flip-flop on me, as Ovitz was doing?

5:30 p.m. I'm on the phone to Los Angeles Mayor Richard Riordan, one of the people on Ovitz's list. He happily consented to an interview the first time I made the request, and now he is eagerly extolling Ovitz's virtues as my cell phone rings. "Mr. Ovitz is on the line." *Great . . . What do I tell the*

Mayor? What do I tell Ovitz? More importantly, what is Ovitz going to tell *me?* I quickly get off the phone with the city's top politician and wait for Michael Ovitz to come on the line.

I listen to that voice again. Just as angry as the last time. Just as upset with me. But now he's leaning toward not cooperating with me, he says. All those phone calls to his office the day before have "spooked" him. He promises to phone me tomorrow with his final decision. I greatly doubt whether I will ever hear from Michael Ovitz again.

Wednesday, March 20. No phone call from Ovitz. Surprise, surprise . . .

The pause in my schedule gives me a chance to reflect on what is happening. Ovitz cares about his image. I have a book to write. How can I ever reconcile his problems with mine? I now know that under any circumstances I am going to write this book. But I don't just *want* Ovitz's cooperation, I *need* it. You don't research a book about Michael Ovitz and expect anyone close to him to agree to be interviewed unless he says it's okay. Nonetheless, I'm determined to try to carry on my research even without his cooperation. I begin phoning numerous people not on the Ovitz list. A few days pass. No phone call from Ovitz. Not much in the way of response from those I have reached out to, either.

Monday, March 25: 5:40 p.m. In 20 minutes the 68th annual Academy Awards will be beamed out to hundreds of millions of people all around the world. It's the biggest day of the year for Hollywood. The last thing in the world I am expecting is to hear from any Hollywood personality. Many have spent the day in beauty salons, many trying on their Armani tuxedos. Returning a phone call to an author would be the lowest of priorities on Oscar night. As for Michael Ovitz, I picture him as being on his way to the ceremonies, hoping that The Walt Disney Company, of which he is president, will have a great night.

The phone rings. By now, that has become a sound I'm not at all fond of. The last few times I've heard it, an angry voice has come on the line to tell me that I'm being too zealous and too aggressive. I have been hoping for some silence.

"Michael Ovitz wants to talk to you," the voice on the line says. This can only be a joke. *Twenty minutes from now, the Oscars begin. Why would he phone me? What is there left to say, anyway?*

A friendly male voice comes on the line. Calm. Easy to listen to. It sounds a lot like Michael Ovitz's voice. After a few seconds I conclude that it really is Ovitz on the line, but a new Ovitz, an easier one to talk to. He acts almost as if our last phone call never took place. He never says that he has changed his mind and will indeed cooperate with me. I can tell by his tone that he is giving serious thought to helping me with this project. He asserts that if he does decide to cooperate, I will have to take my time in phoning people on the list, to prevent them from discussing the project with one another. He remains concerned that his cooperation with the book will become news. He wants to keep thinking about whether he will cooperate, and he will phone me in a day or so.

April 12, Decision Day. Ovitz phones to say that he now is prepared to go ahead and cooperate with the book. He agrees to meet with me the following month, so that I can conduct the first formal interview.

He invites me to dinner at his home in Los Angeles on May 29. Given my past ups and downs with Ovitz, all sorts of worst-case scenarios ran through my head. *We will have dinner, all right, but it will be with his wife and three children, and there will be no actual interview.* Or: *The dinner will turn out to be one of those famous repasts chez Ovitz where I'll be sandwiched between Dustin Hoffman and Warren Beatty but again, there will be no actual interview.*

As I pull up to Ovitz's home in the Brentwood section of Los Angeles, I search for a batch of cars and to my relief find none. After being let in, I see Ovitz, who introduces me to his wife Judy. Then he and I go off for dinner in his living room, just the two of us at the table. Judy and the three Ovitz children occasionally drop by the table, but for the next two hours he answers numerous questions about his childhood, college days, and the early phases of his business career. In the following months we get together frequently: twice in July at his Disney office in Burbank; once in September over the phone; once in October over lunch at his home; twice by phone in January 1997, and twice more that same month in his New York City apartment. I also accompany him on his private jet from Chicago to Bermuda on October 12, 1996, where he gives a speech to the American Magazine Publishers conference. We have ample time to chat during the plane flights.

All through my research and my many conversations with Ovitz, I retain a clear sense of how remarkable it is that I actually have obtained Ovitz's cooperation. For this has been not only Hollywood's most powerful figure, but also its most secretive. Throughout his career, which has spanned two decades, he has refused almost all requests for interviews with journalists and authors. In the few conversations he *has* held with this or that member of the media, almost all of them were conducted on an off-the-record basis. Not wanting to get on the bad side of a man who controls so much of the flow of Hollywood's business, nearly all of his close acquaintances refuse to talk publicly about Ovitz without first getting his permission to do so. As a result, though the media have a huge appetite for details about Ovitz's life and career, scarcely any details ever emerge in print.

Making the project even more exciting, the period of my research turns out to coincide with one of the most convulsive in Ovitz's career. He has barely begun working as president of The Walt Disney Company when I introduce myself to him by letter. Over the next year, as I meet extensively with him, as well as interview his business colleagues, his wife Judy, and his parents David and Sylvia Ovitz, Michael Ovitz embarks on a new phase of his career by helping to run one of America's most important entertainment companies. The experiment proves to be an unsuccessful one. He spends the year largely avoiding the media, but cheerfully submitting himself to lengthy interviews with me about all phases of his business career. He calls our sessions "therapeutic" but it is only when his troubles at Disney deepen toward the end of 1996 that I begin to understand what he means: By taking him back to the past, to his glory days, I am unintentionally helping him to put his current agonies in perspective.

It takes me a while to appreciate just how important it is to Michael Ovitz that I meet with the people on his list. As I expected, many call Ovitz first, to check whether it's okay for them to be interviewed. One interview subject says he has phoned Ovitz three times, because, although Ovitz had told him in the first two phone conversations that it was all right to talk to me, he still can't believe that Ovitz actually has approved the interview! Sculptor Joel Shapiro tells me that he has called Ovitz and said, "I assume you don't want me to see him." To which Ovitz replied, "Actually, I do." Earvin "Magic" Johnson told me that Ovitz had called him five times to make sure that Johnson did see me.

On December 13, 1996, one day before his fiftieth birthday, Michael Ovitz resigned as president of The Walt Disney Company. We had not spoken in the weeks leading up to this momentous decision, for I had begun work on the early drafts of this book. Five days after he resigned, he asked an aide to phone me. Clearly, he wanted me to understand that he wasn't feeling gloomy or depressed over the Disney departure.

Indeed he felt, according to his aide, relieved. He had many offers to contemplate, and he planned to take a few weeks' vacation, then call me to resume our interviewing.

Meanwhile, as word of his multi-million-dollar severance package spread, the name Michael Ovitz was being bandied about at every water cooler in America. People were both astounded and annoyed that the package was so astronomical. As was his custom, Ovitz said nothing at the time. He didn't speak in public about the severance issue, nor for that matter about anything connected to his last year at Disney. (During his entire 14 months at Disney, he gave no one-on-one interviews.)

And yet throughout his tumultuous year at Disney, Ovitz had conducted a series of lengthy interviews with me. In the early interviews he made no overt comment that reflected his inner feeling: that he was not long for the Disney job. Later on, however, he began to hint that he might be leaving Disney, by suggesting to me that something big was in the works for him but that he could not speak about it quite yet.

Then, in December 1996, came the departure from Disney, the controversy over the severance pay, and Ovitz's public silence about all of these matters. Throughout January we continued to talk, but I knew that if he ever did agree to talk about his year at Disney, it would only be at the very end of our interviews. When I at last broached the subject, he asked me if I really planned to include the Disney experience in the book. "Oh yes," I said, "there's no way I can omit such a crucial part of your career." He said that he wanted to think about what, if anything, he wanted to say on the subject, and that he would let me know. Eventually he did decide to talk to me about it. When we met at his New York City apartment, I began firing questions at him. To my amazement, he talked with great candor and emotion about the dreadful 14-month period he had just gone through. He was as angry with himself as he was with those others who had in fact brought about his downfall at Disney. In some ways he was his old frenetic self again, scheduling our interviews on days in which he ran from one meeting to the next. But there was no question that this was a chastened Michael Ovitz, proud of what he had accomplished in the past but uncharacteristically angry at himself for having dived so precipitously into the Disney experience.

1

The Aspen Blues

SEPTEMBER 5, 1996.

Michael Ovitz has been sitting in the conference room at the Little Nell Hotel in Aspen, Colorado, for the past few hours, listening to one person after another address the crowd. He's feeling pretty good, better than he's felt for many months. Outside the air is fresh and cool, and a gentle wind is blowing in off the mountains in the distance.

For the past few days, the 100 senior executives of The Walt Disney Company have been meeting in order to hold a discussion of business ethics. No one really wants to deal with the topic. Most of the executives simply are wishing that today's meeting will end soon, so they can get out into that fresh mountain air.

Ovitz wants out too. Not just out of the conference room, but out of the whole damned company. The last few months have been a hell for him. Few outside the conference room know just how bad it has been for him. But he knows, and he can't tell from one day to the next whether he'll be able to take the abuse any longer.

He wants to tough it out. And every once in a while there are indications that Disney Chairman Michael Eisner may be willing to keep Ovitz on and to make the thing work. When Eisner is in a good mood, as he has been these past few days at Aspen, Ovitz thinks that maybe, just maybe, he'll survive in his new job. Maybe the worst really is over.

To the outside world, Ovitz's first year as president of The Walt Disney Company seemed to be going all right—the road had proved a bit bumpy, to be sure, but not one that couldn't level itself out over time. Ovitz seemed bound for success in the new job. He had rarely failed during his long career, and there was every expectation that, as one of the most powerful figures in Hollywood and someone who seemingly could do no wrong, he was destined for ever more power, more glory.

Indeed, to all those who were looking in at the Disney entertainment empire from the outside, the odds seemed to be at least even that Michael Ovitz would take over the entire company from Chairman Michael Eisner, thereby raising his illustrious career to even grander heights.

The two men had been close friends for 20 years. They and their wives often had vacationed together, and when Eisner had been hospitalized two summers earlier with serious heart problems, Ovitz had rarely left his hospital bedside.

Nearly a year earlier, Eisner had handpicked Ovitz to become the company's president, and his heir-apparent. When the appointment was announced, the entertainment industry reacted with considerable surprise, if only because Ovitz continually had insisted that he never would work for someone else. For 20 years he had run Creative Artists Agency, the talent agency he and four other talent agents had founded, and over the past decade it had become the most formidable institution in Hollywood. Undeniably, Ovitz had been Hollywood's most powerful figure of the late eighties and early nineties, and now he was going to work for the new holder of that unofficial title.

It wouldn't be easy, for either man.

When he offered the job to his friend, Michael Eisner had promised Ovitz that he himself would carry out only ceremonial functions as Disney Chairman, thereby complying with his wife Jane's urgent plea that he take it easy and not tempt fate any further after experiencing such a serious setback. Jane had pressed her husband to hire Ovitz precisely so that Eisner could step back from the day-to-day running of the entertainment giant. Thus, Eisner insisted to Ovitz that it would be Ovitz who handled the day-to-day operations of the Disney empire.

And yet, it was not to be. Rather than stand down, Michael Eisner, sensing that he was cured, worked harder than ever and remained very much the man in charge at Disney. Eisner even canceled plans to take a vacation during the month of August 1996.

By April 1996, six months after he had begun the Disney job, it was clear to Ovitz that he had made a terrible mistake. From that point on, life became a living hell for him. It was filled with an unsubtle whispering campaign against him, staged by certain Disney executives; mounting attacks in the media; and worst of all, Michael Eisner's cold indifference toward him.

And yet, two months later, in June, Ovitz and Eisner had gone on a bicycling vacation together through the Loire Valley in France, and they had talked at length about how best to work out the kinks in their relationship. All through the summer, Ovitz kept hoping that Eisner would transfer his power to him.

And now, as he sits around a table on this September afternoon in Aspen, with Eisner seated at his side and Sandy Litvack, Executive Vice President, and Joe Roth, head of the Disney film studio, sitting across from him, Ovitz is beginning to feel optimistic.

It's hard to figure where that feeling can have come from, for as Ovitz gazes around the room at the crowd of executives, he feels at best like an outsider, at worst like some unwanted intruder. The Disney executives, most of them men, are seated six or seven to a table, and clearly they're getting itchy to leave the stuffy confines of the conference room and enjoy the magnificent mountainous surroundings.

But Michael Ovitz isn't quite ready to throw in the towel just yet. No way.

Perhaps it has been the encouraging words he heard from Michael Eisner when they were bicycling through the Loire Valley in France.

Or maybe it's Ovitz's stubborn streak, a trait that has led him to keep after movie stars day in and day out, until they have collapsed under his artillery barrage and signed themselves up as clients of his vaunted talent agency.

Or his conviction that, no matter how much venom his critics spit out in their attacks upon him, he is tougher than they are, he can outlast them, he will not give them the satisfaction of bringing him down.

And so, when it is Michael Ovitz's turn to make some off-the-cuff remarks to close the session for this day, he decides to give the executives an old-fashioned pep talk. Remaining seated in his chair, he talks about how important it is for there to be a level of trust in the company; there have been press leaks of late, and those have to stop. Internal matters have to remain just that: *internal.*

As he speaks, emotion begins to fill his voice.

And then it becomes clear to the others that he is referring to leaks that have been aimed at hurting him personally. Though he speaks only for five minutes, it seems as if he's rambling, going on for too long. Especially since Michael Eisner's comments, earlier on, lasted just a few minutes.

Wrapping up his thoughts, Ovitz urges the executives to support one another and, when they do talk to the media, to make sure they talk positively: The enemy, he says, should be outside, not inside. He hopes to nurture some sense of unity, if that is at all possible, and when he has concluded his remarks a number of executives approach Ovitz to say that they have appreciated what he has had to say.

Things are looking up. Ovitz breathes a little easier.

That evening, he and Eisner host a dinner. The mood is light, and the two men are back to their old habit of bantering with one another. For the first time in months, Ovitz feels that the troubled relationship just may find a way to resolve itself, and he will be able to stay on.

The next morning a fax arrives for him at his home in Aspen, and it contains a startling message. It's as if someone has thrown cold water on his face. The fax has come from a friend of his in New York, and it notes that one of the New York tabloids has carried an article saying that Ovitz has lambasted the Disney staff for talking to the media. He quickly recollects the hour at which yesterday's meeting ended, then calculates the time difference between Aspen and New York. He immediately realizes that someone at that meeting had enough time, an hour and a half before the newspaper's deadline, to run to the telephone and call someone at the newspaper.

Michael Ovitz feels betrayed.

For years he ran retreats at Creative Artists, and never once was there a leak. His staff at CAA knew better. Anyone foolhardy enough to talk to the media would have been fired on the spot. But the Disney executives feel no such fear of Ovitz, and he realizes that his pep talk has had no impact at all.

His words have been twisted out of shape and leaked to the media—precisely what he was asking the executives *not* to do. His hopes of remaining at Disney vanish the moment that fax arrives at his home. He keeps gazing at the fax, trying to decide whether he is more angry at Eisner or at himself. Somehow, it doesn't seem to matter.

Then he tries to analyze what has gone wrong.

This is stupid. *I have made the biggest mistake of my business career. It was* stupid *to think I could come in and change the culture at Disney.*

He thinks of his years of friendship with Michael Eisner.

He can't figure out why Eisner brought him into the company if he knew he was going to treat him with such disdain, promising him the world but delivering nothing. Ovitz goes to his desk and looks for some paper. He writes a six-page letter to Michael Eisner, the nub of it being the following few words: *This isn't going to work for me. We should talk about it.*

Four months later, on December 13, 1996, The Walt Disney Company announces that Michael Ovitz is leaving his position as president "by mutual consent." The phrase is a piece of diplomatic fiction. Ovitz never wanted to leave, he simply felt that he had no choice.

The Ovitz-Eisner breakup was big news everywhere, especially when it became clear that Michael Ovitz would receive millions of dollars in severance pay. One report in the *Los Angeles Times* suggested that Ovitz would get $50 million in cash and three million shares of stock options worth another $40 million—for a total of $90 million. Other reports put the figure as high as $120 million. As it turned out, the actual figure was even higher: a staggering $128 million!

The severance-pay controversy began to overshadow all other aspects of the story, including the issue of what Ovitz would do next. The columnists had a field day, berating Michael Eisner for rewarding someone so generously for essentially failing at a job. One columnist even went so far as to suggest that Eisner pay Ovitz the severance pay out of his own pocket, to save shareholders the burden of underwriting it.

Ovitz's departure from Disney began to loom very large for average Americans who previously had never heard of Michael Ovitz, as they expressed strong, decidedly negative opinions about his being rewarded so massively for failing at a job that had lasted only fourteen months. Once the most powerful figure in Hollywood, Michael Ovitz now had become "the guy Disney paid all that money to just to get rid of him." It was a low moment in his career, to put it mildly. Probably the lowest, and certainly the most controversial. The man who had ruled Hollywood had become an object of scorn. All sorts of questions were asked: How had he let this happen? How could he have risen so far and yet plummeted so dramatically? What would become of him? Was the curtain coming down for good on the career of Hollywood's most intriguing personality, or would it rise again?

2

King Ovitz

For Michael Ovitz, life only really seemed to get under way when he stepped onto the Universal Studios lot at the age of 17. Yet the real Michael Ovitz could be seen even earlier in life. He was an inquisitive child, to the point of sometimes being overbearing. A cheerful youngster, he was never a loner, always a joiner; he worked hard at whatever he did, and seemed to have natural leadership qualities. He credits his parents with always being there for him, always believing in him, always demanding that he try to do his best. He says that his father, David Ovitz, has been his only true mentor.

The early lives of Michael's parents, David and Sylvia Ovitz, paralleled the experiences of hundreds of thousands of other European Jews born early in the twentieth century.

Michael's paternal grandparents, Leon and Molly Ovitz, had been born in Vienna. Their son David was born in Chernovitz, Romania, on August 23, 1920, while the Ovitz family was on their way to board a ship that would take them to the United States. Six months later the Ovitz family arrived at Ellis Island. They settled in Chicago.

Michael's maternal grandfather, Morris Klene, was born in a town in Russia near the Crimean Sea, and his maternal grandmother, Sarah, was from Bialystok, in northeast Poland. At around the turn of the century Sarah's father reached New York with four of his five daughters, and five sons. Morris and Sarah, Sylvia's parents, arrived in the United States soon thereafter and settled in Chicago, where they opened a bakery. Sylvia, Michael's mother, was born on July 2, 1921.

David Ovitz met Sylvia through a cousin when both were in the eighth grade in Chicago. The two saw one another often, began dating in high school, and were married on May 17, 1942, in Chicago. Soon thereafter David began a three-and-a-half-year stint in the army, serving during World War II in Africa and Italy. Meanwhile, Sylvia worked for Science Research Associates, a vocational guidance testing service that developed college tests. Returning to the United States after the war, David began to work for Seagram's, distributing liquor all around Chicago to chain stores, bars, and clubs. They settled down on Chicago's north side, and their first son, Michael Steven, was born on December 14, 1946, at Passavant Hospital. Michael's brother Mark (now a television producer) was born on November 6, 1951.

Michael spent six months in a kindergarten, graduating from the Haugan School in May 1952. He was five and a half years old. That September the Ovitz family, including Sylvia's mother Sarah, moved to Encino, California, in the San Fernando Valley, in order to be close to Sarah's family and to take advantage of the town's new and inexpensive housing. The neighborhood in Encino, bordering another Los Angeles suburb, Van Nuys, was idyllic, a small enclave of 100 homes. Michael's elementary school was just four blocks away.

David Ovitz had long sought to run his own business and indeed was all set to become a partner in a liquor/grocery store—the Freeway Market. Unfortunately, six months after he arrived in Encino, the underwriters of the business pulled out and the project collapsed. A friend with a wholesale rug business asked David to come to work for him, which he did for the next three years. In 1955, David rejoined Seagram's as a liquor distributor. Sylvia was a housewife.

As a child, and in later years as well, Michael had an especially close relationship with his maternal grandmother Sarah. She was often, according to her daughter Sylvia, Michael's principal caretaker: He was like her child. Sarah was fluent in Yiddish, but because she had arrived in the United States at the age of nine, spoke English well. She and the boy conversed in English, never in Yiddish. "There was real affection between Michael and my mother," Sylvia Ovitz recalls. "He would sit in her room on her lap on her rocking chair, rocking with her and watching television." Sarah took him for long walks in his carriage. If David Ovitz tried to discipline his son, the little boy simply ran to his grandmother who rescued him from punishment. "He could do no wrong as far as my mother was concerned," says Sylvia Ovitz. "When I hit Michael on the behind, my mother would say: 'Your hand should fall off!' "

Michael was enrolled in a small elementary school located in a country house; it was small enough, Sylvia says, that "we knew all the parents." One of the brighter students at the school, he remained there through sixth grade, and graduated at the age of 12 in 1958. His mother was President of the Parents–Teachers Association. His father was an organizer of the town's Little League baseball program. His parents' activist attitude spurred Michael to be a joiner. "If there was something to be in," Sylvia Ovitz says, "Michael was always in it. But he wasn't a pushy kid." He was a member of the Cub Scouts for three years; in sixth grade he gave the Boy Scouts a try, but he didn't like it and quit after about a year.

In his childhood albums, one photograph shows Michael in a cowboy costume; another, sporting boxing gloves; and in a third, a group photo of his Little League team, on his white T-shirt is emblazoned "Teamsters 389 Indians." He looks like a happy kid.

Much of the Ovitzes' family life centered around baseball. "It was a way of life for us," says Sylvia Ovitz. Michael's father played a major role in creating Encino's Little League program—Encino Baseball, Incorporated—which eventually embraced 500 families. David Ovitz coached, umpired, and helped to divide the youngsters into teams. At the age of nine, Michael began to play in the program, at first in the American League, one of the program's four leagues. David and Sylvia never missed a game. Talented enough to make the all-star team, Michael was only a fair hitter but an excellent catcher, a position he filled throughout Little League and into Pony League, for the 14-year-olds and up. Why catcher? "He liked to be in the game all the time," David Ovitz observes. Clearly, Michael also liked to be in the center of things.

From age 9 to 13, Michael attended Hebrew school twice a week at the Valley Beth Shalom Temple. When he turned 13 in December 1959 he celebrated his Bar Mitzvah. The Hebrew school curriculum was of course focused on the biblical lands of Palestine, 10,000 miles away from Los Angeles—sufficiently foreign and exotic, one would think, for a young boy growing up in Encino. Maybe so, but not for Michael Ovitz. Thanks to a teacher named Miss Hillel, who wore braces on her legs and lectured about the Hindus and the Buddhists, he became mesmerized by another part of the world: the Far East. Not exactly what David and Sylvia Ovitz had in mind, when they sent their eldest son off to Hebrew School . . . But Michael couldn't help but be smitten by Miss Hillel's talk of Japanese culture. And in high school gym class, Michael encountered Japanese youngsters who seemed far more mannerly and polite than their American counterparts. One more reason for Michael to become entranced with Asian life.

From the time Michael was nine years old he held odd jobs, always wanting to make extra spending money. His parents didn't encourage him to work, for as they saw it, it was unnecessary. But working was Michael's idea. Though his childhood seemed idyllic, he still wanted to escape from the seemingly difficult life of his parents in their tract house (for which they paid $8,000) in Encino. Mostly, he didn't want to grow up poor. Beyond that, Michael liked making money and, his mother noted, he always liked having nice things. She believed that came from living in a neighborhood where middle-class and wealthy people dwelled, "and so," she concluded, "he always liked to look for something better." The neighborhood was a melting pot in the sense that Irish-, Italian-, and African-Americans, Jews, Catholics, and Protestants, all lived there.

And yet environment may not explain Michael's ambition as well as does his burning desire to be independent. "I've been working since I was nine years old," he says, apparently eager to make it clear that he has been standing on his own for most of his life. He began delivering *TV Guide*, walking around the neighborhood and selling the popular magazine for twenty-five cents an issue, getting a small portion of the proceeds. Later, when he was 13, he delivered the *Los Angeles Times*, and he also bagged groceries at a supermarket.

In 1958, Michael entered the seventh grade at the Portola Junior High School in Tarzana. He remained there for the next three years, through the ninth grade.

Michael loved to gab, to question, to be part of the conversation. "He'd do all the talking from the time he could speak," David Ovitz remembered. Especially at the dinner table. But the one place where he seemed unable to contain himself was in the classroom. Every class at Portola seemed to contain one "eager beaver" who knew all the answers, who raised a hand even at the first whiff of a question from the teacher. That of course was Michael Ovitz. His hand never seemed to rest on the table, it was always in the air. If the teacher asked a question, he had an answer. The other 25 students would just have to wait their turn. At first the teachers found Michael's inquisitiveness an appealing trait. But that didn't last for long. They soon began to look upon him as being a real pest.

At any rate, eventually they summoned David Ovitz to school in order to complain about his son's annoyingly excessive level of zeal. They told David that he had to calm Michael down, to get his unruly son to ask fewer questions. He was being unfair to the other students. David Ovitz listened politely, then went home and informed Michael that his teacher had summoned him to his school. Then, having come to a decision that may well have been pivotal to Michael Ovitz's future success, David proceeded to encourage his son to keep on badgering his teachers! It seems possible at least that, had David Ovitz punished his son at that important juncture for annoying his teachers, the young man would have turned into a meek, shy, and decidedly less intense and curious figure, not the Michael Ovitz everyone would come to know. But we know one thing for sure: Michael's hand waved on and on.

In the fall of 1961, Michael entered Birmingham High School in Van Nuys, California where 10 percent of the 3000-member student body was Jewish. One of his Jewish classmates was Michael Milken, whom Michael Ovitz got to know, but not well. In the 1980s, as the pioneer of junk-bond financing, Milken helped to reshape American business before he was convicted for the part he played in the insider-trading scandals.

More serious than most of his peers, more driven, Ovitz was not a brilliant student, but he did take advanced science courses in his junior and senior years and did do well in them. Toward the end of his junior year he participated in the California Museum of Science and Industry's annual science fair. Michael's exhibit on "salt-water demineralization" won the top prize. Not the most popular of students, he still managed to impress fellow students with his air of self-confidence and by his lack of bluff. "What he said he would do," says close high school friend Steve Stearns, "he would inevitably do. He didn't make promises he wasn't going to keep." That earned him lots of respect, but no great amount of affection.

As a member of the gymnastics team, Michael practiced on a side horse in his garage. He won some modest acclaim for his feats, and earned a letter during his junior year. On March 13, 1964, the school newspaper wrote: "With stars such as Mike Ovitz . . . and a new motto, 'The harder the conflict, the more glorious the triumph,' the Birmingham gymnastic team may surprise everyone and place high in the league finals." He also played tight end on the junior varsity football team.

From the age of eight, Michael Ovitz had wanted to become a doctor. In later years he suggested that his parents had pushed the idea on him, just as many Jewish parents want their children to become a physician or an attorney. Yet his parents contend that the idea was all Michael's. He himself, when a teenager, indicated that a family doctor had been the catalyst here. But no matter who had planted the notion in his head, the young man was highly enthusiastic about what he assumed would be his future profession. Michael did not just "visit the doctor's office," he interrogated the family doctor, Dr. David Rottapel, exhibiting so much curiosity that the physician once told David and Sylvia Ovitz: "I want to buy a piece in him right now, because he's going to be somebody great." He befriended his mother's cousin, a doctor who owned the Beverly Hills Doctors Hospital, and found work in its restaurant, clearing dishes from the tables. The job bothered Sylvia Ovitz, for she thought it beneath her son. She also didn't like to have him working for family.

When Michael applied for a college scholarship, his essay insisted that his burning desire to become a doctor was fueled not by avarice, but by humanitarianism: "I am not, by far, saying that I will not make money as a doctor, for I am aware that most doctors do. But I am saying that the money I make as a doctor will be secondary, and my work will be my primary concern." A revealing assertion: Money mattered to him—mattered enough for him to begin taking on odd jobs from the age of nine—but other things mattered even more. He noted in the essay that it was Dr. Rottapel who motivated him to become a doctor: "Ever since I was eight, I talked to him about my desire to be a doctor. . . . He invariably encouraged me. I suppose that the real precipitate of all of my experience is my desire to help humanity and thus help myself."

Michael seemed very much in charge of his own affairs, and very eager to thrust himself into the center of things: taking the position of catcher in the Little League; badgering his teachers with endless questions; selling *TV Guide* without any parental pushing; exploiting visits to the doctor in order to learn about all aspects of being a physician. . . . All indications of an activist mind, of a young man with enormous self-initiative. Yet despite all that self-confidence, Michael displayed little in the way of leadership qualities.

Others, however, spotted them in him, and nurtured them. One day, during his junior year, the school principal called him into his office. "We have only one candidate for school vice president," he explained to Michael. "We can't let that happen. We want you to run for it too." Although Michael was flattered by the suggestion, he worried, when he learned that a close friend was his main rival for the post, that the contest would ruin their friendship. Relationships, later to figure so hugely in his business career, mattered a great deal to Michael even at this early age. In the end, he decided that this particular friendship could withstand the heat of school politics. He entered the race and won by a vote of 802 to 431. "What a victory!" were the words his mother inscribed next to a high school newspaper article in Michael Ovitz's childhood scrapbook.

IN LATER YEARS, Michael Ovitz would remember his parents more for what they didn't have than for what they did: They didn't hold college degrees and, in his view, they didn't have a lot of money. But Michael's father holds a special place in his life. When asked who are his role models in business, Ovitz says that his inspiration has come from his home: "People impute I had certain role models, but I took bits and pieces that I had seen. The largest role model for my business life was my father. My father had no formal education, and when I grew up he and my mom instilled in me values and a certain moral philosophy and made me aggressive. And more importantly, my dad showed me how to deal with people, how to leverage situations, how to negotiate, how to take care of people."

Ovitz has retained a vivid memory of his father's garage filled with sample bottles of liquor, which the distilleries gave to salesmen: "My dad knew when to slip a guy a free bottle of booze. It was all street stuff, not stuff you learned in college." His father was clever, never giving away cases of liquor but only the odd bottle here and there. When David Ovitz decided that it was time to give someone a gift, he didn't choose that person's birthday or wedding anniversary—he gave the gift only when it was unexpected. Virtually anybody could find their way onto David Ovitz's gift list: a gas station mechanic, a gardener, whomever he met on his daily rounds. "We'd be in crazy places," Ovitz recalls, laughing at the sight of his father leaving the driver's seat and heading for the rear of the car. "My dad would open the trunk and pull out a bottle. They always loved my dad."

Ovitz continues to admire his father, however, as much for his sage advice as for the clever way in which he dispensed gifts when out on the road. He remembers his father taking him aside, soon after he won another election that made him president of his high school, and telling him: "People will hate you for being successful. If you want to be perceived as a king, you have to act like one." Ovitz calls that the best advice he has ever been given. David Ovitz wanted his son to become a king, or at the very least to become the best that he was capable of being. His only concern was that Michael would not set his sights high enough. Once, when he had arranged for his son to work weekends at the Continental market, bagging groceries, David asked the manager to place Michael next to the oldest "box boy" in the market. He wanted to discourage his son from becoming a box boy for life. The tactic worked. Returning home one day, Michael informed his father that, after watching the man next to him stuff food into bags, he would never let that happen to him.

For someone whose entire adult life was to be centered upon Hollywood, the young Michael Ovitz displayed surprisingly little interest in the movies. To be sure, he expended some of his earnings on the pleasure of movie-going, spending seventy-five cents on the Saturday-afternoon movies, week after week, just as every other kid his age did. But for him Hollywood was background music, not a steady, thundering drum in the foreground of his daily life.

He rode his bicycle near the RKO studio lot, or past the homes of Clark Gable and John Wayne, but that didn't bring the studios and the famous actors any closer to his real life. Some of the dads of the children in his Little League program were actors; Dennis Weaver, for instance, had two children who were enrolled in the program. And he did visit the drama department at Birmingham High School in order to watch play rehearsals, but he never joined the department. One of the budding actresses he watched perform was Sally Field, who noticed Michael because he struck up a friendship with her brother Rick. But the actress felt no inclination to befriend young Ovitz. For one thing, he was a grade below her; for another she was shy, whereas Mike seemed to know everyone.

When Michael Ovitz graduated from Birmingham High School in the winter of 1965, he was 18 years old. At a senior breakfast on January 28, he was given an award of merit for being the "most spirited" student and "class con artist." None of the judges deigned to explain their decision. That spring he enrolled in the University of California at Santa Barbara; hoping to complete his college studies as quickly as possible, he attended summer school at the University of Southern California. He still wanted to become a doctor, but that wouldn't last for long.

Michael Ovitz broke into the entertainment field through a Little League connection: one of the parents, Herb Steinberg, was an executive at Universal. The studio was about to inaugurate tours, and Michael asked Steinberg if he could apply to become a guide. He was one of hundreds who sought the prized jobs that would go to just five men and five women. Steinberg hosted Michael at the studio for a formal interview, and hired him on the spot. Given two months to wander the lot, he became acquainted with the surroundings, asking an enormous number of questions of the people he met. Then, on June 21, he began a job that paid

$250 for the entire summer. He worked six days a week, often putting in 14-hour days.

Suddenly, all thoughts of becoming a physician vanished. He longed to become a part of the entertainment industry. Whatever it was that had excited him about the medical profession, did so no longer. Of course, he was not the first young person to become suddenly "turned on" by Hollywood. But others, when embarking on a career in the entertainment world, were sobered by the risks and perils involved. Ovitz had no such fears. He always assumed that he would succeed at whatever he attempted to do. Embarking on a career in Hollywood would be no different. Still, it was hard for his mother, who had thought that "Dr. Michael Ovitz" was the sweetest-sounding phrase imaginable, to reconcile herself to the fact that her son would become "one of those Hollywood types." Sylvia Ovitz joked with Michael that perhaps he had seen blood, and had decided he couldn't stand the sight of it. No such thing. It was Hollywood that he had seen, and a bad case of love at first sight that he had caught. "The year at Universal ruined me," he acknowledges.

Eager to be in Los Angeles, he transferred from the Santa Barbara campus to UCLA, where he enrolled as a sophomore in September. Through his contacts in the liquor industry, David Ovitz had learned that one of Seagram's rivals, the Jim Beam Company, provided college scholarships that paid for tuition and books; he helped his son to receive one of these scholarships. Initially Michael had enrolled in the advanced premed program, but now he believed that he was carrying too heavy a course load in math and the sciences; he switched his major to psychology, with a minor in business. The business courses had less impact upon him than the psychology classes, as his mother noted: "He could psychoanalyze me every single day. He could always tell you what you should do, what you were doing wrong." As part of his psychology schoolwork, Michael worked with autistic children: "It's the single most frustrating thing you can do. You can't fix them. You can only love them."

One day, sitting at a table in the Student Union, he peered across the room and spotted a freshman named Judy Reich, seated by herself at another table, reading. Others in that situation might perhaps have dreamed of approaching the young woman, sweeping her off her feet, and marching down the aisle with her. Yet while others dream, Michael Ovitz acts. He walked up to Ms. Reich and boldly introduced himself, as if it were the most natural thing in the world to do. Today Ovitz has only one explanation to offer of that brave foray to the other side of the student union: "I thought she was absolutely gorgeous." Though ten other seats near her were empty, he asked if the seat next to her was taken. She said no. He sat down and began talking to her. He learned that Judy Reich had been born in Berkeley, California, that she liked to sing, and that she was in the non-Jewish sorority house on campus, Kappa Alpha Theta, sister sorority of Zeta Beta Tau, Michael's fraternity. Phoning her a few days later, Michael asked her out for coffee. He took her to a jazz place, but Judy, only 17 years old, was under-age and could not enter the premises. So instead Michael took her to a pizza parlor up the street. They stayed out late that night, talking, then dated on and off over the next few years. They dated other people, but remained close. Judy was voted the official sweetheart of Michael's fraternity.

Michael and Judy were married on August 3, 1969. Because her father was Jewish but her mother was not, Judy was not considered to be Jewish according to Orthodox Jewish law, which traces Jewishness through the maternal line. Therefore, she volunteered to convert to Judaism just before the wedding. Michael and Judy Ovitz were married at the Valley Colonial House, a Los Angeles catering hall.

DURING HIS JUNIOR year, Ovitz signed up as a counselor for a program called Uni Prep in the UCLA dorms, a week-long orientation period provided to incoming freshmen. He and another student, a young man named Frank Marshall, were responsible for the students on one dormitory floor. Ovitz and Marshall, later to become a major Hollywood producer, shared a room. Marshall recalls that Ovitz struck him as being charismatic and filled with leadership qualities, and an inspiration to the incoming freshmen.

That year, Ovitz found weekend work that thrilled him. He was hired as second-in-command to the operations manager of the studio tours at 20th Century Fox, his assignment being to help design the tours. Near as it was to the UCLA campus, the job proved to be highly convenient. Ovitz had been asked to come up with ways to attract more tourists. Even at this early age, he was wheeling and dealing. As he prepared to contact Grayline bus tours, a Universal customer, he knew he needed some lure if he was to steal away this account. Why not offer Grayline a large discount? What did he care as long as he got the account? Grayline went for the Ovitz deal, and the man who would be called "the most successful negotiator in Hollywood" closed his first big deal, winning the account for Fox. When his boss left for another job, Ovitz became operations manager, and soon had 75 people working under him. He was paid $200 a week for the 50 hours a week he was working, a grand sum for a mere college student.

Increasingly self-assured, Ovitz announced one day that he planned to seek the presidency of Zeta Beta Tau. The members were taken aback. Candidates for that high office usually were selected out of the most popular members. Ovitz was liked well enough, but he seemed too quiet, too reserved, too serious. Still, the fraternity brothers respected him. They especially liked the fact that he played defensive end for the fraternity football team, even though he was small: five feet nine inches. In time he became one of the team's best players. He also played catcher on the fraternity softball team.

Michael was quite aggressive in his pursuit of the fraternity presidency. In an unprecedented move, he actually campaigned for the position, and ran on a platform. No one had done that before, only because no one had thought the job worth campaigning for. He was always searching for ways to boost the fraternity house's image. He pledged to make ZBT the best house on campus, but to reach that goal, the fraternity brothers would have to get their grades up. Praiseworthy performances in sports would no longer be enough. Although hard to believe, the brothers actually *liked* Ovitz's emphasis on studies! He won handily.

Ovitz proved to be an activist president. Running in effect a small business, he presided over a $75,000 annual budget, most of which went for staff and food. He took on himself the big task of refurbishing the fraternity house (while installing the members in a motel), and worked closely with the contractor. In the UCLA yearbook for 1968, the page depicting Ovitz's fraternity house carries a large photo of him dressed in a blazer and white turtleneck, hair unusually short for the late 1960s. "Under the reign of brother King Ovitz," the text went, "the empire of Zeta Beta Tau once again reached a great climax."

Ovitz kept up his friendship with Frank Marshall during his senior year, when they served together on the Fraternity Presidents' Council (Marshall was President of Alpha Tau Omega). Both men talked about going to law school, though Ovitz was more gungho than Marshall. After graduating from UCLA in February 1968, Ovitz entered Loyola Law School the following September. At first he seemed to be enjoying his studies, but gradually he lost interest, dropping out in June 1969. Sylvia Ovitz suspects that he simply missed holding down a job.

OVITZ WAS NOW 22 years old. He had a far better idea of what he did *not* want to be than of what he wanted to be. He did not want to become a doctor—and he did not want to be poor: "I was desperate to move ahead. I didn't want to live the life I lived as a child. I wanted to be in a different world," The world of Hollywood. Friends had told him that it would be nearly impossible for him to break into the entertainment business. Yet he had incredible determination: "I had this insane attitude that anything is doable." It was as if he had been born with the gene for optimism. Photographs of him from this period reveal not just a smile, but a look of self-assurance not to be seen on the faces of most 22-year-olds. Quite clearly, "failure" was a thought that never crossed that mind.

3

A Deal a Second

LIKE ANY OTHER child in America, Michael Ovitz spent Saturday afternoons watching movies. But he had no urge to produce, direct, or act in them. What had always excited him was being up to his eyeballs in business, whether that meant delivering newspapers, bagging groceries at supermarkets, managing a major studio's tours, or arranging for his fraternity to remodel its quarters. As of 1969, and his twenty-second year, he had no firm idea as to what aspect of business truly appealed to him. All he knew was that he desperately wanted to avoid taking some drab, routine job that would keep him from stretching his wings.

Applying for a job at a major studio seemed like a terrible idea. Once on the job, he would feel pressured to stay there for life, unable to explore other facets of the business world. During his time at Universal and at Fox, he had kept a curious eye on the talent agents. And the more he inquired into what they actually did, the more he talked to them directly, the more attractive their work began to appear to him: "I liked their access. They saw movie guys, not just TV guys, and I thought: 'What a fantastic way to learn the business. You get paid for learning how to handle artists, and learning the business side of the business.'" And best of all, a guy wouldn't be trapped for life doing the same thing over and over.

Ovitz always was thinking ahead. Thus, he decided that he would apply for a job as a talent agent now, stay on the job for four or five years, then move on and perhaps start his own business. He had no specific business in mind, but most likely it would be something in the entertainment field. Restless Michael Ovitz had begun to reinvent himself—even before embarking on a career.

He applied to two talent agencies, the William Morris Agency and Creative Management Associates. Freddie Fields founded CMA in 1961 and went on to become the most powerful motion-picture agent in Hollywood, one able to boast of handling such top-drawer clients as Paul Newman, Robert Redford, Steve McQueen, James Caan, Dustin Hoffman, Ali MacGraw, Al Pacino, and Barbra Streisand. The first to respond to Ovitz's overtures was the William Morris Agency. Founded in 1898 in New York City by William Morris, it was the world's oldest talent agency. Over the years its clients had included Eddie Cantor, James Cagney, Katharine Hepburn, Al Jolson, Will Rogers, Marilyn Monroe, and Frank Sinatra. Ovitz went in for an interview and obviously made an impression for he was offered a position in Morris's mail room. He jumped at the opportunity, forgetting all about his MCA application. He couldn't care less that he was starting at the bottom. He had done more than get a foot in the door—he was inside the building. He began work in May 1969.

The William Morris mail room: an institution in its own right! For the mail room at William Morris was to the entertainment industry what basic training was to a marine. It was in the Morris mail room that future agents began their training, spending a year or two distributing and collecting the mail, dropping off scripts to clients, and in general keeping the paper flowing. Grunt-work at best, and paying the paltry sum of $75 a week. Hardly a lot of money to King Ovitz who had been earning $200 a week at Fox. But he felt that at last his career had been launched.

Michael Ovitz approached his new mail-room job in much the same spirit as a marine is forced to confront basic training: doing "all right" was not going to be good enough. Ovitz was determined to be the best mail-room clerk William Morris had ever employed. As well as delivering packages, agent trainees were expected to learn the lay of the land in Hollywood. He who had conducted studio tours, he who had remodeled fraternity houses, had no desire to spend hours or even days studying geography. Nor would he be content with doing nothing for one or two years other than delivering the mail. He decided to master both Hollywood's landscape and the intricacies of mail delivery within the first few weeks. That would leave him free to take on other, larger challenges.

In later years, Ovitz loved to tell friends that the strategy he had employed in the William Morris mail room—racing through the trivial tasks in order to make room for the larger ones—wasn't that complicated. Maybe so. But that hardly explains how he learned the routine so quickly. The answer has to do with Ovitz's being a very driven young man. He always made sure he got to work by 7:00 a.m., two hours before anyone else, and hung around until 11:00 p.m., long after most of the Morris agents had gone home. During those quiet early and late hours he made up his mind to learn as much as he could about the entire agency business. It was as if he had enrolled in a rigorous college course.

As an employee of the greatest talent agency in the world he could, without much energy or stealth, cast his eyes over the most intriguing, revealing documents in the entertainment world, especially those inter-agency memos and contracts pertaining to planned film and television projects for Morris clients. All he had to do was find the time to read the stuff. "I didn't know what the others did," he says of the rest of the mail-room staff. "I didn't care. I just moved past them like a lightning rod. I wish I could say it was a sheer plan of genius, but it was just common sense. It was just being available and in proximity to these people; then you had to seize an opportunity."

He did just that, after most others had gone home. Each evening at 6:45 p.m. the senior executives, including Abe Lastfogel, then Holly-wood's top agent, left their offices and got together at this or that watering hole for dinner, returning to the Morris office at around 10:30 p.m. It was during those long dinners that Ovitz peered through the memos and con-tracts. There was nothing unethical about what he was doing, for after all, he did work for the same company. And yet poring over each and every document with an eagle eye wasn't exactly part of his job description. Still, everyone was too busy to ask why a 22-year-old mail clerk was slowly and intently making his way through some of the most sensitive material in Hollywood. Many at Morris assumed that Ovitz simply was doing his mail-room job more diligently than others usually did. Others may have found the young Ovitz's extracurricular pursuits to be more than a bit abnormal, but he was simply trying to ascend through the Mor-ris ranks as fast as he could.

Ovitz found all of the memos and contracts fascinating, but he could learn only so much from them. He needed to get a feel for how the Holly-wood talent agency business worked and the people at Morris who seemed the best-informed about the business were the Morris in-house attorneys. And so he visited every attorney at William Morris and, knowing that they sometimes gave lectures on their work, asked them to turn over their lecture notes to him afterwards. "I drove people crazy, I drove people out of their minds," says Ovitz proudly of his aggressive quest in search of what made Morris tick. "But they liked it. I was this brash, inquisitive lunatic." The same brash, inquisitive lunatic who a few years before was driving his teachers crazy by means of an endlessly flapping hand.

A lunatic, perhaps, but a giant sponge as well. He could absorb so much simply because he loved every aspect of agenting. He loved the constant action, the telephone calls, the meetings, the hot pursuit of projects and clients. And Morris itself was filled with glitter and glamour. It was all so thrilling. At any moment author Sidney Sheldon, actor Steve McQueen, or television producer Aaron Spelling might walk in. Everyone seemed to be *running,* and Ovitz couldn't wait to join the race: "I loved the business. It was incredible. A deal a second. It was constant, perpetual motion." The business seemed to embrace so many aspects of life that fascinated him: art, commerce, money, people, current events, history. "I realized I could be anything I wanted to be, I could make myself over in the business."

But it wouldn't be enough just to make himself over. He had to make sure his bosses knew of his progress. To that end, he sat down one day and wrote a memo to a superior, Chuck Booth:

> Re: Progress Report—Michael S. Ovitz
>
> First in a series of short reports to keep you posted on my progress in the training program. I have read, discussed, and digested some thirteen things, including notebooks compiled with respect to creation, negotiation, and services of some *Smothers Brothers, Glen Campbell Goodtime Hour, Rowan and Martin Laugh-In.* All deal memos; various treatment, scripts and synopsises (sic) for proposed WMA [William Morris Agency] projects. I have also been keeping my eyes open for new talent that we might be interested in representing. I have achieved this by watching as much local and national television as possible and whenever my financial situation permits, to attend small clubs and school (UCLA, USC, etc.) plays, festivals, and student workshops.

Brashness is the word that comes to mind. Ovitz was after all a mere fledgling in the Morris training program, and it is not at all clear that his bosses had any interest in keeping up with the every move of "that kid." But he wanted to impress them, and so he wrote the memo.

W HATEVER THE REASON, and regardless of whether a memo such as that one helped or hurt him, it wasn't long before Michael Ovitz had caught the eye of the top people at Morris. He had served in the mail room for a mere 100 days before he was made an assistant to the president of the Agency, Sam Weisbord. That had to set some kind of record. Not only did Weisbord run the Agency, he was head of the television department as well.

For all the zeal that young Ovitz had exhibited in the mail room, he sensed that he would have to work much, much harder now that he was no longer a clerk, now that he was breathing the rarified air that the *agents* breathed! Determined to be the best assistant Weisbord had ever had, Ovitz tried to anticipate what his boss was about to ask him to do—and then do it before he was asked to. Weisbord responded warmly to his assistant's enthusiasm. Ordinarily, it would have taken a mail-room clerk such as Ovitz three to four years to be promoted to agent. Weisbord made him an agent after he had been with the Agency for a total of seven months. All those hours spent poring through Agency documents had paid off at last.

In January 1970, Ovitz was assigned to the music area, but he quickly discovered that he wasn't cut out for such work. As his first assignment as a music agent, he drew the job of handling Sly and the Family Stone, a hot "funk" act. Sly and the group were due to perform at the Los Angeles Forum one evening. Sly was nowhere to be found, and forty-five minutes late for the appearance. Frighteningly for him, it was Ovitz's task to make sure that the show went well, and that included making sure that it started on time. Seeming very much out of place in his three-button knock-off suit from Bullock's Department Store and his wing-tipped shoes, Ovitz thought he looked "like a Federal agent" as he walked around the Forum. When he finally located some members of the group in a locker room nowhere near the stage, he introduced himself but was greeted coolly.

"Hey, man," Sly Stone blurted out, "go take care of my band."

The request seemed so amorphous that Ovitz was afraid to ask Sly what he meant for him to do to take care of his band.

"You're late for the concert," Ovitz said, hoping to sound stern, but unfatherly.

"I don't give a shit," said Sly. "Go take care of my band."

Ovitz then located other members of the group in another locker room. He pushed the door open a crack. "I saw things I couldn't believe in a public place," he said later. He has never described exactly what it was he saw, which suggests that he really did not fit in with rock culture.

One band member, drinking champagne right from the bottle, turned to look at Ovitz and yelled: "Narc!" (narcotics officer).

Within seconds, the whole band was screaming at Michael Ovitz. What a way to get started in the agenting business!

Shutting the locker room door behind him and heading for the nearest exit, Ovitz got in his car and returned to the Morris Agency. He then wrote a letter to his superior, stating that he felt he should explore other opportunities than music. The next day he was transferred to the television department. "Sixties rock and roll wasn't for me," he notes of that first, unfortunate agenting experience. Being labeled a "narc" appears to have soured Ovitz on working closely with not-so-conservative types such as Sly and his "family."

In looking for work for its clients, the television department had concentrated its efforts on nighttime television. That was where the action was. The biggest programs and talent gravitated toward prime-time programming. Morris agents did not take daytime television seriously, even though the networks were profiting nicely from daytime shows. Searching for a way to make his mark, Ovitz realized that he could draw attention to himself by helping to find work for his clients on daytime TV. He began to sell Morris talent to game shows and soap operas, and the strategy paid off: The money began to roll in. He then expanded his labors so as to handle variety shows, thereby finding work for writers, choreographers, cabaret artists, and directors. Within 18 months, thanks to Ovitz's efforts, the William Morris Agency had become the force to be reckoned with when it came to the selling of talent to daytime television.

Ovitz built up an impressive client list, including talk-show host Merv Griffin and game-show producers Chuck Barris and Bill Carruthers. Having produced two highly acclaimed game shows—*The Dating Game* and *The Newlywed Game*—Carruthers was sedulously wooed by Ovitz, who then managed to lift his career to new heights. Carruthers found that Ovitz "had a vision. Mike never looked at anything in its separate pieces. He looked at the whole piece, then figured out how to put the pieces together to make the whole. Even at that young age he was very, very cool, somewhat calculating, but he had a great grasp of where he was going. I don't mean 'calculating' in a negative way. You could see the way Michael's mind worked. I always felt he was two steps ahead of anyone else."

One of the personal characteristics that helped Ovitz to stay two steps ahead of the others was an instinct for spotting new talent. One night he happened to be watching a local television comedy show called *Loman and Berkeley*. He was particularly drawn to a fellow who had performed a sketch about a roller-skating rabbi who hailed from Salt Lake City. The man Ovitz had cast his knowing eye upon was both a struggling young actor and a struggling young comedy writer, and Ovitz made a point of learning his name: Barry Levinson. The next day Ovitz picked up the phone to the aspiring actor/writer, introduced himself, and told Levinson that he had seen his sketch about the rabbi and thought it very funny. He asked him if he would like to do some comedy writing for network television. Levinson couldn't believe his luck. Ovitz put him in touch with the producers of a new show that CBS was airing in the fall, *The Tim Conway Comedy Hour.* And that was how Michael Ovitz helped to launch the career of one of Hollywood's most successful directors. Of his early conversations with Ovitz, Levinson says: "It was all so casual. There was no kind of hustle. Quiet and simple."

Howard West, an agent at William Morris, arranged program packages for television networks. From time to time he noticed Michael Ovitz around the Morris corridors, and he found it especially refreshing that Ovitz arrived very early in the morning, just as he did. It also gave West a chance to chat with the young agent. The young man's combination of neat appearance and aggressive style appealed to West. He found him to be industrious and thirsty for knowledge. West decided to keep a close eye on him.

Then one day, West discovered that Ovitz was not especially happy with the work he was doing. There wasn't enough of it, and what there was he didn't find sufficiently challenging. Eager to learn more, he was itching to broaden his horizons. His prayers were answered when Phil Weltman, the man in charge of agents at Morris, urged Howard West to find himself an assistant. West immediately said "Michael Ovitz," and Weltman agreed. Ovitz's career now seemed ready for takeoff.

And yet Michael Ovitz thought that whatever he might decide to do in the future—and it wasn't at all clear that he would remain an agent for much longer—a law degree would come in very handy when seeking more senior positions in the entertainment industry. One day in the fall of 1970, Ovitz, a few months short of turning 24, announced that he was leaving the William Morris Agency to return to law school. Helping to support him was his wife Judy. During the week she worked for an advertising company, and on weekends she sang in the lounge for PSA Airlines, a commuter airline. Earning $300 a week, she was making far more money than her husband was.

Alas, several months later Ovitz had grown tired of his law studies, just as he had the first time around. He called Howard West and acknowledged that he had made a mistake about law school. Could he please come back to William Morris? But it wasn't that simple. Loyalty to the organization was a deeply ingrained aspect of corporate culture at Morris. A person hired to work in the mail room, and then quickly promoted to agent, was expected to remain at Morris for life. There was no time off for good behavior and no one who quit ever dared to ask for his or her job back.

Thus, when Howard West brought Ovitz's request to rejoin the Agency to Norman Brokaw and Sam Weisbord, the two senior managers at the firm, both were determined to bar Ovitz's return. William Morris wasn't a revolving door, they explained to West; one could not leave one day and expect to be welcomed back a few months later. And Brokaw and Weisbord did have history on their side: *No one* had ever been permitted to come back to William Morris after quitting or being fired. But West believed that Michael Ovitz had some special qualities not found in most talent agents, and that it would be a real shame to lose him. For one thing, Ovitz had developed some especially close relations with the network buyers. For another, it wasn't as if Ovitz had gone to work for a competitor; he had simply enrolled in law school.

Howard West made all of these compelling arguments to his superiors and, fortunately for Ovitz, he was a man who carried a good deal of clout at the company. He was considered to be one of William Morris's chief rainmakers, and so senior management actually broke its long-held-to tradition. Michael Ovitz was grudgingly permitted to return to the William Morris Agency. He had beaten the system.

While Ovitz had been away at law school, no one at Morris had bothered to pay any attention to the young comedy writer, Barry Levinson. In the meantime *The Tim Conway Comedy Hour* had been canceled, and Levinson's career seemed to be going nowhere. Then one day, out of the blue, he received yet another phone call. "Hi. It's Michael. I'm back at William Morris." Ovitz immediately signed Levinson as a comedy writer for a show starring the comedian Marty Feldman. Michael Ovitz was back in business, and so was Barry Levinson.

THE MAN AT Morris who loomed largest for Michael Ovitz was Phil Weltman. As the person in charge of Morris's agents, he served as mentor to all of those young people like Ovitz who were coming up through the ranks of the organization. Weltman loved the business, but he had come to it in a roundabout way.

Weltman grew up in the Stuyvesant Heights section of Brooklyn. He went to New York University, but quit after two years in order to take a job on Wall Street as a trader in a small government-bond house. His work day usually being over by 4:00 p.m., he frequently wandered over to the William Morris office to visit his friend Sam Weisbord. Liking what he saw at Morris, Weltman left Wall Street to become a trainee at a starting salary of $25 a week, $70 less than he had been earning as a bond trader.

Now that he had risen to a senior position at Morris, it was his job to teach the young agents the ropes. He knew all the slurs that routinely were tossed at agents, knew they were called lazy and greedy, knew that many thought them no better than hucksters and parasites. And he acknowledged that many of those labels did stick.

But Phil Weltman loved the talent-agent world, and he believed that by means of just a bit of fine-tuning, agents could be trained to be more businesslike, more professional. To do that, he had to set high standards, and to whip his agents into shape as if he were a drill sergeant cracking the whip over a group of marines. No one at the Agency was tougher than Phil Weltman. He allowed his agents one mistake—*one*. "If you make another one," he told them, "don't come back here." And he meant it. His agents called him "a drill sergeant," and Michael Ovitz always had an image of "Sergeant" Weltman barking out orders, screaming, shouting. It didn't matter to Weltman if he humiliated an agent. He demanded results.

Weltman didn't think the talent-agency business was all that complicated. To do a good job, an agent simply had to follow a few basic rules. Weltman knew all-too-well that the most frequently-heard complaint among clients was "I can't get ahold of my agent." Hence his number-one rule was: Get back to everyone! If a client phoned an agent but didn't get through, the call *had* to be returned by the end of that business day. As long as the agent could get to a telephone, no exceptions to this rule were allowed. If the agent truly was out of contact, a secretary had to call the client in order to inform him or her as to when the agent would be returning the call. No client ever would complain to Phil Weltman about a Morris agent. Not if Weltman had anything to do with it.

He kept what was almost a mother's ever-watchful eye on his brood of young agents, Ovitz among them, until he was certain they could handle deals on their own. Unlike most other senior managers at talent agencies in town, Weltman was eager to give his junior agents the responsibility of handling clients, in order to get them some hands-on experience. Yet fiefdoms did exist at Morris. An agent would almost fanatically guard his access to his clients, insisting that he and he alone would take care of all their professional needs. Weltman preached a different ethic, teamwork. Agents sharing information, sharing clients. It required a whole new way of working, and to many of the senior agents, it sounded like a recipe for disaster.

At 6:00 p.m. every day Weltman's door always was wide open. His agents could march into his office to discuss anything. While he couldn't prepare them in advance as to how to deal with all aspects of a negotiation, he did caution his agents not to worry if buyers found the fees they were being asked to pay to be unreasonable. "Be prepared for wild ranting from the buyer. You can always come down." Once a deal had been struck, Weltman insisted that a written confirmation go out the same day. If this meant that the agent had to stay at his desk until late into the night, so be it. For this way of doing business meant that if the buyer later sought to renege on the deal, the Morris agent simply could wave the confirmation letter around. Weltman told his "boys" to model themselves after Abe Lastfogel: quiet, self-effacing Abe. One could do far worse than emulate his enthusiasm and his passion, and his belief that the client always, always comes first.

In the course of his career, Weltman nurtured a number of agents who went on to become some of the most influential figures in Hollywood—among them Barry Diller, Joe Wizan, Robert Shapiro, and Ron Meyer. Weltman was intensely proud that these men—he called them his "boys"—became the heads of studios. And when a visitor came calling at his office in the spring of 1996, to talk about Michael Ovitz, Phil Weltman, long departed from Morris and then 88 years old, had this to say: "Everything Michael Ovitz did, he did perfectly. I asked him if he needed any help, but he never did. I never had to instruct him." No reprimands from the drill sergeant. (Sadly, Weltman died in January of 1997.)

For all the early success he was enjoying at the time, Michael Ovitz sensed, as did a number of his colleagues, that the William Morris Agency had its share of problems. For one thing, the senior executives and agents appeared to be prospering, but they were slow to share their wealth with the less experienced agents. Then too, it was an arena of clashing egos, a place where competition among the agents was fierce. Despite constant assertions on the part of senior executives that Morris was one big, happy family, many agents seemed to be out strictly for themselves. Yet those agents who found the egos too headstrong, or the pace too stressful, did not quit Morris, nor were they fired. Morris didn't believe in downsizing; indeed, it sought to reward loyalty by letting its agents remain in place, almost regardless of performance. Few wanted to leave, few were forced to. Accordingly, promotions were slow in coming. Thus Morris was not exactly made to order for every young, ambitious agent.

Clashes between the younger agents and senior management were inevitable. One such clash occurred when the bosses decided to make the motion picture and the television departments two separate units. Michael Ovitz and other young agents, grasping the fact that television was becoming a medium powerful enough to begin to produce its own movies, thought the decision foolish. Ovitz and other agents urged senior management to reverse the decision, but to no avail.

Another focal point of controversy: the percentage level of commissions that Morris charged for television packages. Morris executives insisted that the commissions remain at 10 percent; a few agents, however, Ovitz among them, thought that a 10 percent commission was too high: The agents were getting paid twice as much as their clients. Again, Ovitz and his associates failed to convince the powers that be. Feeling themselves to be less and less important to senior management, junior agents such as Ovitz were growing increasingly frustrated. They felt that they were bringing in a good percentage of business to the Agency, while getting too little recognition for their success.

Adding to their frustration was the growing rivalry between Morris executives on the East Coast and the young agents on the West Coast. For a long while those East Coast executives had been in the habit of virtually dismissing the West Coast as a source of revenue for the Agency, particularly since the company was doing well. But now the television business was shifting away from the East Coast toward California: Not only was it the hub of production, but it was where the programming decisions were being made. And all of that new business, to the chagrin of the bosses in New York, was being handled by a small group of upstart agents working out of Los Angeles. Three of those upstarts figure prominently in this story.

Michael Rosenfeld had turned 40 years old on June 28, 1974. Hailing from Philadelphia, Rosenfeld had gone to Penn State. His father was a cab driver turned state senator. Michael's dad smoked three packs of cigarettes a day, and died at the young age of 47. Michael, who was 20 at the time of his father's death, always believed that, had his father lived longer, he would have become a federal judge. The father had hoped that Michael would become an attorney; but blessed with a creative touch, the young man was more at home in the world of music and theater than in that of law. He played the piano, wrote music, scripted college shows. Given both his love of conversation and his creative impulse, Michael Rosenfeld thought he had the makings of a fine Hollywood talent agent. He began in the William Morris mail room on February 4, 1957.

Two and a half years later, Rowland Perkins began working in the same mail room for $45 a week. Perkins was born 12 days later than Rosenfeld on July 10, 1934. He went to UCLA, where he majored in business and minored in theater arts; he then spent two years at UCLA's law school, but never obtained a graduate degree. Rowland's parents thought it odd that he should take the job at Morris. And yet within a few months, after a few clerks had quit, their son was put in charge of the mail room. Three months later he became assistant to Stan Kamen, one of Morris's top talent agents and the longtime executive vice president of the William Morris Agency. A little over a year later, Perkins was made an agent and assigned to the television talent department. He then ran the television packaging department. It was at that moment in his career that Michael Rosenfeld caught his attention.

Since 1970, Rosenfeld had been running the motion picture talent department, handling minor actors and feeling less and less productive and creative. He blamed it on senior management, and its unwillingness to let people like him handle the top actors. Perkins knew that Rosenfeld aspired to handle more creative assignments. It also was clear to him that Rosenfeld would be happier packaging television deals than handling film talent. And indeed Rosenfeld jumped at the chance when, in 1972, Rowland Perkins asked him to join a group of industrious agents who would be packaging and selling talent to television companies on the West Coast.

As for Bill Haber, he had been with William Morris since 1964. At first he ran the television talent department, then in 1973 he began to package prime-time television shows. Perkins and Haber grew to be quite friendly. Perhaps the most important link between all three men is that they were serving as William Morris's liaisons to the West Coast network programming executives: Perkins was responsible for CBS, Bill Haber for NBC, and Mike Rosenfeld for ABC.

This talented trio was feeling increasingly frustrated by the Morris environment. "We were starting to feel this piling up of bodies," says Mike Rosenfeld. No one ever seemed to leave Morris, and promotions occurred slowly. Gradually the three men came to believe that it was "us against them," "them" being their Morris superiors back in New York. Jealous of their success, the East Coast executives treated them badly. The trio's sin: performing so well.

Yet for all their disgruntlement with the Morris executives and system, Perkins, Haber, and Rosenfeld knew that one did not just leave William Morris, any more than one divorced one's children. Still, without either planning or quite realizing just what they were getting into, they became unwitting allies in a cause that had no name, a minor revolution that had no leader, agenda, or timetable. These three close friends simply were getting together once a week at some meeting place away from the office, mostly to talk about ways to improve their business. And they knew in their hearts, as they talked, that they all felt they had been carrying the ball for Morris on the television side, and felt as well: "Why do it for them, when we can do it for ourselves?"

It was the summer of 1974. Lingering in all three minds was an unspoken fear that one day the bosses in New York would do the unthinkable and put one of their own in charge out on the West Coast. Allowing those minds to roam more freely, the three men got together one day and began to ask themselves how one goes about opening a talent agency. *Where does the financing come from? Who performs which functions?* The ideas flowed casually. Nothing sinister. Nothing conspiratorial.

As they were departing at the end of the day, Haber said solemnly: "Once you start talking like this, once that kind of conversation begins, it doesn't stop." Now he *did* sound conspiratorial, as if they had stopped being talent agents and had turned into a band of revolutionaries. Perkins thought the whole conversation had been half-fantasy, half-serious. After all, for William Morris agents this was tantamount to treachery; it was not at all clear to him that any of them had the nerve to walk away from Morris. Rosenfeld, however, admitted to himself that Haber had expressed what all three of them were feeling. The seeds of revolt had been sown. Did they have the courage to nurture them?

U NBEKNOWNST TO THE three would-be defectors, others at William Morris also were planning to jump ship. One was Ron Meyer. A former Marine from West Los Angeles, Meyer joined Morris in 1969 and went on to succeed Bill Haber as co-head of the television talent department, before becoming an agent in Morris's motion picture department. Prior to coming on-board at Morris, Meyer had been working for a veteran agent named Paul Kohner whose clients included John Huston and Ingmar Bergman. It was Phil Weltman who had lured him away to Morris. Ironically, had Meyer applied to the Morris mail room on his own, he probably would have been turned down, since he was a high school dropout. But Weltman liked the young man, and that was enough.

However, in early 1974, Meyer was feeling that the future at Morris looked bleak: "Everyone was healthy and alive, and the bosses were not about to relinquish their hold on the company. There was no room for a young person to move through the ranks." And yet there may have been other causes for Meyer's discontent. His associates from that period have suggested that he was having a hard time adjusting to his new spot in the motion picture department, and for that reason wanted to leave Morris. Whatever his motives, he wanted to start his own mom-and-pop agency. He simply was convinced that he and some of the other Morris agents could do better on their own.

If the future at Morris looked bleak to Ron Meyer, he admitted that it looked less bleak for Mike Ovitz. It was no secret that Ovitz was ambitious, and certainly no secret that Morris's senior executives thought the world of him. Of all the younger agents, Ovitz appeared to be the most likely to gain the crown, especially since Sam Weisbord had such great affection for him. Weisbord thought of Ovitz as being almost a son. Meyer had to ask himself, *Would Ovitz jeopardize a possible leadership position at Morris in order to take the risk of joining a startup agency?* Perhaps not. But he knew how hungry Ovitz was, and knew that it might well be years before the Morris veterans would deign to pass the torch. As a close friend to Ovitz, Meyer sensed some unique qualities in him, and believed that he would make the ideal partner for his envisioned new enterprise: "We complemented each other. We were formidable."

In March, Meyer invited Michael and Judy Ovitz out to dinner. He broached the idea of starting a new talent agency, and by the end of the evening, Ovitz seemed convinced. "Mike was smart enough," said Meyer, "to see that it made sense. It was the right time to leave Morris, to do something different. Here was an opportunity to become a co-captain of a ship within a reasonable amount of time." Throughout his childhood and into his early adult years, Ovitz had felt himself to be qualified to serve as a leader and now he hungered to play that role. But he knew that if he was to lead, he would have to leave Morris. The thought didn't bother him much. Yes, he had been treated as something of a "fair-haired boy" around Morris, but he also felt many of the same frustrations that the other junior agents did, with regard to Morris's crusty and overly traditional tone.

And so Ovitz and Meyer were propelling themselves in the very same direction as Perkins, Rosenfeld, and Haber, each set of would-be defectors unaware of the other. And yet the five men all did have one thing in common: They all worked for Phil Weltman. He was their anchor, their mentor, more like a father to them than a boss. Whatever harsh feelings they might be harboring toward Morris, they certainly didn't blame Weltman for the agency's faults. Perhaps out of loyalty to Phil, the five, still operating in two separate factions, felt no great need to rush away from the agency. They also knew that they were better off putting as much thought and planning as they could into any possible move. So for the time being, their conspiratorial thoughts remained only that: thoughts.

Meanwhile, others at William Morris were talking quietly to the five men and learning of their discontent. A few of these agents were asked to join the future defectors. One of them was Jerry Katzman. He declined, and didn't do too badly: As of 1997, he was President of the William Morris Agency.

Another agent, Fred Westheimer, was asked to join the defectors as well. One day Westheimer and Meyer were sitting together in a booth in Frank Musso's Restaurant, in West Hollywood. Meanwhile, Michael Ovitz was sitting on his own at the counter, eating a salad. At one point Westheimer got up and joined Ovitz and they began to talk—and to share Ovitz's salad. The topic of discussion was leaving William Morris. But still, they took no action.

For Rowland Perkins, events of the fall of 1974 helped to clarify the role of the young West Coast agents vis-à-vis their New York bosses. When the job of head of the West Coast television department opened up, Perkins, by now vice president of creative services, seemed a shoo-in. After all, Phil Weltman had been grooming him to take over that department, and Perkins had done good work in his deal-making with the networks' West Coast programming executives. But Perkins's very success proved to be his undoing: Jealous of his achievements, the New York executives wanted to bring him down a peg or two, and so they gave the job to Larry Auerbach, one of their New York colleagues. That was the last straw. Perkins now was ready to think the unthinkable. But could he and the others *really* leave the William Morris Agency?

4

Now, Perkins, This Is Treason!

I T WOULD BE no easy task to jump the good ship William Morris. For one thing, the five agents were making way too much money to simply walk off without good reason. Rowland Perkins was the highest paid of the five, at $80,000 a year. Michael Rosenfeld earned $60,000. Michael Ovitz, Ron Meyer, and Bill Haber raked in $50,000 apiece per year. And still, the five would-be defectors continued to talk about leaving.

Ever since that fateful dinner the previous March, Meyer had kept after Ovitz doggedly, feeling strongly that Ovitz was the right partner for him. They talked about setting up a two-man agency, but hadn't yet decided whether to call it the Ovitz-Meyer Agency or the Meyer-Ovitz Agency. Meanwhile, Perkins, Rosenfeld, and Haber deliberated as their discontent simmered. As time went on, the would-be defectors more and more came to feel that they were carrying an ever-greater load for the agency, making the deals that kept the agency prosperous but not being recognized for their work. But they weren't quite ready to make the leap. That is, not until something very disturbing occurred.

That happened in early December of 1974. Sam Weisbord, executive vice president, walked into Phil Weltman's office. The time was 3:00 p.m. Weisbord got right to the point.

"You were put in the computer and found wanting." In other words, Weltman wasn't a big enough rainmaker.

At first, Phil was confused. A few seconds passed, and then the meaning of the words began to sink in. Weltman was being fired. True, he was 65 years old, perhaps the right time for others to retire, but certainly not for him. He was fit as a fiddle, and felt that he could still make a significant contribution. The dismissal was all the more horrific because Weltman considered Sam Weisbord to be his closest friend. And now, when he had given 35 years of his sweat and his devotion to Morris, he had been told he was no longer needed. What a company!

Abe Lastfogel's wife Frances cried uncontrollably when she got the news that Weltman had been fired. But the executives in New York had felt the ground shaking under their feet. They saw the balance of power shifting to the West Coast, and for whatever crazy reason, blamed Phil Weltman for that shift. At any rate, he had to go.

What the East Coast Morris executives hadn't taken into account was the unique authority and respect Weltman commanded among a certain pivotal group of young Morris agents. Despite his tough, drill-sergeant exterior, he had been like a father to them. Ron Meyer had lost his father at a relatively young age, and Weltman became the father he never had. Thus, it soon became clear that the young agents were not going to take Weltman's ouster lying down.

Weltman broke the news to Michael Ovitz and Ron Meyer at one sitting. Meyer always had considered Weltman to be a very major reason for Morris's success, "the knot that held the whole sweater together," as Meyer himself put it. "If Phil had stayed," Meyer noted, "the company would have been a different place. Once he was gone, the whole place would change for the next twenty years—and it did. Firing him was clearly the single biggest mistake the agency made." Michael Ovitz was taken aback as well, for Weltman was the one true mentor he had at Morris: "He was a Jewish drill sergeant, and he trained all of us. He kept us in line. He was a great father figure. Then he turned sixty-five and they fired him. It just shocked us. I was twenty-six, and I'll never forget it." Walking out of Weltman's office, Meyer turned to Ovitz and said: "This is what they're going to do with us." Phil Weltman's dismissal was about to ignite the greatest revolution in Morris's history.

Rowland Perkins returned from vacation shortly after Weltman's dismissal. Lunching at The Brown Derby with Weltman soon thereafter, Perkins found him to be depressed. For years Weltman had preached to Perkins and others that William Morris was one big happy family, and he had been caught in a lie. Perkins was sympathetic, and dwelled on that cruel and inhuman phrase that Sam Weisbord had used: *Put in the computer and found wanting.* How terribly unjust it all was, Perkins thought: If anyone knew the meaning of family it was Weltman, the generous boss who lined up the deals only to pass them off, gift-wrapped, to the younger agents so that they could add the ribbon and the card and call them their own.

At this point in time, Meyer and Ovitz were on one track, Perkins, Rosenfeld, and Haber on another. And yet all five knew one another, and what they knew, they liked. Rosenfeld, when he was still in the movie department at Morris, had spoken several times with Ovitz, telling him on one occasion: "You know, you would make a very good movie agent. They're wasting you in daytime television." Rosenfeld intended the comment to be a compliment—movie agents were at the top of the pecking order among Hollywood talent agents—and Ovitz took it as such. At root, Michael Rosenfeld simply sensed that Michael Ovitz, with his energy and self-confidence, would one day be a superb leader. Rowland Perkins began to notice Ovitz as well, appreciating his tenacity and thoroughness and his ability to grasp ideas quickly.

Both groups of would-be defectors had whispered their plans to Howard West. He was sympathetic, but believed that they might not make it on their own if they set up two separate agencies. He encouraged the five men to unite. After all, their only client of any repute was Sally Struthers, who was then playing Archie Bunker's daughter on the CBS sitcom *All in the Family,* the top-rated show in America for the fourth straight season. West's advice made sense. But before Ovitz and Meyer had the chance to approach the other three, Bill Haber broached the subject with Meyer: "The three of us are leaving. Would you like to join us?" Meyer hesitated. While he was certain that he would make no move without Ovitz, he wasn't convinced that he and his ally should join forces with the other three men. And that's what he told Haber. "Think about it," Haber suggested.

Soon thereafter, Michael and Judy Ovitz went to dinner with Michael's parents. He told his parents that he was considering leaving William Morris to help found a new talent agency. He must have sounded less than 100 percent confident, for David Ovitz, perhaps remembering how much he had always wanted to start *his* own business, offered nothing but encouragement. "If you're working for someone else, you can get fired. If you have the opportunity to go into a business for yourself, *do it.* If you don't make it after five years, you're still young, you can do it again." Those words, delivered so simply but so effectively by his father, were precisely what Michael Ovitz had needed to hear. This was the most crucial decision of his career thus far, and he had, characteristically, taken his time in deciding whether to take the plunge. But now with his father giving his blessing, Michael Ovitz was ready to join the revolution.

By the end of December, he and Ron Meyer had begun to huddle in secret talks with the other three agents. At times they met at Rowland Perkins's home in Bel Air. For one of their crucial meetings they chose a restaurant called The Golden Bull, at the corner of Sawtell and Pico, a place rarely used by agents and thus likely to assure them of privacy. The five began to talk in specifics about their roles in the new agency. Their thought was to set up an all-service agency, one that would handle television and film performers and anyone else in the world of entertainment, and thus take a broader approach than Morris, which had begun by handling vaudeville performers only. The dinner at The Golden Bull came off better than any of them had expected. It seemed that the new agency, which once had seemed only a far-off dream, was about to become a reality.

Bitter feelings about the overly rigid hierarchy at Morris were uppermost in the minds of the defecting five, and therefore the last thing they wanted to do was to quibble over the positions and titles each would have in their new venture. Ovitz proposed that the five men should become equal partners in the new agency, regardless of seniority. One might have expected the other four to defer to Perkins, who was second-oldest of the five and had the most seniority at Morris; but in fact all five agreed that the egalitarian approach was the way to go. With that decision behind them, the time seemed to have come to put their new partnership under contract. But that meant going to a lawyer—and paying a lawyer-like fee.

Morris agent Fred Westheimer, who had been especially close to Meyer, Rosenfeld, and Haber, had been invited to join the men at The Golden Bull as a possible sixth partner. Westheimer wavered. All that he had ever wanted was to be a successful agent, and he was that now. Helping to run a fledgling agency had never been part of his game plan. He was being asked to throw away all that he had built up at Morris, and start from scratch. Michael Ovitz, by now definitely committed to leaving Morris, called Westheimer that evening and said this: "The Morris office is like heart-attack city. Eventually it's going to kill you. It may be its own worst enemy." Still, Ovitz said he wouldn't blame Westheimer if he stuck with Morris. "We could fall on our asses. We could all be begging on the street corner. It's certainly a risk." Westheimer decided to stay put, and as of 1997 he still is an agent at the William Morris Agency.

At a meeting at Rowland Perkins's house the five agents sealed their fate, shaking hands on the new partnership. But they still weren't quite ready to walk out the door. Some loose ends needed to be tied up: the network schedules had yet to be completed, and it was almost time for the end-of-the-year bonuses to be given out. "We needed every dollar," says Michael Rosenfeld. They agreed to make their move in March. That would give them ample time to secure a line of credit, locate office space, and at last announce their departure to the Morris executives. It felt good to them that they were moving so slowly and methodically. So much needed to be done, and they wanted to get everything just right. They realized that at first business would be slow. After all, they could count on only a few major clients joining them at the new agency. One would be Ron Meyer's client, the actor Jack Weston; another was Ovitz's, sports broadcaster Kelly Lange; and the third was Haber's, television producer Lillian Gallo. Weston, Lange, and Gallo weren't exactly Newman, Pacino, and Redford. But it seemed like a decent enough start.

Right at the beginning of 1975, Michael Ovitz lunched with his college friend Frank Marshall, who had embarked on a career as a movie producer. Confiding in Marshall, Ovitz explained how he and his four partners planned to go into business for themselves, convinced that there was room in Hollywood for a middle-sized talent agency, especially now that television was more and more becoming a force to be reckoned with in town.

"How are you going to do this?" Marshall asked, revealing his skepticism.

Admitting that it was a gamble, Ovitz tried to put on a good face: "We're going to work for the clients. We won't take commissions for a year. Our wives will help in the office. We'll make this work."

Michael Rosenfeld wasn't as confident; he passed some sleepless nights. But there seemed to be little to get panicky about. They had plenty of time—or so they thought. In fact, their best-laid plans were about to go very astray.

T HE TROUBLE BEGAN when Michael Ovitz, canvassing banks in his search for the best terms of credit, walked into a bank and spoke to an executive about opening a credit line for the new agency. Somehow, word of Ovitz's explorations got back to William Morris. None of the five partners was ever to know for sure how Morris found out, but some suspected that a bank officer had informed Julius Lefkowitz, the William Morris Agency's outside accountant, who in turn could have told his brother Nathan, the Morris president. Some partners had a different theory, one that fingered Fred Westheimer as the informant. He certainly knew of their plans. And Sam Weisbord had provided an unintended hint that it might be Westheimer, when he said aloud that more people at Morris should have the kind of integrity Fred Westheimer possessed.

Tuesday, January 7, 1974. Michael Ovitz was away on a skiing vacation. It was the first time that he and Judy had gone somewhere and put Ovitz entirely out of touch with the office. They had driven five hours to Mammoth Mountain in the California Sierras. Ron Meyer was home sick with the flu; Michael Rosenfeld, Rowland Perkins, and Bill Haber were working in their offices.

In the morning, Rosenfeld called New York and spoke to the attorney for one of Morris's larger clients. The attorney—who had good contacts at Morris, and had learned of the five agents' secret—told Rosenfeld: "Mike, they know you're leaving. That's all I'm going to tell you. I can't say anymore. I'm just warning you that they know you guys are leaving."

Rosenfeld was stunned. How can this be? A dazed Rosenfeld collected himself and thanked the man for the information. He immediately called Rowland Perkins, and said mysteriously: "Don't be surprised if you hear from somebody today."

Perkins and Rosenfeld decided to carry on routinely by lunching at a restaurant on Sunset Boulevard. When the pair returned to Morris, there was a message for Perkins telling him that Sam Weisbord was looking for him.

Rosenfeld called Bill Haber to warn him: "I'm sure they know, and Rowland just got a call from Weisbord. So be prepared."

Perkins dreaded the meeting with Weisbord. If Rosenfeld's information was solid, and Weisbord already knew of their plans to leave, the meeting would be a disaster. For he and the other four partners to leave Morris, Perkins knew, would be regarded as an act of treason. No one ever dared to leave William Morris to set up another agency. It simply wasn't done.

When Perkins reached Weisbord's office, Weisbord at first said nothing that would suggest he was onto their secret. Then he asked Perkins to join him for one of his well-known walks along the streets of Beverly Hills. Weisbord loved to walk. They set out from the Morris office on El Camino and reached Charleville, then meandered through some side streets: Camden, Bedford, and Rexford. At one point, almost casually, Weisbord let on that he knew very well what Perkins and the others were planning: "Morris Stoller [Executive Vice President of Morris] told me he understands that five of you are leaving the company. Are you really leaving?" Weisbord sounded hurt, confused.

"Yes," Perkins said quietly. "This is something we were going to come in and talk to you about tomorrow."

Weisbord suspected that the five originally had planned to do no such thing. He grew angrier by the minute.

"Now, Perkins," he fumed, waving a finger in his walking-partner's face, "this is treason!"

"Stop it!" Perkins almost shouted back, an uncharacteristic act for the normally taciturn agent. Silence ensued. The two men walked back to the office without uttering another word. There seemed to be nothing more to say.

Meanwhile, Mike Rosenfeld sat in his office, unsettled at having been found out and now more nervous than ever about joining the new venture. While he had a great deal of faith in the other four men, he knew that there was no guarantee the new agency would pan out. He had set aside some money for his 14-year-old son Michael Jr. in a joint bank account. Just recently he had told his son that he wanted to put aside the money—several thousand dollars' worth—as a fund that could be used to pay the household's bills in case things got tough at the new agency.

Rosenfeld thought he had better warn Ron Meyer, who was at that moment suffering at home with a 103° temperature. When Mike reached him on the phone, Ron was so ill that he could hardly speak. Nonetheless, Rosenfeld's warning proved to be of use. A few minutes later, Sam Weisbord did indeed call Meyer.

"Is it true that you are leaving?" he barked, knowing the answer but needing to hear it directly from Meyer. "Yes," said the sick man, his voice cracking, "it is true."

Next Weisbord called Bill Haber into his office and asked him the same question. He got the same response.

Summoned next to Sam Weisbord's office was Michael Rosenfeld. "Well, are you leaving?" Weisbord asked impatiently.

Rosenfeld was too frightened to get the word *yes* out of his mouth. It was as if his vocal chords had frozen. He could only manage to nod uncomfortably.

"Is it true you're taking important clients from us?" Weisbord demanded to know.

No, insisted Rosenfeld, he and his partners had no plans to raid the company.

Then Weisbord laid it on thick. "Half of every dollar we paid you was for loyalty."

The remark sent Rosenfeld into a tirade. For 17 long and hardworking years he had been loyal. He could hardly contain his anger. "You should be sending us off with a parade, because William Morris trains the best agents in the business. You should be sending us off proud of us, and wishing us well. We can never do enough damage to destroy William Morris even if we wanted to, and we don't. That isn't our goal. Our goal is to build our own company. We will be likes fleas shitting on an elephant. That's the damage we'll inflict."

Maybe so, but the fleas were jumping ship. And Sam Weisbord was by no means placated. He knew what the loss of these five star agents would mean to Morris. The William Morris Agency was hemorrhaging, and he wasn't sure if it could stand the loss of blood.

Most upsetting of all for Weisbord was the news that Michael Ovitz was among the traitors. Ovitz had been almost a son to him, one in whom he had placed great hopes. In time, he might even have run the whole show. Not in the near future, of course. But given all of Ovitz's boyish charm, easy self-confidence, and drive, Weisbord was certain he could have brought him along, built him up into a true leader. Few other agents at Morris possessed so many of the right leadership qualities.

Feeling miserable at being discovered, but relieved that the five could now at least operate out in the open, Mike Rosenfeld had one more urgent chore to perform.

Knowing that Michael Ovitz lived only a half-mile from him (both were then living in the Los Angeles suburb of Sherman Oaks) and was due back that evening from his skiing weekend, Rosenfeld rushed over to Ovitz's home. Eager to let Ovitz know that Sam Weisbord had talked to all of the five except him, Rosenfeld stuck a note on the back door: "Please call me. You are no longer working for William Morris. Rosenfeld."

When Ovitz returned home and saw the note, chills coursed through his body. He had tried to sound optimistic in front of his four partners, even predicting that within a year they all would be making money. But now the actuality of leaving the safe harbor of William Morris hit him like a thunderbolt. He was frightened—very, very frightened. He knew that he was—or rather, had been—the fair-haired boy who had Sam Weisbord in his corner and a bright future at Morris. "I had a good career going," he recalled, "and I was scared about leaving." He phoned Rosenfeld, but kept his panic to himself. He pressed his optimism button in order to make himself sound confident and cheerful, and Rosenfeld thought to himself: "This guy is tough. Nothing bothers him." If he only knew . . .

The two men agreed that the five new partners should meet the next day—after all, they had a company to establish. But Ovitz still faced the highest hurdle of them all: Looking Sam Weisbord in the eye one last time. He knew how persuasive Weisbord could be, but Ovitz doubted that the Morris executive could make him change his mind. Yet he did feel unsettled, and who knew, anything *could* happen.

The meeting was brief and, as Ovitz had feared, exceedingly unpleasant: "He was just totally abusive to me. He kept criticizing me for the decision to leave." Years later, Ovitz suggested that Weisbord perhaps had had it in his power to retain both him and Ron Meyer, had the Morris executive simply opted for a softer, kinder approach at that critical moment in their careers. "There was a fifty-fifty chance that if he had put Ronnie and me in the same room and said, 'You are my guys. You have a future here at the company,' we would have both stayed." Ovitz said he learned a great deal from that conversation: "It taught me that until someone is out the door, don't assume that he's out the door. There might be a way of keeping him."

The meeting with Weisbord had done little to relieve Ovitz's fears: "I was scared, but not scared enough not to go ahead."

WEDNESDAY, JANUARY 8, 1975. Suddenly, all of their planning had taken on an urgency that the quintet had hoped to avoid. No longer did they have the luxury of taking several months in which to plan their departure. The Morris executives expected them to be out of their offices in two days. A brooding cloud hung over the five men. The realization that they were about to strike out on their own when in command of almost no resources, gnawed at them. All five understood that it might be quite a while before they could draw a salary. While most of them did own their own homes, none had the discretionary capital with which to invest in a new business. "We had no money," Ovitz recalls. "We had no business, no systems, no organization. I mean nothing." Well, not quite nothing. Michael's father provided typewriters and other supplies. And the partners' wives agreed to volunteer their time at the office.

When one hears the founding days of the new agency described in such stark terms as those Ovitz used just now, it only serves to make the agency's later achievements seem all the more amazing. And yet Ovitz is exaggerating when he suggests that the five partners had no resources whatsoever to draw upon. For they possessed the most important resource of all, an unlimited supply of enthusiasm. They also had access to a whole array of complementary talents, as well as years of experience in the agency business. Indeed, over the past years they had been among Morris's best performers.

Perhaps most important of all, each of the men had been trained and nurtured by Phil Weltman. The reason that fact is so crucial is that it would be the ethic of teamwork and loyalty which Phil had drilled into each of these five men that would uphold all of them throughout the trying days ahead. These were men who genuinely liked and respected one another, and who were determined to create the kind of convivial surroundings that had been conspicuous only by their absence from William Morris. However much they may have worried, they must have known that they really did have a great deal going for them.

Yet the realization that their departure was now so very imminent—two days, rather than three months—was truly disconcerting: "It was sort of like being in the twilight zone," Ron Meyer remembers. "We didn't have any clients or offices or money, but I knew we were talented and energetic, we were good, and we believed in each other. I had no choice but to be optimistic. I knew we'd find a way to make a living."

It seemed as if there were a thousand details to wrestle with—all at once. One had to do with the issue of surviving the next few months. Ron Meyer had no money. In order to join the new organization, he had to borrow some funds from a cousin. Mike Rosenfeld now was ready to turn to the joint account he had set up with his son. Then there was the procural of office space; fortunately, Perkins and Rosenfeld were on friendly terms with television producer David Wolper.

Early on that Wednesday morning of January 8, 1975, Rosenfeld called Irwin Russell, Wolper's number two. "We're leaving Morris," he said bluntly. Somehow, Rosenfeld knew that Jimmy Komack's old office, at 3rd and La Cienega, was free. Komack was a well-known producer associated with Wolper Productions. "If you could help us out," Rosenfeld pleaded, "even with just that one room with a couple of phones, we'd be grateful." Although Wolper was friendly with all five partners, he felt uneasy about helping the five men, concerned that were he to do so he might endanger his good relationship with William Morris. He checked with Morris executive Lou Weiss, who raised no objection. Wolper then got back to Rosenfeld and told him that the five men could remain on the premises rent-free for a reasonable if unspecified amount of time. That was fine with the five, for they had no desire to remain in Komack's old office for long. Their goal was to set up their own shop as soon as was humanly possible.

Other details of the transition still needed to be worked out. Mike Rosenfeld and Rowland Perkins worried that Morris might demand that the two men return their company cars immediately, and not give them the option of purchasing them: That would be an early sign that their departure was going to be bumpy. But two senior Morris executives permitted Rosenfeld and Perkins to purchase the cars at a fair price.

Possessing as all of them did, of course, given their line of work, a keen sense of public relations, the five understood that their departure from William Morris was going to be big news. Never had so many agents from a powerful Hollywood talent agency like William Morris left at once. Never before had so many defected simultaneously with so little financial support. Knowing the Morris style as well as they did, the five were certain that the top execs would spin the story in their own favor, describing the five's departure as an act of betrayal and treason. Thus, the defectors wanted to make sure that their own version of events was given the proper hearing in the press. To that end they prepared a press release, and Rowland Perkins personally delivered it to *Daily Variety* and *The Hollywood Reporter.* It was a smart move. For sure enough, the "trades" then called Morris to verify the startling news.

On the next morning, Thursday, January 9, the public learned the news for the first time when *Daily Variety* ran a story on its front page headlined "Five Top Television Agents Exiting WM to Form Own Agency; Move Called Amicable."

In the article, Sam Weisbord is quoted as saying: "They're all good men. They have been trained in the tradition of the William Morris man. These are men who want to try to go out for themselves and build a business. We have no animus. However, the superstructure of the TV department at WM remains intact. We are powered by an enormous top level of manpower."

No animus?! Privately, Weisbord and other senior executives at Morris were steaming. Jerry Katzman, a young agent at William Morris at the time, recalls that "The Morris office was a place where you were born, bred, and died. What these five men did was treacherous in some people's minds." Morris's senior executives certainly were eager to see the five defectors fall on their faces. They even spread tales that the five men had been dismissed for stealing typewriters! Some junior agents played down the loss, predicting that their beloved William Morris wouldn't suffer because "those guys aren't executives, they're shoe-leather agents." Rowland Perkins, upon hearing of that phrase, took it as a compliment!

When he was interviewed for the article, Michael Rosenfeld sought to scotch any notion that theirs was a disgruntled departure, but he certainly did hint at the real reason they had for leaving: "The guys really want to do their own thing. The size of the company [WM] and the way it's set up doesn't allow it. We love the company; we feel we are leaving home, but we want to make it on our own. There is no dissent and no hostility. We are very sad about leaving the company, but excited about forming our own." On the next day, Friday, as if to show the whole entertainment world that the defections hadn't fazed its ongoing operations in the least, the William Morris Agency ran a full-page advertisement in *Daily Variety* which stated that it was "delighted to represent *The New Smothers Brothers Show* and wishes Tommy and Dick . . . the best of luck."

On that same Thursday morning, *The Hollywood Reporter* ran a page-one story of its own ("5 WM Agents Form New Firm") that provides a fascinating insight into the pecking order of the five at that time: "Less than a month after his accession to a vice presidency, a sixteen-year veteran of the William Morris Agency is leading an exodus of himself and four other key WMA agents in order to set up shop for themselves." In other words, it was Rowland Perkins leading the exodus, not Mike Rosenfeld, not Ron Meyer, not Bill Haber, and most important of all, not Michael Ovitz.

In his comments, Perkins candidly acknowledges that the key factor spurring him to act at this time has been the recent shakeup at William Morris, the one that gave the New York executives more direct control over the running of the West Coast operation. But he insisted that the chief incentive was the desire of the five men to run their own business. "What basically prompted us," Perkins was quoted as saying, "was primarily wanting to set up our own business. We've been talking about this for some time."

The *Reporter* article made it clear that the quintet posed a potent threat to William Morris: "They are expected to make a sizeable dent in the William Morris list in the process."

Michael Ovitz was seen as being merely one of the minor players in this drama, and was relegated to only two sentences of description in the article: "With the company six years, Ovitz has handled the major load of WMA's coast daytime packaging operations. He has been additionally concerned with prime time programming, and has represented many writers."

As the industry gradually became acquainted with the new endeavor, the founders went to work trying to ensure that their new agency got off to an auspicious start. The best way to do that seemed to be to merge with an established literary agency, and thereby give the new endeavor a ready-made client list. Michael Rosenfeld contacted his closest friend Rick Ray (the two owned a plane together). Rick was a partner at Adams, Ray, and Rosenberg, a well-respected literary agency with its own full list of screenwriters, television writers, and authors. "We would have gone from a client list of almost nothing," says Rosenfeld, "to an entire client list belonging to a very fine, boutique literary agency." On Friday, January 10, the last day on which the five new partners would be employed at the William Morris Agency, Michael Rosenfeld and Rowland Perkins lunched with Rick Ray and Lee Rosenberg at Frascati, a restaurant on Sunset near Doheny. While on the surface the merger sounded like a good idea, the partners of the literary agency were too disdainful of the talent agency business to let the deal go down. "I will never negotiate a parking space at a studio for an actor," Sam Adams insisted. Rosenfeld recalls that Michael Ovitz favored the arrangement, and indeed all five partners, when the merger fell through, were disappointed. And yet in later years, Rosenfeld considered the five to have been fortunate *not* to have brought

Adams, Ray and Rosenberg on-board as partners. For given the literary men's deeply engrained distaste for the talent-agency business, "it might have destroyed us," Rosenfeld believes.

On Monday, January 13, 1975, the new company opened up for business. Punchy from their massive exertions of the previous week the five partners knew they still had a ton of work to do. They still had no formal name, but they were working on that. The tasks were divided up. One partner searched for permanent office space; another for stationery; a third for phones. The afternoons were devoted to drumming up business.

The five would have preferred to go leaderless. They had had their share of bosses at William Morris. It was the bosses who had fired their mentor, Phil Weltman; who had prevented Rowland Perkins from running the West Coast television operation; who had turned William Morris into a place that stifled rather than nurtured enthusiasm and creativity. Had they gotten their wish, the new agency would have run itself. In those early moments of euphoria and idealism, the five men saw the new venture as almost a mythical commune where everyone was free to toss out ideas, decisions were made collectively, and no one reigned supreme—in short, the "one big happy family" that Morris was supposed to be but wasn't. Alas, for legal reasons, corporate officers simply had to be chosen, but the partners were determined to choose in the most random way possible.

Because of his seniority at Morris, Rowland Perkins was made president. Ovitz became a vice president, as did Ron Meyer. Bill Haber became secretary and assistant treasurer, and Michael Rosenfeld, treasurer and assistant secretary!

It was also at this stage that the five drew up a partnership contract with buy-and-sell arrangements, spelling out what would happen to the firm if one of the partners left it.

A secretary was hired. The five men spent $200 on some used office furniture, one piece being a conference table that they picked up from a discount store; they brought card tables and folding chairs from their homes. A few days later Michael Rosenfeld looked at the other four partners as they did their business while seated on folding chairs at the card tables, and thought to himself: *It looks like we're "booking," but not actors. It looks like we're "making book"!*

It was quite a comedown for the hotshot ex-Morris agents. Just a few weeks earlier they had been working out of plush offices and some of them had driven Agency-purchased cars. Now they were paying rent for small offices and still didn't have any permanent furniture. And yet the sweet smell of success was in the air nonetheless. And the man who filled the place with that optimism was Michael Ovitz.

"There was," observes Mike Rosenfeld, "a synergistic cloud that enveloped us all. We just worked seven days a week, around the clock." And Ovitz set the pace. "Just to watch Ovitz was enough, if anybody had any doubts about our succeeding. This was not a man who was thinking about failure." A feeling of isolation also spurred the five on. Ron Meyer explains that "there had been people at Morris who had been our friends, and they were no longer our friends. Every day we thought we were going to war a little bit. At the start William Morris was out to discredit us and hurt us. We felt that if they're coming at us, we better push even harder and go after them. The best defense is a good offense. And that never stopped. Once we adopted that position, we didn't know how to do it differently."

Pretty much affirming Meyer's observations, Sam Weisbord, as interviewed in the January 22, 1975, issue of *The Hollywood Reporter,* sounds extremely defensive—and bitter: "The Morris Office is an institution. It is grounded in granite for seventy-six years. We have withstood wars, vicissitudes of every kind, deaths, departures. You name it, we've undergone it. The company stands at the apex of its powers today. It is leaner, tighter, better than it has ever been. We have built our team. Fellows who want to leave for reasons of ambition or whatever reason in no way affect the power superstructure, the basic core of our company. To repeat myself, we're stronger now than we've ever been."

Despite the early hope of all five partners that they might find a way to turn the new agency into a commune of sorts, and despite the fact that Rowland Perkins and Michael Rosenfeld were his seniors, Michael Ovitz, though only 28 years old, had quickly emerged as the de facto leader of the organization. "I just automatically took over," Ovitz noted. "It wasn't preordained. It just happened. I came in like a pilot with a checklist of what we had to do. I just basically organized the business from day one." Ovitz recalled the advice his father had given him when he was 17—"If you want to be perceived as a king, you have to act like one"—and took that to mean that gaining the respect of others was central to success in business. "You don't get respect unless you first command respect," he noted. "You can't ask someone to do something you won't do yourself. You have to be first out of the foxhole if you want to lead in battle." When a task had to be done, Ovitz said to himself, "I'm going to do it," and the other four all said, "Great." And before anyone realized it, Ovitz knew more about the business than any of the others. He began to look after the others, but that entailed making sure that everyone fulfill his particular function. "Are all the bases covered?" became a favorite Ovitz question.

Ovitz took advantage of the fact that the other four partners were neither natural-born leaders nor particularly ambitious. But Ovitz himself had both the leadership abilities and the raw ambition, and nothing seemed likely to stop him from taking over the new agency, although he had been a very junior partner at first.

THE ACTOR DEAN Jones, star of numerous films including *That Darn Cat* (1965) and *The Love Bug* (1969), dropped by the agency on one of those first days of business. Jones had been a client of Phil Weltman, and he had close ties to all five partners. To Jones, the five men were doing something important, for they had an opportunity to set an example as to how a talent agency should be run. Seated around a makeshift conference table with the partners, Jones suddenly suggested that they join hands and pray. Ovitz looked around at the others, wondering what the hell this had to do with founding an agency. But he went along.

"May God bless this agency," Jones said, leading the prayer. "You have a chance to establish a company with integrity. You are building your reputations in the industry. And you can be known as men who keep your word. You have the example of Phil Weltman as a man of integrity and discipline. You can become an honorable theatrical agency. Power can flow out of that, the right kind of power. Amen."

After the prayer, Jones stayed around to talk. He liked what he heard. None of the five partners had pie-in-the-sky expectations. "Dean," said one of the five, "if we can have ten clients apiece, and if we eventually could make as much as $65,000 a year each, we'd be ecstatic."

FINALLY THE NEW agency had a name: Creative Artists Agency (CAA). On Thursday, January 23, 1975, the name appeared before the industry for the first time when *Daily Variety* ran a front-page story entitled "Ex-WM Agents Form Creative Artists Firm." A similar story appeared in *The Hollywood Reporter* that day. The *Reporter* article indicated that officers already had been chosen: "Actual chain of command is indicated in the designation of corporate officers, according to company president Rowland Perkins; Mike Orvitz [sic] and Ron Meyer are v-p's, Bill Haber, secretary and assistant treasurer, and Mike Rosenfeld, treasurer and assistant secretary." Yet the communal aspect of the business was still seen as being the most striking one: "The five founders will be equal partners and constitute the board of directors. None will specialize in specific jurisdictions."

To the directors, the new name sounded strong, professional, and, most important of all, different from "The William Morris Agency." But it caused trouble nevertheless. CMA's executives, disturbed that "Creative Artists" was too close for comfort to "Creative Management," fired off a cable of protest to CAA. Ovitz and his partners even began to hear rumors that CMA wanted to file a lawsuit over the name. And indeed, a debate over whether to file such a suit was raging at CMA. Around the time that CAA had been formed, Marvin Josephson's firm, Marvin Josephson Associates, had bought CMA from Freddie Fields. But when Fields, who planned to continue to work for Josephson, heard about the name CAA, he became irate. His pride was hurt, and he got Josephson on the phone.

"Marvin, you've got to stop them. You're calling yourself 'Creative Management.' And this is 'Creative Artists.' "

Josephson sought to calm Fields down, explaining that he was planning to put the word "International" in front of the phrase "Creative Management."

But Fields persisted: "You've got to stop it."

"I don't think it matters," Josephson said. "It can't hurt us." He simply didn't feel threatened by the CAA five. There would be no lawsuit.

By January 23, 1975, two weeks after the five partners had moved into the Wolper office on La Cienega and 3rd Street, they were on the move again. This time to permanent quarters a few blocks away, in a fifth-floor office in the Hong Kong Bank Building at 9300 Wilshire Boulevard at Wilshire and Rexford.

Trying to appear serious and professional, each CAA partner gave himself a private office, to go along with the conference room, mail room (ironically but also perhaps inevitably, modeled after the one at William Morris), and reception area. Of course the one part of the office that needed to look attractive was the reception area, so the partners asked one of their clients, an art director, to decorate it. Still, Ovitz strove to keep all costs down. Legal and accounting fees were kept to a minimum. The only overhead was rent, as well as those office supplies above and beyond the ones that David Ovitz had provided.

The most serious indication of rampant frugality was the presence of the partners' wives, taking turns answering the telephones one day a week. The partners had literally been left to their own resources. "We were just five guys with briefcases," says Rowland Perkins, "standing in an empty space. But at least now we had space and phones, and we were feeling good."

It was time to officially let the world know that there was a new kid in town.

On January 24, the new agency announced its formation by taking out a full-page ad in *The Hollywood Reporter.* The ad said simply: "Established 1975, Creative Artists Agency, Inc." And it was signed: Bill Haber, Ron Meyer, Michael Ovitz, Rowland Perkins, and Mike Rosenfeld. At the bottom of the page was the address, 9300 Wilshire Boulevard, Beverly Hills, California 90212. This advertisement was in a real sense the first calling card left by CAA, and the sense of equality was conveyed by the way in which the names were given in alphabetical order. The same advertisement appeared in *Daily Variety* on January 31.

THE NAME OF the game was attracting clients. The more famous, the better. While Michael Rosenfeld had promised Sam Weisbord that he and his partners would not raid William Morris, there was nothing to prevent Morris clients from switching agencies on their own. Often a client felt a loyalty for his or her agent, not for the agency where the agent worked. Ovitz and his partners had been relying upon Jack Weston, Kelly Lange, and Lillian Gallo, all of whom had indicated that they would be with CAA from its inception. Weston's commitment alone had, as Ron Meyer recalls, been a major reason for the five agents to form the new agency. But at the last minute, all three Morris clients got cold feet. The new partners were deeply disappointed, but there wasn't much they could do. Some 20 other Morris clients, not as well known as the first three, did leave Morris to join CAA at its founding. Unfortunately, none of those 20 could pay commissions to CAA until after their obligations to Morris had run out over the next year or two.

One of those 20 clients was William Conrad, the actor best known for playing an assortment of character roles, often mustached, cold-blooded heavies or detectives. He and Ernest Borgnine were the best known of CAA's initial clients. From 1971 to 1976 Conrad starred in the hit TV series *Cannon,* playing an overweight private eye. When he was still at William Morris back in the summer of 1974, Rowland Perkins had signed Conrad to a three-year contract.

Conrad had been out of town when the five had left Morris. On his return he phoned Perkins at Morris to take care of some routine business, only to be told by the departing agent that he and four other Morris agents were leaving to set up their own talent agency.

"I want to come with you," the television star said, without giving it a second's thought.

"That's fine, we'd love to have you!" Perkins proclaimed enthusiastically.

Would William Morris mind?

Perkins suggested that Conrad call Sam Weisbord and ask to be released from his obligations to Morris.

Conrad did just that.

"Bill!" said Weisbord. "So good to hear from you. Funny, we've been having long talks about you here in the last few days. We'd like you to come in. We have to decide on your career."

"That's why I'm calling you," Conrad suggested. "You know what my relationship has been with Rowland Perkins. I really want to go with him. I'd appreciate it if you would let me out of our agreement. You can keep whatever commissions you're entitled to."

The phone went dead-silent for a full minute. When Weisbord finally resumed the conversation, his tone had decidedly changed.

"Not a chance, Bill. You're not leaving until the end of the three years. It will be over my dead body."

"I don't think I want to do that," Conrad commented unemotionally. "I'll talk to you later."

Conrad did join CAA, and the five partners made sure that they paid Morris whatever commissions were owed to Conrad while his three-year contract with Morris remained in force. (Actors like Conrad routinely paid agencies 10 percent of their earnings.)

Among the other clients who switched from Morris to CAA in those first days were Talia Shire, Francis Ford Coppola's younger sister, who played Sylvester Stallone's shy girlfriend in *Rocky* and Al Pacino's sister in *The Godfather, Part II;* veteran actors Burgess Meredith and Debbie Reynolds; the popular musical group The Jackson Five, out of which of course superstar Michael Jackson was to emerge; Barbara Feldon (Agent 99 on the defunct spy spoof *Get Smart*); and Chad Everett (Dr. Joe Gannon on the CBS series *Medical Center*). Rowland Perkins also lured William Morris clients Larry Hagman (who would go on to play J.R. Ewing on the long-running [1978–91], highly-rated TV series *Dallas*) and Fess Parker (who played Davy Crockett in a 1954–55 TV show).

One month before founding CAA, Michael Ovitz had begun to woo an up-and-coming 29-year-old Morris client named Rob Reiner, who had been enjoying great success in the role of Mike "Meathead" Stivic, the often-exasperated son-in-law of Archie Bunker in *All in the Family*. The son of legendary comic actor and writer Carl Reiner, Rob won Emmy awards in 1974 and 1978 for playing the "Meathead" role. After he had informed Reiner of the plan to establish a new talent agency, Ovitz asked him to switch his allegiance. Reiner, finding Ovitz to be "persuasive and forceful," and not bothered by his aggressiveness, agreed. Ovitz pursued other cast members of *All in the Family* and snared Sally Struthers, the actress who played Gloria Stivic, the Meathead's wife. "When Michael mentioned to me that he was going to start his own agency," said Struthers, "I didn't have to think about it for two seconds."

Some performers, like the actor George Segal, affiliated with ICM at the time, took a wait-and-see attitude, while still making it clear how pleased he was that CAA existed: "Before, it was Morris or ICM. Hertz or Avis. Now we have a choice," he told Rowland Perkins. Segal eventually did become a CAA client.

And yet CAA's first few months generated more optimism than revenue. No one understood CAA's dilemma better than Michael Ovitz. He was handling the day-to-day finances, and he knew that the company had to build up its revenues. He thought that one good way would be to find more work for Bill Carruthers, the daytime game-show producer who had been an Ovitz client at William Morris. Ovitz had secured a major deal for Carruthers at Warner Brothers, one that had the game-show producer developing and selling daytime shows. When Ovitz asked Carruthers to move over to CAA, he was pleased to make the move. Within the first few months of 1975, Michael Ovitz sold two daytime shows, one on behalf of Carruthers to CBS called *Give and Take,* with Jim Lang; another on behalf of Bill Naud to ABC called *Rhyme and Reason,* hosted by Bob Eubanks. To Carruthers, Ovitz could do no wrong: "He was driven. He had a great ethic and a great business sense. Michael would create avenues for you that you hadn't thought about yourself. You sensed that he had taken responsibility for your career." Carruthers felt in debt to Ovitz. He had a chance to repay that debt when Ovitz asked Carruthers if he would give his wife Judy work as a model on *Give and Take.* Carruthers wasn't thrilled by the request. "I had three models on the show and it troubled me that I would have to let one of them go to put Mike's wife on the show. But I would have cut my arm off before refusing to do what Mike asked."

Ovitz was indeed smooth, as in getting Carruthers to fire someone in order to make room for Judy Ovitz while still not making the producer feel steamrolled. Thanks to the agent fees streaming in from the daytime game shows, CAA was able to stay afloat through the fall of 1975. When it came to television programs, if a talent agency like CAA was involved in the packaging of such programs, the fees paid to the agency could be substantial, far more than the fees paid for individual talent. Ovitz remained in daytime television through 1975, all the while accumulating more and more mainstream clients.

The agency made important inroads into the television packaging side of the business by putting into practice the policy they hadn't been able to sell William Morris executives on: a reduction of the customary fee charged for television packaging from 10 to 6 percent. As a result, within a few weeks of founding the agency, Ovitz had sold television packages for *The Rich Little Show* and a program featuring The Jackson Five. The 10 percent fee charged by Morris was "too rich," Ovitz notes, "people couldn't afford it. When we cut our television fee from 10 to 6 percent, it increased the volume of our business, so we wound up making far more than if we had charged the higher rate."

ONE EVENT THAT came during the latter part of that year gave Rowland Perkins the feeling that CAA was indeed on the right track. Actor Chad Everett wanted desperately to do a movie for television. He had never done one before.

One evening, Ron Meyer said to the partners as they sat around the conference table, "I've got good news and bad news." He had received an offer for Everett to do a movie for $50,000 that would require only two weeks of the actor's time. A very good deal indeed. The partners were thrilled, for in those salad days of the fledgling firm a $5000 commission would have been almost the equivalent of a million-dollar fee. The bad news, however, Meyer said, was that "we can't let him do it."

Ovitz and the three others listened in amazement. Had Ron Meyer gone crazy? What could possibly be so important as to keep CAA from buying into such a deal?

"The script stinks," Meyer said with finality.

Absorbing his words, the other partners, who also had gone over the script, had to admit that Meyer had a point. They urged him to give Everett the bad news.

As far as Perkins is concerned, that represented an important turning point for the new agency. If the partners could coolly appraise the merits of a deal and then decide whether it was a good one or a bad one for a client and act accordingly, CAA would be moving in the right direction. "I knew we were doing business the right way," Perkins says.

CAA was off to a reasonable start. But it was still far from Michael Ovitz's dream of being the greatest talent agency in Hollywood. So far

such talk seemed mere hyperbole. The problem confronting the five partners at that time was not how to create Hollywood's top talent agency, but
simply how to reach the point where they could begin to collect salaries.
All one could say as of then was that the founders had put together a
modest startup venture, nothing more. Ovitz had his dreams, but there
was no real reason to assume that he would fulfill them in the near future.
Nonetheless, he had some very clear ideas as to the best ways to take the
agency to the next level, and he was about to act upon them.

5

Master Illusionist

As of August of 1975, Michael Ovitz's roster of clients didn't include a single star that could light up a movie marquee. Oscar-winning *Godfather* star Al Pacino had signed with William Morris's Stan Kamen, as had a no-name actor, armed with a nice little boxing script, by the name of Sylvester Stallone. Kamen had his sights on Robert Redford and director Sydney Pollack as well. If CAA was to become the flagship agency that Michael Ovitz hungered for it to be, it would have to start handling the careers of some real stars, not run-of-the-mill television actors but film stars who already were household names. Of course the problem was that the biggest stars were in the habit of signing on with the biggest agencies, the William Morrises and ICM's of the world, not with some faceless, struggling startup called Creative Artists whose agents drew up their contracts on the tops of folding tables.

But now Ovitz was ready to make his move. On an evening in June, six months after CAA's founding, the five partners were gathered around the conference table to discuss the company's future. Ovitz had concluded that the only way in which CAA could become a breakthrough agency was by acquiring some top-flight film clients. He announced this to his colleagues and then added: "You guys should really stick to TV. That's where you're selling shows. But I'm going to start to get myself known in the motion picture business."

Ovitz's decision to seek film stars as clients was part of a broader restructuring of CAA that seemed like a good idea if the agency was going to make a serious bid at expansion. The original egalitarian impulse had proven to be a source of fun but also of chaos, as each of the five partners had tried his hand at everything. But now their client list was growing, and there were only 24 hours in a day. None of the CAA partners could bring himself to admit it, but for all of their criticism of the bureaucracy at William Morris, its compartmentalization did make sense. In August the five partners went on their first weekend retreat to Lake Arrowhead, north of Los Angeles; it was just the five of them, and they held business meetings in between long walks in the rustic surroundings. It was on that weekend that they decided to hire more support personnel and to divide up the responsibility for the "covering" of the networks, i.e., for the finding of work there for CAA clients. Perkins took CBS, Haber NBC, and Rosenfeld ABC, just as they had back at Morris. Ovitz and Meyer would take the much more daring plunge into the uncharted waters of the film business.

Michael Ovitz wished that he could simply pick up the phone and ring a major film star, ask for a meeting, and then rely upon his personal charm and formidable powers of persuasion to entice that star to become a client of Creative Artists Agency. But he knew that there could be no phone calls, no meetings, no chance to turn on the Ovitz charm. For the stars simply had no idea who Ovitz was, nor did they care to find out. Thus, he needed something that would cause them to sit up and take notice of the agency. He needed some leverage that he could use to win the stars over with, and he had an idea. If he could get his hands on some exciting literary properties and then put together a whole film package including a script, producer, and director, perhaps he could lure some big-name stars to CAA.

The first step was to get ahold of such marketable literary properties, and as it turned out, the time was ripe for Ovitz to hunt them down. The studios had all but abdicated their old function of putting feature films together. In the old days, up until the Sixties, the major studios had purchased a literary property, hired a screenwriter, linked up a studio executive with the screenwriter, approached a director, and then cast the film. But the studios no longer had that wide variety of talent under contract—such talent now was represented by the agents, which placed the agencies in the ideal position to put a film package together.

Ovitz decided to spend 10 days of each month in New York City, visiting the top literary agents in town. Time after time he made "handshake deals" with them, some 80 in all. But no literary agent was more important than Mort Janklow, and Ovitz wanted nothing more than to come to an agreement with him.

One day in the spring of 1975, Michael Ovitz picked up the phone in Los Angeles and reached Janklow's secretary. She told the literary agent that a man named Michael Ovitz was on the line. Janklow was puzzled, for the name meant nothing to him. Still, he took the call.

"You don't know me. My name is Michael Ovitz. Four other guys and I have left William Morris and we've started our own agency. We have in fact rented space. We are working on bridge tables. Our wives are manning the phones. We are going to build the biggest agency in 10 years. And I've decided that you are one of the keys to our success."

Janklow didn't quite know what to make of the brash young man. His hype was vintage Hollywood, but Janklow sensed something in Ovitz's voice that was different. Was it sincerity? An infectious enthusiasm?

Ovitz said that he was prepared to fly to New York for no other reason than to meet with the literary agent. "I'll take only a half-hour of your time." Ovitz admitted that the flight across-country was no small undertaking for the fledgling agency: "I want you to know the stage we're in now. The expense of this trip is a factor for me."

Janklow was softening. "His directness was appealing," Janklow would say years later. He decided to see Ovitz.

When he reached Janklow's office, Ovitz placed his watch on the desk and then spoke for exactly 30 minutes, as promised. The more Janklow listened, the more impressed he became, finding Ovitz to be a bright, hard-working man who knew the business very well: "He was very intense, very buttoned. His thought-process was very organized. He seemed very determined. He had a very clarified view of what he wanted to do, especially for someone that young in a field that is traditionally more salesmanship than substance. He seemed a very substantial man. I liked him."

Ovitz wanted to take Janklow's literary properties and turn them into television or feature-film projects. He told Janklow that the future of the talent-agency business lay in the concept of packaging. In the past, Hollywood talent agencies had acquired a client first, then looked around for a script for the client. Ovitz wanted to reverse the process, by finding the script and then pooling his talent agency's clients into a complete package that would be sold to a film studio. "That," said Janklow, "was a very astute judgment in the late 1970s. Ovitz recognized that the game had shifted from the star being everything to the vehicle being everything, and the star being part of the vehicle."

Ovitz asked Janklow if CAA could represent the literary agent in California. Janklow said that that would be premature.

Ovitz then asked the literary agent if he could call him every Thursday at 10:00 a.m. Janklow said yes, and Ovitz began to phone at precisely that hour once a week. Janklow still wasn't sure what to make of the young man, but he certainly was persistent and disciplined: "You could set your watch by his phone call."

"Hi, Mort, how are you? Got anything for me?" Ovitz would say. Whether or not Janklow had anything, Ovitz would fill him in on the latest moves at CAA: We've just signed so and so, we've just rented more space in the building.

It went on like that for about a year. Lots of phone calls, but no business. Then Janklow decided to test Ovitz's ability to sell a manuscript to television or film. Stuart Woods had sold a novel called *Chiefs* to Norton. Woods then asked Janklow to take him on as his agent. Janklow sold the paperback rights for $300,000, then sold the movie rights; but a year and a half had passed and the movie option had expired; the project seemed dead in the water.

The next time Ovitz phoned, Janklow told him about the faltering project: "I have something you can try, but an attempt at a movie has been made by the producing unit which I sold it to. Still, this is an opportunity. It's a very dramatic property."

Ovitz asked Janklow if he really liked the property. "Yes!" said Janklow enthusiastically.

"Then let me try. I'd love to try."

Janklow mailed the book to Ovitz, who read it the next day and agreed with Janklow's positive assessment of the book. Despite Janklow's pessimism about the book's prospects, Ovitz had some thoughts on how to sell the project. With the help of partner Bill Haber, who lined up Charlton Heston, though not a CAA client, to star in a film based on the book, Ovitz sold the project to CBS. Janklow was both surprised and thrilled. Janklow had failed to win CBS's agreement to air a weekly series based upon the book, but the network, now impressed that Ovitz had Heston on-board, decided to back a mini-series. *Chiefs* turned out to be a huge hit and it launched the Ovitz-Janklow relationship, a connection that would lead to CAA's profitable involvement in the television mini-series format.

IF HE WAS going to woo the Redfords and Stallones, the Streisands and Newmans, Michael Ovitz knew that he had to become more visible. For who was he, after all? Just a kid of 28, not a real mover and shaker. He knew that, and what was worse, so did everyone else. The Hollywood pecking order placed movie agents at the top because they dealt with the glamorous world of the big screen. Television agents were quite literally beneath them, second-class citizens. Sue Mengers, ICM's formidable agent of that period, did her best to keep CAA's agents in their place by referring to them disparagingly as "the TV boys." She might as well have called them "minor leaguers."

Ovitz wanted to reach the top of the pecking order, and fast. But how to get there? It had taken the major talent agents many years to scale the heights. How could he expect to make a name for himself overnight? But even if the challenge did seem daunting, Ovitz wasn't rattled. A serious challenge had never fazed him. He seemed to warm up to a good challenge, in fact. He remembered what his father had taught him: If you want to gain people's respect, you have to command it. The best way to command respect in Hollywood, Ovitz decided, was to create the illusion of success. Hollywood, he had concluded, was all about cosmetics, first impressions. Thus, if he could just make the industry believe that he and his new agency were a force to be reckoned with, CAA would be glad to build itself up on a superstructure of illusion.

What Ovitz needed was to gain instant recognition as "a player." But with few resources and little reputation, it wouldn't be easy. He conceived of a ploy that might just win him some much-needed attention. In Beverly Hills there is a restaurant called La Scala on Little Santa Monica Boulevard and Beverly Drive. John F. Kennedy used to hang out there, and Paul Newman and many other Hollywood glitterati still did. Sure, it was a hole-in-the-wall, but that only seemed to give it a special aura. It had red booths and Ovitz thought it a horrible place, but an agent's motto has to be, "When in Hollywood, do as the movie stars do."

One evening in spring of 1975, Michael Ovitz walked into La Scala, all cocky swagger. He walked right up to Tony, the maitre d', a guy who could easily distinguish the Somebodies from the Nobodies. Tony had no idea who this person who was approaching him was, and kept his guard up accordingly. Dancing around in Ovitz's head was a bold plan which, if executed perfectly, would propel him swiftly into the world of Hollywood's power players. Suddenly but also casually, as if he did this every day, Ovitz pulled a $100 bill out of his pocket. Tony was keeping a careful eye on Ovitz, and when he saw the Benjamin Franklin note he was at first confused: Why is this Nobody behaving like a Somebody? Then Ovitz did something that amazed Tony: He tore the bill into two equal pieces, handing one half to Tony. While the occasional $100 here and there wasn't going to push CAA into bankruptcy, every dollar counted in those days, and it's a safe bet that Ovitz's partners wouldn't have looked kindly on the ripping up of large bills in order to indulge a mere whim. Ovitz was aware of that, but thought this risk a calculated one.

"This is for you," Ovitz said, turning on the charm as a smile crossed his face, and acting as if it were the most natural thing in the world to rip $100 bills in two. "I'm building a business, and I'm coming back here with my wife later tonight. I want the best booth in the restaurant. In the future I will be coming with guests. Not tonight. I won't have any guests tonight. Just my wife. You take good care of me, and you'll get the other half."

To Ovitz's delight, Tony proceeded to give him one of those "Okay, I'm going to buy into this" looks. By means of a big grin and a bit of body language, Tony made it clear that Ovitz would get his way this evening, but was still on probation. The clear but unspoken message was, *You'll get your table, but you'd better be as important as you're acting like you are.*

When Michael and Judy Ovitz arrived at La Scala later that evening, Tony, eager for the other half of that $100 bill, ushered the brash young man and his wife to the front stall. Ovitz was secretly thrilled at how he had managed to pull the wool over the eyes of the maitre d'—and of all those who passed near the front stall. Trying to look as if he belonged in that prized spot, Ovitz thought to himself: *I have no money. And yet the Who's Who of the industry are passing by our table and looking at us as if we're somebody important. But I'm a* nobody. Yet it is out of such small deceptions that great talent agencies arise—or so Michael Ovitz hoped.

Every once in a while Ovitz recognized someone he knew—not a big star, but someone with whom he could chat briefly—and he was glad he could send such signals that he was indeed well known around town. He wanted to be noticed. That was enough—for now.

"Going to La Scala," Ovitz would say years later, "was all about image," and the illusion of success.

So was buying the Jaguars. During the summer of 1976, Ovitz was looking for ways to make it appear that CAA was doing well. "We made a strategic decision," said Ovitz, "to take the excess cash we had and buy five Jaguars." Four of the cars were four-door; Ron Meyer got a two-door because he wanted a sports model. Ovitz's was navy blue, Haber's maroon, Perkins's white, and Rosenfeld's silver-gray. Ovitz found a car agency from which he was able to get all five cars for a hefty discount, paying $15,000 for each car. The partners arranged to get customized license plates that had CAA and their initials on them. Ovitz's was CAA-MSO. Rosenfeld's was CAA-MR, Meyer's was CAA-RM, and so on. "Sure enough," recalls Ovitz, "within a week we're driving them around and everyone is saying, 'Look at how great those guys are doing.' Which was exactly the effect we wanted the cars to have. We wanted to create confidence. But it was baloney. It had nothing to do with our abilities." It had to do with creating an illusion, and Ovitz was becoming a master illusionist.

But illusion was one thing, reality another. And the reality of CAA at that time was that the agents had to be frugal. Ovitz wasn't afraid to spend in a good cause, but he did continually remind his partners that every few hundred dollars could well have a bearing on their agency's survival. And yet on one occasion, frugality went out the window, and the experience taught Ovitz to be even more careful about how CAA should spend money.

The occasion was an evening hosted by a pair of CAA clients, Joe Bologna and his wife Renee Taylor. Bologna, an actor and screenwriter had married Renee Taylor, an actress and screenwriter, in 1965. In 1968, they had written and starred in a Broadway comedy, *Lovers and Other Strangers*, which had been made into a 1970 feature film of the same name. When Bologna and Taylor offered to take the five partners to dinner, Ovitz responded favorably, for while the partners didn't have to count every single penny, a free dinner was a free dinner.

Ovitz reserved a private room in the expensive Chinese restaurant Jade West in Century City, and passed the word to his partners that Taylor and Bologna would be treating. On arriving at the restaurant, Ovitz told the maitre d' that "the guy with the big cigar," pointing to Bologna, would be picking up the tab.

The dinner was marvelous, filled as it was with good conversation and laughter. Finally the maitre d' came over with the $500 check, and plunked it down on a plate in front of Bologna, as instructed. Seated right next to Bologna was Diane Perkins, Rowland's wife. Without a second's hesitation she snatched the check off the plate and proclaimed with great pride: "We never let a client pay for dinners." Bologna made no effort to grab the check back.

Rowland Perkins turned red. Michael Ovitz turned white. The other CAA partners turned other colors, as their faces froze in bewilderment. Diane Perkins, quite unaware of the embarrassment she was causing, handed the check to Bill Haber, who passed it to Mike Rosenfeld, as if it were too hot to touch; Rosenfeld passed the check to Michael Ovitz, who turned it over to Rowland Perkins. Years later, Michael Ovitz would stress that talent agents must be professionals. This dinner at Jade West would provide the aspiring professional with a good lesson in how *not* to seem professional. Not knowing whether to laugh or cry, Perkins paid the bill, feeling that he had no choice. For all the rest of that evening, the tone among the five partners was funereal. Michael Ovitz *fumed* all the way home. . . .

FRONT TABLES AT La Scala; Jaguars; making deals with literary agents like Mort Janklow. CAA was moving right along, but not fast enough for Michael Ovitz. In 1975 its gross billings had been only $2.5 million and its revenues only $200,000. Ovitz recorded no income for 1975 when he filed his income taxes. By May 1976, 16 months after its founding, CAA was debt-free, but it had to find ways to raise its revenues substantially. Michael Ovitz continued to search for ways to attract high-priced talent, but that was easier said than done. CAA now had a decent-enough list of clients, including Sally Struthers, Ernest Borgnine, The Jackson Five, Debbie Reynolds, Candy Clark, Buddy Hackett, Chad Everett, William Conrad, Burgess Meredith, Yvette Mimieux, Karen Valentine, Angela Lansbury, Eva Marie Saint, Rich Little, and a host of writers and producers. But there were more prominent names out there that Ovitz was hungry to sign as CAA clients. For one thing, CAA needed cash. The partners still were not drawing a salary. And daytime television clients couldn't bring in enough income to keep the place afloat for much longer. Ovitz needed some film stars, and he needed them *now*.

He turned to a friend, a business manager named Ed Traubner, who in turn put him in touch with a veteran talent agent named Martin Baum. Over the preceding year Baum had been running his own small but prestigious talent agency, with a roster of movie talent that Ovitz envied. Baum had been a partner in Baum & Newborn, a Broadway talent agency at which Sue Mengers, the high-powered talent agent, had once worked. He had gone to Hollywood and headed the West Coast office of General Artists Corporation. When, in 1968, the ABC television network had decided to enter the film-making business, it made Baum the president of its Motion Picture Division. He went on to sponsor Bob Fosse's film *Cabaret* and a pair of Sam Peckinpah pictures, *Straw Dogs* and *Junior Bonner.* Three years later Baum became a producer at United Artists, where he made another Peckinpah film, *Bring Me the Head of Alfredo Garcia.* He then set up his own talent agency, the Martin Baum Agency. While the agency at that time was doing quite well—among his clients were Carroll O'Connor, Sidney Poitier, Julie Andrews, and Blake Edwards—Baum didn't like working in a mere two-person office (just he and a secretary); he found it lonely. He was 52 years old, and ripe for a change. Traubner called Baum and suggested that he meet with Ovitz: "You might find you have things in common."

Ovitz met Martin Baum, but had mixed feelings about bringing him on-board as a new partner. Yes, his track record was superb, and yes, he would bring a nice list of movie stars with him; he also would open some doors to the film industry for CAA. He had been quite a famous agent in his day and rightly so, for he was a born salesman. In short, Martin Baum had just the kind of experience that CAA needed. And yet Ovitz viewed that real strength as being a real weakness as well, for he asked himself, *Why make room for a 52-year-old guy when his best days probably are behind him?*

As for Baum, all he knew about CAA was that it had no film business—and he did. It had Michael Ovitz, who had a nice way about him, a good sense of humor, and seemed very self-sufficient. And it had four other partners who, if they proved to be as friendly and enthusiastic as Ovitz was, would help relieve Baum's loneliness. At any rate, the meeting between the two men ended with an unofficial agreement that they would look at each other's client lists and then decide if there was any reason to collaborate.

Baum met with the other CAA partners. While he liked them, he found their offices shabby. Six weeks later, Ovitz showed him the offices into which CAA planned to move in September. Century City was more modernistic, and consisted of a group of high-rises in the center of Beverly Hills; it had become the business capital of Hollywood. The new offices at 1888 Century Park East were on the fourteenth floor of the Tiger International Building, headquarters of Flying Tiger Airlines. The card tables would be replaced by modern office furniture. Baum thought that the new office space, triple the size of CAA's present offices, and its decor, represented a marked improvement over the old quarters.

Ovitz looked over Baum's client list carefully. On it were some of the entertainment industry's bigger names: Sidney Poitier, Julie Andrews, Blake Edwards, Carroll O'Connor, Richard Harris, James Clavell, Joanne Woodward, Harry Belafonte, and Dyan Cannon. Securing Dyan Cannon as a client would be an especially big coup for CAA, as she was such a major actress. She had won the New York Film Critics award for best supporting actress of 1969, for her portrayal of the uptight Alice in *Bob & Carol & Ted & Alice*. She was nominated for an Oscar for that film.

What especially appealed to Ovitz, however, was the fact that Baum was earning as much in fees as all the CAA partners together. Ovitz told him that he could have any office he chose if he came on-board, but Baum wavered. When he asked his friends what they thought, the friends wondered why he would want to join CAA: His client list was more impressive than theirs, and they were nothing more than an upstart, unproven agency.

Baum too had a good many doubts, and to relieve them he began to see a psychiatrist three times a week. Upon learning that Baum had an offer to join CAA, the psychiatrist advised Baum to accept it. CAA's youthfulness and Baum's experience seemed likely to prove a compelling mix. Baum relented, and quickly told Michael Ovitz. But it looked as if the patience of the other four partners had already run out. Ovitz confessed: "Marty, now my partners are having difficulty accepting you. They find you a difficult guy. If it takes you this long to make up your mind, they're nervous about what this means." Baum returned to the psychiatrist, who volunteered to meet with CAA's partners. When he did, the psychiatrist suggested that Baum's procrastination hardly constituted a character flaw; rather, it revealed that he was not a man to make a major decision lightly. Convinced by that argument, three of those other four partners dropped their objections. Only Bill Haber, troubled by Baum's seeming indecisiveness, had not come around, but he was willing to talk to Baum. They met at Baum's office on Sunset Boulevard.

"Marty," Haber began, "I've talked to ten people about you, and ten out of ten say we shouldn't make a deal with you."

Baum laughed. "I must be doing something right. If everyone loved me, I wouldn't be a good agent."

Haber couldn't help but join in the laughter at that one. The two men shook hands.

Baum met with Ovitz one more time. Ovitz explained to him that the partners now were ready to bring him in as a co-manager, granting him a one-sixth partnership in the business. Suddenly, Ovitz's tone turned harsh. The difference in their ages notwithstanding, Ovitz believed in telling it like it is: *We're giving you a full partnership, we're going to take care of you, you'll never be poor again, but we'll expect you to work like crazy in return.*

There were to be no laggards at CAA. Baum said he had no intention of being a laggard.

Marty Baum became the sixth partner of Creative Artists Agency—an equal one with the other five—on September 30, 1976. Bill Haber decided to throw a party for Baum at Haber's beach home at Malibu, and to invite both CAA's and Baum's clients. At one point during the party, Baum looked up into the sky and saw an airplane flying over the house with a banner attached. It read: "CAA Welcomes Marty Baum." It was then that he knew that Haber truly had recanted.

On October 11, 1976, the merger became public. An advertisement ran in the 'trades' to this effect: "The Martin Baum Agency and Creative Artists Agency announce the merging of their two companies to continue under the name of Creative Artists Agency."

Soon afterwards, Baum landed actor Rod Steiger, of *Dr. Zhivago* fame, as a client for CAA. Ovitz was confident that Baum could bring more star-power to the agency. Accordingly Ovitz sent him to the south of France, where the actor Peter Sellers was living. Baum's mission, a costly one for CAA, was to sign the film comedian as a client. Renting a car and driving to Sellers's home, Baum spent the weekend with the actor and made progress in convincing him to join CAA as a client. Baum served another crucial purpose at CAA, that of introducing Michael Ovitz to a number of important Hollywood business figures, including a good many producers and entertainment attorneys.

The merger with Marty Baum was a major turning point for CAA. Now for the first time it could boast of a client list that contained the names of some of Hollywood's most important film stars—still not of the caliber of a Paul Newman or a Robert Redford, but a sufficient array of talent to encourage Ovitz and his team in the belief that marquis clients were at last within their reach.

6

Pretzels, Tennis Balls, and Soapsuds

Though it seemed self-evident that CAA eventually would have to hire more agents if it was going to join the ranks of the other major talent agencies, some of the partners wondered whether such expansion would be wise. Bill Haber, for one, thought that the agency was just the right size the way it was. He liked its intimacy, and cherished the familial atmosphere; he also feared that a larger agency might bring on a William Morris–like bureaucracy. Michael Ovitz found it startling that his partners seemed to want the agency to remain in neutral. Whenever Bill Haber or anyone else voiced such conservative thoughts, he chose not to argue with them but kept his cool, and went ahead anyway with plans to enlarge the agency.

Amy Grossman was the first to benefit from Ovitz's expansionist dreams. She had graduated as an English literature major from UCLA in June of 1975, and then joined up at William Morris as a secretary the following September. Yet she quickly discovered that she much preferred giving dictation to taking it. In short, she wanted to become an agent, but William Morris had become increasingly distasteful to her. There was, she remembers, the horrific caste system, with the most important agents occupying the first floor, the next important the second floor, and so on. She was working for the youngest agent at Morris, and the whole agency struck her as being very dark and secretive and unfriendly. Executives still were embittered by the memory of the treasonable actions taken by the five defectors. She had never met any of the five men, but she quickly learned from Morris agents that they were very bad people—"Nazi piranhas," as she puts it! Unfortunately for Grossman and her dream of becoming an agent, the executives weren't about to put a secretary through the mail-room training program; nor did she have any great desire to deliver the mail: "I wasn't that type of girl. I wasn't going to get my fingers inked."

Then one day, Michael Rosenfeld phoned her. A television producer whom she had dated had passed the word to Rosenfeld that Grossman was interested in leaving Morris. CAA needed a secretary. Was she interested? Though she was only 21, she blurted out that what she really wanted to be was an agent. Well in that case, Rosenfeld told her, come meet the partners, you have nothing to lose. And she did. As soon as she entered the CAA office she noticed the palpable difference: "Everyone was walking in and out of the offices, laughing, giving high-fives. They were all so excited and open and sharing. They were alive. You didn't have to be a genius to see the difference between CAA and Morris."

She began to work at CAA as a secretary on September 30, 1976, the same day that Marty Baum arrived at CAA. The following January she was promoted to agent.

Next to benefit from Ovitz's interest in expanding the agency was Laurie Perlman. Her first encounter with CAA occurred on the beach. She was 23, and had recently graduated from USC's film school. Much like the younger Michael Ovitz, she wanted to get into the entertainment business, and thought that agenting would be the best way of getting in on the ground floor. She had applied to William Morris, ICM, and Adams, Ray, and Rosenberg, and was waiting for replies. A male friend who was with Laurie on the beach worked for the Columbia Pictures story department. He was reading a script that CAA had submitted to Columbia, hoping that the studio would want to turn it into a motion picture. Laurie noticed that the cover on the script was made out of cheap-looking recycled paper, and didn't even sport the CAA logo: "CAA was so poor they couldn't even afford a cover with the official CAA logo yet."

Not put off, she applied to CAA and met with Michael Rosenfeld. She told him she wanted to be an agent.

Rosenfeld immediately noticed how attractive Perlman was. "You're very sweet," he said, "but we're really not used to having agents who are as feminine as you are."

She decided that Rosenfeld was testing her, that an agent was supposed to sell and that he merely wanted to see how well she would sell herself to him. She spoke for 20 minutes about how there was a new breed of woman coming into the work force, and that in their own way these women were even more formidable than those who had gone before them. "We just wear our femininity a little differently," she explained to Rosenfeld, who remained noncommittal about hiring her. Impressed by his honesty, Laurie phoned him every two weeks. In the meantime, ICM had offered her an agent-trainee position. She sent a telegram to Rosenfeld informing him of that fact, and asking, "What do I have to do to get another interview?" Rosenfeld showed the telegram to Ovitz and the other partners. Now they were impressed. Rosenfeld offered her a job. CAA still had no agent-trainee program, but Laurie felt that her prospects of advancement were better at CAA than at ICM.

Though Laurie Perlman hadn't started working yet, the CAA directors invited her to join them at a Christmas party given by Sid and Marty Kroft, two producers who had been Michael Ovitz's clients ever since the Morris days. It was late December 1976, and CAA's continuing condition of frugality prevented it from sponsoring its own Christmas parties. The party was held in the Krofts' offices at a large soundstage in the San Fernando Valley. It was there that Perlman had her first chance to talk to Michael Ovitz. "He had a strength, a solidity, and a twinkle in his eye. There was a humor about him. He doesn't let everybody see it. It's not his public persona."

Now CAA had seven agents—the five original partners plus the new one, Martin Baum, plus Amy Grossman—and one agent trainee, Laurie Perlman. Perlman began to do work for Ron Meyer, spending half a day with him and half a day in the accounting department. She and another accounting-department employee typed the checks that were made payable to the clients, less the 10 percent that CAA kept as its fee.

For CAA's first full two years, the partners took no salaries. They lived off savings, and drew money from the business in order to handle their expenses. But by the end of 1976, the agency's financial situation had sufficiently improved for Ovitz and his associates to give themselves salaries. But while the CAA client list had grown to include 90 clients, the entire list fit on one four-column page, with one column for writers, one for actors, one for producers, and one for directors. And CAA's reputation was little more than that of a small, struggling talent agency. Senior studio executives didn't rush to the phone to take calls from Michael Ovitz and his partners. Yet it was crucial that Ovitz and his team reach those executives, in order to find out what projects they had in the works. Ovitz understood that, and he encouraged his five partners to search for ways to get the attention of these executives. He gave them few directives in this regard, which gave them a good deal of latitude.

One major target was a 32-year-old studio executive named Sherry Lansing, who had spent the previous year as executive story editor at

MGM. She held the highest non-acting job a woman could attain at a major Hollywood studio. Born in Chicago in 1944, she had graduated from Northwestern University's theater department and had once been a minor actress.

Bill Haber, who had no experience with the motion picture side of the business, nonetheless took Michael Ovitz's advice and began to approach senior studio executives, those at MGM of course being high on his list. Deciding to start with someone other than the head of the studio, he called Sherry Lansing. He introduced himself and asked if he might meet with her for lunch or dinner, in order to learn about the acting roles that needed to be filled in MGM's current film projects.

Polite but brief, Lansing said that her assistant Susan Merzbach usually answered such queries. "That's the way we do it for everybody" was her way of trying to end the conversation.

"Well," said Haber, "I don't want to be like everybody."

"I don't mean to be offensive," she said, but repeated that she could not meet with him.

"Then," said Haber, trying to sound friendly, "I will shower you with gifts. Then you won't think I am like *everyone else*."

And thus Haber quietly retreated. But that didn't mean he was going to take no for an answer. Rather than the customary champagne, Haber began to send Lansing cases of Evian water. Silence. Since he wanted to be seen as different from others who tried to build a relationship with Lansing by sending her more traditional gifts, he sent over huge containers of pretzels. Then salt. Then tennis balls. He became obsessed with the idea of enticing her into joining him for a meal. Every once in a while Lansing felt obliged to phone Haber to thank him for the gifts, but she had trouble getting through to him. He got word to her that he would not be taking *her* calls until she agreed to have a meal with him. Lansing was stymied. She didn't know what to make of Haber. He certainly wasn't like *everyone else*. When she finally got Haber on the phone, Lansing urged, "Can't we meet, please? Come to my office."

I'm afraid that won't be possible, said Haber. She had to agree to a meal, or there would be no meeting.

Some time after that, Marty Baum brought Peter Sellers in to CAA for a meeting. Though Sellers was then near the end of his career, he still would be an important catch for the new agency. Baum made sure that all six partners attended the meeting, which was held in the conference room opposite the reception area; the room had lots of windows, which meant that it afforded a clear view of the reception area.

Halfway through the meeting, Michael Rosenfeld looked out in that direction and saw something extraordinary out of the corner of his eye. Emerging from the elevator was a young man. What made him a bit different from other young men was the fact that he was naked, except for the towel that covered his private parts and the soapsuds in his hair, as if he had just walked out of a shower.

The receptionist looked up at the man and gawked, half in confusion and half in fright.

Spotting the group of people in the conference room, the young man walked over, whipped open the door, and demanded to know "Who's Bill Haber?"

Peter Sellers, a man who was no stranger to wackiness (remember *Dr. Strangelove?*) stared at the visitor and wondered what on earth kind of a place CAA really was. A moment later, the young man held up a sign that read: "OK, we give up. We'll have dinner with you." He then dropped the towel, placed the sign on the table near Bill Haber, and scampered off. Michael Ovitz and his colleagues were tongue-tied, to put it mildly.

The least tongue-tied seemed to be Sellers, who acted as if the unexpected visitor had done nothing more than serve coffee. "Let's carry on," he urged the agents. And so they did, with Sellers quickly announcing that he was looking forward to having CAA represent him.

Moments after the meeting had broken up, Mike Rosenfeld paid a call on Bill Haber in his office.

"What the hell was *that* all about?"

Haber explained everything, from the tennis balls to the pretzels to the towel-clad visitor. *Why the towel and why the soapsuds?*, Rosenfeld asked anxiously. *Those*, Haber explained, *were evidently meant to remind him that he had once told Lansing he would* shower *her with gifts. Why did the young man* drop *the towel?*, Rosenfeld queried. *Well*, said Haber, *it must have been Lansing's way of admitting that she was* throwing in the towel *and was ready to meet him over a meal. . . .*

Haber picked up the phone and called Sherry Lansing. She agreed to have dinner the following week, but she insisted that her assistant, Susan Merzbach, would be joining them. "I'm intrigued!" Lansing admitted.

No one was more shocked by those conference-room antics than Michael Ovitz. He himself was capable of employing unorthodox methods in order to achieve his aims, but not quite *that* unorthodox. Nonetheless he encouraged Haber to carry on, full-steam-ahead. "Good luck!" he said, hoping that Haber's dinner would go well both for him and the firm.

Haber teamed up with Rosenfeld to map out a strategy for The Great Meal. "Let's do something really special," Haber suggested, and Mike Rosenfeld, who flew planes, proposed that they *fly* Lansing and Merzbach to the dinner. Haber, a highly reluctant, white-knuckle flyer, would have preferred to go overland to his dinner, but had to admit that *he* was the one who had said "something special." They decided that they would fly to Santa Barbara.

Haber arranged for Lansing and Merzbach to be picked up by a limousine in front of MGM's famous Thalberg Building. A red carpet was rolled down the building's front steps. A violinist stood by, serenading the two women as they approached a limo replete with champagne and flowers.

With a turbulent weather system approaching from out of the north, Haber had nixed Santa Barbara. Instead he had asked Rosenfeld to fly the four of them from Los Angeles International Airport to Van Nuys. When the limo pulled up to the terminal at LAX, Haber was waiting and introduced the two women, by now giddy from drinking champagne, to a man wearing a blue shirt, dark blue tie, epaulets, and wings: "He's our pilot, Mike."

"Pilot Mike, pilot Mike," Sherry Lansing kept saying. "From now on, that's your name." He looked like he worked for American Airlines.

Sherry Lansing insisted upon being home by 10:30 p.m. "Not to worry," Haber replied. "We'll have you back in plenty of time."

"Are you taking us to Las Vegas?" Lansing asked. "I won't go to Las Vegas." But Haber wouldn't reveal their destination.

It began to drizzle. Pilot Mike told everybody not to worry. The flight lasted only 12 minutes, and the two women laughed all the while. Lansing couldn't believe what was going on. What a stunt Haber had pulled: flying her to dinner! She loved it.

Once they had deplaned at Van Nuys, Rosenfeld, still posing as Pilot Mike, asked Haber if he might join him and the two women at dinner, at the 94th Aero-Squadron Restaurant, a popular airport eatery. Haber agreed happily, and the four of them got into Rosenfeld's Jaguar. Unable to keep up the pretense any longer, Pilot Mike took off his pilot's pin and said, "I'm Mike Rosenfeld, Bill's partner. I'm not a charter pilot, we set you up." Lansing thought the stunt was the funniest thing that had ever happened to her. She thought Haber and Rosenfeld were adorable. The dinner went extraordinarily well. More violinists showed up at the table. The four walked out of the restaurant over yet another red carpet, which led to the very same limousine the women thought they had left behind them at LAX.

Over the coming days, Sherry Lansing told everyone she met about her wild and wacky evening with "those guys at CAA," and she promoted them as being bright and funny, creative and outrageous. She became one of the agency's biggest boosters, and word spread that Michael Ovitz's operation was dynamic and one to keep an eye on. Hollywood execs began to hear the whole weird tale, from the pretzels and tennis balls to the soapsuds and the falling towel, and to inquire of Haber and Rosenfeld: "Aren't you the guys who flew Sherry Lansing to dinner?" The incident put CAA on the map. Michael Ovitz was in charge of a bunch of zanies, but zanies who knew what they were doing.

Of COURSE, HAD the CAA partners been nothing *but* a bunch of zanies, their reputation would have been imperiled. But they had something else going for them, a rare commodity that Hollywood loves: the ability to charm the pants off people. They were all irresistibly persuasive. And they were all so enthusiastic and knowledgeable, and seemed so loyal to one another, that clients really *wanted* to entrust their careers to them. Ovitz was the driving force of the business. He involved himself in everything from the finances to the hiring, from deciding how the office should look to taking care of the long-term strategic thinking. While the other partners did take the business seriously, Ovitz alone seemed to be on a mission. Only he seemed to hunger to gain ascendancy over the industry.

On a cold night in 1976 Michael Ovitz and Mike Rosenfeld left the Sherry-Netherlands Hotel in New York City and headed for a restaurant where they were to meet an important literary agent for dinner. As the two walked into the restaurant, Rosenfeld asked Ovitz, "How much money would it take to make you happy? Ten million dollars? Twenty million dollars?"

"You don't understand," Ovitz replied. "It's not about money. The money will flow. It's about power and influence." As Ovitz's power and influence over the entertainment industry grew in the subsequent years, he always tried to convey an impression that he wasn't hungry for power per se. According to him, it was respect that he was always in search of. Yet this comment to Rosenfeld, made early in Ovitz's career, strongly suggests that power was in fact his ultimate goal.

In his quest for power and influence Ovitz seemed to be fearless, willing to pick up the telephone and approach anyone at all, unconcerned by the prospect of being turned down. He wasn't afraid to speak his mind, to voice opinions, to come to firm decisions. His mind raced from one subject to the next, creating an impression that he was impatient to the point of growing rude. Yet what others failed to understand was that Ovitz prided himself on getting in as much business in one day as possible.

That goal allowed for no idle chitchat, and often demanded that Ovitz make the difficult decisions that had to be made.

Ovitz's icy demeanor led some to turn to Ron Meyer in search of solace and reassurance. Ironically, it was this ex-Marine who became the "good cop." People liked Ron's patience and kindness, and he gained the reputation of being a guy who knew how to smooth ruffled feathers. He spoke softly, and his voice generated none of the tension that Ovitz's did. Even if Meyer was forced to be the bearer of bad tidings, he always did so in such a way that the person he bore them to didn't get upset with him. It was said of him that he could get through 100 phone calls in a day, most of them brief to the point of curtness, and still never sound dismissive. While it was Ovitz who directed things from on high, Meyer was looked upon as being the key to the agency's day-to-day operations. Meyer prided himself on being much more "street-smart" (his own phrase) than Ovitz was, while Ovitz was far more studied in his approach. "The combination worked," Meyer notes.

Bill Haber had the same relentless, persistent nature as Ovitz, but the other partners had a difficult time figuring him out. They called him "oblique," a good word perhaps, for someone who could manage to get at Sherry Lansing in such a clever and roundabout fashion. He had none of Ovitz's flair for the confrontational. It was unthinkable that Ovitz ever would dream of flying Sherry Lansing to dinner, for instance. He simply would have kept phoning her until, by a slow campaign of attrition, Lansing gave in.

Michael Rosenfeld, the oldest of the five original partners, was the most creative of them, a man of music who played the piano and had scripted college shows. He shared some of the same wackiness with Haber (this, after all, was Pilot Mike), and some of the same problem-solving ability with Ovitz, but he differed from the others in being the most garrulous of the bunch. He saw this as his strength, and enjoyed boasting that he had the gift of gab. He also had a marvelous knack for spotting talented young men and women of real potential. One of his main tasks at CAA was the hiring of personnel.

Rowland Perkins was the group's elder statesman (though technically Rosenfeld was 12 days older), the most avuncular, the one with the longest track record in the talent-agency field. Yet he had never pushed himself to the forefront. He was every bit as hard a worker as Meyer, Rosenfeld, and Haber, but there was only one Michael Ovitz, and that was a simple fact that Rowland Perkins had the grace and the good sense to acknowledge very early on.

One of Amy Grossman's most vivid memories of those days is of the regular weekly staff meeting, held every Monday at 7 p.m. Because these sessions, conducted around the large, round, wooden conference table, tended to run on for three hours or so, dinner usually was brought in. Before Martin Baum became a CAA partner, pizza and beer was the usual fare. But in the Baum era, there might be soul food from South Central Los Angeles on one Monday night, Russian cookery from a certain restaurant on Sunset on the next. And good wine replaced the Coke. "I elevated their tastes," Baum recalls with great pride. "I introduced them to the world of better living."

Even at this stage—20 months into the new venture—the partners resisted giving any one partner too much power over the others. No one, not even Michael Ovitz, actually "ran" the meetings. Somehow the week's business just got done, as anyone who wanted to speak did so and was intently listened to.

Amidst a sea of sushi or soul food, the partners tried to devise new ways of snapping up major talent. It was no easy task. Still, Ovitz and his five partners had at least two things going for them that few other agents possessed: an enthusiasm and zeal that were contagious, and a willingness to do almost *anything* to get a new client.

One whimsical incident occurred in 1976, when Ovitz was doing everything he possibly could to get a pair of highly talented writer/producers named Carol and Nigel McKeand to commit to CAA. Both were from England, and both possessed dry senses of humor. As they and the partners sat around the conference table one day, the McKeands were saying little, and even less about whether they would sign up with CAA. Ovitz and his colleagues felt that they had just about talked themselves out. There was simply nothing left to say.

"What's it going to take to get you to sign?" Michael Ovitz asked finally. "Does somebody have to get up and tap-dance on the table?"

And then, before anyone could even think of trying to stop him, Ovitz shocked those in the room by leaping out of his chair and up onto the conference table, where he did his pathetic best to tap-dance. The fact that he was no Gene Kelly hardly mattered. He had shown that he was prepared to make a fool out of himself if it would help him to land a client—and the McKeands loved it. "We're signing," they said.

That tap dance proved to be both easier to execute and easier on the nerves than some other CAA efforts at winning over clients. On one occasion Ovitz and Rosenfeld were flying to Las Vegas, where they hoped to sign a client. Always keeping a careful eye on CAA's budget, Rosenfeld persuaded Ovitz that they would save some dough if Rosenfeld piloted his two-engine plane to Las Vegas, with Ovitz as passenger in the copilot seat. The plane took off and, reaching a speed of 180 miles per hour, moved across the Mojave Desert. Suddenly the door next to Ovitz flew open and there came a loud whooshing noise. Imagining that he was about to be sucked out of the plane, Ovitz was scared to death, and thought that the worst might happen. Rosenfeld knew better. At 10,000 feet, the plane was too low for any such tragedy to occur. Sensing no imminent danger, Rosenfeld grabbed the door handle and pulled the door shut, then tried to turn it to a closed position. No luck. But at least the noise had abated.

"You need to hold this handle for the balance of the flight!" Rosenfeld shouted to Ovitz. "It's not dangerous!"

Sure, right, Ovitz thought, *not dangerous.* But sensing that he had no choice, Ovitz grabbed ahold of the door handle with his right hand and had no trouble keeping it in a closed position for the next hour until they had safely landed. Still, once they were back on terra firma, it took Ovitz ten minutes to regain his composure. He had been prepared to do almost anything that would procure a new client for CAA, but this nerve-shattering experience caused him to radically reconsider the value of pursuing clients with Pilot Mike at the helm. Tap-dancing on tables was about as high off the ground as Michael Ovitz cared to get. . . .

In 1977, a project came along that would turn the tide for CAA. It was this project that caused Ovitz and his partners to really begin to believe that the agency was bound for glory.

The incident concerned the novelist James Clavell, who had been associated with Martin Baum for many years. In 1971, as President of ABC Pictures, Baum had made a film called *The Last Valley* that Clavell wrote, directed, and produced. Baum had served as his agent four years earlier when Clavell wrote, directed, and produced the hit Sidney Poitier movie *To Sir With Love.* Then, in 1975, there came the publication of Clavell's best-selling novel *Shogun,* the story of English sea pilot John Blackthorne's struggle to survive, and to come to grips with an alien culture, after being shipwrecked off the coast of Japan during the early 1600s. Confronted by both vast cultural differences and darkly tangled political and religious intrigue, Blackthorne seeks to bring his Western instincts into line with Eastern traditions. He befriends a Japanese warlord who aspires to be the supreme military dictator (or shogun) of the country, and falls in love with his translator.

The novel had been on the Hollywood market for three years, as efforts were made to turn the massive novel into a two-and-a-half-hour feature film. But its 1395 pages and 60 characters simply proved too many for anyone to get a handle on, and a screenplay was shelved. Having befriended Clavell and become a big fan of the novel, Michael Ovitz yearned to breathe life into the faltering Hollywood project. If the novel was simply too broad and sweeping for the big screen, why not present it as a TV mini-series? Ovitz and ABC Television had done much business together of late, so he pitched the idea to ABC, at first to only a lukewarm response. Americans, the executives told Ovitz, were not about to spend 10 or 12 hours in one week watching the Japanese on television! Ovitz then made a pitch to Diane Berkeley, the person in charge of mini-series production at NBC. "She fell in love with the concept," Ovitz recalls, but there was the major problem of what to do about the lengthy conversations of the Japanese characters in the novel. If the Japanese actors spoke in English, it would seem odd. Ovitz's proposed solution was to let the actors speak in Japanese, and use subtitles. "Everyone thought we were crazy," he recalls, but his proposal was accepted and NBC committed itself to air *Shogun* in five installments over a 12-hour period.

CAA received $1 million in commissions for *Shogun*—four times as much as its largest fee prior to then. This was CAA's first major television deal, and it provided the agency with enormous visibility. *Shogun* starred Richard Chamberlain as John Blackthorne, took three years to produce, and was shot on location in Japan at a cost of $20 million, with $1 million going to Clavell for the film rights. That made it the most expensive mini-series as of that time. Appearing from September 15 to 19, 1980, *Shogun* was a great hit. The five episodes of the mini-series ranked as the top five shows of the first week of the new season, and gave NBC the highest-rated week in its history. *Shogun* was the second-highest-rated mini-series ever, second only to the legendary *Roots*.

AMONG THE CLIENTS whom Ovitz pursued the most doggedly were the film directors. Ovitz had a special appreciation for these people, for he believed them to be smarter than most actors and actresses and also more articulate, more fully conversant with their profession. He was comfortable in their company and found it easy to talk with them, far more so than was the case with actors and actresses. Ovitz also was realistic, and understood that the time still was not ripe for CAA to sign top movie talent. The agency simply was not in that league yet. "We couldn't sign big clients," he says now, looking back to CAA's founding years. "Why would a big client go with us? Who were we?"

As a result, Ovitz devised a strategy that he hoped would lure famous actors and actresses over to CAA's side. It had to do with merging with Marty Baum; with securing really fine movie scripts by keeping in touch with Morton Janklow and other literary agents; and with strengthening relationships with key studio executives like Sherry Lansing. But it also had to do with getting the names of some important directors onto CAA's client list. For Ovitz sensed that nothing was more compelling to the major actors and actresses than a good script coupled with an outstanding director.

One of Ovitz's first directorial finds was a former off-Broadway actor named Richard Donner. A New York City native, Donner had begun by directing documentaries, industrial films, and commercials. After directing episodes for *Wanted Dead or Alive* and other television series, he began to direct feature films in the early 1960s, specializing in action adventures. In 1976 he had just finished making the movie *The Omen*, starring Gregory Peck and Lee Remick, when he signed up with a young literary agent named Steve Roth from the Ziegler-Roth agency. Donner then was paid $1 million to direct the film *Superman*, starring Christopher Reeve, and its sequel which at that time was the most money ever paid to a director.

It was at around that same time that CAA hired away Steve Roth, attracted by his list of movie clients, including Richard Donner. When he informed Donner of his decision to switch agencies, Roth urged him to meet with the folks at CAA. Yes, they were beginners on the feature-film side of the business, but Roth thought that Donner should give some serious thought to letting Michael Ovitz and his team represent him.

Not surprisingly, Donner wasn't entirely sure that he wanted to go with CAA. After all, the new agency had been largely about TV up to that point, and his career was now all about movies. What was more, now that he had done *The Omen* and was doing *Superman*, his career certainly seemed to be going places. He was understandably concerned that CAA perhaps lacked the connections and the clout to find the right projects for him now that he was a star director.

But what the heck, no harm could come from meeting with the CAA directors. Donner did so, and showed the six partners some footage from the *Superman* film. Throughout the screening he kept glancing over at Michael Ovitz, who seemed the most impressive of the bunch. He was, in the director's mind, very bright and aggressive, and he had a wonderful manner when he made a pitch. Ovitz seemed to be convinced that he could move Donner's career ahead, and that of course was music to Donner's ears. Somehow, Ovitz intuited that Donner wanted to direct a classier kind of movie, one with less action and more meaning. Donner had been talking to other agents as well, but none of them had seemed to grasp the fact that he was tired of making action movies. Much to Donner's chagrin, all that they pitched to him were thriller and horror films.

"It's time for you to do a small, intimate picture," Ovitz advised. "You've done big films. Now let's show them that you are an intimate director, and that your career in film will be as diversified as your television career was."

Donner was hooked.

"I'll go with you," he said to Ovitz. "But I'm not entirely sure. I'm going to go on a handshake, not a contract." Donner went to work on *Inside Moves,* a film about a disabled young man who botches a suicide attempt and then goes on to make friends in Max's bar with other handicapped people. It starred John Savage and Diana Scarwid. The movie did not win critical acclaim, and Donner became known in later years for such action hits as *Lethal Weapon* and *Lethal Weapon 2*. Still, Ovitz had read Richard Donner superbly at a critical juncture in the director's career, and that special Ovitz intuition had been enough to turn Donner into a CAA client.

Thus, Michael Ovitz had a gift for looking at a director's work and immediately sensing whether the director had a bright future; if so, he wanted to be a part of it. He would pick up the telephone and hope that the personal chemistry would be right, right off the bat. Of course, things didn't always work out quite that quickly or smoothly. As with Michael Crichton, a well-established author, the prospective client had representation and had no desire to switch agents. So Ovitz's aggressiveness did not always pay off as quickly as he would have hoped.

Michael Crichton was sitting in his living room one night in 1978 when the phone rang.

"You don't know me. My name is Michael Ovitz. I've seen your movie, *Coma,* and it was terrific." Crichton had directed the film based upon his own book.

"That's very nice," Crichton answered out loud, and then added to himself, *whoever you are. . . .*

And with those few words, the conversation ended. Both men appeared to understand there was nothing more to talk about.

Michael Crichton was not just one of the most prolific men in America, but one of the smartest as well—he had graduated *summa cum laude* from

Harvard, then taught anthropology at Cambridge University. He went on to pick up a medical degree at Harvard. He had published six paperback thrillers under the pen name of John Lange before he proceeded to put out highly-touted novels under his own name, including *The Andromeda Strain* and *The Terminal Man.* After several of his books had been turned into films by other people, he decided to direct a television movie based upon his 1972 novel *Binary.* Since then he had directed several more films based upon his own books.

In 1979, Crichton's phone rang again.

"You probably don't remember me. My name is Michael Ovitz. I've just seen your movie *The Great Train Robbery,* and it's terrific." This time Ovitz identified himself as one of the leaders of Creative Artists Agency.

Well, Crichton thought, this is kind of an interesting guy, pleasantly aggressive. He assumed that Ovitz was making some kind of an overture vis-à-vis representing him. Crichton's agent had been Bob Bookman at ICM, but Bookman recently had gone to work for Columbia Pictures and now there was no one at ICM with whom Crichton felt close. It was at around that time that Crichton had decided to put himself on the open market, and began to meet with the top agents in Hollywood.

But Crichton found that he was disappointed by their seeming reluctance to sell him in his own right. While they acknowledged his success as a writer/director, the agents subtly conveyed their doubt that Crichton's name alone appearing on a film would suffice to make it a success. His movies still needed star power to pull them over the top.

Meanwhile, Michael Ovitz kept calling, so finally, deciding that he had nothing to lose, Crichton agreed to meet with him. Ovitz immediately understood what Crichton was looking for in an agent, so he made it clear that he thought Crichton's name alone *was* enough to make a hit. Sure, Ovitz told him, stars once all but controlled the movie business, but those days were long gone. "Now, the writers control things; the people like yourself who can create material and execute it, they are the ones who are in charge."

The Ovitz pitch hit home for Crichton. He also liked the fact that Ovitz and his colleagues at CAA worked out of small offices in Century City, in contrast with the large, showy offices favored by almost all the other agents. And based upon what Crichton had been hearing around town, the CAA agents were making some pretty sweet deals for their clients. Crichton thought to himself: *I've got no idea what's true, but Michael seems brash and savvy, and he's telling me what I want to hear. And that's interesting.* When he signed up as a client at CAA, Michael Crichton felt good about it.

Ovitz still reserved a special place in his heart for comedy, both on television and on the big screen. He loved the new humor of the 1970s—less slapsticky than the Milton Berle/Sid Caesar variety of a few decades earlier, yet just as zany and with far more sting and controversial bite to it. He loved the new TV hit *Saturday Night Live,* and a number of its stars, including "Blues Brothers" John Belushi and Dan Ackroyd, had become CAA clients. In sync with that kind of comedy, and believing that the rest of the country was as well, Ovitz naturally inclined toward a young man named Ivan Reitman. The Czech-born director had begun directing and producing movies in the early 1970s, and he met Ovitz for the first time in 1979 when he was directing *Meatballs.* That was his second American film; *Animal House,* which he had co-produced the year before, was his first. Reitman had lived in Canada since the age of four and then had settled in Hollywood. For a long while he went without an agent, but once he decided to seek one out ("It seemed like that's what people did here") he spoke to three, one of whom was Ovitz. At the time Reitman had an idea for a film comedy that he wanted to call *Stripes,* about a sergeant who trains a platoon of misfit volunteers. No script, just an idea. Reitman wanted to continue to direct, but he hoped to increasingly be perceived as more creative than his previous films may have suggested that he was. Ovitz set up a meeting with the young director, and yet again seemed to intuit Reitman's hopes and dreams without needing to be told about them. Reitman signed with CAA.

But even now that he had Ovitz as his agent, Reitman continued to try to make his own production and directing deals. Eager to talk to Reitman directly, Michael Eisner, then president and chief operating officer at Paramount Pictures, sought him out, hoping to lure the young director over to Paramount. By the end of their conversation Eisner had proposed that Reitman direct three movies and produce five others, over the next five years. Reitman thought he had a firm commitment, budget and all, but asked for some time to think it over. Meanwhile he relayed the information to Ovitz. Although Ovitz had a hard time figuring out why Reitman was talking directly to Eisner, he made no mention of his perplexity, saying only: "That sounds interesting. Let me go and talk to Eisner."

But when Ovitz and Eisner got together, the agent realized that Reitman's description of the deal with Paramount had been overdone.

Calling Reitman back the next day, Ovitz explained: "You know, the way Eisner is describing it, is not the same." The fact of the matter is that both men had heard Eisner correctly. Eisner had indeed been genuine in offering the long-term deal to Reitman, but he had recanted after his studio colleagues had resisted the proposal.

"What do you mean?" Reitman asked Ovitz, clearly disappointed.

"Well, he was very interested in making *Stripes* as your next picture, and basically after that it was a development deal."

"No," said Reitman. "I was very clear that these were 'put' pictures [i.e., films that a studio guarantees will get made]."

"Well, something happened over night."

"You don't know me very well, but I am very clear about these kinds of things."

"You know what we'll do?" said Ovitz. "I've already called Frank Price [then the head of Columbia Pictures]. Why don't you present *Stripes* to him and see if he wants to make it, and we'll just sell it right under Paramount?"

"Is that wise?" Reitman asked Ovitz.

"Yeah, it will teach Paramount a lesson. We'll show them you're a desirable commodity to the industry." Thanks to Ovitz, Reitman did meet with Price at the Columbia boss's home the very next morning. Price loved the premise behind Reitman's idea for *Stripes:* "I want to make a deal. We're making that picture."

In the ensuing years, whenever Reitman attended Michael Eisner's New Year's Eve parties in Aspen, Colorado, Eisner, as part of his lengthy toast, always made sure he reminded Reitman that "Michael Ovitz stole you away from me to Frank Price."

Stripes, starring Bill Murray and Harold Ramis, was released in 1981, and went on to become a huge hit.

7

Hollywood's New Rainmakers

THE SIGNING OF such directors as Richard Donner, Michael Crichton, and Ivan Reitman gave a much-needed spark to CAA's reputation. But somehow, the high-priced movie talent was still reluctant to come over to the agency. William Morris's Stan Kamen remained the most prominent talent agent of the day, representing such stars as Warren Beatty, Jane Fonda, Richard Gere, Robert Redford, and Barbra Streisand. Ovitz was eager to attract some of these stars, but CAA remained a small business, with only 19 agents (compared to William Morris's 150) and 200 clients (most of them from television) with revenues of $90 million by 1979. Ovitz had been running the company de facto for so long that his colleagues at CAA naturally thought of him as being the man in charge, though for the past four years he had only been a vice president. To formalize the ongoing reality, the partners elevated Ovitz to the post of president. It was a title he would retain for years to come.

Ovitz never once stopped thinking about signing major clients, but he knew he needed a fresh and imaginative approach if he was to reach into the upper echelons of Hollywood. He decided that he would get to the people behind the stars, since the stars themselves had no incentive to deal with Ovitz directly. Noticing that some entertainment attorneys in town had taken on a new role, that of managing the careers of their star clients, Ovitz began to sense that his best way of getting closer to the big stars would be to build some strong relationships with their attorneys. The attorneys' film clients looked to them for advice not only on legal matters, but also as to which scripts to read and which movie projects to take on. Even when these actors did have agents, they listened more intently to their high-powered attorneys than to anyone else. Ovitz's hope was that they would heed their lawyers' advice and become CAA clients.

Only the really big entertainment attorneys exerted such major influence upon their film-star clients that they could send them without protest to a relative "nobody" like Michael Ovitz: Gary Hendler, Barry Hirsch, Bert Fields, Jack Bloom, and a few others. While Ovitz sought to befriend these attorneys, other talent agents in town saw no advantage to cultivating such people. And Ovitz certainly was taking a risk: If he came off as too arrogant or bothersome, any of these high-powered attorneys could smear CAA's name in such a way that it might stay smeared. But that wasn't about to deter Ovitz from trying.

One day in 1979, as he was walking in the lobby of the building that housed CAA's law firm, he glanced at the building's directory and a name caught his eye: Gary Hendler. He had heard of the attorney, of course, and now saw that he worked at a law firm just four floors above CAA's office. Hendler had a cash-rich tax practice and had signed some of the biggest celebrities in town, including Sydney Pollack, Robert Redford, and Paul Newman. Ovitz took the elevator to the eighteenth floor and asked if he might meet Hendler. The two men greeted each other and Ovitz invited Hendler to dinner. They became great friends and began to talk about sharing clients. Ovitz certainly was eager to do so, since he saw gold in the talent-rich Hendler client list and was eager to share clients with the entertainment attorney.

One of Hendler's clients, and friends, was a Scottish actor named Sean Connery.

The son of a truck driver and a charlady, Connery had dropped out of school at the age of 15 to join the British navy. All the while building up his body, he worked at such odd jobs as bricklayer, lifeguard, and coffin-polisher(!) before finally becoming a swimming-trunk model and, in 1950, representing Scotland in the Mr. Universe contest. His acting career began in 1951, when he landed a part in the chorus of the London production of *South Pacific*. Making little headway as an actor over the next decade, his luck changed when he was chosen to portray James Bond, the dashing secret agent of the Ian Fleming novels. When *Dr. No* appeared in 1962, Sean Connery's Hollywood career was off and running. There followed a string of James Bond films, including *From Russia with Love* (1963); *Goldfinger* (1964); and *Diamonds Are Forever* (1971). Connery continued to make movies throughout the decade, but by the end of the 1970s his career had begun to hit the shoals. "At the time it wasn't that easy to sell me," Connery recalls. "They weren't breaking the door down for my services."

Connery decided it was time to be represented by someone in Hollywood. He had had some dealings with ICM in Europe, and had been in touch with Stan Kamen of William Morris. But now he turned for advice to a friend, Mike Medavoy, who in 1978 had co-founded Orion Pictures. Medavoy recommended that Connery seek out attorney Gary Hendler. Connery heeded that advice and became a close Hendler friend. It was Hendler who put the actor in touch with Michael Ovitz.

Connery auditioned other agents as well, but he preferred Ovitz. While Connery knew that Ovitz was making a pitch, he also felt that the agent sounded sensible: "He wasn't making any great, monumental claims. He said that he wanted an office that would have the best writers and directors, with the best actors and actresses. He foresaw the idea of packaging. Putting together creative and talented people was very much in his game plan. Nobody talked quite that way to me. They all talked about how good they had done in the past."

The signing of Sean Connery with CAA on February 23, 1979, was a watershed event, marking the first time that the agency had managed to snare a top Hollywood talent. Ovitz's dreams for the agency were still far from being realized, but with the signing of a genuine movie star, CAA certainly had made a giant leap forward. Never mind that Connery appeared to be treading water for the moment. Ovitz viewed that as a challenge. And now that he had Connery in his client stable, he could kick off pitches to prospective clients by saying, "Hi, my name is Michael Ovitz. I represent Sean Connery." Perhaps because he was CAA's first big client, Connery always would retain a special place in Ovitz's heart. For instance, he was one of the few clients to be provided with office space at CAA. And Connery ate up all of the personal attention that Ovitz showered him with. But the actor was most impressed by Ovitz's troubleshooting displayed during the filming of *Never Say Never Again* (1983), the last Bond film that Connery was to make. Connery was having a personal problem with the producer, Jack Schwartzman. Ovitz the problem-solver went into action, appearing on the set and resolving the problem at once. "Michael was very good in terms of dealing with problems like that," explains Connery. "I've never had to call an agent to come on the set since then."

THE NEXT BIG film star to move into Ovitz's orbit was a young man from Cleveland with one of the most recognizable faces on the big screen. The son of a Jewish sporting goods store owner and a Catholic mother of Hungarian descent, Paul Newman entered Kenyon College in Ohio with the idea of studying economics, but switched to drama. It was the praise he won for his initial appearance on Broadway in 1953 in *Picnic* that led to a Warner Brothers film contract. His first screen appearance, in 1955, in *The Silver Chalice,* made no impact, but eventually he would win acclaim for his portrayals of boxer Rocky Graziano in *Somebody Up There Likes Me* (1956) and of Billy the Kid in *The Left-Handed Gun* (1958). Also in 1958, Newman received an Oscar nomination for his role as the embittered alcoholic Brick Pollitt in *Cat on a Hot Tin Roof.* Newman's expressive blue eyes and rugged physique were to make him a huge star in the 1960s. He was nominated for Oscars for his work in *The Hustler* (1961), *Hud* (1963), and *Cool Hand Luke* (1967).

In the late 1970s, CAA's Michael Rosenfeld had been representing Newman's wife, Joanne Woodward. She liked the agency, and thus, even though a few other agencies were desperately trying to sign Newman, his wife's recommendation that he join CAA carried the day. He became a CAA client in 1980, a time, Newman recalls, when he was thinking about doing things other than acting: "The business was changing. I was kind of a dinosaur. I was really losing interest in acting and that whole rat race." Heavily into his auto racing at the time, the actor was interested in doing a movie only if it was a great one. Michael Ovitz, aware that Newman's career had been floundering after such films as Robert Altman's *Buffalo Bill and the Indians* (1976), and *Slap Shot* (1977), pitched the actor: "If an agent doesn't do anything for you, it doesn't cost anything. I truly believe I couldn't do a worse job than you are doing for yourself." Ovitz took over his career and managed to obtain roles for Newman that had been slated for other actors or at first didn't seem right for him. For instance, it was thanks to Ovitz that Newman was chosen to play the lead opposite Oscar-winner Sally Field in the 1981 film *Absence of Malice.* The movie deals with journalistic ethics, or the lack thereof. When the leader of a long-shoremans' union disappears, a female journalist (Field) throws a spotlight on someone (the Newman character) wrongly accused of causing the man's disappearance. Newman's character, as Newman describes him, had been written as "a half-Mafia, Italian kind of character," and the actor had never before been cast as an Italian-American. Thus Ovitz suggested that the name of Newman's character be changed to Gallagher, and that he be made an honest liquor distributor rather than an underworld sort. Now the actor seemed right for the role.

The adding of Paul Newman's name to CAA's roster gave the agency's reputation yet another tremendous boost. Ovitz and his colleagues clearly were on a roll, and the Newman signing showed the industry that the acquisition of Sean Connery had been no fluke. Ovitz and Newman became fast friends, and on a number of occasions the agent watched him race cars. Newman also took to Ovitz's business style: "He's a cross between a barracuda and Mother Teresa. He's a tough and crafty businessman, and I mean that in the best sense of the word. He's sly like a fox, but that's the only way you can survive in that agency business. But he also has a kind of generosity of spirit that people are not accustomed to seeing. He says funny things, but he doesn't know that they are funny. I expect he'll own most of southern California in the next seven or eight years. I hope it's not the part that slips in the ocean. He's a lot like drivers in automobile races. There are a lot of guys who know how to lead races, but they don't know how to win them. Ovitz is like a driver who knows how to lead a race and how to win. He's a great mediator."

Ovitz's own star was now on the rise, and as his family began to grow, he had even more reason to cheer. On October 9, 1980, he and Judy had their first child, a son they named Chris. A daughter, Kimberly, would follow on July 10, 1983; and another son, Eric, was to be born on December 18, 1986.

Ovitz's well-cultivated relationships with Gary Hendler and other attorneys were beginning to pay off handsomely. Ovitz had hit upon a winning formula when he began to mix with an attorney like Gary Hendler, for both men wanted to share clients for the good of all concerned. Hendler's close friend John Calley, one of the production heads of Warner Brothers at the time, recalls that "Hendler thought any time he could get a client with Michael Ovitz, he was doing his client a great service."

In addition to Hendler, Ovitz had targeted Bert Fields as being one of those hotshot entertainment attorneys capable of steering film clients his way. Not long after the founding of CAA, Ovitz sought Fields out. They went to lunch, and Fields was impressed by his luncheon partner's intelligence and energy. In the course of the meal, Ovitz pulled out a dollar bill and presented it to the attorney. Fields, accustomed to receiving somewhat more generous fees in payment for his services, was bemused. Still, he waited patiently to discover what Ovitz was up to. "I'd like to pay you a dollar a year not to sue me," leaving Fields wondering whether the talent agent was serious or not.

And sure enough, Ovitz did send Fields a dollar a year. As Fields tells the tale of Ovitz's offer, he makes it sound as if Ovitz were joking. But was he? Who knows, but it certainly was a clever ploy. If anyone were to approach Fields and ask that he take legal action against Ovitz or CAA, Fields would have to admit that he had a financial relationship with the talent agent that would preclude him from taking the case.

Fields and Ovitz began to send each other movie scripts, and naturally, when Fields took on a young Los Angeles native by the name of Dustin Hoffman as a client, he urged the up-and-coming actor to think seriously of taking on Ovitz as his agent.

Ovitz himself had begun to take notice of Hoffman when he made a spectacular film debut in Mike Nichols's 1967 cult classic *The Graduate*. Hoffman followed up with stellar performances in *Midnight Cowboy* in 1969 and *Lenny* in 1974. In 1979 he at last grabbed an Oscar for his lead role in *Kramer vs. Kramer*. Prior to *The Graduate*, Hoffman had mostly relied upon managers and attorneys rather than agents, of whom he thought little. But with his sudden stardom after *The Graduate*, Hoffman felt he needed more "sophisticated representation," and thus agreed with Fields's suggestion to meet Ovitz.

At their first meeting, in 1978, Ovitz had made no impression on Hoffman at all. Accompanied by CAA colleague Steve Roth, Ovitz let Roth do all the talking. Later, when Fields asked Hoffman what he had thought of Ovitz, all the actor could say was, "I don't know, he didn't say a word." Fields did not let up. A year later, while Hoffman was filming *Kramer vs. Kramer,* Fields arranged for the actor and Ovitz to have a quiet dinner. Joining them were Judy Ovitz and Hoffman's soon-to-be second wife, Lisa Gottsegen. There was much to talk about: Dustin and Lisa wanted to have children; Judy was pregnant with the Ovitzes' first child. It was the beginning of a long-standing friendship.

"I liked him," says Hoffman, "because I felt he was atypical of an agent. He was quiet. He seemed smart." Ovitz recalls telling Hoffman at that dinner: "We are totally new in the movies and we will dedicate ourselves to you. We'll kill for you." Ovitz explained to Hoffman that an actor of his caliber didn't need an agent to find him work; he could get all the offers he wanted. Ovitz then asked Hoffman, "What do you think makes a good agent?" "Well, it all starts with material," the actor replied. To which Ovitz replied, "We'll get you material." Hoffman sensed something genuine in Ovitz, and he was hooked. When Hoffman became a CAA client in 1980, the agency had three of the biggest names in Hollywood: Connery, Newman, Hoffman.

Still, Ovitz's appetite for big-name talent kept on growing. He now set his sights on another Hendler client, an up-and-coming young director named Sydney Pollack. After acting in television plays in the late 1950s, Pollack turned to directing in the early 1960s. His *They Shoot Horses,*

Don't They?, of 1969, won Pollack an Oscar nomination as Best Director. Four years later he was to direct Robert Redford and Barbra Streisand in *The Way We Were*, a love story set against a backdrop of political activism.

As the decade of the 1980s got under way, the director was being represented by the small, elite Ziegler Agency. When Ovitz phoned the director at his home, Pollack had no idea who he was. Ovitz asked Pollack if he might pay him a call, but the director was noncommittal. Ovitz then waited and phoned every two weeks, each time asking for an appointment. After a while, Pollack relented and agreed to see him: "Michael was so thoroughly persistent and undaunted that I started taking meetings with him." The director assumed that someone so persistent would make an effective talent agent. Pollack's career had, in his own words, "moved like a turtle." The list of films that he had directed was credible enough, but thus far contained the names of no blockbusters. Thus, while he was eager to move his career ahead, he had no evidence that Michael Ovitz could help him, beyond his tenacity.

When the two men finally did meet, Ovitz didn't promise the director that he would give his career a major boost, only that he would do his best. "He talked about my career and what he admired about it," Pollack recalls. "He would've been a fool to say, 'I can do this while someone else can't.' Mike wasn't stupid." Ovitz spent most of the time talking about how much he wanted to represent the director. Pollack found the agent interesting and intelligent, but didn't know what to make of him: "He wasn't effusive. He was not a guy who jabbered in your office. Usually when someone is all over you, they talk nonstop. They're effusive. Mike has always been slightly subdued and quiet. I didn't like or dislike it. I noticed it and it set him apart." Pollack explained to Ovitz that he had no reason to switch agencies, and that he liked the feeling of familiarity that one got only by staying with one agency over a long period of time. After they had met several times, Pollack told Ovitz: "I'm impressed with what you say, but there's nothing wrong with where I am." Yet more and more, Pollack was feeling himself drawn toward Ovitz: "There was something about him that was decidedly different from any other agent I had talked to." After their fourth meeting, Pollack was ready to commit himself to Ovitz, and the director signed on with CAA on March 9, 1981. Many of his friends asked him if he was crazy, but as Pollack says now: "These were people who didn't know Michael Ovitz."

Pollack's friendship with one of the great film stars of the era, Robert Redford, proved to be highly fortuitous for Ovitz, since the director introduced Redford to the agent. The son of an accountant, Redford attended the University of Colorado on a baseball scholarship, but he dropped out of school in 1957 in the hope of becoming a painter or an actor. He made his Broadway debut two years later in a minor role in *Tall Story*, which led to a starring role on Broadway in 1963 in Neil Simon's *Barefoot in the Park.* Redford's Hollywood career got under way in 1965, but he only became a major star four years later when he played the Sundance Kid to Paul Newman's Butch Cassidy in *Butch Cassidy and the Sundance Kid.* The top-grossing movie of 1969, at $46 million, it made Redford a worldwide celebrity. Four years later he teamed up with Newman again in the even bigger hit, *The Sting,* which garnered $78 million and an Oscar nomination for Redford. In 1976 he portrayed *Washington Post* reporter Bob Wood-ward in *All the President's Men,* the story of the aftermath of the break-in and burglary at the Watergate apartment complex that led to President Richard Nixon's downfall. And yet, while the movie was the fifth biggest of the year, at $30 million, Redford's personal drawing power appeared to be slipping. Several less-than-spectacular efforts followed: *A Bridge Too Far* (1977), *The Electric Horseman* (1979), and *Brubaker* (1980).

Redford had been using William Morris's Stan Kamen as an agent, but now he felt that he needed to jump-start his career. It was then that Syd-ney Pollack matched Redford with Michael Ovitz, who wooed the blond-haired superstar away from William Morris and signed him with CAA on March 25, 1981—just 16 days after Ovitz had signed Pollack! The twin signings of Pollack and Redford forever changed the way in which CAA was perceived in Hollywood. No longer was it looked upon as the distant third to William Morris and International Creative Management; in fact, it was moving ahead with incredible speed to challenge both of the larger agencies. Ovitz's conquest of Sydney Pollack and especially of Robert Redford had quite simply put CAA on the map, to stay.

ONE EVENING IN the early 1980s, Gary Hendler was pouring out his heart to Michael Ovitz at Scandia, a restaurant in Los Angeles. While he did have his highly successful tax practice, Hendler felt lonely, with no partner with whom to share his excitement. He also felt overburdened. While Hendler never came out and directly asked Ovitz to help him, the talent agent listened to the attorney's woes and decided to try to alleviate them.

That evening after leaving the dinner, Ovitz phoned another attorney friend, Barry Hirsch, an entertainment attorney who also had a booming business but had been voicing to Ovitz complaints of much the same kind as Hendler's about his burdensome and lonely law practice. Ovitz thought that he might be able to solve both men's problems by making one simple suggestion.

He invited Hirsch to breakfast the next morning, and proposed that he and Hendler merge their law practices. The two men immediately cottoned to the idea. "They wanted companionship. They saw what I had with Ronnie Meyer and Bill Haber." Within a week, Hendler and Hirsch had decided to join forces. As the matchmaker of their "marriage," Ovitz would go on to maintain strong ties to the new law firm, which eventually would add a third partner to become Armstrong, Hendler and Hirsch and to emerge as one of the most powerful entertainment law firms in Hollywood. Over the coming years, Ovitz the matchmaker was to reap enormous dividends from this lawyerly alliance: Ovitz, Hendler, and Hirsch ultimately shared 50 clients, among them Robert Redford, Sean Connery, Sydney Pollack, Barbra Streisand, and Francis Ford Coppola.

EVERY ONCE IN a while, as he sought to sign an actor, Ovitz used the direct approach. Such was the case in July of 1981. Ovitz and Ron Meyer were vacationing at the Kahala Hilton in Hawaii with their wives and children. This was going to be the weekend when the two partners got away from the daily grind of toiling away in Hollywood's star factory. Ironically, however, and as yet unbeknownst to the agents, right under their noses one of Hollywood's hottest properties was on vacation as well. Staying at the same hotel was a cocky young actor and writer named Sylvester Stallone, then represented by Stan Kamen of William Morris.

The 35-year-old Stallone grew up in a poor, broken home in that supertough area on the West Side of Manhattan known as Hell's Kitchen. He got tossed out of 14 schools in 11 years, and worked as zoo attendant, pizza-maker, and movie usher, all the while hoping to make it out to Hollywood as an actor. He played some bit movie parts, but his acting career had begun to sputter by the mid-1970s.

It was then that Stallone decided to write a screenplay of his own. This of course became *Rocky*, the story of a down-and-out boxer who overcomes seemingly insurmountable odds in taking on the heavyweight champion of the world. Stallone also starred in the 1976 film, and the movie surprised everyone by capturing the Oscar for Best Picture. Stallone also had been nominated for Best Actor and Best Screenplay. Three years later he would star in the sequel, *Rocky II*.

Meyer learned through a Stallone acquaintance that the star of the *Rocky* movies was staying at their hotel. When asked if he would like to meet Stallone, Meyer jumped at the chance. Ovitz and Meyer planned their assault carefully. Playing it cool, they took their magazines and books to the beach and acted like tourists. Spotting Stallone wasn't hard: He was the only one wearing a *Rocky* jacket! Eagerly, they approached him.

Ronnie Meyer made the pitch, while Ovitz stood there and tried to look important. No small feat, since he was clad in loud clothes, a beach hat, and wore sunglasses. Meyer and Stallone wound up taking a long walk on the beach, and they hit it off. The fact was that Stallone was worried about his career. He had just appeared in a pair of films, *Nighthawks* and *Victory,* and both were box-office flops. Meyer urged him to consider CAA: "My attitude was that whatever he was doing could have been better, and we were aggressive; we would give him much more time and attention and focus than he was getting." Stallone obviously was impressed with Meyer and Ovitz, though his personal manager had warned him that CAA agents were no better than any other agents in town. Three days later he dropped Kamen and signed with CAA. Agents at William Morris complained privately that Ovitz and Meyer had employed unfair tactics, in thus swooping down upon Stallone and capitalizing upon his career doubts. For Ovitz, those slow spells in a career represented the very best moment in which to grab a new client.

Acquiring major movie stars such as Connery, Newman, Redford, and Stallone was one way to let the world know that CAA was the "hot" new agency in town. Another way was to take lesser-known names and earn their eternal gratitude by securing fat contracts for them.

One case in point was a young man named Armyan Bernstein. He had arrived in Los Angeles in 1975, hoping to make it as a screenwriter. What was it that distinguished Bernstein from many others just like him in Hollywood? On the surface, not much. But he came armed with self-confidence—having written some plays for campus playwriting festivals back at the University of Wisconsin—and with a couple of screenplays in hand. He had been born in Chicago, and graduated from college in 1970 with a B.A. degree in history. For an entire year Bernstein lived the life of a mountain man and a recluse, in a cabin in the Colorado wilderness. Then in the early 1970s he became a broadcast journalist. After writing his screenplays he showed up in Los Angeles, knowing no one and having no idea at all as to how to get anyone to read his material.

One day, when Bernstein was sitting around a table with some friends, one of them told him that he simply had to find an agent.

"Who's the best?" he asked.

The most famous agent at that time was Stan Kamen. It just so happened, that someone at the table knew Kamen, and he promised to deliver Bernstein's two screenplays to the Morris agent. But then someone else said: "You know, there's a group of guys who have just broken away from the William Morris Agency. They're new, and young, and just starting out. Maybe you should go see them."

To Bernstein, the Morris defectors sounded like the more logical choice for him than the stratospheric Stan Kamen, who after all dealt only with the biggest clients. Thus it was that Bernstein decided to check out CAA. One day in early 1975 he appeared at the old offices in the Hong Kong Bank building. He was immediately struck by how small the offices were, and by the fact that the agents were sitting at card tables. The first CAA agent Bernstein met was Michael Rosenfeld, who chatted with him and told the wannabe screenwriter what he was aching to hear: that CAA could help him to make it in the business. "You've come to the right place at the right time," Rosenfeld said encouragingly. The agent boasted that among their clients were Rob Reiner (still doing *All in the Family* at that time) and a great comedy writer named Barry Levinson. Bernstein liked what he heard.

He was introduced to Michael Ovitz and Ron Meyer as well; they too left him with a good feeling: "Mike Rosenfeld was like the uncle you wished you had, and Ronnie was like the brother you wished you had. Mike Ovitz was something else. He's not easily defined by these family relations. He was like no one I had ever met before. He knew what he wanted to do, where he was and where he was going. And he seemed to know where you were and where you were going." His style was comforting to Bernstein, who admitted to Ovitz that he was searching for inspiration and support and feeling somewhat adrift at the moment.

Soon, CAA helped Bernstein sell one of his screenplays, *Thank God It's Friday*, for $25,000 to Motown, which, in turn, made a deal with Universal Studios to make the movie. Released in 1978, the film starred Debra Winger, Jeff Goldblum, Donna Summer, and The Commodores.

Bernstein had a new screenplay he particularly wanted to sell called *One from the Heart*. Ovitz and Bernstein met one Friday, at which time the agent told the writer that he loved his new project and planned to send it to all the studios: "We're going to have an auction, and hopefully by the close of business Monday night, you're going to be rich." But auctioning a screenplay wasn't a common practice at that time, and Bernstein had his doubts that Ovitz could live up to his promise.

As of that Monday morning, Bernstein had heard nothing from Ovitz or Rosenfeld, and therefore he decided to call CAA.

"So, what's going on?" he asked Ovitz impatiently.

"It's good news, but we don't know yet *how* good. Let us get back to you. Come by here this afternoon." Bernstein did so, unable to contain himself as he waited to hear just *how* good the news might be.

"What's the number you have in mind?" Ovitz asked Bernstein, referring to the amount of money he thought that his screenplay might have garnered.

Bernstein threw out a number that seemed quite high to him: "Seventy-five thousand dollars."

Ovitz looked amused. He had a little twinkle in his eye. Then he asked the young man playfully, basking in this moment of utter triumph, "Would you take three hundred thousand dollars?" A huge smile broke out on his face.

Armyan Bernstein couldn't believe what he had just heard. *Three hundred thousand dollars?* The number sounded astronomical. He looked at Ovitz and then at Rosenfeld and thought to himself: "Am I really worth this much money?"

The point was that it didn't matter how much Armyan Bernstein himself was "worth." What mattered was that Michael Ovitz had secured that amount for him, and it wouldn't be long before the industry heard that Hollywood's new rainmakers were at it again—big-time.

One from the Heart was produced and directed in 1982 by Francis Ford Coppola and was not a commercial or critical hit. Still, Michael Ovitz had delivered for Armyan Bernstein—and that was all that mattered.

AARON SPELLING HAD been a moderately successful television producer during the late Sixties and the Seventies. Starting with *Mod Squad,* a counterculture police drama, in 1968, Spelling had produced a number of reasonably successful crime-related dramas, including *S.W.A.T.* (1974), *Starsky and Hutch* (1975), and *Charlie's Angels* (1977). He then turned to a more elaborate format, producing the long-running series *Dynasty* (1979).

At one point in the late 1970s Tony Thomopoulos, then in charge of ABC Television, called Michael Ovitz to say that Aaron Spelling was looking for new representation, and Thomopoulos believed that the two men should meet. Ovitz and Spelling got together and the producer agreed to become a CAA client. It was a big moment for the agency, since Spelling would become CAA's biggest cash cow over the years. Spelling always had wanted to produce feature films as well as television programs. Thanks to CAA, in 1983 he was able to produce his first film, *Mr. Mom,* which starred Michael Keaton and was directed by John Hughes. Spelling's relationship with CAA was advantageous to both parties: CAA provided him with ideas for new television shows, and Spelling helped the agency to obtain clients. "It was a great partnership," Ovitz recalls. "He paid us the most money of anybody in the company." Each year, dating from the late 1970s, Spelling ranked as one of the five highest-fee-producing clients. He was CAA's most successful television client by far. In 1984, the agency's biggest commission came from Bill Murray and *Ghostbusters;* in 1993, from Steven Spielberg and *Jurassic Park;* but each and every year Spelling was among the top fee-producers for the agency. And of course, in the 1990s, Spelling would go on to produce such smash television hits as *Melrose Place* and *Beverly Hills 90210.*

THE TIME AT last had come when Michael Ovitz no longer had to woo major prospective clients. The tables had been turned. An actor or actress now had to have an impressive resumé, and the potential to have an even more impressive future, if he or she was to have a shot at becoming a CAA client. Ovitz and Meyer may have found Sly Stallone on the beach, but they had no intention of scavenging the streets and beaches for all their new talent.

So it was strange, very strange, when, one day early in 1981, CAA agent Paula Wagner got a phone call from movie producer Stanley Jaffe, asking her and Ovitz to take a look at a film called *Taps* that he had just completed. It featured a 19-year-old actor whom Jaffe really admired. The young actor had been in one movie (*Endless Love*) before *Taps*, but it had received lukewarm reviews that didn't suggest that he was to become the next James Dean or the next anyone else. Sure, the girls thought he was strikingly handsome. But heartthrobs like that came and went, and Michael Ovitz couldn't afford to waste his time or energy on such flashes in the pan.

Still, Ovitz and Wagner had enough respect for Jaffe to get interested when the producer suggested that they take a look at the young actor's performance in *Taps*. Wagner and Ovitz rented the film, and both were quite taken by the teenager. They let Jaffe know that they agreed with his positive assessment of the young actor, and Jaffe then arranged for Ovitz and Wagner to meet the young man, a virtual unknown at that time.

The actor's name was Thomas Cruise Mapother IV. Born on July 3, 1962, in Syracuse, New York, Thomas suffered as a boy both from dyslexia and from the breakup of his family. He lived for brief periods in Louisville, Ottawa, and Cincinnati, where he attended a Franciscan seminary. Finally settling down with his remarried mother in Glen Ridge, New

Jersey, he quit the wrestling team in the aftermath of a knee injury and began to act in his high school's productions. Eager to become a professional actor, he moved to New York City in 1980 and made a professional decision to drop his last name. Prior to his film debut in *Taps* in 1981, he managed to eke out a living as a busboy and maintenance man.

Few meetings would end up meaning more to Ovitz than his first with Tom Cruise. It was apparent to Ovitz, when he met the young actor in his office, that Cruise lacked self-confidence, and wasn't at ease in the Hollywood world. Ovitz could easily just have been polite to the young man, spoken briefly with him, and then escorted him out of the office before returning to his bigger-name clients. But he spotted something in Cruise, a star power that came forth despite his lack of polish, or maybe because of it. The young man was only 19 years old, but Ovitz sensed that he had a bright future—a very, very bright future—ahead of him. "He sat down on the couch across from us," Ovitz recalled, "and we were knocked out. He had this quiet energy. His eyes sort of danced. He had this infectious smile. He was the single politest man I'd ever met. No arrogance or cockiness. I just fell in love with the guy. He was terribly centered. He just wanted to be an actor."

And Cruise, for his part, was equally taken with Ovitz. "I liked Michael Ovitz immediately," Cruise told the author. "He was very nice to me, very warm and encouraging." And that meant all the more to Cruise, since he knew about the big CAA signings of late, as did just about everyone else who followed the careers of the top Hollywood talent.

Ovitz asked Cruise for the names of some of his favorite actors.

"Dustin Hoffman and Paul Newman" was the reply. To Cruise, both actors were legends.

"You should work with some of these people," Ovitz said casually. It was his way of saying: *Stick with me, and I'll make your dreams come true.*

"Oh, that would be kind of amazing," Cruise replied. "That would be great." *That would be shocking!* was what he meant.

Cruise couldn't even grasp the concept of being in the same movie with someone of Paul Newman's stature. "Paul Newman is like in another universe," he thought at the time. "I had no idea of what working with him would be like."

Ovitz cautioned the young actor that if he was going to work with the truly great directors he might have to pass up certain projects in order to be available for the ones that a Scorsese, Kubrick, or Levinson would direct, "and that will take some guts."

Tom Cruise signed with CAA on March 10, 1981. In the following December, *Taps* was released.

Cruise knows that in his first few years at CAA he wasn't one of Ovitz's huge stars, yet he is grateful to have been treated as such: "He didn't treat me any differently. I wasn't making him that much money compared to Paul Newman, Dustin Hoffman, or Sydney Pollack, all those guys who were making a lot of money for him. He probably made a few grand on *Risky Business.*" That's a reference to the hit film that launched Cruise's career when it appeared in 1983. "Michael Ovitz," Cruise added, "wasn't a snob, or pretentious at all. He made me feel like I had a home at CAA, and with him."

Most likely, by 1983 Michael Ovitz had realized that "Tom Cruise" was certain to become a household name—perhaps not overnight, but probably within the next few years.

Cruise found Ovitz to be dynamic and very bright. They shared an interest in video technology and talked about the subject often. The two men clicked. Ovitz told the young actor that he should call him at any time if he had a question, even at home. And once, Cruise did call Ovitz with a problem: He wanted to ensure that a studio would market one of his films properly. "The next thing you knew," said Cruise, "there was no problem." Ovitz had promised to come up with the answer, and he had. Sometimes Ovitz called just to find out how things were going, and Cruise also appreciated the fact that Ovitz always returned his calls promptly. "Many times," he says, "I've called him and he's been incredibly helpful." Ovitz always knew what was happening in Cruise's career. The actor liked that as well.

What sealed their relationship was Ovitz's reliability: "Everything he said he would do—like calling me—he always did. He would just go out of his way. He had a way of making you feel really special."

With so many signings rolling in, in March 1981, CAA began to place advertisements in the Wednesday and Thursday editions of *Daily Variety*, announcing which stars it had just signed. Soon all of Hollywood was in on the new guessing game: *Who did CAA get their hooks into this week?*

CAA was having a great year back in 1981. The partners earned more than they had ever dreamed they would: $500,000 apiece. Thus it comes as no surprise that one of them, Michael Rosenfeld, decided to retire in 1982. After Rosenfeld's departure, Ovitz remained an equal partner along with Bill Haber, Rowland Perkins, Ron Meyer, and Martin Baum.

Now that he had put together a solid roster of clients, Ovitz was in a position to exploit the selling technique of packaging as never before. By offering a studio a ready-made film package that came replete with director, screenwriter, and stars, he made it extremely hard for a studio to say no to him; he also ensured work for many of his clients. The first major film project CAA packaged was *Tootsie* in 1982, one of the most popular films of the 1980s. Attached to the project were such notable CAA clients as actors Dustin Hoffman and Bill Murray and director Sydney Pollack. Throughout the rest of the 1980s, CAA would package some 150 movies.

Since packaging gave him such leverage with the studios, Ovitz regarded the sales technique as a powerful tool for gaining business, one that had the effect of getting larger and larger fees for his clients. But others bitterly complained that CAA's packaging strategy unfairly hiked the prices that studios had to pay for actors. Ovitz scoffs at the criticism. He is proud that he figured out a way to boost his clients' take. "It's one hundred percent correct," he says gleefully. "CAA set the pricing standard. That was our job. We were agents, and agents get as much as they can for clients. That's what we did. We controlled the prices in the marketplace. My theory was, if you had all this talent under one roof, you could benefit from it."

But while Mike Ovitz may not have seen anything wrong with packaging his clients, some of the once-mighty studios felt that they were being strong-armed into accepting CAA packages on a take-it-or-leave-it basis. For years the studios had called all the shots, deciding which actors would play which roles. Now Michael Ovitz's CAA had become the decision maker, practically dictating to the studios who would star in which films and how much the stars would be paid. While the studios could always refuse to accept a CAA package, their executives had a good reason not to seem snappish: The next time around, CAA just might pass them up. Ovitz held the studios hostage. And while some executives kicked and screamed, most went along. It was all but impossible to say no to a CAA offer, because it provided a near-guarantee that a movie would open big, thanks to its packaged stars. An entertainment lawyer by the name of Lee Rosenbaum was to learn all of this one day in 1982.

Employed at Embassy Pictures, a startup company trying to produce feature films, Rosenbaum took part in negotiations with CAA to obtain film stars for the movie version of the long-running Broadway hit, *A Chorus Line*. The film rights belonged to Polygram, which commissioned Embassy Pictures to get the movie made. CAA packaged the two producers, Cy Feuer and Ernest H. Martin, Richard Attenborough as director, and actor Michael Douglas in the lead role; Arnold Schulman was brought in as the screenwriter. What Rosenbaum learned at that time was that CAA was far deeper into developing and producing projects than the studios were; CAA put movies together, while Embassy simply funded them: "Embassy got to say, 'We like the script, or we don't, Attenborough is great, or he's not.' But CAA really put that movie together. I learned that CAA was different from ICM and William Morris, neither of which really packaged movies in order to get jobs for their clients. The CAA philosophy was about getting as many of their clients into a package as possible, and getting the movie made."

Rosenbaum went on to represent Columbia Pictures in the early 1990s, in the negotiations that led to the making of the film *Bram Stoker's Dracula*. Jim Hart, a CAA client, had written a script based upon the Bram Stoker novel. CAA wanted two of its clients, Francis Ford Coppola and Winona Ryder, to direct and to star in the movie, respectively. Sitting across a table from Rosenbaum were three CAA agents, a CAA business affairs person, attorney Barry Hirsch, and a Hirsch law firm associate. The six people laid out the package that Columbia would have to buy into: Winona Ryder would get $1 million, Coppola, $5 million. The budget for the film would be $25 million. "What else do you want to know?" asked one of the CAA agents. . . .

Ovitz's ability to package major film projects that featured his heavy-hitting clients gave Ovitz a decided advantage in terms of getting the attention of the studios. Few could compete with him. Marion Rosenberg, an agent who tried to do so, recalls how difficult it was for her: The best she could hope to do was to talk to a development executive or a casting director as she sought to find work for a client, whereas all that Michael Ovitz had to do was call the head of a studio. It was far more effective, she says with a wistful sigh, to be in a position to tell a studio chief over the telephone, "This is what I'm offering, take it or leave it," about this movie package or that, than to be forced to deal with lower-level studio executives: "Most agents like myself had to pull many strings before we could get to the person who could say yes. Ovitz cut through all that." Moreover, he had not only the script, but the director and the stars to offer the studio as well. If she had a good script, Rosenberg notes, she couldn't simply drop the proper directors and stars into place; she had to speak to their agents, and "that put me at a disadvantage."

No doubt. And there is equally little doubt that it helped Michael Ovitz to become even more powerful.

8

A Shroud of Secrecy

Now that he had so many major film stars in the CAA stable, Michael Ovitz could turn his attention to "growing" the talent agency. Rather than hire away older, more experienced talent agents from the other agencies in town, Ovitz preferred to build up a corps of his own home-grown agents, men and women who would absorb the CAA corporate culture right from the start, a culture that was almost entirely a reflection of Ovitz's personality and style. As he sought to develop that corporate culture, one of Ovitz's chief goals was to reverse the largely negative stereotype of the old-time Hollywood talent agent. For what he wanted above all was for CAA talent agents to be respected. "I hated the disrespect for the profession," he says. His aim was to inject a new professionalism into the agency business, in the hope that that would not only dissipate the disdain felt toward all agents, but make CAA agents simply indispensable to all Hollywood deal-making.

In order to do all of this, Ovitz wrapped CAA's corporate culture and business operations in a shroud of great secrecy. The more secretive CAA was, the more mysterious, and the more mysterious, the more awe-inspiring its agents would seem. It was easy to shield the agency from public scrutiny: CAA was, after all, a privately-owned firm with no public shareholders, and hence under no obligation to reveal its mode of operations or its finances. Though he sometimes came under pressure to take the company public, Ovitz had little incentive to take such a step. "I ran the company based on total secrecy," Ovitz explained. "If we had gone public, the fabric of the company would have unraveled. I did a lot of things for people. I loaned money to people a great deal, and bailed people out of jail. I always paid for everything. Because of SEC [Securities and Exchange Commission] rules I would have had to report all of this, and I didn't want to. If we had gone public and I had wanted to give Tom Cruise an expensive gift, I wouldn't have been able to without hearing back from some shareholder. I didn't want that." At any rate, avoiding the limelight now became one of Ovitz's trademark characteristics.

Secrecy was seen as being vital to the agency's interests, for once word leaked out that CAA had just obtained $5 million for a client to star in a film, for instance, other CAA film clients might feel themselves to be justified in demanding the same or a similar amount for their own services in a film. Or if William Morris or ICM discovered at an early stage that CAA was putting together a package to sell to a certain studio, those agencies might try to make preemptive strikes of their own. Thus, while it is common for many private companies to jealously guard their privacy, Ovitz turned secrecy into a powerful psychological weapon, surrounding CAA with a mystique that led others to believe that exciting, intriguing things were going on behind its closed doors.

CAA talent agents reinforced that image by the way in which they appeared in public, whether at movie premieres, fancy restaurants, or elsewhere. Rarely appearing on their own, but usually in groups of four or five, the agents projected an image of strength and purpose. They never spoke about Michael Ovitz except to praise his skills in the most general terms; never did they discuss how he ran the business, or what CAA's clients were up to. Always they sought to deflect public attention away from themselves and onto their clients. To attract publicity, an agent was taught, was to risk incurring the wrath of clients, who were afraid that the media spotlight would begin to glare upon the agents.

Because so little was known about CAA's business tactics, and because its agents seemed so all-powerful, the myth grew up that CAA agents were the *übermenschen* of Hollywood, a group of exceedingly zealous, aggressive warriors who seemed to pop up everywhere and to require no sleep. As CAA moved from strength to strength throughout the early Eighties, agents elsewhere tried to lay bare CAA's operations—but the institution remained an impregnable fortress. And the loyalty and discipline displayed by Ovitz's agents only served to enhance CAA's mystique.

Not even the lowest-ranking employee at CAA was made to feel comfortable about leaving the agency. Josh Bycel took a $300-a-week job as a clerk in the mail room at CAA in the fall of 1993, and wasn't even on the agent track. After a month, Bycel left CAA to take a higher-paying job ($500 a week) as assistant to a film agent at ICM. Pleased with himself that he had found a better job, he was taken aback by the bitter reaction of Arlene Newman, CAA's director of human resources: "I wish you wouldn't have come here if you were going to go to ICM." Later, Bycel would admit that he had been naive: "Leaving for ICM was not something you did at CAA. It was like leaving the Dodgers for the Yankees."

Keeping a low profile came naturally to Michael Ovitz. His childhood and early-adult years had made it clear that he had no lust for the limelight. He deliberately chose to work in the least public segment of the entertainment industry, and he genuinely (and naively, he would later admit) hoped to become a major business figure without attracting public attention. "Michael," says his close friend Arne Glimcher, president of the PaceWildenstein Gallery in New York, "knows who he is. He doesn't need the media telling him who he is. The media would get angry when he didn't give interviews, but his concept was 'we are not the stars.' " People interpreted his privacy as arrogance, and his shyness as imperiousness.

Even in the smallest things, Ovitz enjoyed being furtive, even conspiratorial. Nothing pleased Ovitz more than to track down a friend and send a gift and then, when the friend asked him how he had tracked him down, become silent. He seemed to be distinctly uncomfortable when under public scrutiny. Whenever he was interviewed, he supplied only the scantest of information about his personal life. And he seemed to experience almost a physical revulsion upon being photographed. Working behind closed doors, and leaving others with the feeling that he was a man of a thousand secrets, gave Ovitz an adrenaline charge. When David O'Connor joined the CAA mail room as an agent trainee in October 1983, he found Ovitz to be "sort of spectral. You didn't see him roaming the halls a lot. His was the one office whose door was always closed. We'd put fresh water in his pitcher and restock his cabinet with nuts and put drinks in the refrigerator, but I didn't see a whole lot of him. He'd say hello in the hallways, but he always seemed purposeful. There wasn't a lot of conversation. There was a general sense of awe."

Even Ovitz's business friends had a hard time penetrating his inner shell. Producer Norman Lear calls him "circumspect, careful, measured in his affections. He'll only unbend in flashes." Rarely did he unwind even before those closest to him. Al Checchi, the co-chairman of Northwest Airlines whose friendship with Ovitz began in the mid-Eighties, guessed that only once in every nine months or so would Ovitz disclose a confidence to him, and even then prefacing the comment, only halfjokingly, with, "This is a private conversation. If you ever repeat it, I'm going to kill you." After four years of such threats, Checchi politely suggested to his friend that perhaps by now he had built up enough trust that the threats could cease.

Reporters had no luck breaching the CAA fortress or accessing its general. Agency policy was to treat journalists as if they didn't exist. "You can only create fires," co-founder Rowland Perkins notes, in explaining why even journalists engaged in simple fact-checking were shot down. For years, CAA had no spokesperson. From CAA's perspective, there was no need for one. Ray Kurtzman, the director of business affairs, had formally been charged with handling the media, but that was a fiction. David O'Connor was an assistant to Ovitz from 1984 to 1986. Whenever O'Connor received a call from a journalist he referred the caller to Kurtzman's secretary, who had clearcut instructions to say that Mr. Kurtzman did not speak to the press.

The result was that the public at large knew almost nothing about Michael Ovitz. Even those in the entertainment industry had only a superficial impression of him. All that most had absorbed about him were the myths and the mystique. Marion Rosenberg has been a Hollywood talent agent since 1979, and now owns her own agency. But like so many of the agents in town, she has only a fleeting recollection of the man: "There was always a perception of immense power. Ovitz was always there, but I never heard the man open his mouth. I cannot tell you what Mike Ovitz's voice sounds like. I've never heard it, either in person or in public. Agents tend to socialize with one another. But he really didn't. Certainly I saw pictures of him at fund-raising events. I used to see him at lunch in various restaurants. But this was not a ubiquitous man, somebody who was out and about. That helped him immensely. There's nothing more powerful than silence, than knowing what you know and keeping it to yourself and letting it out to just a handful of people. That's immense power."

I F NONE OF CAA's corporate culture was accessible to outsiders, CAA's agents knew full well its basic shape and form. For Ovitz drilled it into them, sometimes overtly by barking out orders, more often implicitly by setting a personal example. He set the highest standards imaginable, and then expected his agents to emulate him. It was his goal to work harder than anyone in the office. Armyan Bernstein, the client whose screenplay Ovitz had sold for $300,000, once phoned him at 9:00 a.m. "Oh, you're in early," Bernstein quipped. Sounding insulted, Ovitz replied, "I accomplish more before you get to the office than you do all day." Then Ovitz broke out in laughter. Bernstein knew that Ovitz had been joking, but only partially: "With Mike, the feeling is, 'You can't work as hard as I do; don't even try.' "

On his way to work each morning he was on the car phone, arriving at the office every day except Wednesdays by 9:00 a.m. On Wednesdays he arrived at 7:45 a.m. to prepare for the weekly staff meeting 45 minutes later. He often remained in the office until 7:30 or 8:00 p.m., then went to dinners and screenings. The hard-driving Ovitz was unable to back-pedal, even when close friends such as Dustin Hoffman would tease him about his zeal. "Mike," Hoffman would say, "how many three-by-five cards are you writing as you listen to me on the phone and say, 'Oh, that's interesting.'? How many calls do you have waiting for you? Am I your one-hundred-seventieth call today?" He spent more evenings out than at home, his wife Judy often accompanying him to premieres and other swanky parties. By the time he arrived at his office in the morning, Ovitz already had his day organized, with a lengthy list of priority items that he would turn over to assistants to handle. The list might include such to-do items as who should receive a gift, who should get a certain manuscript. He looked over the log of phone calls to be made, and prioritized them with a red pen. The more red dots next to a person's name, the higher the priority.

Reaching for the telephone was almost an automatic reflex for Ovitz. While on the phone, he skimmed the daily newspapers. Rick Kurtzman, a former Ovitz assistant, remembers Ovitz remaining on the phone for six-hour stretches. He was determined never to waste a minute. And with so many phone calls to make, so many tasks to assign, he put himself under enormous pressure. Others felt sorry for him, but he thrived on it. "The gift I would give him," says art consultant Barbara Guggenheim Fields, "would be to make an appointment for dinner with him and cancel it, so he could spend it with his family." But Ovitz probably would have rushed back to the office to make more phone calls. "There were no hours," Ovitz says, as he recalls his nonstop quest to outlast everyone else in the office. "The agents came in early and left late, because people tried to beat me and stay later. It wasn't complicated. There were no time cards. You would get in the building at 8:00 a.m. and stay until 8:00 p.m., and the place was cooking." Ovitz's goal was to turn CAA into the busiest agency in town, an efficient energy-cell that never stopped humming.

David O'Connor joined the CAA mail room in October of 1983, and became Ovitz's assistant 18 months later. The thing that most impressed O'Connor about CAA was the phenomenal pace that Ovitz set for everyone: "He worked harder than everyone else. He was so disciplined about that. He returned all of his phone calls, or had me or some other agent handle them. He would go crazy with me if he found that a call had not been returned or something else hadn't been handled. He was very diligent in making sure that everyone on the outside felt that the company took care of them. He treated everyone with a tremendous amount of respect."

Michael Rosenfeld Jr., son of the CAA co-founder, began to work in the CAA mail room in 1984. He recalls that Ovitz had no qualms about expecting agents to work around the clock, seven days a week: "He didn't say it. He implied it." Everyone got the message, no one seemed to complain. Michael Rosenfeld Sr. recalls that no one took vacations, no one missed a day: "If you got up in the morning, and you thought you didn't feel good, you still dragged yourself out of bed and down your front stoop, and if on the front stoop you fell and broke your leg, you crawled on your hands and knees, and you came to see me and I would tell you if you had a headache and if your leg was broken. *You* didn't make that decision." If anyone felt even a momentary inclination to goldbrick, they only had to glance at the workaholic Ovitz and his partners, who never seemed to slack off. *Never.*

"There was a certain intimidation," recalls Amy Grossman, who began with CAA as its first agent trainee in 1975, became an agent, and remained with the agency until February of 1992. "Those guys didn't let up. No matter how many phone calls they received, they returned them. Somehow those guys never got sick; they never had a doctor appointment; never left papers at home; never came upon an accident on the road that prevented them from getting to a meeting on time. Agents [at other firms] felt they had no screen to hide behind. If they [the leaders at CAA] could do it, why couldn't you? The [CAA] management wasn't at the [swimming] pool; they'd gotten there [to a deal] earlier, faster than you. They were the best. So you're going to be awed, intimidated, by somebody who does something so well. They were *so good.*" And you're going to make sure you never screw up. To Ovitz, "screwing up"—which often translated into "losing a client"—was sinful. "This was a guy who didn't want to lose, ever," says Mike Rosenfeld Jr. "If a client was lost to the agency, it was unacceptable to him." Ron Meyer used to say that you didn't really become an agent until you lost your first client. If Michael Ovitz ever heard that thought voiced, he must have found it odd—and dangerous. He was unwilling to lose, and he expected his agents to feel the same way.

Ovitz expected his agents to be as fanatical as he was. He often said that agenting was a business based upon appearances. Thus, his agents had no product to sell other than their clients and themselves. "The product," Ovitz explained, "was service. We always had to look like we had better service, and had more information, and were more aggressive, and we were really on top of everything."

He hoped that his agents would make him their model, and while he knew they would sometimes fail to get a client, he insisted that they at least give it their best shot. "The only sin that we could commit as employees," says Amy Grossman, "was the sin of omission. No one got into trouble for trying something, taking a chance. You got into trouble for *not* trying to drum up business, for not returning calls. If you did something so horrible it cost the representation of a client, it was okay as long as you had good intentions." In an earlier comment, Mike Rosenfeld appeared to suggest that Ovitz would not tolerate the loss of a client under any circumstances. He was exaggerating. Yes, it is true that Ovitz didn't want to lose even a single client; but as Amy Grossman indicates, if a client did fail to sign with CAA, Ovitz would take it out on the agent only if he or she had been lax or indifferent. As Grossman notes: "If you sat around, that wasn't going to work. I don't remember anyone being lazy."

Indeed, the mere fact of being around Ovitz and his team spurred people into action. "You felt energized," said Amy Grossman. "You wanted to do your best. Wanting to please Michael Ovitz was an enormous motivational factor for the entire staff. You felt privileged. He had the right balance of inaccessibility and accessibility. It was tantalizing to be with him. He'd come close, and go away. You never got enough of Mike to get sick of him." He encouraged agents not just to do their best, but to stretch themselves beyond their comfort zones. And it worked. Richard Lovett, an assistant to Ovitz, later an agent, and currently CAA's president, recalls: "Michael's presence was so strong that everyone wanted to perform for him; if Michael asked you to do something it was the first thing you did, and you did it better than anything else you were responsible for doing."

For the agent trainees working out of CAA's mail room, Ovitz's frenetic pace wasn't off-putting. They were young, and they knew that this "basic training" was a prerequisite for becoming a full-fledged agent. Even the fact that their expensively-earned college degrees seemed to have brought them to nothing more than delivering the mail was viewed as being an acceptable embarrassment. After all, in a few years and with a little bit of luck, they would be CAA talent agents and thus hold the most prized jobs in all of Hollywood. Simply knowing that Michael Ovitz himself had begun his career in the mail room of a talent agency made these agent trainees feel special. And they were special, to Michael Ovitz. He believed that, by putting these trainees through the same paces he had gone through, he was building up a new breed of talent agents as enthusiastic and disciplined as Michael Ovitz. While the tasks that mail-room personnel carried out were often menial, their journeys around Hollywood were designed not only to get the mail delivered but to educate the trainees about the town's geography and its key players. Nor was the mail-room program all grunt-work. The trainees slowly gained exposure to CAA's talent agents, and they were encouraged to converse with them about their work. Trainees harboring lofty ambitions hoped for the chance to be mentored personally by Ovitz; hence, the job of being Ovitz's personal assistant was the most prized assignment in the office. One such trainee was David O'Connor.

During the spring of 1984, David began to notice that Ovitz's office was calling upon him more and more to carry out tasks for the boss: He took films over to Ovitz's home in Brentwood for weekend screenings, drove him to the airport on a number of occasions. *Perhaps,* O'Connor thought, *Ovitz is testing me, checking whether I'm good enough to become his assistant.* Needless to say, O'Connor was thrilled—and enticed.

Then one day Ovitz's office rang O'Connor, to say that the boss wanted to meet the trainee. O'Connor waited around all day for word that Ovitz was ready to see him. As of 7:00 p.m., Ovitz was meeting with Robert Redford in his office. The door remained closed until 8:30 p.m. Finally Ovitz's assistant told the trainee to go home, that there would be no session with Ovitz on this day. Disappointed and confused, O'Connor went home, wondering whether he would ever hear from Ovitz again.

A few weeks passed. It was now a Friday afternoon in April. Again Ovitz's office rang the trainee. Again O'Connor was told to stand by for a meeting with Ovitz, scheduled for 4:00 p.m. This time, O'Connor was escorted into Ovitz's office right at four. It was the first time he had been in the office when Ovitz was there. Still on the phone, Ovitz waved his hands, motioning his guest in. O'Connor headed for a chair in front of Ovitz's desk, but Ovitz pointed to a couch. Ovitz then seemed to stay on the phone forever, making the young mail-room staffer increasingly nervous. Trying to calm his trembling nerves, O'Connor told himself: *I've got to sell myself to this guy.* Then, as if he were holding a conversation with himself, he replied, *Wait a second, the ball is in* his *court. He* phoned *me.* That helped a bit, but O'Connor remained jittery.

Suddenly, Ovitz was off the phone and coming around the desk to take a seat near O'Connor. Ovitz's back was to a window, whereas the young man was looking directly into the bright sun. Trying to make out Ovitz's face, O'Connor could see only shadows. *Great,* O'Connor thought to himself. *The ball may be in his court, but I can't even see his face.*

"So, what's up?" A common way for Michael Ovitz to start a conversation.

What's up? What do I do with that kind of question? the trainee asked himself.

Clearly this wasn't the time to chitchat about how he had dropped off five scripts this week, or just bought a birthday present for Sly Stallone. If he really was in line to become Ovitz's assistant, this was the time to make it clear just how much he wanted to work with Michael Ovitz, and how much he enjoyed being at CAA. David spoke rapidly. Meanwhile, unbeknownst to him, Ovitz had secretly pressed a hidden buzzer on his phone three times, and in walked an assistant. They chatted for a while, and then the assistant left. O'Connor resumed his pitch. Then, just as covertly, Ovitz buzzed another assistant in. The assistant chatted briefly with Ovitz, then departed. O'Connor returned to his pitch. For a third time Ovitz reached clandestinely for the buzzer, and an assistant arrived to say a few words with the boss. O'Connor thought little of the interruptions until some weeks later, when an Ovitz assistant confessed the truth: Ovitz had been testing David's nerves, to see how well he coped with distractions. That was all. Ovitz had had no real need to meet with those assistants about anything.

David O'Connor obviously passed the test, for he became Michael Ovitz's assistant that very month. A six-month trial period ensued. Though he knew he was expected to be a quick study, the trial period was full of bumps. "I was to service him like he services his clients, and I just didn't get it," O'Connor recalls. "I didn't get it at all. If I didn't follow up before he followed up for me, there was always hell to pay." Realizing that he was being more of an irritant than a help, O'Connor constantly feared that he was about to be fired during his first few months as Ovitz's assistant. In time, however, O'Connor improved, and Ovitz gave him more slack. "If I couldn't get something done completely," said O'Connor, "Ovitz wanted to know that I had taken the task fifty yards down the field." Ovitz suggested that O'Connor turn in typewritten notes to him, explaining which tasks had been done, which had not. In that way, O'Connor grew into the job. In September of 1986, David O'Connor became a full-fledged agent at the Creative Artists Agency.

JAY MOLONEY WAS a native of Hollywood, California. He had entered the talent-agency business because of his father, screenwriter Jim Moloney. Jim had been a client of CAA's Marty Baum, and once had written a script called *The Fiendish Plot of Fu Manchu* in which Peter Sellers took an interest. In the summer, at the end of Jay's freshman year at USC, Baum arranged for the 18-year-old to work in the mail room at CAA for two months. The experience hooked Moloney, who quickly decided that he wanted to become an agent. Although his preference was to quit school immediately and enter CAA's agent-trainee program, the USC student ran into resistance from the agency's executives, who thought he was too young and would let him work only part-time. Upon returning to USC, Moloney befriended Richard Lovett, who at that point in time had been assigned to CAA agent Fred Spektor. Thanks to Lovett, Moloney became an assistant to Spektor, skipping the mail-room-trainee program entirely. In time, Moloney became friendly with Ovitz's secretary Donna Ensom, who often asked him to get lunch for her and, later, to answer Ovitz's phones when she was away from her desk. Moloney's goal was to become full-time assistant to her boss, because "the opportunity to work for Michael Ovitz was the best job in show business for someone getting started."

In 1984, Moloney began to run other errands for Ovitz, and that led to his being chosen as an extra assistant. It was a great time to be at CAA. Moloney says: "We all felt that we were the guys in the white hats, and all the studios were our friends; the only enemies were the other agencies. It was an amazing time to be there." Ovitz was beginning to spend time with non-Hollywood players, and the effects were telling. Moloney recalls Ovitz returning from investment banker Herb Allen's highly secretive annual conference at Sun Valley, Idaho, where a veritable Who's Who of American business attended seminars and chatted breezily with one another during the off-hours: "It was one of the first times I saw Michael truly blown away. Something clicked for him about what was next for him, spending that kind of time with that level of talent and intelligence and power."

In 1986, when Ovitz's executive assistant David O'Connor was promoted to agent, Moloney stepped into David's shoes. His first few months on the new job were anguishing. He was expected to do all that he had been doing as a junior assistant—which took up a good 30 hours a week—plus all the tasks of the executive assistant. And because Ovitz increasingly was preoccupied with developing relationships outside of Hollywood, he made it clear to Moloney that all of the day-to-day tasks relating to clients had to be done perfectly. "The biggest crime I could commit," Moloney remembers, of his arduous breaking-in period under Ovitz, "was to waste his time."

Jay will never forget one Friday toward the end of 1986. That was the day on which he misworded a telegram, signed by Ovitz, meant to congratulate Danny De Vito upon being nominated for a Golden Globe Award for his role in *Ruthless People* (1986). The only trouble was that Jay had congratulated the actor for his role in *Down and Out in Beverly Hills*, a film in which Nick Nolte starred but De Vito did not even appear! Within moments of receiving the telegram, De Vito had Ovitz on the phone and was ribbing him about the error. As soon as he had put down the receiver, Ovitz turned upon Moloney: "I don't know if this is going to work out with you. You're young, and you seem to be a little bit over your head." Perhaps, Ovitz seemed to be implying, Moloney should do a mail-room stint before he tried again to tackle his present job.

Moloney, 20 years old and eager to keep working for Ovitz, phoned him at home on the very next morning, a Saturday. "If I can't work for you in this job," the young man proclaimed boldly, "I don't want to work here. I think I need some help, but I don't want to go backward. If you don't give me another chance, I will have to leave the company."

Ovitz appeared to be impressed by Moloney's boldness and persistence, traits which he himself possessed and in spades. He promised to think about what the young man had said.

In fact, the subject never arose again. Soon after his conversation with Moloney, Ovitz added another assistant to his staff, Dan Adler, thereby spreading out the onerous workload.

Ovitz put his assistants through hell. He made them feel, almost from the first minute they began working for him, that they weren't long for the job. Perhaps Ovitz was thinking of Phil Weltman's old adage: *You are allowed one mistake, that's all.* He set the highest standards in everything he did, and he expected his assistants to come up to those standards almost immediately. When they didn't, he barked. When they improved a little, he shrugged his shoulders indifferently. But finally, when he deemed that they were good enough to be promoted to full-blown agent, he treated them as if they were his own sons.

David O'Connor and Jay Moloney were among the fortunate ones, for they came through the system whole and intact. But the pressures on other young recruits sometimes were overwhelming. Some found that they lacked the needed drive and dropped out when it became clear that they were never going to make it out of the mail room. Those who did graduate from the mail room became assistants to agents and, after another trial period, full-blown agents. A new agent who did his or her job well could expect higher pay than at any other talent agency in town, longer hours, and real job security. Ovitz hated to fire anyone. He saw such a step as an admission of failure on his part. As far as he was concerned, someone with a good head could always be trained to become a successful agent. If a person was coming along too slowly, Ovitz believed that it was always possible to slot that person somewhere else, and that in all likelihood, that would take care of whatever problem had existed. He wanted his agents to feel a fierce loyalty to their agency, and on those rare occasions when agents decided to leave of their own accord, he took it very personally.

BLUMBERG

In the CAA corporate culture, teamwork was just as highly valued as were secrecy and hard work. Probably even more so. Nearly everyone in the talent-agency business talked a good game, vis-à-vis sharing clients and sharing information, but very few played one. At William Morris a petty competitiveness had prevailed, with the senior agents keeping their clients to themselves and preventing the younger agents from learning the ropes and helping the agency. Ovitz was determined that the internecine warfare that had been the rule rather than the exception at his old agency would be replaced at CAA with an "all for one, one for all" spirit.

Ray Kurtzman, who worked at William Morris before he was put in charge of CAA's business affairs, recalls that at Morris, if someone signed a big star, "that agent would husband him and everybody had to go through the agent. Mike Ovitz didn't believe in that. He believed that you should surround yourself with agents who could talk to the actors directly. And anyone who had an idea could call the actors directly. It was unheard-of at most agencies. But at CAA, that policy not only made people feel really good about themselves, it also gave them a tremendous experience so that they were capable of dealing with situations that younger people at other agencies could not."

John Calley, who served as president and chief operating officer of United Artists in the early 1990s before he became president and CEO of Sony Pictures Entertainment, notes that Ovitz prevented tiny pockets of power from cropping up within CAA, that the agency appeared to speak with one voice: "Ovitz had enough confidence to know that by giving a 28-year-old agent the day-to-day access to an artist like Mike Nichols, he wasn't going to lose Mike Nichols." Ovitz made sure that younger agents like David O'Connor got to deal with CAA's major clients, and eventually O'Connor did in fact begin to represent such industry heavyweights as Sean Connery, Robert Redford, and Sydney Pollack.

Team sports became the perfect metaphor for Ovitz, and he often attended Los Angeles Lakers basketball games. While other fans at the Forum screamed and hollered whenever Magic Johnson swished one of his magnificent hook shots, Ovitz got his kicks from a Laker fast break, as the team moved down the court, passing the ball off to one another and always searching for a way to get the ball to the towering, agile Johnson underneath the basket. Ovitz relished nothing more than that split-second when Johnson had to decide whether to pass off or to take the shot himself. Often Johnson passed off, thereby getting the assist, helping the team to score, and teaching the valuable lesson that teamwork can pay off more handsomely than individual showmanship.

In order to reinforce that lesson, CAA made a point of rewarding those agents who provided assists as much as, if not more than, those who were in charge of a certain area of the business. As Bob Goldman, CAA's chief financial officer, explains: "Agents were constantly reminded that they would not be compensated on the basis of what they did as an individual but on what they did on the whole. Older executives were encouraged to work with younger associates, and if they didn't they were criticized. The younger associates loved it because it gave them great access to the clients."

At other agencies, agents made their mark on the basis of whom they were able to sign. But CAA's team approach allowed for some agents to be rainmakers and for some to concentrate exclusively upon servicing clients. Amy Grossman never signed a client throughout her long career at CAA, but she provided great service to many of them. In 1988, when she was only 34 years old, she was paid the astonishing sum of $500,000. "It was socialistic," Ovitz observes, "because the compensation was based on how well *everyone* did. That's how teams do it. If you win the Super Bowl, everyone gets the same amount of money."

The importance of the concept of teamwork at CAA meant a lot of things in terms of the day-to-day operation of the organization. It meant joining forces to make sure that all phone calls were answered. It meant whole-heartedly accepting CAA's egalitarian style, with its lack of formal titles other than president, its lack of name plates on doors, its alphabetically-ordered agent directory. It meant agents going out in groups of four or five to film premieres or to lunch with important clients, in order to show solidarity and strength and loyalty to one another. "We constantly found ways to show strength in a community by having groups of agents out together at premieres and parties and restaurants," notes Richard Lovett. "Agents were expected to be wildly aggressive. Out every night, being wherever the show-business action was happening, being at the heart of activity. We practiced the art of being well coordinated, of doing our homework always."

They sure did. Indeed, it got to the point where CAA agents always seemed to be traveling in packs or, even if seeming to be alone, speaking with "one voice"—the voice of CAA, which in effect meant the voice of Michael Ovitz. The image that Hollywood had of the Ovitz agency was not that of the lonely agent turning up at someone's office for a nice, quiet meeting, but of a group of young agents, all incredibly well dressed, all talking the same talk, all determined to make their mutual presence felt. These smoothies were well coordinated all right, right down to the finely-honed pitch they would deliver to clients. Once, three CAA agents each arranged, unbeknownst to the other two, to have a one-on-one lunch with the same prospective client, which ended up occurring upon three successive days. At precisely the same point in the conversations, each of the agents looked up from his food and proclaimed with great emotion: "You are the most exciting talent I've come across in my career!"

Another important thing that teamwork meant at CAA was never bad-mouthing another agent in public, but rather resolving all differences behind closed doors. Dirty laundry was never to be aired outside of CAA. Laurie Perlman, one of CAA's first agent trainees, recalls attending a CAA retreat at which Ovitz went around the room and asked each person for a candid comment about the agency. When it was Perlman's turn she spoke up loud and clear, imploring the more senior agents to act with more civility, if and when they felt it necessary to chew out a junior agent. "We need to speak to each other and still leave each other with our dignity. Sometimes we don't do that." Ovitz liked Laurie Perlman's phrasing on that occasion so much that he frequently used it in his future briefings to agents. "What made CAA different from the other large agencies," says partner Marty Baum, "was the feeling that the entire company was behind you. You were part of a family. If anyone did well within the agent ranks, we all prospered. It was a source of pride when any of us would get a deal. People at other companies fought with each other because the money wasn't distributed equally to agents. An agent would be jealous of anyone else getting a financial gain from a booking. But at CAA, we had five agents working on one deal."

The high value that Ovitz placed upon teamwork also required of his agents that they engage in honest debate about their labors. On new CAA agent Bryan Lourd's first company retreat, he and other agents sat on uncomfortable chairs in a ballroom in La Jolla. "Let's talk about why the motion picture department isn't communicating well with the television department," Ovitz said, by way of opening the session. For the first 5 or 10 minutes, agents seemed hesitant to talk, but Ovitz was having none of it: "We're not going to waste each other's time. We're here to make each other better. We trust each other. I want to hear from everyone, from trainees as well as agents." Slowly, and one by one, agents and trainees began to open up. This, Lourd couldn't believe. Whenever he had tried to speak out at such meetings elsewhere, he had quickly been made to believe that he had stepped out of line. "At CAA if you had an opinion, even if it was unpopular, but it was good, you were celebrated for being courageous and having a good idea."

It wasn't long before CAA's teamwork approach had become the envy of the other agencies. "Ovitz," says Gavin Polone, "was smart enough, unlike other agencies like mine at ICM, to recognize that the best way to build an agency was to build the careers of other people under him. At United Talent Agency, where I worked later, the major agents were too insecure to help build other people's careers. So the momentum would sputter. They couldn't build on it. There was no one with any focus or vision like Michael Ovitz."

Ovitz ALWAYS WAS seeking to enhance the image of the talent agent. Thus, in order to make CAA agents seem more professional, appearance was considered to be a very important part of the corporate culture. Ovitz believes that agenting is a serious business, and back then he wanted his agents to appear serious, and dress seriously. There was no written CAA dress code, but by way of setting an example, Michael Ovitz dressed well, yet conservatively. "You knew exactly where he shopped," says Laurie Perlman. "He had Gucci loafers, an Allendale suit, and this was in the days before all the designers. He gave a lot of care to his dress, and he expected it in kind." As for the women, again there were no specific guidelines. But Laurie Perlman felt that she had to wear suits and muted colors, and never anything sexually provocative.

CAA's agents picked up Ovitz's signals, all right, since they opted for dark Armani suits, white Sulka shirts, and skinny black ties. And if someone missed the signal, Ovitz was quick to get that agent to toe the line. Bob Goldman always felt there was a kind of informally enforced dress code, certainly more so than at other talent agencies. He remembers instances in which Ovitz actually would purchase men's suits for agents and charge it to the agency, to underscore the point that appearance mattered a great deal. Such overt tactics were used sparingly, however; most CAA staff members came up through the ranks, so it became second nature for them to dress well.

Dan Adler began work in the CAA mail room in September 1986, then became assistant to Ovitz and then a CAA agent. While working in the mail room, he delivered a package to an office outside the building for the first time. From behind the receptionist's counter someone looked up at him and said, "You must be a CAA trainee." The fancy shirt and tie gave away the fact that he was one of Michael Ovitz's troops, not one of those less nattily attired fellows from the messenger services.

Ironically, it was only Ron Meyer, one of CAA's co-founders, who played fast and loose with the Ovitz dress code. Like many others in Hollywood he found the wearing of a coat and tie to be distasteful, preferring to don sweaters and slacks instead. Ovitz's attempts to bring Meyer into line with the agency's more formal style became a vintage bit of comic Hollywood folklore. So much so, in fact, that when the two men performed a scene in a private video put together for Warner Brothers chief Terry Semel's fiftieth birthday celebration, playing the roles of Batman (Ovitz) and Robin (Meyer), they made fun of their differing dress styles—and everyone in the audience got the joke!

"Ronnie," asked Ovitz, dressed as Batman, complete with the CAA logo on his uniform, and noticing that Meyer was wearing only a sweater and slacks, "why do you dress like this?" Why wasn't he dressed as Robin?

"This is my uniform," replied Meyer. "I thought we were going to be just Batman and Ronnie."

Ovitz EXPECTED A great deal from his agents: long hours and high performance, as if they were playing in the Super Bowl every day; 100 percent devotion to the job. But if the corporate culture was going to be so demanding, Ovitz understood that his agents deserved to be compensated for exhibiting such strong loyalty to the organization. Thus CAA agents were paid far better than any other agents in town. "We were very fortunate," says Bob Goldman, "in that we always did so well that it was very easy to compensate people very generously. So we put our money where our mouth was." Some agents reportedly were earning the astronomical sum of $1 and $2 million a year.

Other agencies used an objective measurement when paying agents, calculating salaries as a percent of total revenues earned that year. CAA, on the other hand, paid its agents on the basis of Ovitz's subjective judgment as to how well the agent had performed that year. Bonuses formed the bulk of yearly incomes. But bonuses were given not for individual performance, but for team play. Even agents who had pulled off some spectacular coup were not specifically rewarded for having done so. Though rumors floated through Hollywood that Richard Lovett had been paid $1 million for signing Tom Hanks, the truth, as David O'Connor relates, was that "you never got paid a bonus for any one specific thing. And if you had a great year one year you wouldn't be rewarded, or if you had a bad year, you wouldn't be punished." O'Connor's bonuses usually made up 90 percent of his annual income, and "it was sort of an understanding that you'd get paid at least as much the next year, unless something surprising happened."

The hard-work-for-high-pay approach worked remarkably well. CAA agents remained at their jobs far longer than other Hollywood agents. And there was another interesting phenomenon that everyone commented on, but few could figure out. Perhaps it had something to do with the high degree of job satisfaction. It was the fact that so many CAA agents and employees got married to one another. Some dozen marriages occurred, including those between agents Rick Nicita and Paula Wagner; agents Robert Bookman and Amy Grossman; agents Mike Rosenfeld Jr. and Sonya Goumas; agents Dan Adler and Jenna Park Adler; agent Jeff Jacobs and CAA executive Stephanie Kahn-Jacobs; agent Bryan Loucks and CAA librarian Shannon Nelson; and agents Jack Rapke and Laurie Perlman. If such marriages aren't necessarily the best way of gauging job satisfaction, they certainly do give a good indication of the familial atmosphere that Ovitz had striven so hard to cultivate. But what they reflect, above all, are the demands that were placed upon CAA agents. It was very simple: One was expected to be on the job day and night, with no time off for a social life. Thus it became natural and inevitable that candidates for marriage would end up being narrowed down to the people whom one ran into day after day on the job. And then too, Michael Ovitz prized loyalty above almost any other human quality. What better way to show Ovitz that you were being loyal to him and to his firm, than to marry within the CAA family? It was as if these agents were saying: "See, daddy? We're *never* going to leave home!"

9

I *Am* a Control Freak

THOUGH HE WAS only 58, Stan Kamen had seemed tired of late; some of his friends thought he might be ill. At any rate, he certainly didn't seem like his old self. His Saturday-afternoon parties, filled with big-name movie stars, were no more. Kamen's terrible secret was that he was dying of AIDS. Some in the Hollywood community knew that he was gay, but none spoke about it openly—and certainly not to reporters. Two other William Morris executives, Sam Weisbord and Morris Stoller, also were ailing, both from cancer. Thus it was that one of Hollywood's great institutions seemed to be falling apart.

Stan Kamen tried to hang on to some of his more important stars such as Jane Fonda, Barbra Streisand, Chevy Chase, Jill Clayburgh, Al Pacino, Goldie Hawn, and Diane Keaton. But Kamen's list was hemorrhaging. Soon he lost Gregory Hines and Rock Hudson. Then, worst of all, Jane Fonda. Toward the end of 1985, Michael Ovitz declared that, for as long as Stan Kamen was ill, as a gesture of respect he would refrain from signing any more of his clients. He didn't want to appear to be taking advantage of a dying man.

All the while, Ovitz kept talking to potential clients, visiting them on the set of this or that picture, making a point of being helpful wherever and however he could. But many of these prospects had no idea just how relentless Michael Ovitz really was, in terms of bearing down on anyone he had made up his mind to target as a future client. "He would stop at nothing," recalls Laurie Perlman. "There was no such thing as humiliation or rejection. If he was going after a client, there was no such thing as anything getting in his way. He would talk to the person directly. He would find out who their best friend was. He would find out who they worked with last. He would find out where they hung out and hang out there—there was nothing he wouldn't do to get what he wanted. He was a master at knowing how to put someone on the defensive and gaining the best out of the situation. He was a master at pushing any situation or any human to their limits. All the while he would be stroking, giving a compliment, always skillfully trying to get the most out of the person. He knew how to make you feel seen, make you feel heard, and yet get whatever he needed."

Even Stan Kamen's clients were glad to be seen in Michael Ovitz's company for word had begun to spread that Ovitz was getting incredible contracts for his clients. That alone made him an attractive dinner partner. Whereas Stan Kamen had seemed more of a friend and confidant, Ovitz came across as the tough-minded businessman, a guy who was always armed with a business plan for a potential client's career. Although few ended their dinners with Michael Ovitz by announcing that they were ready to abandon Stan Kamen in favor of CAA, it was by means of these get-togethers that Ovitz acquired a powerful back-up position, in case the client's relationship with Kamen should suddenly go sour.

Many were surprised by the meteoric rise of CAA. One of these was Michael Crichton. He had a pet theory that talent agencies in Hollywood rise and fall like the tides. All during the early 1980s he had watched CAA rise, and was sure that by the mid-eighties it would begin to fall. "I had accepted that one of the verities of Hollywood was that no agency was on top for more than three to five years and then it fell," he explained. "It was like kind of a sea movement, the tide came in, the tide went out. It just seemed as if there was so much instability that no one could achieve power. So I assumed that by 1985 or 1986 CAA would be on the downslope, and of course it wasn't."

Because CAA was so secretive, almost no one outside the agency had any idea what made the place run so smoothly. On the surface it seemed a "well-oiled machine"—a favorite CAA phrase. To Graydon Carter, editor of *Vanity Fair*, "It had the quiet hum of crisp efficiency. You wished the government ran like this. There was no panic, just quiet efficiency and money being turned over. You imagined the Rothschild bank in the nineteenth century. Everyone tried to model themselves on Michael Ovitz. He knew how to get things done."

Behind the veil of secrecy, however, Ovitz was making a major effort to ensure that CAA ran, as he liked to say, "with the precision of a Swiss watch." This was no easy task, for there were many disparate components to CAA—with agents working in film, television, music—and the competitive pressures coming from the other agencies were enormous. Yet Ovitz loved the melee, loved nothing more than to be in the thick of the fight. When things were going well at the agency—as was generally the case—the office was a beehive of activity, with phones ringing and people coming and going. Agents checked in with one another, clients were on the verge of signing, deals for film or television or music projects were about to be closed. "It was fantastic," Ovitz recalls. "Every day I could create the day for myself."

This was the exciting world of agenting, and it was the world that Ovitz knew and loved best. He had no inclination to be a movie or television producer. Working on just one project at a time, as most producers did, struck him as being inhibiting and limiting. He wanted the freedom to roam from one project to another, to view the bigger picture—and most of all, to ignite and re-ignite his creative energies with each new day.

Ovitz remembers asking the novelist James Clavell what he liked about sitting in a room and writing all day. Clavell told him that "Every day I get transported to another world I get to make up." That explanation appealed to Ovitz, for he too felt that, when working as an agent, he could transport himself to other worlds. Agenting allowed him to be creative, to "travel"; to employ a metaphor from the art world, what he loved was his sense of "the canvas" on which he could paint his ideas and dreams: "I was free, and on my own to be creative." He thought of himself as painting a picture, but not just any picture; one by George Seurat, made up of thousands of dots. When one looks at a Seurat, Ovitz notes, there is no single dot in the painting that means anything; but if you look at all the dots together, then those dots create a picture. So it was with agenting. The signing of one client, the packaging of one film, didn't add up to the fulfillment of one's hopes and dreams. But when taken jointly, such moments did. As an agent, Ovitz said, "I got to create a picture and a company and an image."

Creating that picture, and making sure that the company ran smoothly, required organizational skills, and demanded that all sorts of decisions be made that would keep CAA on top of all show-business trends and television and film projects. It was the mastering of all those details, both large and small, that got Ovitz's adrenaline going: "I enjoyed the organizational parts of the business, and never stopped for twenty years. Every system in the company I created. We had the most sophisticated set of systems imaginable for billing and backup communication. No one had ever heard of the systems we set up; nothing fell between the cracks." Thanks to Ovitz and a Harvard Business School whiz kid whom he hired, Sandy Climan, CAA began to do sophisticated financial modeling long before that became the fashion in the entertainment industry. Making use of computer-compiled spreadsheets, Climan put together models that helped CAA to prepare for negotiations vis-à-vis various film projects. Ovitz adds: "CAA ran like a Swiss watch. It was no accident that the business grew as it did. We made a five-year plan every year. There was always a total plan."

For that reason and many others, Ovitz was considered by most to be simply the best agent in town. And that fact alone inspired other agents to emulate him. One of these was Richard Lovett. After graduating from the University of Wisconsin, Lovett joined CAA in 1982, in the mail room.

Since he showed promise, Lovett was assigned as an assistant to CAA agent Fred Spektor. Ovitz thought Lovett capable, and liked the fact that he was helping out with Spektor's clients. Thus in 1985, at the age of 25, Lovett was promoted to agent. He loved the excitement and enthusiasm and buzz of CAA: "The place had something going that was unstoppable at that time. Michael had reinvented the way agents did their business," especially with regard to the team approach. What really drove CAA, however, Lovett said, was the man at the top: "There existed a cult of personality. Michael is a rare breed in that he is a true leader. He had a vision for himself and for the company. Everyone took it for granted that he saw things that other people didn't see; that they could believe in him; potential clients and clients felt that too."

Ovitz involved himself in everything, and even his closest business friends describe him as being a "control freak." Bob Goldman observed that Ovitz "has a need to control everything. He wouldn't sleep at night if there was some area he wasn't totally aware of and in control of. He would review expense reports. He would be concerned about little items if something wasn't attended to properly."

In the spring of 1979, Rick Kurtzman got a taste of Ovitz's micromanaging. One day, soon after he had become Ovitz's assistant, he mailed submissions for the *Diner* film project to the studios, believing that to be more cost-efficient than using a messenger service. When Ovitz discovered what Kurtzman had done, he made him wait at the mailbox outside of CAA's Century Park East building and wait for the mailperson, so that he could retrieve the envelopes. "It was one of the less stellar moments of my life," Kurtzman recalled. It was also one of the best examples of what a perfectionist Michael Ovitz could be, when it came to the training of his agents. Then again, one person's perfectionist is another's fanatic. But Ovitz probably would be proud to admit to being fanatical when it came to the running of CAA. He is proud that the place ran like a Swiss watch, and had no apologies to offer even for those seemingly "fanatical" things he had to do to keep the watch ticking smoothly along.

Yet while he was indeed dead-set upon building the greatest talent agency that Hollywood had ever seen, Ovitz also was mindful of the danger of allowing CAA to grow too swiftly. Indeed, he thought that in many respects keeping it small had its advantages. Thus by 1986, CAA still had only 57 agents (compared to 185 for William Morris) serving around 600 clients. As Rowland Perkins noted, CAA was never going to build up so endless a list of clients as those possessed by William Morris and ICM: "We were careful. We were always worried about quality. We wanted to believe that our clients had most of their careers in front of them. If you hired more clients, you'd have to hire more agents." Accordingly, CAA never bought another company, a move that would have automatically increased the number of its agents and clients. Nor did it ever open a branch office in New York.

THROUGH IT ALL, Ovitz never lost sight of his and CAA's real reason for being: to further the careers of clients. And what Michael Ovitz had a particular knack for was steering an actor's career down avenues that may have looked like dead-ends to the client. That's what he did for Rob Reiner, and for Penny Marshall. Both were well-known actors, and from 1971 to 1979 they were married to one another. Both happily acknowledge that it was Ovitz who encouraged them to become directors, at a time when neither believed that he/she had what it takes.

In Rob Reiner's case, Ovitz promised him that he would help him to get his own production company. He did just that by finding him development deals, first with Metromedia and then with Columbia Pictures and ABC Television. These deals allowed Rob not only to perform, but also to write and to create his own shows. In 1978 as *All in the Family* was coming to the end of its hugely successful seven-year run, Reiner tried his hand at creating and starring in his own comedy series based upon Jewish immigrant life on the Lower East side at the turn of the century. It was to be called *Free Country*, and Reiner would play an 89-year-old man looking back upon his life. Unfortunately, the idea had little appeal for ABC: Ovitz and Reiner met with Michael Eisner and Fred Silverman and sought a commitment for six episodes, but the ABC executives were only lukewarm about the idea; Ovitz and Reiner pushed and pushed and finally got the series launched.

Reiner saw something of himself in Ovitz; both of them were, in Reiner's view, tenacious bulldogs who doggedly pursued something they wanted until they got it in the end. Rob had watched Ovitz in action across the negotiating table, and he admired his tactics: "Michael takes these very tough positions and makes the other side think there's no room for negotiation. He's able to test the limits and sometimes even go over the limits, but he knows how far he can go. He never leaves a penny on the table. He'll never let anyone get the best of him. He also does it gentlemanly. He doesn't do it with rancor. He's tough, the toughest negotiator I've ever seen. It was very clear in the room that at any moment we'd get up and walk out. It was clear he wasn't going to get pushed down. He never showed weakness."

Reiner made a successful debut as a film director with *This Is Spinal Tap* in 1984, an hilarious spoof of rock documentaries that has rightfully become a cult classic. He later emerged as the highly acclaimed director of comedies and dramas. The coming-of-age film *Stand By Me* (1986) set the pattern, with Reiner being seen as the director of films that were both critical and commercial successes. Such films included *The Princess Bride* (1988), *When Harry Met Sally* (1989), and *A Few Good Men* (1992), which won several Oscar nominations including one for Best Picture.

Even when Reiner was busily forming Castle Rock Entertainment early in 1988, Ovitz continued to advise him: "I didn't utilize Ovitz as a traditional agent. I'd make my own deals, but every time I made a picture we'd have lunch and he'd say, 'This is what the market will allow. This is what someone of your stature should be getting.' We talked specific numbers. He didn't do the actual negotiating. He was always very accurate. My partners never had any problem, because they came up with the same numbers." Ovitz did not take the usual 10 percent agent fee from Reiner. Rather, Castle Rock had a special arrangement with CAA: The agency would help to find material for the studio, and for that service CAA would receive $50,000 for every Castle Rock film and $200,000 for those Castle Rock films which Reiner himself directed. Reiner added: "Ovitz wasn't really my agent. I never signed papers with him. The agency operated in a very loose way in that regard, but it was regimented in other areas. They basically said, 'If you like it here, fine.' They don't hold a gun to your head and say 'You have to stay.' "

If Rob Reiner had always dreamed that he might someday enter the production side of the entertainment business, his wife of the 1970s, Penny Marshall, had no such aspiration. She had wanted to be what she in fact became: a successful working actress. She attributes almost entirely to the influence of Michael Ovitz the fact that she later became a successful director as well.

Penny Marscharelli was born in Brooklyn in 1942, the daughter of an industrial filmmaker and a dance coach, and younger sister of the man who would go on to become a director-producer-writer and the creator of *Pretty Woman*—Gary Marshall. She dropped out of the University of New Mexico so that she could dance and perform in summer stock. Competing on television's *Ted Mack's The Original Amateur Hour,* Marshall then appeared in the 1967–1968 season of *The Danny Thomas Hour,* and regularly on a number of television shows. Her breakthrough role, of course, was that of Laverne on the long-running hit situation comedy *Laverne and Shirley* (1976–1983), which was created by her brother Gary and produced by her father Tony. Penny directed some of the episodes.

Marshall met Michael Ovitz when she was out looking for a heavy-hitter as an agent: "I had a nice agent, but I needed a big gun," she recalled. As of January 1976, *Laverne and Shirley* was America's top-rated TV show, and Marshall naturally was eager to capitalize upon her success. One manager whom she interviewed wanted to take a 15 percent commission on her earnings. Not only did Ovitz plan to charge her 10 percent, but he told her that "you deserve more," while promising her that she would get it when he renegotiated her contract.

With a twinkle in her eye, Marshall admits that she drove Ovitz crazy. "I told him I also wanted a washer-dryer in my contract."

"Penny," responded Ovitz, "you can buy one of those."

"I don't care. I want them to like me and give me a present." Ovitz included the washer-dryer in her contract. In subsequent years, Marshall had Ovitz ask for more such "presents" to be included in her contracts, including pool furniture, a bicycle, and a paid vacation—all of which she eventually received, but not all at once. Ovitz asked that Marshall be given one of these presents a year, figuring that the studio would not agree to give her all the gifts at once.

She and Ovitz had their disagreements. He liked to show up on the set to make sure that all was going well. On one such occasion, Penny was fuming because 20 pages of the script had just been changed. "I didn't need any hand-holding," she recalls. "I wanted him to negotiate on my behalf, but I didn't need him around all the time. When I saw him on the set that time, I said 'Get out. We're working.' " Whenever Ovitz met Penny Marshall on later occasions, he would rib her: "You're the only one who ever kicked me off a set." When he visited her on the set of *A League of Their Own,* in Evansville, Indiana, the temperature was an appalling 120°. Ovitz deplaned, traveled to the set, felt the heat, and asked Marshall, "Are you crazy?" He then returned to the plane. Visiting her on another occasion on the set of *Awakenings*—an actual mental institution in Brooklyn—he said to her, half-serious and half-joking, "You pick the worst places to shoot." Marshall recalls: "He was scared; we were all scared."

But generally they got along. She liked the fact that she could talk to him "as a person." And Ovitz liked Marshall because she didn't take advantage of him. "You don't complain to me about the business. You talk to me about other things," he once said to her.

And all during that time, Michael Ovitz told anyone connected with Penny Marshall that she was perfectly capable of directing. She herself hadn't given it any thought. Yes, she had directed a few episodes of *Laverne and Shirley,* but it was fairly routine for stars of sitcoms to take a crack at directing an episode or two. "He spread the rumor that I could direct, and all of a sudden I was being talked up as a director." When Penny tried to suggest that directing wasn't for her, Ovitz told her: "Even if you were the biggest actress in the world, you'd work maybe three to six months a year. You'd get bored, whereas if you're directing, it takes longer."

In the mid-1980s, *Jumpin' Jack Flash,* starring Whoopi Goldberg, was in production. Ten days after shooting began, the director was fired for not getting along with Goldberg, who then asked Marshall to take over. Ovitz wanted to negotiate a better deal for Marshall. She told him, "Don't, I don't know how to direct. Ask for less." Ovitz said he couldn't do that, he would be too embarrassed. But Marshall forced him to renegotiate her contract so that she would receive a *smaller* amount than before! "I'll never do that again," she says now, as if Michael Ovitz had succeeded at last in teaching her a valuable lesson.

In ADVISING PENNY Marshall to take up directing, Ovitz was going on instinct. And as often as not his instincts were uncannily on the mark, as shown in the case of Marshall and dozens of other clients whose careers he nurtured. Such instincts can never be pinned down analytically but other aspects of Ovitz's behavior are more open to analysis. And the best place to start, in any effort to discover just how Michael Ovitz gained his phenomenal success, is a small (131-page) book called *The Art of War,* a 2000-year-old military tract written by the Chinese philosopher warrior Sun Tzu. Ovitz himself points to this little book as being the main source of his business strategies. The publisher of the 1988 paperback edition touts the book on its back cover as being "still perhaps the most prestigious and influential book of strategy in the world today." And once the word was out that Ovitz was a devotee of *The Art of War,* the book enjoyed a resurgence of popularity within the entertainment industry. The curious-minded, unable to discover much about how Ovitz functions by intently perusing the newspapers and magazines, hoped to gain some insights into the Ovitz magic by checking out Sun Tzu's tract.

Sun Tzu's main advice is for generals to try to win battles without shedding blood. Although he never says that "War is hell," that is what the Chinese philosopher clearly has in mind when he suggests that it is best to avoid fighting if possible. "It is never beneficial to a nation," he writes, "to have a military operation continue for a long time." The successful warrior is the man who best knows how to prevent violence: "One who is good at martial arts overcomes others' forces without battle, conquers other cities without siege, destroys others' nations without taking a long time." Sun Tzu counsels that the warrior should remain detached, reserved, and calm when facing adversaries: "Those who are good at knighthood are not militaristic," he writes. "Those who are good at battle do not become angry, those who are good at prevailing over opponents do not get involved." And finally: "Best of all is when your troops are held in such awe that everyone comes to surrender. This is preferable to winning by trickery, violence, and slaughter."

Of course the question then becomes, how to create a situation in which one's troops are held in such awe?

Ovitz understood Sun Tzu to mean that warriors should try to appear as powerful as possible, in order to frighten off potential rivals. Warriors don't necessarily have to *be* powerful, to *possess* great strength, to actually *have* mighty armies on their side. They only need to *seem* to be powerful. Accordingly, the creation of an illusion of power generally will suffice to obviate lengthy and messy controversies and battles. The way for Ovitz to win such bloodless battles in the talent-agency business was to instill fear into his rivals, the fear that Ovitz would indeed turn his power against those rivals if he felt that to be necessary. How best to instill that fear became Ovitz's chief challenge, how to make his rivals believe that he had "a stick at his side" (his own phrase) and might at any time choose to raise it against them. Ideally Ovitz never would have to do so, for as Sun Tzu decrees, the warrior's goal is to avoid fighting as much as possible. "Ninety-nine percent of all my confrontations and altercations," Ovitz explained, "were about not picking up the stick. People perceived that they might get hit, that I had actually picked up the stick." He often told his agents that each of them possessed just such a stick by his or her side. "You must create the impression that you will use the stick if necessary. But the minute you use it, you will have lost."

For Ovitz and CAA, it was hard to convey an impression of omnipotence during the agency's early years, for that was a time when the CAA client list was small and Ovitz still was mastering his trademark technique of packaging. But Ovitz adopted one piece of advice from Sun Tzu as he sought to build up an illusion of power: Exploit the notion of _enigma._ "Those skilled in defense hide in the deepest depths of the earth," Sun Tzu wrote. "What enables a good general to win without fail is always having unfathomable wisdom and a modus operandi that leaves no tracks. A military operation involves deception." By being secretive and enigmatic, Ovitz managed to create a mystique surrounding CAA, a mystique that suggested that CAA agents had special gifts, possessed a kind of magic, that those agents were the best in town and got the best deals for clients.

Ovitz suggested that his strategic approach to business was "not that complicated." As he speaks those words he reaches for four books on his desk that he suggests are "the foundation" of his strategy: Sun Tzu's _The Art of War;_ Lao Tse's _Tao Teh Ching;_ and Aristotle's _Ethics,_ volumes I and II. "That's fifty percent of it," he says, referring to the four books. "I'll give you the other half." His strategic approach, he then noted, was to combine Eastern philosophy with Western team sports. "Read _The Art of War_ and the _Tao Teh Ching,_ get it flavored by a little of Aristotle, and watch the Los Angeles Lakers do a fast break. It's like watching a Swiss watch work as they drive down the court, five guys; Magic Johnson would look, fake, and rarely take the shot. That was my philosophy. Total precision as a team. Watch any kind of team sports. Precision teamwork. No egos. _The Art of War_ may be the most important book you'll ever read to understand business. These team sports are precision sports where one doesn't work without the other. Eastern philosophy stresses the foundation in unity and order. There's an order to the universe. Look at history, the great nations had a sense of unity and place. The leaders cared about the people. The leaders are very sacrificial. I have an ego as big as anyone else's, but I learned to sublimate it."

Ovitz truly believes that Hollywood is one big battlefield, and he sees himself as one of its generals. He has no trouble wielding power. Thus it never bothered him to be called "a control freak," for he _wanted_ others to sense that he is in command—in _full_ command. "People say you're a control freak," a reporter for _Time_ magazine once asked him. "What's wrong with that?" Ovitz snapped back. "When I get on a plane, I don't want a laid-back pilot. I want a pilot who is a control freak, who is paying attention to every single detail of his job. . . . Ask my clients if they want a laid-back agent or a control freak." And what he wanted to control more than anything was the perception people had of CAA, to make sure that others thought of his "troops" with the greatest amount of awe imaginable.

But in order to do that, Ovitz had to make people believe he was trust-worthy, a man of his word. He worked hard at that. "If he said he would do something," says Jerry Perenchio, chief executive officer of the Chartwell Partnership Group and a former partner of producer Norman Lear, "he would do it. If he said he'd get back to you, he would. You never had to fol-low through. He was meticulous." And Ovitz made sure that all of his CAA agents functioned with the same meticulousness. "We felt," Ovitz says, "that the critical ingredient of a service business was follow-up. Period. If you told someone you were going to do something, do it. Period. We had this system. It started where we'd write handwritten notes. The rule was that it was incumbent upon a person who got the note to be actionable on it. If everyone was that responsible, the system would amplify itself to the hundredth power. People don't follow up with anything in other places. No one could compete with us."

Follow-up, Ovitz understood, was Building Block Number One when it came to getting results, and he knew that results were what counted above all else. Signing a client; putting clients into a film project; arrang-ing for a screenplay to be turned into a television mini-series. If he was to succeed in creating even the illusion of power, he had to come up with such real results, had to demonstrate that CAA could do better for its clients than anyone else in town could; and, above all, had to provide evi-dence on a continuing basis that when things were at their bleakest, the wisest step was to turn to Michael Ovitz. "If Mike had a technique," explained film producer Kathy Kennedy, "it came to light best when peo-ple weren't willing to speak to one another in the course of negotiations. He would get a dialogue going. He got the parties on the phone or got them in a room." And then he got results. He obtained those results through a rare mix of skills that are evident to Michael Crichton, who describes Ovitz as being "unusually smart and disciplined. You don't see that combination. You don't see that many smart guys who stay disci-plined and focused and clear about what they are trying to get accom-plished, about what's in their best interest, and their client's." According to literary agent Mort Janklow, "People signed on with Ovitz not because he loved them, or he gave them a big party, or showed them around, or introduced them to girls, or anything that Hollywood became famous for, but because of the sheer level of his competence."

Actor Dustin Hoffman understood what Ovitz's competence had done for the entire talent-agent business. "The word *agent* wasn't a pejorative after Ovitz came to town. He gave the name a dignity because he com-manded respect. He commanded respect because of the time he put in and because he got back to you. Other agents didn't get back to you."

Few other agents possessed that special mixture of persistence and creativity that Ovitz displayed every day on the job. When he felt confident that he was right—even if others whom he respected, disagreed—Ovitz never let up. Such was the case when Ovitz sought to interest Sydney Pollack in a film that Dustin Hoffman and director Hal Ashby had been working on, and that had already been sold to Columbia Pictures. The movie Ovitz had in mind was a comedy, and a seemingly very silly one at that, and Pollack wanted no part of it.

Pollack felt that he had a reputation to preserve. He had worked hard to be regarded as the director of serious films, beginning in 1969 with *They Shoot Horses, Don't They?*. Four years later he enhanced that reputation for seriousness by directing *The Way We Were*. Pollack was quite aware that his career was advancing slowly—no blockbusters so far—but he had no complaints. He liked doing serious movies. He saw no reason to change course.

But Ovitz possessed enormous self-confidence, enough to tell important directors such as Sydney Pollack what was good for their careers. Now, in 1981, Dustin Hoffman had mentioned to Ovitz that he and director Hal Ashby were about to go into preproduction on the comedy to be called *Tootsie*, but that Ashby had suddenly been forced to leave the project. Hoffman was going to play the lead role of Dorothy Michaels in the film.

Despite Pollack's hesitations, Ovitz had faith that Pollack could turn out a wonderful film.

"It's a one-joke picture," Pollack said at one point, trying to sound decisive, as in *I don't want to do this picture*.

Ovitz would not relent. His instincts told him that the Pollack-Hoffman combination would prove to be unbeatable.

"The script doesn't work," the director said simply, wishing that he could end the phone conversation right there, politely but quickly.

"Ignore the script," Ovitz suggested, taking one of his most favored tacks. Any other agent would have been suitably impressed by the fact that someone had spent thousands of dollars to get a script into shape. Not Michael Ovitz. If there was an obstacle in his path, his policy was to pretend that it didn't exist.

"Go to work with Dustin, and make it your own. Make it what you want to make it."

Hmm, thought Pollack, *talent-agent talk. Or to be more accurate, Michael Ovitz talk*. He wasn't impressed.

"I don't have a personal vision to make a picture about a guy in drag. That's just not on my mind."

It was on Ovitz's, and he wasn't about to yield on this one. Five more times he phoned Sydney Pollack and urged him to direct *Tootsie,* and five more times, Sydney Pollack said no.

And then Pollack began to think: *It's happening all over again. The phone calls. The pressure. The charm.* Ovitz was proving to be just as persistent as he had been when trying to snare Pollack as a client some months earlier. What was *with* this guy, anyway? Didn't he *ever* let up? Pollack didn't know, but he sure hoped so.

One day in Las Vegas, Ovitz came upon Pollack, who was in town with Paul Newman for an auto race. Of course, Ovitz hadn't really "come upon" the director at all. He had searched him out.

"Look, here's what I've set up for you," the talent agent began, as if the five last phone conversations had never existed. "I want you to work for one week with Larry Gelbart and Murray Schisgal [both screenwriters] and Dustin. I will get you paid for one week of your full directing salary. After the week, the studio will own any ideas you come up with, and you can decide whether you want to do this picture."

Pollack knew when he was beaten. He still didn't want to make the picture. But it seemed that saying "Yes" to Michael Ovitz was far easier than saying "No." Perhaps if he just went off for a while and made a pretense of being interested in this film, Ovitz would back off.

Fine, he told Ovitz, he would spend a week with Dustin Hoffman, Larry Gelbart, and Murray Schisgal. They would close themselves off from the world in Pollack's Malibu apartment, and try to make the movie work. But he wasn't promising anything. Pollack doubted greatly whether they would succeed, but at least after a week Ovitz would quit phoning about this damned project.

The director, the actor, and the screenwriters got down to work. Hoffman brought the bagels, Pollack a huge tape recorder. Each day they spoke their thoughts into the tape recorder. They tried one way of doing the movie, then another. Pollack watched Dustin Hoffman play the role of Dorothy Michaels. Hoffman made one terrific woman, but Pollack had a few suggestions. Try it this way, Dustin, try it that way. Bit by bit, Pollack was getting into the movie. He actually was getting excited.

Precisely what Ovitz had hoped for had happened: The work had become its own lure to the director, and he had been hooked. The four emerged from the beach shack and Pollack indicated to Ovitz that he was ready to do the movie. The agent quickly notified Columbia Pictures that *Tootsie* was ready to be launched.

When *Tootsie* was released in 1982, it won 10 Oscar nominations, including Best Picture, Best Actor (Hoffman), and Best Director (Pollack).

It was the second-highest-grossing film of the year, earning $95 million. (Little wonder that it wasn't the top-grosser. That honor went to one of the highest-grossing films of all time, *E.T: The Extra-Terrestrial,* which brought in nearly $230 million in that year alone.) Pollack appeared in the movie as a high-powered talent agent. At one point, as the camera pans around Pollack's office, one can see on the wall the logo of Creative Artists Agency!

Ovitz was just as insistent a decade later, when he tried to convince Sydney Pollack to direct a film based upon John Grisham's 1991 best-selling legal thriller, *The Firm.* Pollack was hesitant, doubtful that the Grisham tale could be translated into a plausible movie. In the novel the main character, Mitchell McDeere, a young lawyer, joins a law firm in Memphis. He discovers that the firm is a money-laundering front for the Mafia, but decides to stick around in order to get rid of them. While Pollack understood that its plot had helped to make the novel a success, he was concerned that moviegoers wouldn't find McDeere heroic enough. Pollack was troubled by the fact that in the novel McDeere chose to stay on at his job even after learning that the firm was corrupt. "I was worried whether it would work in film, because the hero was as corrupt as everyone else. He swindled the FBI, swindled the firm, ended up homeless, rootless, all of which works in the book. But I didn't have confidence in it as a film story. I didn't want to do it." Also, Pollack sensed that Grisham's millions of fans would be furious with him for any and every change he as the movie's director might make in the novel's plot. "It was a very dangerous project," Pollack said.

Michael Ovitz set aside all of Pollack's arguments. Once again, he simply wouldn't let up, or let go. " 'Persuasive,' with Mike," Pollack says, "is never one phone call. He's like a dog with a bone. He just won't let it go. He doesn't abandon things or give them up. He decided that I should do *The Firm,* and no matter how many times I said no, he would wait a while and call me up again and start all over."

Over the phone one day, Ovitz told Pollack: "Making a movie like *The Firm* is what this business is about. You can make a successful commercial picture and buy the time and financial security to make another kind of picture. You will make a good picture. You won't compromise aesthetically. Tom Cruise [who was to star in the film] is terrific. You two will work well together." What ultimately convinced Pollack to direct the film was not any one thing that Michael Ovitz had said to him but rather, in Pollack's words, "the intensity and persistence of his attitude, and the degree of his conviction." Released in 1993, the Paramount-produced film received two

Oscar nominations for Best Supporting Actress (Holly Hunter) and Best Original Score. It grossed over $77 million, thereby making it the fourth largest box-office attraction that year.

Investment banker Herb Allen is aware that many people viewed Ovitz's tactics—all that aggressiveness and tenacity—in unfavorable terms. But Allen believes that such tactics are an inevitable part of a successful Hollywood agent's style: "Michael Ovitz built a great business by being programmed and deliberate. A lot of people see that as a negative but it fits him, it's his style. If you're an agent, you have to pick up the phone. How else are you going to get to anybody? At the heart of what Michael will always do is to be an agent. Some critics will say, 'Stop agenting me.' By that they mean Ovitz is pushing too hard, lobbying for something that they think is not in their best interest and he's just out there to collect his ten percent. Mike spent his whole life being an agent, and he was the best one who ever lived. He made a lot of careers and a lot of money for a lot of people including himself, which is a nice way for the system to work."

OF COURSE, TENACITY doesn't always come easy, not even for a Michael Ovitz. For instance, getting people on the phone can sometimes be a problem—especially when they're just about to head out to sea.

As of the early summer of 1977, Frank Marshall, Ovitz's former classmate from UCLA, was a fledgling producer, a protégé of director and producer Peter Bogdanovich. Seeking to become an independent producer, he had just made his first deal to produce and develop, with Tony Bill, *The Sting II,* for Universal. Then, in mid-June, Marshall was asked to produce a film to be called *The Driver.* Set in downtown Los Angeles at night, the film focused upon the world's best getaway driver. But Marshall hated the idea of 10 weeks of night shooting in downtown L.A. He would rather have spent the summer sailing. Tony Bill owned a sailboat, and he and Marshall raced twice a week.

A week later, Marshall was on the dock at Marina Del Ray, getting his boat ready to sail, when the pay phone on the dock began to ring. It turned out to be Michael Ovitz on the line, and Marshall couldn't believe that Ovitz had tracked him down—and to a pay phone on a dock, no less!

"I need to give you some advice," his college classmate began. "You should do *The Driver.* It will be good for your career. Larry Gordon and Walter Hill [the executive producer and director] are good people." Marshall began to reel off the same old excuses for not making the picture.

"No, no, no," Ovitz said. "Do the movie. You really need to think about this. As your friend and agent, I tell you that you should do the movie. You should do a major studio movie like this one." Marshall did so, and his career accelerated. But what always impressed him, even more than the excellent advice Ovitz had given him, was the agent's ability to unearth him in the most obscure place imaginable.

Ovitz didn't hesitate to turn his aggressive tactics upon another superstar, actor Kevin Costner. Soon after graduating from California State, Fullerton, where he had studied marketing, Costner took up acting. He certainly got off to a cold and clammy start, as the corpse in the opening-credit sequence of the 1983 movie, *The Big Chill*! Four years later he would rise to stardom portraying a charismatic Russian spy in *No Way Out* and Eliot Ness in *The Untouchables*.

Given the remarkably successful year he had just had, all of the major Hollywood talent agencies were trying to lure Costner away from International Creative Management. At around the same time the actor was trying to get financial backing for a western that would focus upon the relationship between a lieutenant in the Union army and the Sioux Indian tribe. Costner had met producer Jim Wilson and writer Michael Blake in 1981 during the filming of *Stacy's Knights,* starring Costner. Five years later, encouraged by Wilson, who knew of his love for the American frontier, Michael Blake published a novel called *Dances with Wolves*. Blake and Wilson were both hoping that the book would provide the basis for a screenplay of a film they wanted to produce, with Costner as its star. The novel depicted the Sioux Indians as the good guys and the white men of the American cavalry as brutal enemies of the Sioux and hence, the bad guys. Only Lieutenant John Dunbar (Costner's character) admired the Indians, and wound up being adopted by them.

Costner approached his close friend, Armyan Bernstein, by now a Hollywood producer, and Bernstein in turn asked Michael Ovitz what he thought of the project. Bernstein thought that the screenplay was brilliant, and he had great faith in his friend Costner's ability to carry the movie off. But Bernstein's partner Tom Rosenberg wasn't enthused by the prospect of backing a three-hour western in which the Indians would speak in Lakota with English subtitles. Others must have had similar doubts and fears, for all of the other major studios had turned down the film project.

"Do it," Ovitz said to Bernstein. "Give Costner the money to do this."

But in the end, Bernstein and Rosenberg decided against it. Ovitz remained excited about Costner's project. "I should represent this guy," he told Bernstein, who offered to put the agent in touch with Costner if

Costner was agreeable. The actor, however, was reluctant. Finally Ovitz did get the green light, but he had trouble getting Costner on the phone. "Man, this guy is persistent!" Costner reported to Bernstein. "He's called me ten times in two hours."

Ovitz asked Costner to come into the office for a meeting. He did so, and the two men discussed the actor's project. By this time Costner was close to giving up all hope of ever getting this film made. But Ovitz remained confident that he could sell the film to a studio. Costner signed with CAA on June 20, 1989, and eventually Ovitz placed the film with Orion Pictures. When it was released in 1990, *Dances with Wolves* earned more than $81 million at the box office, making it the fourth-biggest movie of the year. It became one of the most highly acclaimed movies of its era, as it won an incredible 12 Oscar nominations and 7 actual Oscars, including Best Picture, Best Director (Costner), and Best Screenplay Based on Material from Another Medium (Michael Blake).

0VITZ SHOWED HIS customary tenacity when he was trying to match directors up with stars. At least, when it was a case of CAA directors and CAA stars, as it generally was. On one occasion he was trying to package a comedy to be called *Scrooged,* and he wanted Richard Donner to produce it.

"Do me a favor, read it," Ovitz urged Donner. "It's going to Paramount. I think you'll love it." Donner read it and found it a funny script with some potential, but he wasn't overly enthusiastic about it.

Ovitz suggested that Bill Murray should play the lead, but Donner still wasn't sold on the movie. That didn't dissuade Michael Ovitz. "If you have problems with the movie, if it doesn't make sense to you, meet with Bill Murray. Then I'm sure you'll want to do it."

One night at 11:00 p.m., Ovitz called Donner at his home.

"You're not going out, are you?"

"No, why?"

"Because Bill Murray's coming over. Brace yourself. He's got your address."

"No," said Donner. "It's too late." Donner couldn't believe that Ovitz was serious. All he could think of was: *This is no way to behave. This takes "casually dropping in" a bit too far.* He was all the more discomfited since he and his producer wife Lauren Shuler had a rule, "Don't bring business home," and since Donner liked to be asleep right after the 10:00 news was over.

But not this night. Tonight, Bill Murray was dropping by.

When the actor arrived, he and the Donners began to talk. First some small talk. Then some serious talk about the movie. Murray was excited about the script, and communicated that to Donner. Despite the late hour, Donner found that he was getting enthusiastic too. (Pollack and Hoffman, the bagels and the tape recorder, all over again . . .)

By 1:00 a.m. Murray and Donner had connected. Donner escorted Murray to the door, then called Ovitz: "Okay, you got a deal. I want to make the movie."

Of Ovitz's antics, Donner would comment years later: "I found him insane, but irresistible."

Scrooged, directed and co-produced by Richard Donner and starring Bill Murray, came out in 1986. It raked in some $80 million at the box office.

O VITZ WAS WINNING over all of these clients—the Rob Reiners and Penny Marshalls and Richard Donners—to a certain extent because all of them spotted in him something that the other talent agents simply didn't have. Yes, they liked his aggressiveness, his tenacity, his charm. But the one quality that really got to them was Michael Ovitz's ability to function at the highest level in so many different areas of life. To them, as to so many others, this was Hollywood's Renaissance Man.

10

Renaissance Man

Plenty of Hollywood figures were competent in one area or the other. But Michael Ovitz believed that if he was to seem to be truly all-powerful, he had to display a wide-ranging competence. It wouldn't be enough to be only a financial wizard; or to have a keen intuition about cultural trends; or to develop the skills needed to converse with a wide spectrum of people. He felt he had to have mastery of all of that—and more. Intensely curious, he tried to acquire as much and as varied knowledge as possible.

Once, Ovitz wanted to buy a telescope. It had become fashionable among Ovitz's friends to gaze at the stars, and Ovitz wanted to be fashionable. He invited Al Checchi, co-chairman of Northwest Airlines, to come along for the purchase. The first stop was a place in the San Fernando Valley that sold three hundred different models of telescopes. Ovitz practically moved in on the owner. Checchi thought they would stay for ten minutes; they were there for two hours: "Michael was talking about the most arcane details. I was almost dying. But he had to know everything there was to know about telescopes, and that's the approach he takes with everything." As they came out of the store, Ovitz explained why he had shopped for so long: "I have to know something about everything, because the people I deal with have such diverse interests."

He is proud of the fact that he has acquired sufficient knowledge to talk intelligently to so many different kinds of people. "Very few people," Ovitz observes, "have been able to keep a dialogue going with a filmmaker and a rock star and an author of a novel and with a politician and a guy who invests in real estate and a guy who owns a high-tech company. There are only a limited number of people who can read a balance sheet, who can talk to a banker, and who can talk to a filmmaker." He was one of them.

But Michael Ovitz didn't just keep a dialogue going with such people; he came up with new and different ways of winning them over to his side. Eschewing the in-your-face brashness of other talent agents, the ones who began meetings by saying, "How can I help you?," Ovitz was slow and subtle, a master of using small talk to soften someone up, injecting doses of humor as tension relievers and rarely venturing into a meeting without having first done his homework. He knew how to flatter potential clients. He made sure that he noted the person's latest book or movie. He liked to say that "someone of your stature" shouldn't have had to do a certain project, or should be doing other kinds of projects. As part of his effort to project great power he often spoke as if he were omniscient, at least about the Hollywood scene. He knew when things were going to happen, and where, and he left the impression that these changes would have a direct impact upon the career of the person with whom he was speaking. He rarely divulged what he knew—that was very much in keeping with projecting a sense of power—but he did talk in great specifics about the person's career, how he planned to shape it and to change it if necessary. If a potential client was an actor and secretly yearned to be a director, Ovitz knew that, and encouraged the person in that direction. If a director had been doing comedies and wanted to be taken more seriously, Ovitz could help him or her to find movies with more serious themes. Coming from other agents, such words failed to ring the bell. When Ovitz spoke them, with all of his remarkable self-assuredness and zest, the bell rang out sweet and true.

H E K N E W T H E value of knowledge in conveying the impression of power, and so Ovitz read voraciously, mostly magazines. Arne Glimcher, President of PaceWildenstein Gallery and one of his closest friends, believes Ovitz to have a photographic memory: "He reads magazines on every subject from audio equipment to car magazines to art journals. I can't get through *The New Yorker* every week, but he gets through ten magazines a day. When we go away on holiday he's always reading." When Ovitz travels he takes three satchels with him: one is filled with business items, one with personal items, and one only with magazines.

Of course, Ovitz also reads books and watches television and films. But back at CAA it was the telephone that allowed him to know about people's whereabouts, new projects, sudden changes of plans—in short, what was happening. He used the telephone with such frequency that it seemed at times to be almost a part of his body. Each day, by his own estimate, he was on the telephone with at least 200 people. He initiated about half of the calls, with the other half coming in to him. He prided himself on being able to find anyone in a moment's notice, and his personal staff gained the reputation of being able to track someone down with the same efficiency as a White House operator. And as the perception of Ovitz's power grew to almost mythic proportions, he found that he had less and less trouble reaching someone. To make oneself unavailable to take a phone call from Michael Ovitz made about as much sense as to turn down a chance to make a million dollars. "He has a way of generating enthusiasm," says entertainment attorney Bert Fields. "So whenever someone gets a phone call from Michael Ovitz, the reaction isn't 'Oh, not him again!' It's, 'Well, let's see what he's up to now.' " When Ovitz phones because he is disturbed about some particular issue, he often begins the conversation by saying, "I'm confused about something," sending out the none-too-subtle signal that the last thing the person on the other end of the line would want is for Michael Ovitz to be confused.

Talent agents feel a strong need to check in with clients on a continuing basis, and Ovitz did that whether the client's career happened to be waxing or waning. "One of the things I really liked about him," says Michael Crichton, referring to some of the less-busy periods of his career, "was that he never stopped calling me." Ovitz had some business acquaintances whom he called once a week, or once every few weeks, for no specific reason other than to keep in touch. Actor Warren Beatty, investor Ron Perelman, and publisher Mort Zuckerman all fell into that category. Ovitz called his close friend, art gallery owner and movie producer Arne Glimcher, every day. If someone called Ovitz but he wasn't available at that moment to take the call, Ovitz always made sure that the person wasn't left hanging. "I got a call once from his secretary to say that he couldn't call me," says Mort Zuckerman. "That's super-efficiency."

A phone conversation with Ovitz is brief and to the point. Ivan Seidenberg, chairman and chief executive officer of the New York–based telephone company, Nynex, spoke to Ovitz once or twice a week, each call lasting only two to three minutes. They might talk about issues pertaining to Seidenberg's field (telephones and communications) or the latest movie. But idle chit-chat, never. Small talk, says Robert Wright, president of NBC, "is like a bumper on the road to him." Ovitz prefers to listen rather than to talk. He loves to ask, "What's new?," and then just sit back and let his conversational partner fill him in. "So much of success in life is listening," says TV producer Norman Lear, "and Michael is a great listener. He's got great antennae." Investor Ron Perelman says that he knows of only a handful of business leaders who, like Ovitz, use the telephone both to acquire information and to pass on what they know, the bad news as well as the good. "Most people," Perelman suggests, "only want to bring you the good news." When at CAA, Ovitz spoke several times a week with a number of people, including entertainment mogul Barry Diller and investment banker Herb Allen. "I'm a Rolodex friend," says Allen, though he is of course much more than that to Ovitz. "At 12:00 p.m. Tuesday, he calls me."

On the surface, these appeared to be just friendly calls. But of course they were more than that. More often than not, Ovitz had picked up a scent and was after a particular piece of information. He knew it, and the person on the other end of the line often knew it as well. Nor was everyone thrilled to get such calls. "Sometimes," says Sydney Pollack, "I didn't take his calls. And he would say, when I finally did, 'Did you get my message? You didn't return my call.' And I would tell him: 'I didn't return your call, Michael, because there's nothing to say. It's just a 'hello' call. All you want to say to me is, 'I'm just checking in. Is everything okay? What's going on?' "

Being persistent didn't always endear Ovitz to his clients. Michael Crichton found Ovitz to be at times "kind of bullying, hounding, calling all the time, pushing, pressing, demanding, sending stuff, kind of a full-court-press mentality. If he wants something from you, he's all over you most of the time." Ovitz would sometimes pick up the phone and ask Crichton, "When can we get together?" Or, Crichton notes, "He gets other people to call, pushing, pushing, pushing. I don't like that. And I tell him. But he does it anyway. He is very abstract, calculating, and very intellectual, and then he badgers; he just kind of pushes to make things happen." Smiling broadly, Crichton notes: "I prefer the intellectual part."

OVITZ HAS UNDERSTOOD far better than many the intrinsic value of having and maintaining strong business relationships. And he works hard at cultivating them. David O'Connor, his assistant from 1984 to 1986, recalls what Ovitz was like when he was trying to make a friend: "We'd send gifts out like you can't believe. He'd find out what the person was interested in. I would call up the person's assistant and find out what the person was interested in. Usually it was a lot of gadget stuff. Ovitz was very respectful whenever he met someone. He'd write a personal note and he'd send a little gift, often something funny, or perhaps the latest gadget. Whatever their interests were. That was a lot of my job. I had catalogues of everything, including the latest exercise equipment that I would get wholesale: Lifecycles and Stairmasters." His CAA agents were encouraged to send gifts to clients as well. Once, in order to woo Madonna as a client, Laurie Perlman asked her assistant, Michael Rosenfeld Jr., to purchase underwear for her birthday from a lingerie store. When Rosenfeld delivered the goods to Perlman, the agent wrote a note and attached it to the gift: "Dear Madonna. Come to the Agency." The singer-actress must have liked the underwear for she soon became a CAA client.

Ovitz's close friend Al Checchi notes that "business is common sense, and when practiced at the highest levels, it is a series of relationships. It is being organized and being strategic. The technical aspects of business tend to be perpetrated at the lower levels. At the top, it's leadership, personal skills, and personal characteristics, and Michael is very accomplished in terms of his personal skills." On occasion it was difficult to figure out why Ovitz was cultivating a particular relationship. Often it seemed as if there was little the person could do for Ovitz in return. But Ovitz believed that in time, many of these relationships would pay off: "I wanted to be the guy, if someone was in trouble at 4:00 a.m., I was the kind of guy they could count on."

Al Checchi exemplifies someone seemingly far removed from Michael Ovitz's world, an unusual choice as an Ovitz friend, not the kind of person who looked like he had much to offer to a Hollywood talent agent. Yet Ovitz sensed that Checchi was just the kind of person he might one day need: someone with broad experience in running large corporations; someone who would be able to advise Ovitz, if and when he made his big move into the world of big business and high finance.

At the time when the two men met for the first time (1984), Checchi had been working with the Bass brothers of Fort Worth, Texas—Disney's largest stockholders. Checchi was one of two non-family partners who oversaw the non-oil business of the Bass family. The Bass brothers began to acquire Disney stock in the 1980s, and eventually they amassed nearly a 25 percent stake in the company. By that time, working along with Roy Disney, Walt's nephew, they had effected a change in Disney's management, selecting Michael Eisner and Frank Wells as the two top Disney executives. From March to August of 1985, Eisner brought Checchi up from Fort Worth to Disney headquarters in Burbank, to do some strategic and financial consulting.

Checchi's arrival in Burbank coincided with a party that Ovitz was throwing to celebrate Eisner's forty-third birthday. Unable to attend the party because he himself was being given a farewell sendoff, Checchi sent his regrets along with a birthday gift to Eisner, a bottle of Chateau Lafitte Rothschild that had been bottled in the year of Eisner's birth, 1942. Soon thereafter, Eisner and Ovitz were on a conference call to Checchi, with Ovitz joking that it was a good thing he (Ovitz) had been there when Eisner uncorked the bottle, for otherwise Eisner would have stashed it in his refrigerator and used it someday to wash down a sandwich. While the two men had grown to be very close friends by that date, that putdown of Eisner as being hardly the sophisticate surely reveals that Ovitz had no qualms about treating his friend dismissively. When Ovitz later served under Disney Chairman Michael Eisner, many people found it hard to explain why the two old friends should be having so much trouble getting along. Had they known about this time when Mr. Ovitz had joked rather unkindly about Mr. Eisner's lack of taste, they might not have bothered to wonder.

Checchi soon returned to his work for the Bass Brothers in Fort Worth, and Ovitz began to call him once a week just to check in. Since Checchi knew little about the film industry, he plied Ovitz with all sorts of questions. In return, Ovitz asked to be let in on the behind-the-scenes details vis-à-vis the corporate maneuvering he read about everyday in *The Wall Street Journal*.

Whenever he visited California, Checchi dined with Ovitz. He boasts that he is one of that select few who have stayed in the guest room at Ovitz's Brentwood home. In October 1985, Checchi decided to leave the Bass brothers' employ and to strike out on his own. That winter, while visiting Los Angeles, he came down with the flu and remained in his hotel room, quite sick. Someone arrived at the door with a large container of chicken soup and a card attached that read: "If this has been curing Jews for two thousand years, there's no telling what it will do for a wimpy Italian." The note was signed "Michael Ovitz." Checchi's reaction was similar to that astonishment which Frank Marshall had felt when Ovitz tracked him to a public telephone on the Marina Del Ray dock. *How on earth did Ovitz find me? How did he know I had come to Los Angeles, had checked into this hotel, and was ill?* Ovitz never did divulge how he found out, but Checchi offers this explanation: Ovitz is omniscient! "Michael is probably the most plugged-in person I have ever known. With him as a friend, you pretty much know he knows where you are most of the time."

As soon as Checchi had arrived in California for good, his friend took a personal interest in helping his family to get settled in. He made introductions for them and helped to get Checchi's three children into the John

Thomas Dye School, a private elementary school, even though it was the middle of the term.

The two men had no existing business relationship, nor did there seem any prospect that Ovitz and Checchi ever would have one. And that fact baffled Checchi. He just couldn't figure out what use he might be to Ovitz, other than as a friend. Then one day in the early 1990s, Ovitz, who was advising the Japanese company Matsushita with regard to its plans to acquire a Hollywood studio, asked Checchi to lend him some of the business-strategy unit at Northwest Airlines. The unit would be given the task of providing a top-down strategic analysis of MCA, a possible acquisition target of Matsushita. (The business strategists did in fact put together a presentation for Matsushita.) "He asked me to assist him in such a casual way," Checchi later would say. Checchi also helped Ovitz to select a law firm to handle the Matsushita–MCA deal.

Ovitz's attentiveness to the needs of his business friends was truly extraordinary.

One day he dropped in to the Manhattan gallery of his friend Roy Lichtenstein, the famous pop artist. When he was in New York with a few hours to kill, Ovitz liked to visit his artist friends just to find out what their latest works-in-progress were, and to keep abreast of the art-world in general. Suddenly, Ovitz's eye was riveted by an advertisement for a Chinese film festival that was posted on a bulletin board. He and the artist began to chat about Chinese action films, which Ovitz said he loved. Lichtenstein noted that he loved them too. A few days later a number of videocassettes arrived at Lichtenstein's studio—needless to say, some Chinese action films, courtesy of Michael Ovitz. "Even the slightest little reference," recalls Lichtenstein, "and he remembers it. Then you would get something in the mail. You have to be careful not to mention anything too much. He's not doing it for any reason other than to be nice, that I can see."

That certainly was the impression Ovitz wanted to convey. And yet the almost compulsive gift-giving did reflect something more than Ovitz's generosity. He was a talent agent, and talent agents provide service to clients. One of the traditional ways of providing that service had always been by bestowing gifts. But Ovitz took the custom in hand and virtually reinvented it, by sending gifts to anyone and everyone whom he might, even at some distant date and for some as-yet-unknown reason, wish to cultivate as a friend, especially as a business friend. It was a trick he had picked up from his father, who used all those liquor bottles in the trunk of his car for the very same purpose.

On one occasion Sydney Pollack was having lunch with Ovitz, and he mentioned something about a CD-ROM he had just heard about. As a waiter brought over the sandwiches, Ovitz reached for a pencil and made a note to himself. The CD-ROM was on Pollack's desk when he got back to his office. Another time, Ovitz was having a drink—his usual malt whiskey—at publisher Mort Zuckerman's home. Ovitz told the publisher about a great 25-year-old malt whiskey he knew about, and Zuckerman said he would be sure to buy some for their next get-together. The next day, a case of the liquor arrived at Zuckerman's home.

On yet another occasion, back when Barry Diller was still at Paramount, Diller was in a meeting with Ovitz. The subject of cars came up and Diller, aware that Ovitz owned a Jaguar, told the agent how eager he was about acquiring a certain kind of Jaguar. The next day Ovitz called Diller, to say that he had researched how Diller might go about getting the car he had in mind. Diller found Ovitz's gesture mildly annoying: *Why is Ovitz making such an effort for me? What does he want?* Naturally, Diller was curious to know; but at the same time, he was impressed that Ovitz had taken the time to look into the matter for him.

Yes, it really could be "dangerous" to admire something in Ovitz's presence. His friend Arne Glimcher was having dinner with the Ovitz family at its Brentwood home. Glimcher spotted a wonderful book on Chinese brush painting, a very hard book to find. He looked over the book carefully, intrigued by the subject matter. A few days later he received a copy of the book from Ovitz, only to feel guilty for having perused the book long enough to send Ovitz into action yet again.

It wasn't simply that Ovitz *wanted* to help his business friends. He actually seemed to be wounded when those friends needed something and wouldn't permit him to help them to procure it. Soon after Al Checchi moved to Los Angeles, he went over to the UCLA campus to work out at one of their athletic facilities. He took out a membership, and then mentioned to Ovitz how glad he was to have found such a marvelous health club. Ovitz chastised him: "You don't have to find a health club for yourself. I've got people who handle things like that."

"But, Michael," Checchi responded, a tad embarrassed by Ovitz's insistence, "I'm not a client of yours."

To Ovitz, that was a mere technicality. Whenever he discovered that one of his business friends needed something he simply took charge, making it *his* responsibility to ensure that that particular need was fulfilled.

Joe Smith, who in late 1986 became chairman and chief executive officer of Capitol EMI Records, had been a close Ovitz friend for years, an Ovitz neighbor at Malibu beach, and the occupant of a CAA office for 18 months in the early 1980s. One day soon after he had become the Capitol Records boss, Smith was in New York for his daughter's wedding. He received a call saying that it was urgent that he contact Michael Ovitz. When he did, he heard the voice on the other line ask, "How could you do this?" "Do *what?*" Joe Smith asked, having no idea at all why Ovitz was so upset with him. "How could you take this job and not tell me about it?" What infuriated Ovitz wasn't that he thought Smith was making a mistake in taking the Capitol job and that Ovitz might have helped him to avoid it, but that one of his agents had learned about Smith's decision before he himself had. Smith was amused. "Michael," said Smith in a calm tone, "where did *you* fit into this? You weren't representing me, so I didn't think I needed to come to you first." But Smith knew it was a losing fight. Ovitz wanted to control things in Hollywood, and knowing in advance who was doing what was part of controlling things; Joe Smith had deprived him of one very tempting opportunity to play that role.

There was no role that Ovitz loved to play more than that of guardian angel. He confided to friends that there was a time to make money in life, and a time to do good deeds. He was always looking for a way to perform a good deed. Hence he was deeply delighted whenever his contacts made it possible for him to break through whatever bureaucracy seemed to be giving a friend trouble.

In the spring of 1986, when entertainment attorney Bert Fields's wife Lydia became ill, Ovitz found out about her illness and told the attorney: "Listen, pal, if I can help, just let me know." Fields didn't like to accept favors from a business acquaintance, but one day his wife was given a medical test at the UCLA medical center that would determine whether she would live or die. Impatient to get his hands on the results, Fields visited the laboratory but was told by the staff that they were closing for the weekend and thus he wouldn't be able to see the results of the crucial test until Monday. "You can't do this to my wife!" he responded furiously, but to no avail. So he called Michael Ovitz and explained the situation. "Stay there, pal," Ovitz instructed him. "In fifteen minutes, the dean of the UCLA medical school is going to be there doing your test." Grateful, but bemused, Fields suggested that he didn't need the dean, all he needed was a laboratory technician. Ovitz asked him to stand by.

Sure enough, within five minutes the dean of the medical school was walking down the hall toward Bert Fields! He asked the laboratory staff where Mrs. Fields's test was, and ordered them to show the results to

Fields right away. The test was negative, but sadly Lydia Fields did die of the same disease in September 1986. When he tells the story, Bert Fields notes: "It's easy to say Ovitz behaved that way because of his relationship with me, but you can't explain his behavior just on the basis of relationships. I think he would be helpful to almost anyone he knew in that circumstance." Of course one aspect of any explanation has to be that Ovitz revels in the idea that he can get things done better, faster, and more effectively than anyone else. And he loves to show others, especially his closest business friends, just how remarkable he really is, and just how extensive is the reach that his power gives him.

WHEN IT COMES to performing a service, hardly any area of business or personal life is deemed by Ovitz to be out of bounds. For instance, on a number of occasions he has played matchmaker. "He talked me into getting married," acknowledges producer Richard Donner, whose wife is producer Lauren Shuler. Ovitz also tried to arrange a match between Bert Fields and art consultant Barbara Guggenheim. CAA agent Bob Bookman had introduced Guggenheim to Ovitz in the late 1970s, when she was just setting out on her career as an art consultant and Ovitz was just beginning to get interested in art. Bookman thought that Ovitz represented a potential client for Guggenheim. And she did in fact become an art consultant to Ovitz, helping him to buy paintings for his Brentwood home.

A few months after Lydia Fields died, Ovitz called Bert Fields to say, "I know it's early for you, but I've got a girl for you. She's involved in art. You'll like her a lot." Fields really wasn't very interested—"It really is early, Mike. I'm not seeing anybody"—and he quickly forgot all about Ovitz's phone call. But four years later, Barbara Guggenheim had just been sued by Sylvester Stallone over a painting. She was planning to have Bert Fields defend her. Just prior to Guggenheim's first meeting with Fields, Ovitz called Guggenheim. "Do you know Bert Fields?" she asked. She was seeing him later that day, and wondered what Ovitz might know of him. Dead silence on the line. Guggenheim took that to mean that perhaps Fields wasn't the right attorney for her. "Is he no good?" she asked finally. Ovitz laughed. "No, that's not it at all. He's fine. That's the guy I've been trying to fix you up with for four years, but he won't go out on a blind date." After hanging up the phone, Ovitz called Fields. "Do you know who you're seeing today?"

Bert Fields and Barbara Guggenheim were married in 1991. He was 62 years old at the time and she was 44. Michael Ovitz and Ron Meyer threw the couple an engagement party. "There are only two groups of people here," Ovitz quipped as he proposed a toast to the happy couple. "Barbara's friends, and people that Bert sued." And what about the legal squabble, the one that finally brought Barbara Guggenheim and Bert Fields together? Stallone gave up the suit.

Ovitz DEFINES HIMSELF not only by his wide array of personal contacts, but also by a rather frenetic eclecticism that keeps him on the go all the time, both physically and psychologically. If any character trait seems to sum up Michael Ovitz, it is a certain restlessness, a need to break loose from the confining nature of Hollywood into other worlds, those of art, of business and high finance, of high technology; a need to think beyond the present to five years ahead, ten years ahead; a need above all else, to continually reinvent himself to push past barriers, to break new ground, to be the pioneer. "He's got to be an innovator," notes Laurie Perlman. "He's got to be in the foreground." If he had no long-term game plan for himself when he was in his twenties, Michael Ovitz still had that sixth sense that told him not to take any job that would prove to be limiting to him in the end. From the very start of his career he always was planning his next move, always bent on improving himself. "My nightmare was to wind up my career as an agent, and not as a principal, having done only one thing in my life," Ovitz comments. Throughout all of his years at Creative Artists, he refused to focus only on the present but kept an eye on the long term.

Because he was restless, because he wanted to transport himself across so many boundary lines, Ovitz naturally found one-dimensional people unappealing. And that meant that he found most Hollywood figures narrow. He wanted to go beyond the world of Hollywood, to get beyond the limitation that he found there. If there was one way to displease Michael Ovitz, it was to talk only movies with him. Whereas if someone kicked off a meeting with him by talking about the latest exhibition at the Museum of Modern Art, or a merger between two business titans then under discussion in the pages of *The Wall Street Journal,* he was totally attentive, and would proceed to happily engage in a long, protracted conversation on the subject.

The fact is that even when Michael Ovitz is *in* Hollywood, he is never entirely *of* it. Not once in his conversations with the author of this book did he speak about how an actor had given a fine performance in some movie, nor for that matter did he mention any movies as being among his favorites. He showed little enthusiasm or respect for actors and actresses; after all, they talked mostly about the movies—*theirs,* in particular! While it isn't possible to draw any clearcut conclusions as to his attitude toward women and while he did hire quite a number of female agents when he was the head of CAA, Ovitz himself made it clear to the author that he is especially disdainful of actresses and for that reason he usually assigned junior agents to handle their careers. He never came out and said it, but Ovitz does seem to share with a number of other male business figures a discomfort in the presence of women in the workplace.

Differentiating himself from the rest of Hollywood always has been of major importance to Ovitz. One way of doing that has been to point to his home life, marking him out as a man of solidity, in contrast with the less serious types who abound in Hollywood. It is important for him to be viewed as a family man. "The single most important priority in my life," he observes, "is my family. I always put my family above business." He has been married for 27 years, yet most marriages in Hollywood, he likes to say, last no more than five minutes. On a Saturday evening in October of 1996, he took the author along with him on a private jet flying from Chicago to Bermuda, where he was to give a speech to a group of American magazine publishers. The first thing he did upon boarding the plane in Chicago was to call home. After he had hung up the phone, Ovitz noted how much he hates to be away from his family on weekends.

A few weeks later, on a weekday at 1:30 p.m. in Los Angeles, at the start of an interview with him at his Brentwood home, Ovitz made it clear that the meeting would have to end by 3:15 p.m. so that he could attend his son Eric's Little League baseball game. He frequently attended Los Angeles Lakers games with his family. A Bar Mitzvah or Bat Mitzvah in the Ovitz family provided a rare occasion for Ovitz to speak affectionately of his family in public. Such diverse Ovitz friends as NBA Commissioner David Stern, movie and television producer Norman Lear, and sculptor Joel Shapiro were impressed upon hearing Ovitz speak so tenderly of his family. That "family values" are so very important to Ovitz seems to tell us that he feels that surviving in Hollywood depends upon differentiating oneself from others who have little respect for those values.

Ovitz's world is unquestionably an eclectic one. He's curious about many things, but it is art and technology that appear to interest him the most. And it seems no coincidence that he was intrigued by Asian culture. He has since acquired a proficiency in the self-defense art of aikido, which turns an aggressor's strength against him. Ever since his days as a gymnast back at Birmingham High School, the five-foot-nine-inch Ovitz has kept himself fit by exercising every morning in his home gym. It was because of Michael Ovitz that Jerry Seinfeld took an interest in aikido for a while. Norman Lear once received a rare invitation to watch Ovitz work out. "He was utterly riveted on what he was doing," Lear reports, "utterly focused." At the end of the session, Ovitz handed Lear a copy of *The Art of War*. Lear walked away from that session marveling at Ovitz's concentration: "the kind you'd see in a great musician, the kind that requires tremendous discipline." And yet Ovitz's interest in martial arts—and his wider interest in Asian culture—was one of those facets of his life that he preferred to keep private. Not even his closest business friends have heard him discuss such subjects.

NOTHING BETTER ILLUSTRATES Ovitz's interest in distancing himself from what he thinks of as being the "narrowness" of Hollywood than his passion for collecting art. Over the past 20 years he has amassed one of the finest private art collections in the United States. It is characteristic of the man that when he becomes interested in something he immerses himself in it, becomes almost a fanatic on the subject.

Yet precisely where his interest in art came from is unclear. "It didn't come from us," says his mother Sylvia Ovitz. "We couldn't afford to buy art." Nonetheless, only a few years after he founded CAA, Ovitz began to think seriously about establishing his own art collection. It was the literary agent Mort Janklow who, sensing Ovitz's interest, introduced him in the late 1970s to Arne Glimcher, head of the PaceWildenstein Gallery in New York. Glimcher promised to take good care of Janklow's friend. When Ovitz phoned and said he would like to come in and look around, Glimcher decided to show him some of the most extraordinary pieces in the gallery. One of these was a Matisse painting. Ovitz asked the price.

"Nine hundred thousand dollars," said Glimcher, without so much as blinking an eye. Though steep for that time, in fact that asking price represents something of a bargain given what any Matisse painting would be going for just two decades later. Ovitz passed on the painting, and then suddenly became very cool toward his host. He soon departed the gallery.

Mort Janklow phoned Glimcher later that day. "What did you do to Mike? He was really furious. He thought you were arrogant. He felt you were trying to put him down by showing him things that he wasn't interested in, or couldn't afford to buy."

A bit exasperated, Glimcher replied: "I showed him all of the master works I had because he was your friend. *You* introduced us!"

A month later, Ovitz was back at PaceWildenstein to see the show of an artist in whom he was interested.

Noticing Ovitz, Glimcher came up to him and remarked: "Mort said you thought I was arrogant."

"I did. I thought you weren't showing me things that I wanted to see."

Glimcher then showed Ovitz a painting by Brice Mardens. It was the very finest of Mardens's paintings, which were to be exhibited at the gallery a month later. Ordinarily, Glimcher would have shown such a painting only to a Mardens collector, but Ovitz asked so many intelligent questions about the painting and the painter that Glimcher was won over. No one had ever put so many queries to Glimcher. How did the painting fit in historically with Mardens's other works? Ovitz asked. Who were the artist's antecedents? How did this painting rate among all of Mardens's works?

Clearly, Ovitz was interested in the painting. Glimcher told him the price, and Ovitz made an offer below that.

"I don't sell art like that," Glimcher snapped.

Ovitz left, but later called Glimcher three or four times to dicker over the price of the painting. Glimcher didn't hold Ovitz's bargaining against him, since that was in fact the practice at other art galleries, just not his. But at last he said, with finality in his voice, "If you want to buy the picture, buy it at my price." And Ovitz did.

Ovitz returned to Glimcher's gallery again and again. African art interested him. Peering at some works from the Yoruba culture of Nigeria, Ovitz asked to be provided with some written material on the culture. Glimcher sent him three books. A month later Ovitz was back at the gallery, peppering Glimcher with such intensely detailed questions that it seemed to him as if Ovitz had memorized all three of the books he had sent him. Arne Glimcher was impressed that the Hollywood agent had actually taken the time to read books about art and the artists.

Ovitz's tastes in art were far more expansive than those of anyone Glimcher had ever met, ranging from Chinese furniture and ceramics, to contemporary sculpture to modern painting. Within each of these disciplines, Ovitz studied the item's history and the market for it and other items of its kind, and then determined where other significant items from the same collection were now located. He sometimes asked Glimcher to track down such items so that Ovitz could purchase them. As Arne Glimcher became friendlier with the man, he began to notice that Michael Ovitz was interested only in the best achievement of an artist, or of a culture. Ovitz was always after the best, his standards both in the business world and in his personal life were the highest possible. He wanted the best of everything, and would settle for nothing less.

Ovitz took enormous pride in being elected, early in 1992, to the Board of Trustees of the Museum of Modern Art in New York City, the first Californian to serve on the board. He had served on the Chairman's

Council of the Museum, invited to do so by MOMA board chairman David Rockefeller.

The walls of Ovitz's home in Brentwood were filled with paintings, some as large as the wall on which they were hung. Yet given the unpretentious furniture, the family photographs on display, and the sounds of children drifting in from elsewhere in the house, a visitor feels that he or she most decidedly is walking around someone's *home*, not an art museum. Nonetheless, in the foyer hangs a Roy Lichtenstein, a larger version of which may be seen in the atrium of the building where CAA presently is located. Off the living room, in a den, is a portrait of Chuck Close's wife, which he painted not with a brush but with his fingers. In other parts of the house were a small Joel Shapiro sculpture in bronze, and another in wood. There were also paintings by Picasso, Jim Dine, and others. The Ovitz art collection had been earthquake-proofed: Sculptures were waxed to tables; one Modigliani sculpture rested on a base that moves back and forth, so that in the event of an earthquake the sculpture would not be damaged. "It wasn't a self-aggrandizing move, it was about extending self-knowledge," says Arne Glimcher, referring to Ovitz's slowly accumulated collection. He lent parts of it to exhibitions and museums, but almost always anonymously. It pleased him when someone to whom he was showing the collection asked questions about the paintings or the artist. If the paintings provoked a lively discussion about art, he was thrilled. He had not amassed all these paintings just to hear a visitor say, "Wow!," and then move on. He wanted his guests to show a real interest in his collection. When they failed to do so, or reacted inappropriately, Ovitz simmered. Once director Richard Donner looked at a painting on the wall of Ovitz's home and asked him jokingly, "Did your kid do that in school?" Ovitz made it clear to Donner, by means of a single disdainful look, that he was not well pleased by that remark. Says Donner: "Mike turned his collection into a multimillion-dollar operation, and I ate my words."

Ovitz spent a good deal of time talking to gallery owners, and to the artists themselves, and a good deal of money in acquiring art. He contends that his main reason for building up such a fine art collection is very simple: He loves art. In his home he has around 2000 books in his art library. On one occasion in the 1990s, he scoured these books in search of a suitable background for the advertisements that CAA produced for Coca-Cola. One advertisement, with Coca-Cola bottles falling out of the sky, was meant to be reminiscent of a René Magritte painting.

One of the many important artists whom Ovitz sought out was Chuck Close. Their friendship was sealed at a dinner at The Four Seasons in

New York attended by Michael and Judy Ovitz, Chuck and Leslie Close, and sculptor Joel Shapiro and his wife Ellen Phelan. Ovitz had bought some of Close's work, including the aforementioned portrait of his wife Leslie. Close was impressed with a quality in Ovitz that others had noted as well: "When he gets involved in something, he jumps in with both feet. Judging by the art he has in his house and how quickly he acquired a lot of it, he's a pretty quick study."

Long before he met Michael Ovitz, Chuck Close had rules about who he would permit to buy his paintings. Close's practice had been not to sell too many of his paintings to any one collector. "When you get a painting of mine, it's a long time before you're offered another one," Close says. "And of course, Mike doesn't like to wait. He's impatient." Ovitz had to wait a long time between the first Close painting he acquired and the second. Close notes that Ovitz has a tremendous pride of ownership about his collection: "It stops being my painting and starts being his painting."

Chuck Close has also discovered that Michael Ovitz pays his (Close's) paintings the honor of bestowing upon them a good bit of his time and thought: "You can tell that he's been sitting and looking at my paintings. He'll ask me what's the optimal viewing distance; and he will watch the way people look at the paintings and talk about that. Clearly these are not things that go on the wall and disappear as kind of wallpaper or background for cocktail chitchat or power meetings." On one occasion, a Chuck Close painting owned by Ovitz was damaged. While others might have ignored the damage, Ovitz became obsessed with getting it repaired. Close was impressed.

Another time, Ovitz wanted Close to paint his portrait. At first Close refused, for it was his firm policy never to paint the portrait of the same person who planned to purchase it. And he knew that if he agreed to paint Michael Ovitz, Ovitz immediately would want to own the portrait. Then, says Close, "I would be working for a living. That probably contaminates my work a bit." But Ovitz kept on asking, so Close had no choice but to keep on refusing. Finally, Close did consent to *photograph* Ovitz.

Ovitz took a liking to Close, and told him that the next time he came to Los Angeles, he wanted to throw him a party. Throwing a star-studded party, big or small, was Ovitz's way of suggesting how important he was within Hollywood circles. Close planned to be in Los Angeles for the opening of PaceWildenstein's Los Angeles branch, with Close's work constituting the first show in the L.A. gallery. Ovitz decided to host a party for the artist, as promised, at his home on September 27, 1995, the day before the opening of his show. "What movie stars would you like to meet?" Ovitz asked Close, and a huge list featuring the biggest names in

Hollywood was drawn up. Close recalls that Ovitz "couldn't stand that someone wouldn't be there. So the party grew and grew." Among those who eventually attended were Dustin Hoffman, Steven Spielberg, Michael Keaton, Tom Hanks, Ellen Burstyn, Jerry Seinfeld, Kate Capshaw, Warren Beatty, Annette Bening, Sidney Poitier, Sally Field, Billy Crystal, and Ellen DeGeneres. Because it had rained the day before, Ovitz had fake grass placed over the real grass on his grounds, so that people's shoes wouldn't get muddy.

As Chuck Close sees it, Ovitz was accepted as an important player in the art world not because he had money and power. "Anyone with money can be a player," observes Close, "but you don't necessarily impress people. Just buying things isn't impressive. A lot of people buy things." Close's point is that the art world had taken note of the fact that Ovitz employed his usual diligence in learning about art, "and pretty soon they couldn't imagine that he hadn't been doing it his whole life."

Indeed, Ovitz was comfortable around artists, and numbered among his closest acquaintances some of the country's leading figures. As we have seen, Roy Lichtenstein was one of them. Lichtenstein somewhat impishly comments that while he knows that Ovitz has a number of artist friends, he (Lichtenstein) has only one friend in the business world, and that is Michael Ovitz. When he is in New York, once every three months or so, Ovitz generally drops by Lichtenstein's studio. "We talk about everything from music to movies," Lichtenstein says with a laugh, "to art in general." Ovitz likes to look at Lichtenstein's present work in progress, an honor the artist won't accord to just anyone. "I think he likes to come and hang out," the artist notes. "He goes from meeting to meeting when he's in New York. I think he kind of relaxes in my studio. It's always surprising that he has the time."

On Lichtenstein visits to Los Angeles, Ovitz has had him over to dinner at his home (four times, as of Lichtenstein's last count). Each time the guest list has been different, but it has included Dustin Hoffman (twice), Warren Beatty, Annette Bening, and Sean Connery. The 16 guests would sit at two tables, 8 at each table. At one point during the dinner Ovitz would get up and say something, and then ask the guests to change places between courses so that each person got to talk with everyone else. Once a magician appeared, and did his repertoire of tricks. "The grownups were fascinated," Lichtenstein reports. On some of those visits to Los Angeles, the artist would meet with Ovitz at a restaurant. On one occasion he dined at Spago with Ovitz and Sean Connery. On another he was joined by Michael Eisner and Ovitz. "They sent this embarrassingly large limo to pick me and my wife Dorothy up," Lichtenstein remembers, noting that Eisner and Ovitz were casually dressed in athletic warm-up suits. Lichtenstein guessed that art would be the main topic of conversation. It wasn't. Nor was entertainment. "I wouldn't have even known they were in the entertainment business, from the conversation."

Another close artist friend of Michael Ovitz's, the sculptor Joel Shapiro, happens to also be his cousin. Shapiro's maternal grandmother and Ovitz's maternal grandmother were sisters. For years before the two met, Shapiro's mother had been telling her son that he had a cousin in Los Angeles who was a talent agent, and that he should look him up. "But," Shapiro says, "of course I would never look up relatives," for he had a nightmarish vision of an overwhelming number of family members descending upon one of his exhibitions. Thus one day in the early 1980s when Ovitz walked into Shapiro's studio at 33 Bleecker Street in New York to see his sculpture, he had no idea that he was in fact related to the sculptor. But he became friendly with him, enjoyed his art, and began to buy Shapiro sculptures.

Ovitz has one of Shapiro's sculptures on the front lawn of his Brentwood home. "Michael is familiar with creativity, so I felt open to him," Shapiro says. For two years, Ovitz was after Shapiro to make him a table for his screening room at home. "I'm a sculptor, not a furniture person," he told his cousin, though he had made many tables to be used for his work. Shapiro finally agreed to take on the task, but could never quite get around to it. Ovitz called him every few months: "What's happening with the table? Are you doing it?" Finally Shapiro did produce a table for Michael Ovitz's office and a sculpture for the atrium of the CAA building that opened in 1989.

For Joel Shapiro, the fact that Michael Ovitz has been interested in his art has added luster to his career. "If he does show interest in you, it's very meaningful. His patronage is nice. He's influential, and people look at him as a taste-maker."

Once he had discovered the family tie to Joel Shapiro, Ovitz summoned his mother to his office. Even though she was his mother, Sylvia Ovitz felt nervous being there, in the lair of the big-time Hollywood agent.

"I'm really upset!" Michael Ovitz told his mother.

"Uh, Michael! What did I do?" She had no idea what he was talking about, but was anxious nonetheless.

Then, smiling, he asked, "Why didn't you tell us we had a famous artist in the family?"

Even Michael Ovitz's mother was intimidated by him.

11

Stepping Out of the Shadows

ARNE GLIMCHER, ONE of Michael Ovitz's closest friends, had wanted to be both an actor and a painter as a youngster. So, as an adult, he moved in the worlds of both art and entertainment, by becoming president of one of the most prestigious art galleries in the United States, Pace-Wildenstein, and by emerging as an important Hollywood producer.

He began his Hollywood career by playing a bit part in the 1982 movie, *Still of the Night,* which starred Meryl Streep and Roy Scheider, and was directed by his close friend Robert Benton (the director of *Kramer vs. Kramer*). He also served as an unofficial adviser to Ivan Reitman in his 1986 film about the art world, *Legal Eagles,* which starred Robert Redford and Debra Winger. Glimcher liked to hang around movie sets and was so keen on the film business that he began buying literary properties that he hoped to turn into feature films. Of course, whenever he wanted to pursue a Hollywood project, he turned to his friend Michael Ovitz, who had been serving as Glimcher's adviser for film projects.

One night, shortly after Christmas 1985, Glimcher was distraught. He had invested two years of his life in trying to produce a movie based upon the life of primatologist Dian Fossey, and word had just gotten out that she was dead—murdered, in fact. He had just arrived in Rwanda and was scheduled to meet with her to finalize plans for the movie. But then the horrible news arrived. For nearly 20 years Dian Fossey had studied the mountain gorillas of Central Africa, founding the Karisoke Research Centre in Rwanda's Virunga mountains. In 1983 she wrote a best-selling book, *Gorillas in the Mist,* based upon her experiences studying the gorillas. Glimcher purchased the film rights to Fossey's autobiography, signing her as a consultant for the film; he made a deal with Universal to make the film.

Glimcher had been captivated by the project, not so much as a vehicle about protecting endangered species but as the story of how a single courageous woman changed the course of history of an African nation. The whole thrust of the movie, as he saw it, was that one person could make a difference. He saw Dian Fossey as a genuine heroine. But, now that Fossey had been murdered, Glimcher was certain that his cherished project had died with her. He couldn't imagine completing it without her. But he hadn't counted on the problem-solving abilities of his close friend in Los Angeles.

On that difficult night the first person Glimcher called was Michael Ovitz. "It's all over," he said despondently to Ovitz. "The project has died with Dian."

"It's not all over," Ovitz said calmly. "It's just different. You'll see. With this notoriety, there's going be an enormous interest in her life story. The project is universal. Her whole life is interesting. You can deal with her whole life. Come back to America, and let's see what we can do with this."

In despair, Glimcher returned to Los Angeles, and was disappointed to learn that producers Jon Peters and Peter Guber were putting together their own version of Fossey's story for Warner Brothers. A script for the Peters/Guber movie, to be called *Heaven and Earth*, had been ordered, and locations already were being scouted in Rwanda. Ovitz had little comfort to offer to Glimcher: "When it comes to a war between Warner Brothers and Universal, and Warner is ready to do the movie and you're not, Warner will win, and there won't be two movies on Dian Fossey's life."

But Ovitz wasn't through by any means. He talked to Terry Semel at Warner Brothers and Tom Pollock at Universal, and won their approval to co-produce the Fossey film, an unusual arrangement indeed. In other words, Warner Brothers and Universal had agreed to do only one movie, in effect combining Glimcher's project with the Peters/Guber movie, *Heaven and Earth*. But when Glimcher presented a $26 million budget, $2 million more than what had been discussed, both studios got cold feet. Then Michael Ovitz went to work. He believed in the project, and was ready to have CAA make a certain sacrifice to get the movie made. Sigourney Weaver, not a CAA client, had been chosen to play the lead role of Dian Fossey. "Here's what you've got to do," Ovitz instructed him. He urged Glimcher to sit down with Guber, Weaver, Michael Apted (the director), and the rest of his team, and figure out how to take $2 million out of the budget.

Glimcher was gloomy. "I don't think we can. We're to the bone on the movie now."

"You've got to." It was Ovitz's routine answer. In other words: When there's a problem, don't get depressed, figure out a way to solve it. Ovitz offered to help: "The first thing you can do is: Don't take anything up front. Take it on the back end. Get Sigourney Weaver to give back half of her fee. Get Michael Apted to do the same." Weaver, who was the highest-paid actress at the time, agreed to be paid less. The others quickly fell in line. Once the budget had been reduced, Glimcher, in London and ready to begin the movie, called Terry Semel in Los Angeles and asked for a meeting. One was arranged at Warner's offices in Rockefeller Center in New York. Attending were Semel (representing Warner Brothers), Pollock (representing Universal), and other executives from the two studios, along with Glimcher and his team.

Glimcher walked into the meeting feeling better than he had for some time, but still not at all certain that he was going to be able to get his movie made. He knew that he had managed to chop $2 million from the budget, but he had no way of knowing whether the studio executives would decide to green-light the picture at the reduced amount.

Terry Semel opened the meeting, consoling Glimcher: "Don't worry, you did your best. We would have made the movie at twenty-four million dollars. It was just pushing it over the edge at twenty-six million. The project wasn't necessarily a movie that would be a blockbuster, so you shouldn't feel bad."

Glimcher: "If we had come in at twenty-four million dollars, you would have made the movie?"

Semel: "Yes."

Glimcher then passed out copies of the new, reduced budget to everyone seated around the table. "Here's our new budget. Here's what we've done. We've cut our fees. I'm taking nothing. We are at twenty-four million dollars."

Glimcher looked around the table and noticed that many of the faces seemed to be turning white. Pollock said that he had to catch a plane to Toronto; he told Semel he would agree to whatever Semel chose to do. Asking Glimcher and his team to wait in another room down the hall, Semel and the studio executives took a half hour before calling them back in and announcing that Warner Brothers and Universal had decided to co-produce the movie.

The first thing Glimcher did was to pick up the phone and call Michael Ovitz. "Bravo," was Ovitz's terse way of congratulating his friend.

On June 1, 1987, the cast and crew of *Gorillas in the Mist* began work in Rwanda. The movie opened in September 1988. It garnered over $80 million at the box office and was considered one of the most prestigious films of the Eighties. It earned five Oscar nominations.

And Michael Ovitz's role in getting the movie made further enhanced his reputation as Hollywood's greatest problem solver.

On February 20, 1986, Stan Kamen, the William Morris agent who had dominated Hollywood during the 1970s and early 1980s, died. Some of his clients already had defected to Michael Ovitz's CAA. The big question was, "What will his remaining major clients do?" These included Barbra Streisand, Goldie Hawn, Warren Beatty, Kirk Douglas, and Chevy Chase. Executives at William Morris were on the phone to Ovitz and to Jeff Berg and Sam Cohn at ICM, begging for time—six months—in which to cement their relationships with Stan Kamen's clients. But Ovitz was in no position, or mood, to promise that he would honor a cease-fire. These people, after all, were free to leave Morris whenever they wanted.

Ovitz was aided by Terry Semel, chairman and co-chief executive officer at Warner Brothers, in winning over some of Kamen's more important clients. Semel admired CAA, and was happy to recommend the agency to the stars he employed. He especially liked the agency's efficiency and straightforwardness: "If you said there was a problem, they would cut right through it and within an hour or two get back to you and say 'It's done' or 'It's not going to be done, let's talk about another idea.' Other agencies had a less hands-on feeling." Upon Kamen's death, Semel spoke to such Warner Brothers regulars as Barbra Streisand, Goldie Hawn, Chevy Chase, and Meryl Streep, making clear to them his hope that they would decide to sign on with Ovitz. "We saw Stan's death as a good opportunity for some of our clients to go to CAA," Semel recalls. "CAA was a good place, with aggressive people who were probably going to lead the 1980s and 1990s in their field. We are the largest producer of movies in the last twenty years, and CAA was building the largest list of stars."

Ovitz sensed that he was getting closer and closer to dominating the movie business in a way that no agent ever had done before. For one thing, he had single-handedly given a big boost to the careers of some of Hollywood's biggest talents. Director Sydney Pollack's career was no longer inching along at a snail's pace. Since Ovitz took him on as a client in 1981, he had directed a couple of blockbusters: *Tootsie*, in 1982, which grossed just under $95 million, and the critically-acclaimed *Out of Africa*, in 1985, which made over $43 million. Ovitz had been just as effective in supercharging the career of veteran Sean Connery. By 1983 it had become clear to Connery, then 53, that his James Bond–moviemaking days were behind him. He could no longer be cast in the sexy-spy mold. Connery needed to find roles that were more in keeping with that of a versatile, colorful, middle-aged actor. And Ovitz hit pay dirt for him by casting him in just such a role: In 1986, Connery won the British Academy Award as Best Actor for his portrayal of Brother William in the film version of Umberto Eco's best-selling medieval thriller, *The Name of the Rose*.

Paul Newman's career also re-blossomed under the magical Ovitz touch. He was nominated for Academy Awards for his performances in *Absence of Malice* (1981) and *The Verdict* (1982), and after a whole series of near-misses, finally won the Oscar (his first) for his role in *The Color of Money* opposite Tom Cruise in 1986.

Ovitz did not get off to a good start with Sylvester Stallone. Miscasting him as a singing cabby opposite Dolly Parton in *Rhinestone*, which proved to be an expensive, embarrassing flop at the box office, Ovitz almost immediately rebounded by placing Stallone in a series of action films that earned the actor as much as $15 million a film. But perhaps Ovitz's greatest success came with actor Tom Cruise. He had told the actor when he signed him in 1981 that there was no reason why he couldn't perform with Hollywood's biggest stars, and Ovitz backed up his words with some of his most effective agenting: In 1986 Cruise starred in both *Top Gun* and *The Color of Money*. In the latter he co-starred with superstar Paul Newman, and both films were box-office hits.

Ovitz's connection to literary agent Mort Janklow also paid off nicely. Ever since their relationship began in the late 1970s, CAA had been using the books of Janklow's novelist clients to initiate 10 hours of television network mini-series, including *Rage of Angels, Mistral's Daughter, Princess Daisy,* and *Hollywood Wives*. Janklow boasts that he and Michael Ovitz have put together more television deals than any three of the studios combined.

Yet Ovitz felt that he needed to accomplish still more if he was to be seen as truly dominating the business. And as he saw it, the only way for CAA to rule Hollywood was to sign the three top actors of the day: Dustin Hoffman, Al Pacino, and Robert De Niro. Ovitz had signed Hoffman in 1980, but Pacino and De Niro remained tantalizingly out of reach. Ovitz had been told over and over again that the signing of all three of those major stars represented an impossible feat, for no single talent agency had ever had the top three actors of the day safely under its wing. But the lure for Ovitz was his recognition of the fact that if he could sign Pacino and De Niro it would become virtually impossible for any other major star to seek representation anywhere other than at CAA. When Ovitz was on the verge of signing Al Pacino as a CAA client, he phoned Dustin Hoffman as a courtesy. "Do you think my signing Pacino would be a problem for you?" he asked Hoffman. After all, Pacino and Hoffman would be competing for the same roles. But Hoffman replied that he saw no problem. And then, on June 25, 1986, Michael Ovitz succeeded in signing Al Pacino.

At the time that CAA was pursuing him, Robert De Niro wasn't represented at all. De Niro had wanted to do a particular film for 20th Century Fox more than anything else he could imagine. The Fox executives hesitated, but Penny Marshall, director of the film, at last managed to convince them to make an offer to De Niro. The offer was too low to satisfy the actor, however, and De Niro withdrew from consideration for the role. Eventually Tom Hanks played the part that De Niro had hoped for in the Penny Marshall–directed smash hit *Big* (1988). Irked by that episode, De Niro eagerly became a CAA client, signing with the agency in the fall of 1987.

Ovitz had done the impossible. And in the wake of Kamen's death, he went on to sign such major film stars as Barbra Streisand, Goldie Hawn, Chevy Chase, and Meryl Streep, as well as the directors Martin Scorsese and Sidney Lumet. Ovitz was on a winning streak that had no end in sight.

Even Sally Field was ready to become a CAA client, after having held out for so long. Ovitz had first tried to win her over as a client in the late 1970s, when she was a rising young actress. After her graduation from Ovitz's own Birmingham High School, Field attended the Columbia Pictures acting workshop and was chosen over 150 other actresses to play the lead role in the 1965–1966 television series *Gidget*. For the next three years she enjoyed an even larger triumph as star of the popular series *The Flying Nun*. Weary of being cast in these relentlessly cute, undemanding parts, Field in 1977 landed the role of a mentally disturbed woman possessing 16 different personalities in the four-hour television series *Sybil*, for which she won an Emmy.

Michael Ovitz called Sally soon after that, and asked if he might represent her.

"Absolutely not," was her reply. She did remember Ovitz from high school, but she had no desire to join CAA, concerned that the agency might not last: "I didn't know if they'd be in business more than an hour and a half." Whenever she and Ovitz met, the conversation drifted easily to recollections of high school friends, but Field remained aloof. Meanwhile, her movie career soared. She won an Oscar in 1979 for her portrayal of a union activist in *Norma Rae,* and another one in 1984 for her role in *Places in the Heart.* (It was then that she won some notoriety by gushing, at the Oscar ceremony, "You *like* me, you *really* like me!") But beginning in 1986, when Paul Newman was starring in *The Color of Money,* Field began to hear some remarkable things about Michael Ovitz: "He was really taking great care of Paul." Believing that her present agent lacked Ovitz's ardor, she communicated that fact to Ovitz, who immediately began to look after Sally. She called him soon after and said: "Now, I'll come with you guys."

By the summer of 1986, virtually the entire Stan Kamen stable of stars had switched over to CAA. It was the equivalent of all the depositors at Chase Manhattan Bank suddenly shifting their allegiance to the Bank of America. If the signing of Hoffman, Redford, and Newman in the early 1980s had helped to put CAA on the map, the acquisition of Stan Kamen's major clients at this later stage catapulted CAA far above and beyond its former rivals. CAA had become the most powerful institution in Hollywood, but still Michael Ovitz remained an enigma within the industry as a whole, and unknown to the public at large. All of that was about to change.

In the fall of 1986, Michael Ovitz was invited by the *Los Angeles Times* to come in and observe Nexis, a new data-retrieval system that scanned newspapers. The newspaper's publisher, Tom Johnson, typed in the name Michael Ovitz, eager to show his guest that not even the mysterious, low-profile Mr. Ovitz could elude the long tentacle-grasp of Nexis. But not a single reference could be found. Johnson was embarrassed. "Never mind," said Ovitz. "I'll be happy if I never appear in Nexis." He was dead-serious. As public-relations specialist Stephen Rivers liked to say: "Ovitz would have been perfectly happy if the next thing written about him was his obituary." Though he was fast becoming the most powerful figure in Hollywood, Ovitz was virtually unknown beyond the town limits, and that's just how the head of Hollywood's hottest talent agency liked it.

A decade earlier, when he was just starting out in the talent-agency business in the mid-1970s, Ovitz had gone to the public library and searched through the card catalogue, and then through microfilm, for the name "Lew Wasserman." Wasserman was chairman and CEO of MCA and its Universal Studio and the most influential figure in Hollywood, but Ovitz noticed how little information there was on him, and how few photographs. And there was a lesson in that for Ovitz. He believed—naively, he later would admit—that, just as Lew Wasserman had done, he could become an important business figure in Hollywood and yet still remain outside the focus of the public eye.

But for the time being, his hope that he could linger on in Hollywood's shadows seemed a viable one. Even if Ovitz had encouraged media coverage of himself and CAA, editors had little interest in him and his fellow movers and shakers in the world of Hollywood business. The very notion of "Hollywood business" seemed an oxymoron to them. The studios generated too little revenue to be of interest to the business media, and, after all, Michael Ovitz was just another agent. The only Hollywood people worth writing about were the movie stars.

By 1984, when Michael Cieply joined *The Wall Street Journal* as a reporter for its Los Angeles bureau, he had already learned from his reporting days at *Forbes* of the media's meager interest in the business side of Hollywood. Cieply's "beat" was not the movie industry per se, only the entertainment companies based in L.A., and he was meant to spend only half of his time covering the movie industry. Then, too, the New York–based entertainment firms—another significant segment of the Hollywood story—were covered by various *Journal* reporters working out of New York. All of this served to constrict Cieply's focus, and to dissipate any enthusiasm he might otherwise have had for "Hollywood business" stories.

Yet an event was to occur in that year of 1984 that would cause the media, for the first time, to take a long, hard look at Hollywood's business side: This was corporate raider Saul Steinberg's "greenmailing" of Walt Disney Productions. Steinberg accumulated 6.3 percent of Disney's shares, then several months later sought to purchase 49 percent of the company for $1.2 billion. In order to get rid of Steinberg, in June the Disney board paid him for his stock, thus providing him with a $31 million profit. Michael Cieply still recalls what was for him the first tangible sign of the heightened media interest in Hollywood: In 1983, *The Wall Street Journal*'s archive contained only three pages of clips on Disney; a year later, there were 33 pages of clips on the company.

Business reporter that he was, Michael Cieply felt liberated. Excited by the media's new interest in the no-longer-oxymoronic "Hollywood business," Cieply now, in the fall of 1986, was confident that if he came up with good Hollywood business stories, his editors would agree to publish them. Thus it was that he began to dig deeper and deeper into the topic, intensifying his conversations with people working in all areas of the entertainment industry. Before, it had been his custom to cover the Hollywood business world one company at a time, taking little note of those larger themes and common threads that bound that whole world together as one. Now, he searched out just such themes and common threads, and, as he did so, he slowly began to notice something strange: Time and time again, one man's name was coming up in all of his conversations: Michael Ovitz. And Cieply noticed something else as well: Those who uttered Ovitz's name always seemed to do so with a kind of awe. They left the clear impression, without saying it outright, that this man had become a very powerful force in Hollywood. From what Cieply could gather, Ovitz had come to wield so much influence largely by taking the unprecedented step of "packaging" an entire film project and selling that project to a studio. Those with whom Cieply conversed generally knew next to nothing about Ovitz beyond that. Often they mispronounced his name: *Ah*-vitz, rather than *Oh*-vitz. None of them knew what he looked like, or sounded like, and certainly none of them had any inkling of how Ovitz performed his magic, or how much of it might be charisma, grand strategy, or just dumb luck.

Regardless, Cieply now was deeply intrigued. For after all, this Ovitz fellow was *only* a talent agent. Not the head of a studio. Not a major producer of films. Since when did an agent wield such power? Cieply knew enough about Hollywood—or thought he did—to find it odd that a mere talent agent—not a studio head, such as Louis B. Mayer in the golden days of old—was being spoken of in such reverential tones. But if he was going to convince his editors to let him do a story on this mystery man of Hollywood, Cieply knew that he would have to do a lot of digging. All he had as of that moment was cocktail-party gossip. He needed some solid facts that would serve to substantiate the hyperbole he had been hearing.

He began with *The Wall Street Journal*'s "morgue." He wanted to find out just how much—or how little—Ovitz had been in the news, and what had been said about him. He searched and searched, but found not a hint of the man. *How strange*, Cieply thought, growing confused. Was this Michael Ovitz worth a story, after all? Based upon his extensive conversations, he had certainly thought so. But if so, why on earth had the media ignored him for so long? Even discounting the media's long-standing lack of interest in such "Hollywood business" people, how could someone this powerful have remained this private for this long?

He decided it was time to speak to his editors in order to let them know what his reporter's antennae had been picking up and to find out if they thought that Ovitz was worth pursuing. Cieply knew that if he had made the same pitch to his editors 10 or even 5 years earlier, they undoubtedly would have made him feel like two cents. But that was then, and this was now. And so, when Cieply presented what he knew to his editors, they urged him to go after the story.

He began with some traditional legwork. Among the people he turned to was an old acquaintance, Irving Azoff, the head of MCA Records and producer of the film *Urban Cowboy*. "Who is Michael Ovitz?" Cieply asked Azoff. Much to Cieply's surprise, Azoff told him that he *knew* Michael Ovitz, and "I'll introduce you."

A short time thereafter Azoff was invited to attend one of those huge Hollywood movie premieres, this one thrown by The Walt Disney Company and replete with a fancy tent-party in the rear of Chasen's. Azoff was reasonably certain that Ovitz would be present, and so he asked Cieply to tag along. Sure enough, Azoff soon spotted Disney Chairman Michael Eisner talking to Ovitz, and he took Cieply over to the two men and introduced the reporter to Ovitz.

"He's from *The Wall Street Journal*," Azoff told Ovitz. "He's going to write about you."

Immediately Ovitz tensed up, as if a cold chill had suddenly swept down upon him. Cieply watched as Ovitz's demeanor changed. Ovitz said nothing at first, but rather seemed to be weighing his words well.

"Well," said Ovitz at last, speaking in low tones as if he didn't want anyone to hear. "I really prefer that you don't write anything about me."

Eisner was enjoying the scene. He knew Cieply by reputation, knew him to be a dogged, determined reporter. He also knew that his friend Michael Ovitz most emphatically did *not* want to see his name in Cieply's newspaper. Thus Eisner thought he would have a little fun at Ovitz's expense.

"You're dead now," said Eisner, speaking as if he were serious. "I know this guy. When *The Wall Street Journal* pulls the trigger, the bullet will come out of the gun."

Growing even more tense, Ovitz seemed to find nothing amusing in Eisner's words.

"Can I call you?" Cieply asked Ovitz.

Ovitz said nothing, but merely gave off one of those "if looks could kill" stares. He was determined to live his life, to conduct his career, well out of reach of the public spotlight. He had kept a tight lid on his career thus far, and he saw no reason to lift it now.

The day after he encountered Ovitz at the Hollywood premiere, the *Journal* reporter phoned Ovitz's office and asked to speak with him. Within seconds, Ovitz was on the line. A good sign, the reporter thought. It wasn't. Ovitz had anticipated Cieply's call, and was ready with his answer even before Cieply asked any questions. He had no intention of being interviewed. Nor did he want to be written about in the press. No threat, explicit or implicit, followed. In fact, Cieply noticed that Ovitz's voice was a bit warmer than it had been the previous evening. "I don't want publicity," he said emphatically. "It can only disrupt my relations with my agency." Ovitz seemed to be expressing concern that his partners would be annoyed with him if they sensed that he was making a play for the spotlight.

The reporter was taken aback by that tack, since he knew he had no choice but to focus upon the top man. That was what business journalism almost always did, zero in on the fellow in charge. And he knew that he would write fairly about Ovitz, giving the story something of a positive spin, for he planned to describe how this all-powerful fellow was pulling all the strings these days in Hollywood. Why on earth would Ovitz object to *that?* And yet Ovitz already clearly was fighting the story tooth-and-nail, behaving as if Cieply and *The Wall Street Journal* had plans to expose him as a criminal.

Cieply wasn't deterred by Ovitz's refusal to cooperate, but he certainly was disappointed, for he knew that the story would be far more interesting if it was based in part upon conversations with the man himself. At any rate, he began to call lots of people around town, and he kept calling Ovitz—but could no longer get through to him.

Just a week later, Cieply and his wife were attending another premiere, this one at Mann's Chinese Theater. In an amazing coincidence, they found themselves sitting one row behind Michael Ovitz. Turning around and seeing Cieply, Ovitz stared, but said nothing. Cieply assumed the worst: *He thinks I'm chasing him.* A week later Cieply traveled to New York, where he breakfasted at The Jockey Club with movie producer David Brown, husband of *Cosmopolitan* editor Helen Gurley Brown. To Cieply's astonishment, in strolled Michael Ovitz. This was the third time in two weeks that Cieply and Ovitz had bumped into one another! Cieply knew that he had *not* been hounding Michael Ovitz, but he feared that Ovitz had already drawn that certainly well-warranted conclusion. Ovitz looked around the room, spotted Cieply, looked extremely uncomfortable for a few seconds, and then darted out of the restaurant.

Still, Cieply wanted to interview Ovitz, all the more so now that he had collected a good deal of information about him. But he knew that his chances of doing so, as of that moment, were nil. Soon after the "bizarre encounter" (Cieply's phrase) at The Jockey Club, the reporter got in touch with Michael Eisner and asked him for his help in getting to Ovitz. Instead, Eisner turned sinister. "If you print this story about

Michael Ovitz," he said in a threatening voice, "it's going to be very bad for you."

To Cieply, Eisner's response was heavy-handed, and made the Disney Chairman sound like a Mafia don in a bad Hollywood movie.

Cieply laughed, hoping to lighten the mood.

Figuring now that Cieply couldn't be scared off, Eisner turned mellow. "Well," he said, his voice less emotional, "if you're going to do this, I'll help you." Eisner explained that Ovitz had no intention of talking to Cieply, but if the reporter were to provide him with some questions, the Disney chairman might be able to provide the answers. Though Eisner never said as much, Cieply assumed that he would ferry the questions to Ovitz and ferry back his answers.

Ovitz's unwillingness to talk directly to a reporter, but willingness to answer his questions by means of a go-between, was an accurate reflection of Ovitz's long-standing stance vis-à-vis the media. As he had said to Cieply, he preferred not to be written about at all. But if that simply couldn't be the case, he wanted to have a measure of control over what was said about him. Thus, Ovitz replied through Eisner to 200 questions that Cieply had handed over to Eisner. The questions ranged from Ovitz's childhood to his business career.

At last, Cieply was ready to write his story. The scuttlebutt from those first conversations had proven to be true: It seemed that Michael Ovitz really was Hollywood's most important power broker. That became the central theme of the story. And Cieply was pleased to find that his editors understood the significance of what he had uncovered. For the story, when it appeared on December 19, 1986, ran on the right-hand column of page one. The headline made it sound as if *The Wall Street Journal* article was introducing Michael Ovitz to the public for the first time, as it more or less was: "An Agent Dominates Film and TV Studios With Package Deals." The opening line of the story got right to the point: "By some accounts, the most powerful individual in Hollywood is neither a star nor a studio chief. He is an agent, Michael S. Ovitz."

Cieply then sought to explain Michael Ovitz to his audience: "The president and a co-founder of the increasingly muscular Creative Artists Agency, Mr. Ovitz is all but unknown outside of Hollywood's clannish creative community. Inside it, however, he is respected and feared, admired and loathed, courted and contended with as are few others." Cieply proclaimed CAA to be "the predominant broker of Hollywood talent and story material," noting that the agency "has a grip on an unusual share of the most sought-after actors and directors in film—Sylvester Stallone, Dustin Hoffman, Robert Redford, Jane Fonda, and Sydney Pollack among them."

The story marked a critical turning point for Michael Ovitz. His hope of remaining outside the glare of publicity had been dashed. His secret was out, making December 19, 1986 one of the most pivotal days in his life. The curtain had risen on one of Hollywood's great untold stories, and Ovitz wondered what it would mean both for him personally and for CAA. Would his power grow or dissipate under the inevitable public scrutiny? How would he cope with all of the attention that the media would increasingly shower upon him? Would the title "the most powerful individual in Hollywood" prove to be a blessing or a curse?

Just how much power did Michael Ovitz *really* possess? Did he, for example, have the power to single-handedly decide whether or not a movie would be made? The answer is no, he did not. Like anyone else in Hollywood who was seeking to promote a movie project, Ovitz had to discuss and negotiate, tempt and cajole—and push and push. What distinguished him from most other "players," however, was the zeal and persistence he exhibited when he really believed in a project. Of course, even such unbridled tenacity couldn't guarantee that a film would get made. Yet it remained true that when Michael Ovitz decided to pursue something, he never let up, and that often it was his persistence alone that became the deciding factor in whether or not a movie got made. Ovitz's dedication to *Tootsie, Gorillas in the Mist,* and countless other films brought those projects to the screen, period. In 1986, the same intensity of dedication brought to life another movie project that became one of the most talked-about films of our time.

A television writer named Barry Morrow had put together a story of a materialistic salesman who discovers, in the wake of his father's death, that he has an autistic brother. Autism is a neurological handicap that afflicts 4 in 10,000 people and is characterized by self-isolating, compulsive behavior. The autistic brother in this story is a "savant" as well; like 1 percent of all autistics, he has an incredible ability to do such things as multiply huge numbers at the drop of a hat or memorize half of a phone book.

Morrow pitched the story to Jon Peters and Peter Guber early in 1986. Peters and Guber liked the story and offered it to Warner Brothers, who turned it down thinking it was just too similar to another film it was making—by the name of *Forrest Gump!* But Robert Lawrence, president of United Artists, bought the story from Guber-Peters after hearing it pitched for just 15 minutes.

Chosen to direct the film was Martin Brest, who had directed the smash hit film *Beverly Hills Cop* (1984). Dustin Hoffman would play the "high-level autistic" Raymond Babbitt, and Tom Cruise would play his brother Charlie. The film, which would rise to such critical and commercial acclaim, was to be called *Rain Man*.

There had been some talk that Jack Nicholson was being considered to co-star with Hoffman. But Paula Wagner, Tom Cruise's agent at CAA, read the *Rain Man* script. "You'll think I'm crazy," she told Cruise, "but you should play this character." She felt, however, that the autistic man's brother, described in the script as being 46, would simply have to be made younger if Cruise, then 24, was going to be given the role. She sent Cruise the script, and then she and Cruise went to see Ovitz. Cruise had competition. Dustin Hoffman wanted actor Mickey Rourke to play the Cruise role. But Ovitz prevailed. "Mike fought for me," Cruise declared, "and they cast me in it."

Not only had Tom Cruise been hungering for just such a dramatic role, but he had yearned to do a film with Hoffman for as long as he could remember. Cruise and Hoffman had first met in a Cuban restaurant in New York a year earlier, as Cruise had lunch with his younger sister. Hoffman was performing on Broadway at the time in *Death of a Salesman*, and Cruise had been having trouble getting tickets to the show. Arranging for Cruise and his sister to see the show, Hoffman not only took care of the tickets but invited the two to come backstage after his performance. "We should work together," Hoffman told the young actor. "Yeah, right," Cruise said to himself, figuring that to be a pipe dream at best.

Back to *Rain Man*. The chosen director, Martin Brest, had tried for months to get excited about the film, but at last concluded that it was still about "two schmucks in a car." He dropped out of the project. Michael Ovitz, on the other hand, had a vested interest in getting this movie made. He had convinced two important clients, Hoffman and Cruise, to commit to the project. Thus Ovitz, along with Tony Thomopoulos, then chairman of United Artists, and Bert Fields, Hoffman's attorney, worked doggedly to keep the picture alive.

Tootsie director Sydney Pollack then was brought in as director, but eventually dropped out. Next up was Steven Spielberg. He had been eager to work with Dustin Hoffman, and he thought the movie felt like a $100 million box-office winner; but he felt obligated to honor a previous commitment to direct the final entry in the *Indiana Jones* trilogy (*Indiana Jones and the Last Crusade*). Pollack rejoined the project but found that he still wasn't happy with the script, especially with the latter part of the picture when the two characters are in a car on their way to Las Vegas. "Each time a director fell out," says Tony Thomopoulos, "it added fuel to the fire, because my management didn't think that a director could find a creative way to deal with this picture." And yet for the better part of a year, and while four screenwriters worked feverishly in an attempt to perfect the script, Ovitz kept Dustin Hoffman and Tom Cruise excited about the project, and true believers in the picture.

Finally, Ovitz turned to his long-time client Barry Levinson. The movie *Diner* had launched him as a major film director in 1982, and then in 1987 he directed *Good Morning, Vietnam,* which was a big hit for Disney. *Rain Man* would be his sixth picture. Explaining to Levinson that Sydney Pollack was having problems with the script, Ovitz asked him to read it and then to consult with Pollack. At the time, Levinson was just off to the desert for a few days of vacation. During the car ride he explained the story to his wife Diana and another couple. They told Levinson that the story sounded great. His wife told Levinson that he should direct the movie, but he explained to her that he was only reading it for Michael Ovitz. Meanwhile, Ovitz was trying to convince Pollack to remain with the project. As Pollack noted: "Michael begged me to do the movie. *Begged* me! But he had no influence, and finally I said, 'I don't want to do it.' " When Pollack pulled out of the project, this time for good, Ovitz asked Levinson to meet with Tom Cruise.

The two met at Cruise's home. Cruise remembers: "We had been working on the project for two years. I was nervous that the project wouldn't get made. The script needed work. 'So you're really going to make this movie?' I asked Barry. And he said, 'Yes, we'll start shooting in six weeks.' " Whereas other directors had seen it as being the big weakness in the picture, Levinson regarded "the second act," in which the two men travel in a car, as being its greatest strength. He saw both the humor and the emotion in it. Thus, when Tom Cruise called Dustin Hoffman, and then Paula Wagner, and finally Michael Ovitz, and asked each of them the same question—"Are we really going to make this movie?"—all of them said "Yes!"

Of Ovitz's role in getting *Rain Man* made, Levinson has this to say: "He believed strongly in the piece. He kept Tom Cruise and Dustin Hoffman together when it kept falling apart from one director to another. He didn't let it die. It's always an easy thing in this business. When an element doesn't work, you abandon the project and go to something else. But he never let it go. He had this kind of conviction that it would work." Adds Tony Thomopoulos: "Ovitz wanted this to happen, and he wasn't going to let anything stop him. It seemed like many a day when it wasn't going to work. But he focused on it and focused on it. We felt like we were two people with our backs against the wall, fighting everybody off. We were propping each other up." Thomopoulos is right about that: He and Ovitz had constantly heard from people in the industry that *Rain Man* should be a TV movie, not a feature film.

So, what was it that drove Ovitz to make such a trouble-plagued movie? What made him feel that *Rain Man* would be a triumph, when so many others had their doubts? "I absolutely loved the script," Ovitz explains. "I loved the relationship between the two guys: the hustler brother who is a total shark but who finds some soul through his long-lost autistic brother." Ovitz also recalls how he worked with autistic children as part of his college psychology program, and had always been moved by their plight. Then, too, the relationship between Raymond and Charlie Babbitt reminded Ovitz of his relationship with his brother Mark: "We struggled in our relationship, but now we're okay." (Since both brothers work in the entertainment industry but one is far more powerful and far more widely known than the other, that struggle certainly is understandable.)

When *Rain Man* was about to be released, MGM revealed that it had less faith in its potential than Ovitz did, for it cut back on the number of theaters in which it would play. Ovitz urged MGM to reconsider that move, and did in fact convince them to increase the number of theaters where the movie would appear. The movie ended up making almost $87 million, and became the top-earning movie of 1988.

"*Rain Man* belongs to a lot of people," said producer Mark Johnson, as he hoisted the Oscar for the Best Picture of 1988 on the stage of the Shrine Auditorium in Los Angeles in the spring of 1989. Also picking up Oscars were Barry Levinson as Best Director, Dustin Hoffman as Best Actor, and Barry Morrow and Ron Bass for Best Original Screenplay. When Dustin Hoffman delivered his tear-filled acceptance speech, he made sure that he mentioned Michael Ovitz and the dedication he had shown in getting *Rain Man* made. Later Hoffman acknowledged that "the film would have been shelved if it hadn't been for Mike Ovitz. It wouldn't have happened without him."

I᙭ WAS RARE for Michael Ovitz to actually discover talent. On occasion he did strike gold, as in the case of Tom Cruise. But on the whole Ovitz thought it safer and far more appropriate for an agency such as CAA to sign established film and television stars as clients, and then push their careers as far as they could go. But every once in a while he did come upon someone whom he thought could become a big star. On one occasion, such a "discovery" was made in his very own home.

When Michael Ovitz met Steven Seagal, the tall, dark, muscular martial arts expert with the distinctive ponytail had no acting experience at all. The most time he had spent on a studio lot was his advising Sean Connery on martial-arts techniques for one of Connery's films. Seagal was born in Detroit in 1952, then moved to Los Angeles at the age of nine. Over the ensuing years he spent many hours developing his martial-arts skills. Indeed, at the age of 17 he traveled to Japan, where, for the next 15 years, he studied and then taught aikido.

Upon returning to the United States, he began to advise Connery. As for Michael Ovitz, he had spent years performing a variety of martial-arts routines, and by this time he was getting a little bored with the techniques he had mastered and was ready to be sold on something new. He had read about aikido, a very advanced form of martial arts, and thought that it sounded like it was worth pursuing. An acquaintance, upon hearing of Ovitz's interest in aikido, told him that he really should meet a young man named Steven Seagal, who had been studying and teaching aikido in Japan for many years. Seagal visited Ovitz at his Brentwood home, and began to give him lessons at $50 a shot.

Like countless others in Hollywood, Seagal aspired to a movie career. But he was broke, and had little hope. Ovitz lent him some money to tide him over, and offered to call Terry Semel at Warner Brothers. Ovitz pitched Semel cleverly: "Clint Eastwood is in his sixties. Here's a guy in his thirties. He moves like a gazelle. He looks incredible. I've got a hunch about him." Ovitz arranged for Seagal to demonstrate his martial-arts skills to Semel in person. Seagal set up an actual confrontation, in which four men attacked him with butcher knives; in Bruce Lee fashion, Seagal sent the four men flying off into the air, and left Semel shaking his head in awe. Once he had dispensed with his adversaries, Seagal walked up to Semel, shook his hand, and walked away, every inch the cowboy hero walking off into the sunset.

Needless to say, Semel was bowled over. On the basis of Seagal's bravura performance, Ovitz and Semel structured a five-picture deal for the aikido instructor. At that time Warner was financing and distributing quite a number of low-budget action movies starring Chuck Norris and others, and Semel figured he had on his hands another big star for such movies. He came up with $8 million to fund Seagal's first movie, *Above the Law*, which appeared in 1988. Other movies starring Seagal quickly followed: in 1990, *Hard to Kill* and *Marked for Death* (one of the top-grossing films of the year); in 1991, *Out for Justice;* and *Under Siege* in 1992, *On Deadly Ground* in 1994, and *Executive Decision* in 1996.

As 1986 WAS winding to a close, Ovitz kept reaching higher and higher. By the end of August, he had finally gained majority ownership of the company he had dominated for the past decade. In June of 1986, Martin Baum had agreed to relinquish his share of the business, and two months later, Rowland Perkins did the same (both remained at CAA as agents). As a result, Ovitz owned 55 percent of the company; Meyer and Haber each owned 22.5 percent.

But even gaining financial dominance of CAA was not enough. He wanted to reach beyond the talent-agency business. He wanted to be on the cutting edge of any and every trend that was shaping American culture and society. He felt sure that the new technologies were going to transform American culture and, specifically, the world of entertainment. Considering himself as he did to be the entertainment world's most insightful entrepreneur, he figured that it made sense for him to link up personally and professionally with his counterpart in the computer world, the young man named Bill Gates.

Head of Microsoft, Bill Gates, in 1987 only 31 years old, was *the* whiz kid of the computer world. By figuring out how to provide personal computers with the necessary operating software to perform a wide variety of functions, Gates had almost single-handedly enabled ordinary people to make real use of their home and office computers. Ovitz was convinced that whatever Gates was doing, and soon would be doing, in the computer field would have many wonderful applications to the entertainment industry, even if he had no real idea as to *how* that was going to happen. It made enormous sense to him to get in on the ground floor, regardless of the direction in which visionaries like Gates ended up taking the computer culture. Ovitz wanted to meet this *wunderkind,* and hoped to do some business with him.

He knew that Sandy Climan, who was helping Ovitz with the financial side of the agency business, was friendly with Gates's colleague Steve Ballmer, and so Ovitz asked Climan to arrange a meeting for him with Gates. Ovitz and Gates met at a Japanese restaurant in Seattle and seemed to hit it off very nicely. Sandy Climan and Steve Ballmer were there as well. The dinner lasted for four hours. Every once in a while Gates and Ballmer would ask in a lighthearted way what on earth a couple of Hollywood talent agents thought they had to do with Microsoft. But as Ovitz talked about the way in which the entertainment world was gear-ing up to embrace the coming technologies, Gates began to sense that perhaps he and Michael Ovitz did have some common ground under their feet. As for Ovitz, he found Gates to be brilliant, and believed that CAA would benefit enormously if it had Gates on, and at, its side. More specifically, what Ovitz had in mind was for Microsoft and Creative Artists to enter into a business partnership to build interactive products that were perfectly in sync with the emerging media technologies. It would be Hollywood and the personal computer taking a ride into the future together. "I wanted to be the Hollywood gateway to Microsoft," Ovitz recalled. "I said, 'We'll be your eyes and ears.' "

Gates was amenable to some kind of arrangement, and even seemed to be prepared to make CAA Microsoft's principal partner in Hollywood. Ovitz, however, thought that Gates had not gone far enough. He wanted Gates to announce at a press conference that CAA would become Microsoft's *exclusive* partner in Hollywood. But that, Gates was not prepared to do. Part of the reason may have been Ovitz's "paltry" offer to earmark "just" $50 million for the new startup joint venture. "I tried to tie him up," Ovitz recalls, "but he was too smart for me. He saw what I was trying to do. I could never find any common ground. His assets dwarfed mine. I didn't have any assets. It was one of the reasons I wanted to get out of the agency business."

Ovitz's aides were disappointed that the project had slipped through the agency's hands; it was to be regretted, they felt, that Ovitz hadn't been willing to compromise a little by agreeing to becoming Gates's principal, but not exclusive, Hollywood partner. That would have enabled the venture to go forward, and there is no telling how far into the future Microsoft and CAA might have gone together. But Ovitz wanted Gates all to himself. He didn't want to share the young phenom with anyone else in Hollywood.

Michael Ovitz had been able to get his way with just about everyone in Hollywood. But on this one occasion, he had been stymied. The battlefield was a Japanese restaurant, and the contestants were the most powerful figure in Hollywood and the dominant figure in the whole arena of the new technologies. Of course these two really weren't engaged in battle at all; they were simply circling one another like two prize fighters, as they tried to figure out whether it made sense for them to join forces in order to better ward off their rivals. Ovitz wanted in, but Gates didn't like the look of CAA's small-time ante. Still, Michael Ovitz wasn't about to back down. Just because he couldn't get Bill Gates to play on his team didn't mean he was going to stop exploring ways of merging Hollywood with the world of technology.

IN APRIL 1995, Microsoft and DreamWorks SKG, the new entertainment group controlled by David Geffen, Jeffrey Katzenberg, and Steven Spielberg, formed an electronic-entertainment joint venture to be known as DreamWorks Interactive. The new 50-50 partnership was precisely what Michael Ovitz had envisioned for CAA and Microsoft.

Then, in December 1996, CAA and Intel unveiled the CAA/Intel Media Lab, hoping to capitalize upon the growing desire on the part of computer software specialists to turn the personal computer into an entertainment medium. This too bore a resemblance to the original Microsoft–CAA deal, as envisioned by Ovitz.

Much of the Ovitz family's life centered around baseball. The fifteen-year-old Michael is third from the right in front in this 1961 photo.

Michael met his future wife Judy Reich when both were college students at UCLA. They were married on August 3, 1969, soon after he began working at the William Morris Agency.

Creative Artists Agency was founded January 1975, and eventually grew to be the most formidable institution in Hollywood. Shown here are the five founders: Rowland Perkins (far left), Bill Haber (third from left), Michael Rosenfeld Sr. (third from right), Michael Ovitz (second from right), and Ron Meyer (far right). Also shown are Phil Weltman (second from left) and Marty Baum (fourth from left).

At their first meeting in 1981, Michael Ovitz thought 19-year-old Tom Cruise had a star-studded future. Ovitz enticed Cruise to become a CAA client by offering to find him work with the biggest actors and directors of the day, and Ovitz delivered on his promises.

By the time Ovitz signed Robert Redford in 1981, the ruggedly handsome actor had already won fame for playing the Sundance Kid to Paul Newman's Butch Cassidy in Butch Cassidy and the Sundance Kid *in 1969. After joining CAA, Redford starred in* The Natural *(1984),* Out of Africa *(1985),* Sneakers *(1992), and* Indecent Proposal *(1993).*

CAA gained great momentum when superstar Paul Newman signed as a client in 1980. He went on to star in Absence of Malice *(1981) and* The Verdict *(1982) and then won an Oscar for* The Color of Money *(1986).*

Michael Ovitz and his staff stand in the atrium of the CAA office building at the corner of Wilshire and Little Santa Monica Boulevards in Los Angeles. Opened in 1989, the I. M. Pei–designed offices have become one of the landmarks of the city.

Having the finest actors on its client list helped give CAA a reputation as the most powerful talent agency in Hollywood. One of those actors, Tom Hanks, starred in A League of Their Own (1992) and won an Oscar for his role in Philadelphia (1993). He is shown here with Michael and Judy Ovitz.

A serious art collector, Ovitz was introduced to the art world by Arne Glimcher (left), President of the PaceWildenstein Art Gallery. In time, Ovitz developed one of the finest private art collections in the United States. Thanks to Glimcher, Ovitz came to know many leading artists, including Julian Schnabel (center).

One artist Ovitz admires is Roy Lichtenstein, who, at Ovitz's request, painted a huge mural that hangs on a wall in the atrium of the CAA office building. Shown here with the Ovitzes are Lichtenstein (center), painter Ellsworth Kelly, and Roy's wife Dorothy.

The President comes calling: One of the more memorable days of CAA history was December 4, 1993, when President Bill Clinton made a fund-raising appearance in the atrium of the CAA office building.

CAA client Marty Scorsese, best known for directing Raging Bull *(1980),* The Last Temptation of Christ *(1988),* Goodfellas *(1990),* and Cape Fear *(1991).*

Ovitz often vacationed together with CAA clients. Here he and Judy appear with Dustin and Lisa Hoffman, along with Diana and Barry Levinson in Aspen, Colorado.

A light moment. Director Steven Spielberg (left), Dustin Hoffman, and Michael Ovitz took time out at a party to do some juggling.

A partnership in name only: Attending the November 1, 1996 premiere of Ransom, *Disney President Ovitz and Disney Chairman Michael Eisner appear, in public at least, to be getting along. In fact, by the time of this premiere, Eisner had arranged for Ovitz to leave the company after the first of the year.*

12

No Photos, Please

Ovitz's dreams of exploiting the new technologies were still off in the future. Meanwhile, he was taking all possible steps to reach his goal of creating the world's greatest talent agency. Although he had of course been the dominant factor in the agency's success thus far, Michael Ovitz was by no means running a one-man show at CAA. He continued to groom a set of agents molded in his image by empowering them to handle major clients, by encouraging them to work together, and by paying them huge sums so as to ensure their loyalty. And he sought to strengthen the agent force by hiring bright new faces. Two of these, Bryan Lourd and Kevin Huvane, had been working for William Morris in February 1988. Lourd represented Candice Bergen, star of the hit TV show *Murphy Brown*. Lourd and Huvane were close friends, so much so, in fact, that they even had made a pact that they would only leave William Morris together. Thus, when Rick Nicita, a CAA agent, phoned Lourd, and Ron Meyer phoned Huvane, asking each Morris agent if he would like to move to CAA, each answered that he would consider leaving Morris only if the other came along as well.

Lourd knew little of CAA, only that it was a "mythical place," and knew even less about Ovitz. Then Michael Ovitz invited him to breakfast. During their three-and-a-half-hour meal, Ovitz asked Lourd about his parents and about art and philosophy, but they talked about agenting only in passing. At one stage Ovitz said encouragingly: "You can do whatever you want to do, as long as you do it well and stay focused and participate for the good of the overall group." Lourd, who had felt alone and astray at William Morris, was excited: "This guy knew more about me than anyone at Morris had ever asked or known in five years. He was inspirational. He could talk about any subject." Two days later, Lourd and Huvane joined CAA.

At Morris, Lourd had grown frustrated, watching helplessly as CAA stole client after client away from his agency. He had no idea how CAA was able to find so many good roles for its clients. All he knew was that his own agency's strategy was faltering. Morris was too passive, he thought, too dependent upon the willingness of studio and network executives to divulge what roles were available in their upcoming projects. The fact of the matter was that getting the studios and television networks to supply such information was very slow going.

But now that he had joined CAA, Lourd found himself plunged into three-hour staff conferences, at which 40 agents sat around a table and employed a very different strategy from the one he had seen at Morris: "The sessions were electric. We talked about what was going on in town and how to control it, and how to use that information to service our clients better." CAA seized the initiative, trying to match actors and actresses with scripts that the agency learned about even before the studios or television networks did. "That was exciting," Lourd says. "It was much more like being a producer." Lourd began to see just why CAA always was snatching clients from William Morris. He found that CAA agents really did share information, and that no one got into trouble for doing so. At first he found the CAA work-style strange, for it was not at all what he had been used to. But in time he warmed up to the concept, and began to work closely with the other agents.

Lourd and Huvane got especially close to Richard Lovett, David O'Connor, and Jay Moloney, three other successful young CAA agents. Lovett and O'Connor had been friends since their days together in the CAA mail room. The five agents were at the same place in their lives: All were young, single, and largely unencumbered, free to attend the required Hollywood events, free to socialize together, and to talk shop hour after hour.

In 1988 the five agents began to meet at one of their homes for three to four hours every Saturday, a social get-together that often turned to business. At first, according to Bryan Lourd, Ovitz seemed confused about why the agents were meeting. Although he had encouraged his agents to work as a team, what these agents were up to may have smelled a bit too much like the plotting that he and his four partners had engaged in back in 1974, when they had defected from William Morris and established their own talent agency. "He was slightly put off by it," Lourd recalls. "But as he saw the results of those meetings, he was happy. He trusted us." Lourd invited him to attend, but Ovitz always said he was too busy.

In fact, Ovitz reacted to the coalescing of these agents with a mixture of pride and unease. He was proud that these young men cared so much about their work that they were prepared to take it home with them. But he was made uncomfortable by their independence, and by the possibility that they would decide to do what he and his partners had done: jump ship, and establish their own agency. As Jay Moloney notes, "There's part of him that's always cautious if he doesn't feel he's in control. He didn't know for sure how committed we were to him, right up to the end." According to David O'Connor: "Michael reacted ninety percent positively to the fact that we were meeting with each other; ten percent of him was a little concerned that we could go off and form our own company." In truth, Ovitz need not have been concerned.

The "Young Turks," as they came to be called, were not about to revolt or defect. They had it too good at CAA. Take David O'Connor. He had started at CAA in 1983, earning $1000 a month as a mail-room agent-trainee. Five years later, as an up-and-coming agent, he was making more money than he had ever dreamed of earning. Some of his fellow agents boasted privately that they were pocketing upwards of $1 million a year. It can be assumed that O'Connor earned close to that same million-dollar mark, whereas the salaries of agents at the other talent agencies weren't even in the same ballpark. Says O'Connor: "Michael was always very mindful to pay you more than you could possibly make in another agency or studio, if he wanted you to stay."

Though the Young Turks were too well paid to contemplate leaving CAA, they remained a source of worry for Ovitz. He would have looked upon their departure as constituting a personal failure. For a person to leave CAA was an act of supreme disloyalty to its leader, Michael Ovitz.

IT WAS IN 1987 that Michael Ovitz signed another major star, a young man who had begun his career in television, then shifted to films. Born in Chicago in 1952, Robin Williams trained on the West Coast as a stand-up comic, and gained fame as the innocent wisecracking extraterrestrial, Mork from Ork, on the television sitcom *Happy Days*. That led to a spinoff, *Mork and Mindy*, which ran for four years on ABC and in 1979 ranked number three in the ratings. Williams had had roles in seven films, but only one was a modest hit, *Moscow on the Hudson*. His career then took a nosedive, but it revived in a big way in the mid-1980s when he played the iconoclastic disk jockey, Adrian Cronauer, in the Disney hit *Good Morning, Vietnam*. Barry Levinson, that film's director, was an

Ovitz client, and Williams began to ask Levinson about Ovitz. While making his next film, *Dead Poet's Society,* Williams met Ovitz for dinner. He complained that he hadn't been getting the best scripts and that, as a result, his career had stalled. Ovitz promised to help, and Williams became a CAA client.

Williams soon did begin to see more interesting material, including a script for the movie *Hook.* "Ovitz," Williams says, "was always looking aggressively for the right scripts. He was trying to find a comedy role for me that would be suitable." Williams also was grateful to Ovitz for supporting him during a difficult period, when he was receiving a good deal of negative publicity for having a romance with his child's nanny (she would become his second wife, Marcia Williams). Marcia appreciated Ovitz's support as well: "Michael made sure to let people know they were doing the wrong thing by behaving unkindly toward me. He didn't stand on a fence." Having someone like Ovitz for an agent appealed to Williams: "There's a great power there. He was the heavy artillery. He was there when you needed a big gun."

If MICHAEL OVITZ was anything, he was consistent. He had come up with a magic formula: taking film and television performers and personally finding projects for them, rather than waiting around for offers from the studios and other outside parties. That had become CAA's modus operandi, and, as long as it stuck with it, the money was sure to keep rolling in. There was, in Ovitz's view, no reason to take on clients outside of show business. That would be to enter uncharted waters, and Ovitz had no wish to stray too far from CAA's traditional fishing grounds.

But one day, something happened to change Ovitz's mind. A tall young man approached Ovitz. Not an actor, but not just any man. In fact, his was the most recognized name in all of L.A. He was an athlete, and he wanted Michael Ovitz to represent him. The only trouble was, Michael Ovitz had no interest in representing athletes.

The man's real name is Earvin Johnson. Most of the world, however, calls him "Magic." Since 1979 he had been the star point guard of the Los Angeles Lakers, and he had been named the NBA's Most Valuable Player on three different occasions. He was unquestionably the most popular figure in all of Los Angeles—which is saying something, since Hollywood's denizens are not exactly unknowns.

In the summer of 1987 Johnson turned 28, and began to think about what he would do in a few years after retiring from the NBA. He had watched in dismay as his close friend Kareem Abdul-Jabbar of the Lakers ran into serious financial trouble, and had vowed to learn from his friend's mistakes. Johnson had talked to his general manager, Lon Rosen, about doing something even more entrepreneurial than what many other athletes were forced to do in their retirement. Perhaps that might assure him of financial security in his later years. But Johnson had no idea how to become entrepreneurial, nor did Rosen; but Rosen did remember reading in the newspaper about a powerful new Hollywood talent agent named Michael Ovitz. Rosen told the basketball star that Ovitz sounded like the ideal person for Johnson to talk to about getting started in business. But Rosen didn't want to approach Ovitz cold. Johnson said he knew someone who could make the introductions: Joe Smith, the Capitol Records chief. He was a big Lakers fan (he had had four seats at Lakers home games for 33 years) and a close Ovitz acquaintance. Over steaks at Morton's, Johnson asked Smith to smooth the way for Rosen to phone Ovitz, which Smith did. Johnson's immediate concern was to get Ovitz's help in improving the terms of the 25-year, $25 million contract that he had signed in 1984. The contract had looked fat and juicy then; now, Johnson believed that he might not have made such a good deal.

"I represent Magic Johnson," Rosen said to Ovitz over the phone one day in September.

The silence at the other end of the line confounded Rosen. Generally when he mentioned Magic's name, the response was significantly more enthusiastic.

Ovitz remarked curtly: "We don't represent sports. We do entertainment." Ovitz might as well have simply hung up. Rosen was stunned by the seeming putdown, and barely heard Ovitz as he explained that the track record of athletes going into business for themselves hadn't exactly been spectacular. Ovitz said that he didn't want to waste his time.

"Why would Magic Johnson want to work with someone like me?" Ovitz asked. *Was Ovitz softening?* Rosen couldn't tell.

"Because," Rosen replied, "he wants to be more than an athlete, he wants to be a businessman, to be marketed as something different. He wants to stand out," Rosen told Ovitz.

There *were* things about Johnson that Ovitz admired, especially the way he handled himself on the basketball court. He was no hog but was always passing the ball, trying to help others on the court. Indeed, Johnson's style of play had become a metaphor for Ovitz's management style at CAA. He wasn't sure what he could do for this man, but he *was* Magic Johnson, and for that reason alone Ovitz thought he ought to at least have the courtesy to meet with him.

Rosen was thrilled to hear that Ovitz would in fact see Johnson.

On the eve of the get-together, Ovitz told his friend Joe Smith: "I'm not going to sell myself to him. Does he know who I am?"

Smith nodded.

"Remember, I'm going to play it cool." Smith saw through all of this talk, and believed that Ovitz just might agree to take on Magic Johnson as a client.

Johnson, all six feet nine inches of him, walked into the meeting in Ovitz's office feeling out of place. This definitely was not home court. He felt strange. But Joe Smith had assured him that Ovitz was a great guy, and would be friendly toward him. He had nothing to worry about.

The agent and the basketball star shook hands. Johnson gave one of his famous grins. Ovitz, a foot shorter than Johnson, looked up at his guest and before the two men even sat down, blurted out: "I don't deal with athletes." He liked to watch athletes, he said, but he didn't think athletes were "into" business, that they were able to commit themselves to it. He had worked with entertainment figures, Ovitz explained, because they brought in more money than any athlete could.

Few people intimidated Magic Johnson. He was big and muscular and powerful, and most people looked up to him—literally.

But now, Johnson did feel intimidated. He felt in total awe of this man who seemed to be putting an end to a meeting that hadn't even begun.

"I want you to help me," Magic Johnson said quietly. "I've always wanted to be in business." It was all he could think to say, even though the words sounded hollow and meaningless.

"Earvin, you want to be in business," Ovitz replied. "Okay, I'm going to talk to you for five or ten minutes." And he did. Ovitz asked some questions, then abruptly said: "A number of people have come into my office. Athletes. But I never represented them. Well, let me think about it." The meeting had lasted all of 40 minutes.

Johnson walked out of the meeting feeling that Ovitz had just shot him down. And the whole meeting had been bizarre. The NBA star wasn't used to having people tell him they had more important clients, who made them more money than Johnson could. "Ovitz was letting me know I'd be a small potato," says Johnson. "I came into his office six feet nine inches tall, but when I walked out I was five-nine. He made me feel that small." It was a learning experience for Johnson. "Welcome to the real world," he told himself. "When you're an athlete, you think you're so big and everybody is happy to talk to you and to do business with you. He just let me know that's not the case. You had to have something going for you other than the fact that you could shoot baskets." Yet Johnson admired the man for having been so direct and honest with him. "I learned a lot from that first meeting."

Johnson assumed that he would never hear from Ovitz again. He forgot about the meeting. It was no fun being humiliated. If Ovitz didn't want him, he didn't want Ovitz.

A few weeks later, Michael Ovitz called Magic Johnson. He said very little, just asked Magic to come in. Now Johnson was confused. Hadn't Ovitz shot him down at that first meeting? True, Ovitz had said he would give some thought to representing Johnson, but the basketball player had assumed that Ovitz was just being polite. Well, if Ovitz wanted to see him, maybe there was some hope after all.

This time when the two men met, the atmosphere was different. Johnson could tell that right from the outset. Ovitz's original hesitancy and discomfort had given way to a genuine warmth. Ovitz talked about everything but business, asking about the basketball player's family, what he wanted out of life. "It was interesting," Johnson recalls. "He wanted to know about *me*." Usually, those who got the chance to talk to Johnson wanted to dwell on his moves on the court. Johnson suddenly found himself opening up to Ovitz about his father and mother, about what it was like growing up with six sisters and three brothers, how he had worked all of his life since he was 10 years old, how devoted he was to his family. Ovitz was indeed being warm and personable, but he also was testing Johnson. Ovitz had always thought of athletes as being one-dimensional, as people who could talk for hours about what they had done or were doing in their sport but who weren't terribly articulate when it came to discussing other aspects of their lives. But as he listened to Johnson, he sensed something different in him. He seemed to care genuinely for his family. He seemed to be a guy who was capable of making a commitment. Ovitz made up his mind on the spot.

"I'm going to take you on."

Again Ovitz was rewarded with the big Magic Johnson grin.

Their third meeting was held at Le Dome Restaurant on Sunset Boulevard. Ovitz and Rosen arrived first, and were soon joined by CAA's Sandy Climan. Five minutes later Magic Johnson strolled in. People in the restaurant stood up and gave him a standing ovation. It happened a great deal to Johnson, but Ovitz was amazed. "That was when we hooked Michael Ovitz," Lon Rosen would say later. Michael Ovitz represented the most glamorous stars in Hollywood. Yet when most of them walked into a restaurant, while some patrons might whisper or stare, they would never actually stand up and applaud. Magic Johnson seemed to be someone very special. For his part, Johnson was equally impressed by Ovitz: "When we started meeting in restaurants, you could see how he positioned himself at his table where everybody knows the flow comes toward him. He didn't want to hide. It was very calculated."

During their meal, Ovitz explained how he planned to market his new client. He saw Johnson as more than an athlete, as someone possessing movie-star-like popularity, and he wanted to market him accordingly. To market Johnson as merely an athlete would have meant finding a job for him in his post-retirement years as a coach, TV commentator, or a company spokesperson. Ovitz had bigger plans for him. But as exciting as these plans were, if they were to be made realities Johnson would require a good deal of polishing. Ovitz began with the fundamentals.

"This is what I want you to do," Ovitz told the basketball star. "Throw out all those *Sports Illustrated*s and all those sports pages. If you're going to go into business, here's how we're going to start. I want you to look at *BusinessWeek, The Wall Street Journal,* and the business section of the *Los Angeles Times.* I want you to start reading. You don't have to read each article. Just read the first and last paragraph. Start learning about business. See what interests you. If you don't find an article interesting, don't read it." Ovitz also told Johnson that he wanted him to study tapes of his own interviews, in order to improve his speaking style. After he had read some articles and perused those videotapes, they would talk again, Ovitz said. Of course Ovitz's assumption was that Johnson knew nothing about business and little about public speaking, but Johnson didn't consider Ovitz's suggestions degrading. He simply was excited to have Michael Ovitz as a mentor.

Soon thereafter, Ovitz sent copies of *BusinessWeek, Fortune, Newsweek, Time,* and *The Wall Street Journal* to Magic Johnson, who began reading the material; he found the whole experience unsettling: "I was intimidated more by Michael than by the magazines and newspapers. He has that way about him that makes you feel intimidated. It took me a lot of time not to feel intimidated, and to turn it into admiration and respect."

At Ovitz's suggestion, Johnson read articles about Japanese business, as well as *The Art of War.* "He makes your mind work," Johnson observes. "He never gives you the answer. He wants you to find the answer." As part of his effort to transform Magic Johnson the L.A. Laker into Earvin Johnson the businessman, Ovitz gave him advice about how to avoid bad business experiences: "You're the best, so you have to associate with the best. No matter how much it costs you, you have to align yourself with the best accountant, the best lawyer."

In 1988, Ovitz helped Johnson to renegotiate his contract with the Lakers. But if Ovitz was going to restructure Magic's contract, it appeared that he would have to find a way of getting around the NBA's salary-cap provisions, which placed strict limits on the salaries that a team could pay its players. In a meeting with David Stern, the NBA Commissioner, Ovitz suggested that the NBA salary cap wasn't meant to apply to players of Johnson's caliber. "He transcends the game," Ovitz said. "Rules are rules," Stern responded, in a friendly manner. Stern recalls that his talk with Ovitz was not hostile: "There was a fair amount of parrying going on, some of it relatively good-natured, but we each had positions to preserve." Ovitz admitted to Stern that if he had been the head of a movie studio, he might have considered a salary cap to be a great idea, but as a talent agent he certainly would never be in favor of placing a cap on fees paid to film stars. Stern was pleasantly surprised to find Ovitz far softer than the image of him painted in the media: "He was direct, grasped the issues immediately. I had read articles that suggested some dark, brooding person. But I never saw that person."

Ovitz did some digging and discovered that the NBA's collective-bargaining agreement stipulated that a personal-service contract could not be spread over more than seven years. The NBA was forced to acknowledge that Ovitz was right about that, and thus he was able to arrange that the Lakers would pay Johnson the same $25 million but over a much shorter period: 7 years rather than 25. The restructured contract complied with the salary-cap provisions, and Johnson now was earning $3.14 million a year instead of $1 million a year as under his old contract.

Ovitz had promised Johnson that he would turn him into something more than a company spokesperson, and he delivered on that promise. In 1989, Johnson was linked up with the Pepsico Company, the parent firm of Pepsi Cola, Kentucky Fried Chicken, and Pizza Hut. Never before had an athlete been offered both the role of company spokesperson and an equity position in the company. Yet Ovitz had convinced Pepsico's executives that letting an African-American basketball star buy a distributorship would be both good for business and politically correct.

Some in Hollywood thought that Johnson would try to pursue a movie-acting career in his post-basketball days, but Ovitz, sensing that Johnson really wasn't keen to make movies, persuaded him to focus on acquiring movie theaters instead.

Ovitz paved the way for Johnson to undertake business deals in Europe as well, including one in 1989 that made him the spokesman for a processed-meat (hot dogs, ham, bologna) company. As the main dealmaker there, Ovitz had the right to take a fee from Johnson, but he waived the fee. For one thing, Johnson had other value to Ovitz, in that he added a new luster to the CAA client list. The media had begun to describe that list as "ranging from Sylvester Stallone to Magic Johnson."

Then, on October 25, 1991, Magic Johnson's world was shattered. It was on that day that he discovered that he was HIV-positive. When Johnson informed Rosen, the issue was broached whether Johnson should make a public announcement. Rosen suggested that they consult Ovitz. Rosen called Ovitz at home and let him know that he had something important to tell him, but that he wanted to do it in person. They agreed that they would talk when they met at an event that both men would be attending that weekend.

When Ovitz heard the news from Rosen, he was shocked. "I need your help," Rosen said. "It's almost impossible to handle." Ovitz called Johnson right away: "I'm here for you, and I'm here with you." He promised to make the best physicians in the field available to him. Ovitz favored the idea of having Magic make a public statement, saying that it would help many other sufferers to hear this celebrity acknowledge his own sad situation. Ovitz also suggested that the basketball star should try to help find a cure for AIDS. "Just having Ovitz there to advise," Rosen would say later, "was something we needed."

On the day of Johnson's announcement, Rosen received seven offers to have Johnson write his memoirs, each for a large sum. Rosen asked Ovitz to handle the deal, who then placed the book with Random House, the highest bidder. Random House agreed to Ovitz's proposal that it publish a separate handbook on HIV-prevention as well. Ovitz himself earned nothing from the deal, donating his fee to charity.

Once Johnson had signed on with CAA, other athletes, hearing of the Ovitz–Johnson relationship, tried to obtain the services of the super-agent as well, but he turned them down. Michael Ovitz had a soft spot for Earvin "Magic" Johnson, but he held steadfast in his general policy of not doing business with athletes.

Over time, the two men became close friends. Johnson kidded Ovitz about his habit of wearing ties all the time, and insisted that the next time they meet, he must not wear a tie. Despite Johnson's teasing, Ovitz could not break his old habits—the next time they met, Ovitz wore a tie! Magic also became friendly with Judy and the Ovitz children. Johnson played ball with Ovitz's son Chris when he was small, and danced with Kimberly Ovitz at her Bat Mitzvah.

Johnson is happy to credit Michael Ovitz for all of his business success: for prepping him for his business meetings, and for teaching him how to talk to executives. He soon overcame the fear he had felt at that intimidating first meeting in Ovitz's office. "Michael taught me more about business than anybody. The reason I am where I am is because of him. I didn't want to be just a jock. He made that a reality for me. Now I'm Mr. Johnson, a businessman. You have to deal with me like that."

Johnson retired from the NBA in the fall of 1991, after learning that he was HIV-positive. He returned briefly in the following fall, but then retired a second time. He returned again in January 1996, and re-retired later that year.

But when Magic Johnson describes his relationship with Ovitz today, the tone is still worshipful: "He taught me how to make people mesh and blend. He jokes with me now. He can loosen his tie now. I still run things by him. I still get representation from CAA. I still seek his advice. I still use the people he had introduced me to when he was still at CAA. He still has a hand in my master plan."

Earvin Johnson now owns two movie theaters—one in Los Angeles and the other in Atlanta—each theater having 12 movie screens. He also owns two shopping centers, and has recently signed a deal with Twentieth Century Fox to produce feature films and television programs. He also agreed to host a late-night talk show five nights a week on Fox television. Johnson owns a T-shirt company, and has a 5 percent interest in the Los Angeles Lakers.

IT WAS MAGIC JOHNSON'S perception of Michael Ovitz as a very powerful man in Hollywood that had drawn the basketball star into his embrace. In the early years of his career, Ovitz didn't have to work all that hard to create that perception. All he had to do was remain secretive and mysterious. Yet by the mid-1980s, it was becoming increasingly difficult for him to remain so hidden. Forces were at work in American society that would not permit Michael Ovitz to bask in his anonymity for much longer. By the end of 1986, when *The Wall Street Journal* printed the first major newspaper profile of him, the media were becoming far more interested in business personalities. And major Hollywood business figures were high on most journalists' "to do" lists. When, around 1980 and 1981, Ovitz began to sign the high-priced talent, few outside of Hollywood paid him any notice. But five years later, as movie stars became more and more powerful and demanded higher and higher salaries, the media's curiosity about the behind-the-scenes personalities who represent film and television stars was intensifying. "We agents were not supposed to become as well-known as our clients," says CAA co-founder Ron Meyer. "But the more we tried *not* to be in the press, the more the press became interested in us." Since Ovitz did think of himself as being a key figure in Hollywood, someone who knew just what was happening all over town, it was only natural that the media would gravitate to him, that it would want to know what he thought about anything and everything connected with the entertainment business.

But because CAA executives and agents had a policy of not responding to phone calls from journalists, the rumors began to fly about just what went on within the hallowed halls of Ovitz's agency.

For instance, someone reported that Ovitz was so hyper-secretive that he had banned all personal computers from CAA, fearing that computer disks containing valuable information about clients might find their way into the wrong hands. (Yes, Ovitz *was* hyper-sensitive about any possible information "leaks." But no, there never was any ban enforced upon the use of personal computers by CAA's employees.)

Someone else reported that CAA agents were being indoctrinated in Japanese business methods by means of rigorous physical exercises that the staff ran through in the atrium of the CAA building that opened in 1989. (Again, not true.)

A third report told of a special elevator in the CAA building, one meant for the exclusive use of the agency's superstar clients. (No such elevator existed.)

Finally, there was a story going around that had Ovitz ordering a custodian to work full-time on polishing the building's doors, to ensure that they were returned to a state of pristine cleanliness after every rush of entries into the building. (The only truth in that report was that there *were* a lot of shiny surfaces in the building. However, there was no custodian whose only job in life was to keep such surfaces shining.)

As a result of all these rumors, it became a commonplace to think of Ovitz as a swaggering, bullying figure who got his way by means of threats and, at times, punishments. His closest confidants, those who had seen him up close, knew that he could be difficult, but they thought the reports of his bullying were exaggerated. "Mike," says one of these confidants, "has an intimidating manner, and that can be mistaken for being threatening. But Mike is not a guy to say 'Do it this way or I'll get you.' He has an in-your-face style and has a controlling personality, but I never saw him threaten anyone." But that was probably because Ovitz cleverly did his threatening behind closed doors.

At any rate, forced as it was to rely upon second- or third-hand sources, the media had to pass along what amounted to mere rumors about Ovitz. But Ovitz himself didn't seem to mind. Even when false information found its way into newspaper articles, the effect was simply to enhance CAA's image, to make it seem larger than life. And as that *was* the effect, Ovitz had no reason to pick a fight with the media. But the minute he sensed any possibility of his image being distorted or sullied, he launched into action.

In 1984, Bob Woodward, who along with fellow *Washington Post* reporter Carl Bernstein had forced Richard Nixon to leave the White House by bringing to light the Watergate scandals, wrote a best-selling book called *Wired*. The book dealt with the life and death of actor John Belushi, and Michael Ovitz had been Belushi's agent at the time of the actor's untimely death from a drug overdose in 1982. When Ovitz learned that the book might be turned into a Hollywood film, he went into action, for he was intensely concerned that the film might portray him and/or his clients in a negative fashion. The book told the story of Belushi's rise to fame as a television and film comedian, and his eventual descent into the drug abyss. It also exposed the long-standing, well-hidden drug habits of some of Hollywood's biggest stars. When Ovitz learned that veteran producer Ed Feldman had obtained the film rights to the book, he contacted a number of his clients who had been mentioned in the book: Jim Belushi, Bill Murray, Dan Ackroyd, Robin Williams, and Robert De Niro. Ovitz then became authorized, on behalf of this group, to convey to Feldman the fact that these five clients would sue if the film sullied their characters. Ovitz hired an attorney and instructed him to tell Feldman: "We're not saying 'Don't make the film,' but if one word is inaccurate, we'll file a lawsuit." Later Ovitz would admit that he had been naive at this time: "I was stupid. I didn't understand. I was totally in love with the entertainment business, and in love with making something of myself. There was a naivete about me that people didn't understand. I didn't know John Belushi had a drug problem. As far as I was concerned, Bob Woodward was out to destroy him. But he wasn't. We had read the book, and the book was exceedingly accurate. I shouldn't have gotten them [the CAA clients] all together and done all that." In the end, the group did not file a lawsuit, and the film was made. One producer who was associated with it doubted that Ovitz really planned to file a suit, but it was troubling enough just to have Michael Ovitz fuming over a project. "While Ovitz couldn't take you to court," that producer says, "he was in a position to hurt your career in the future." Such was the perception of Ovitz's all-pervading power.

But the *Wired* experience certainly does suggest just how far Ovitz was prepared to go to keep anyone from damaging his image. He was always telling his CAA agents and others that power is something that has to be used selectively: If one just goes around threatening people all the time, that tactic will soon prove to be counterproductive. And yet at the time, Ovitz genuinely believed that having his name be part of a film that documented the drug habits of some of Hollywood's major celebrities would do him great harm. And so he ordered his lawyers into action. A decade later, he wasn't feeling very proud of that action. But then again, a decade later he wasn't too thrilled by *many* of the tactics he had employed as part of his ongoing attempt to manipulate and outmaneuver the media.

THE MORE EVASIVE Ovitz was, the more the media began to play a guessing game: What is Michael Ovitz up to? How does he operate? Few knew. Most of those whom journalists interviewed about Ovitz *acted* as if they knew, but all they really had to offer was speculation backed up by a minuscule number of facts. And often they were flat-out wrong about all of it. Ovitz suggests with much frustration that at least 50 percent of what has been written about him has been wrong. He did not say which 50 percent. To suggest that the media had gotten a good deal wrong about him was clever on Ovitz's part. What he was really saying: If you want to write something about me, don't use the media as a guide. So much of it is incorrect. Given the fact that he wasn't about to explain what the media had gotten right, and what it had gotten wrong, Ovitz had the perfect method for keeping the media from writing about him. Or so he hoped. In their own defense journalists undoubtedly would say that if mistakes about Michael Ovitz have appeared in the media, he has no one to blame for that fact but himself: He could and should have taken their phone calls and answered their questions.

As for *The Wall Street Journal* article of December 1986, it stung Ovitz sharply. He told reporter Michael Cieply that the article had damaged his relations with his CAA colleagues, apparently meaning that his colleagues felt a tad jealous that Ovitz was getting all of the credit for CAA's achievements, and they were not. But what must have hurt Ovitz even more was the brutal fact that he was no longer Hollywood's greatest *secret* agent. Slowly but surely, other segments of the media were beginning to track him down. *Spy* magazine was the most dogged and the most critical. Yet no one in Hollywood, Ovitz included, took *Spy* magazine very seriously. Few in town read it. And yet one magazine that *was* read in Hollywood had much more of an effect on Ovitz. This was *Premiere,* founded by Susan Lyne in 1988.

"We had the cheeky idea," Lyne explains, "that we would cover Hollywood as journalists the way I had at *New Times* and *The Village Voice.*" That means, very aggressively. Lyne gave reporter Kim Masters the assignment of finding out what was cooking over at CAA. After Masters had phoned Ovitz a few times, asking him probing questions about life at CAA, Ovitz got in touch with Susan Lyne. There were a few strained conversations, most of them having to do with Ovitz's desire to stay out of the news. "He hated the press," says Susan Lyne. "He just didn't understand why he had to deal with it. He really believed he was a private person, not a public persona." Lyne tried to explain to Ovitz that his fight to remain anonymous had to be a losing battle right from the start: "You are *not* a private individual. You are the head of the largest and most significant talent agency in Hollywood. You may want not to be covered, but that won't happen. Either you find a comfort zone, or the media is going to be very antagonistic."

It wasn't going to be easy for the intensely private Mr. Ovitz to find a "comfort zone," but he did begin to admit to himself that Susan Lyne might have a point. And so grudgingly, with about as much enthusiasm as someone about to jump into a den of wolves, Michael Ovitz decided to shift his strategy vis-à-vis the media, but only ever-so-slightly. "After *The Wall Street Journal* article," he says, "I started to get more attention than I deserved. I decided, rather than try to create a vacuum, that I would talk to these people. The press for me has been up and down. I thought by talking it would be better than not. There was a finite number of people covering the entertainment industry, not like now [1996]. You didn't have the media frenzy that you have now." Still, Ovitz remained uncomfortable, and basically distrustful of journalists. For the most part he refused to grant interviews. And on those rare occasions when he did consent to talk to reporters, he insisted on not being quoted; and even when he had been assured that his confidences were being taken only on a "background" basis, he tended to be vague. "Ovitz was brilliant," says a reporter for a major news magazine, "but you could never learn *why* he was so brilliant from talking to him."

Ovitz still believed that his best strategy was to keep the press from writing about him. And he adopted the unusual tactic of requiring any photographer taking pictures of him to sign a release stating that, once one of his or her pictures had been published, any further use of that photo required Ovitz's permission. "I figured," he explains, "that if they didn't have any pictures, it would be hard for them to write about me. If *Spy* magazine couldn't get my picture, I thought they wouldn't write about me—but it didn't stop them. I dreamt I could be an important business person without anyone knowing about it, which is really naive. But I also didn't foresee that the press had an interest in people behind the scenes."

But steering clear of the media isn't just a business strategy for Ovitz. He seems to feel a deep-seated aversion to having his picture taken, period. "Taking a photo of him makes him horribly self-conscious," says Anna Perez, his spokesperson in the 1990s. One can hardly avoid the conclusion that this intensely secretive man simply doesn't like to be *watched.*

Ovitz ALSO ALWAYS has made it clear that he doesn't want his business friends to speak about him to the media. The strategy, clearly, has been based on the supposition that, lacking any reliable information, a self-respecting editor simply wouldn't be able to run stories on him. Thus Ovitz's friends, when approached about Ovitz by an interviewer, always comply with his wishes, often without even consulting him beforehand. They see no benefit to airing their views of Ovitz in public, even if the comments are flattering ones.

Sometimes the temptation to talk to a reporter is too strong, but even then a chill factor is at work. *Time* magazine reported that when the heads of two film studios, and one of Ovitz's own senior employees, were asked what they thought of him, all three men sang his praises but only "on background," fearful that Ovitz might be angry with them for having said anything at all. And even then all three had second thoughts, calling Ovitz to confess preemptively that they had talked to a reporter. Such is Ovitz's power, that even his friends are frightened to death to say something *positive* about him in the press!

With the media interest in CAA rising and rising, Ovitz took the unprecedented step, in October 1988, of hiring a New York–based public relations firm, Howard J. Rubenstein Associates Inc., which could boast of having as clients such tycoons as Donald Trump and Rupert Murdoch. But even before Rubenstein took over as CAA's spokesperson, he quickly put to rest any hope the media might have had that CAA and all of its clandestine ways was about to become an open book. "The relationship," indicated Rubenstein, "won't be in the traditional way of seeking publicity for CAA." In other words, the CAA policy of not disclosing the details of its operations would remain in full force. Rubenstein noted that there had been too much inaccurate reporting about the agency. Specifically, some reports with regard to CAA's packaging of film projects had been misstated. But what had especially annoyed Ovitz was *Spy* magazine's publication, the month before, of what purported to be the complete CAA client list, one of the agency's biggest and, until then, best-kept secrets. He argued that the listing was inaccurate, and had forced CAA agents to apologize to clients whose names had been omitted. In order to avoid such misstatements in the future, Rubenstein now would be answering reporters' phone calls.

Then, in December of that year, Tina Brown, at that time the editor of *Vanity Fair,* found out for herself that the hiring of a spokesperson had indeed not altered CAA's attitude toward the media. Hoping to do a major profile on Ovitz, she sent him a letter that asked him to cooperate with the story. "I was surprised to hear . . . that you are on the point of 'breaking your silence to the press in *Premiere,*' . . . [which] would be rather like Marlon Brando choosing *Falcon Crest* as a vehicle for a comeback." Brown praised Ovitz's "aura of leadership" and "gifted sense of talent, material, timing, plus, of course, extraordinary business acumen," and even compared Ovitz to the legendary Irving Thalberg. Brown explained in the letter that she was too busy to do the profile herself, but suggested writer Jesse Kornbluth as someone "knowledgeably well disposed toward" Ovitz's CAA. She assured Ovitz that she would be "watching over [the article] and shaping it every step of the way." And yet despite all of that, Ovitz refused to be interviewed, and Brown decided against the story.

Nonetheless, CAA's love-affair with secrecy was beginning to take its toll. Within the agency, people were beginning to question the validity of the "no comment" approach, especially since the effect was to direct what little media coverage there was toward Michael Ovitz, while leaving everyone else toiling away in obscurity. "I think it was a mixed bag," says Richard Lovett, an agent in those days. "It added to a perception of great strength, coordination, purposefulness, and the agents engaged in single-minded work for the clients. But the negative part was that we began to be depicted in the press as agents who were a group of one-dimensional drones marching to order."

By early 1989, Ovitz's sustained effort to keep the media at bay had begun to founder. Big stories about CAA were about to be written, and the only question was whether Ovitz would cooperate with them. And indeed, over the next 10 months the media produced more major profiles (three, to be exact) on Ovitz and CAA than at any time previously. For the *Time* piece of February 13, 1989, entitled "Pocketful of Stars," Ovitz allowed himself to be interviewed—"the first extended interview he has ever given," reported *Time.* But Ovitz was careful not to be too revealing, and largely dwelt on his business philosophy: "Some companies believe that internal competition helps the bottom line, but I'm not of that school. We try to take the paternal approach of the Japanese, who take care of their own, and temper that with Western creativity and ingenuity." In general the *Time* piece was flattering to Ovitz and CAA, noting that "Ovitz and his cadre of agents are Hollywood's new power brokers." Then added *Time:* "Nearly everyone in show business agrees that Ovitz, 42, president of Creative Artists Agency, is probably the most powerful figure in Hollywood." It also noted that Ovitz's clout was derived largely from the 675 names on CAA's client roster, including actors ranging from Paul Newman to Bette Midler, directors from Ron Howard to Martin Scorsese, and musicians from Michael Jackson to Madonna. "Ovitz . . . has shown an uncanny touch for putting stories and stars together," the magazine observed, noting that four box-office hits—*Rain Man, Mississippi Burning, Twins,* and *Scrooged*—had been CAA-packaged deals, along with such television hits as *Golden Girls* and *Beauty and the Beast.* The magazine even quoted Ovitz friends and acquaintances as suggesting that Michael Ovitz was well on his way to becoming a true Hollywood immortal.

Of course, it wouldn't have been easy for the media to write negatively about Michael Ovitz and CAA at this time, since all of those who had disdain for the man felt constrained from airing their grievances. As the most powerful person in town, Ovitz had the power, if he so chose, to use it in order to punish any critic who went public by denying him or her all access to his stable of stars. The mere possibility that he might exact such punishment was enough to silence his critics. And when the media did try to say something negative about Ovitz, the piece generally lacked power, since no Ovitz critic was willing to speak out either on or off the record. When Mitchell Fink, a columnist for the *Los Angeles Herald Examiner,* wrote a piece on April 20 reporting about what some of these critics were saying of Ovitz, all he could do was to note that "rumors" existed:

- ◆ "That certain directors did leave CAA, but on their way out they heard such time-worn Hollywood lines as, 'You'll never work in this town again.'
- ◆ That a certain actor was suing Ovitz and CAA because the agency all but forced him to accept a role in a film that turned out to be a turkey.
- ◆ That a major publication was hard at work on a negative story about Ovitz.
- ◆ That the Justice Department was conducting an investigation of CAA in the wake of *Wired.*

Ridiculous, you say? Perhaps. Hearsay? Almost definitely. But people are talking."

They may have been talking, but Fink was unable to find *anyone* willing to go on record with definitive information about CAA. Which meant that even if some of the rumors were true, no reporter ever was going to get at that truth. Such was the extent of Ovitz's power.

That summer, two more profiles of Ovitz appeared: one in the *Los Angeles Times* on July 2, the other a week later in *The New York Times* magazine. Both talked about CAA in upbeat terms, laying on the flattery and making Ovitz seem larger than life. But as he sat down for the interviews in both cases, Ovitz felt that he was losing control, and he didn't like the feeling. "This is not a comfortable experience for any of us," he told Michael Cieply, who now was reporting for the *Los Angeles Times*. "We really function behind the scenes. . . . If we could convince you not to do this article, that would make us the happiest guys in town." Ovitz chose not to cooperate with *The New York Times* magazine during most of reporter L. J. Davis's research period; only when the article was ready for publication did he agree to a 30-minute phone interview. Both of the articles which appeared that July added to the agency's mystique. "CAA has become one of the most powerful, and least understood, show-business institutions since the old MCA Artists talent agency was broken up under a federal consent decree nearly thirty years ago," Cieply wrote in the *Los Angeles Times*. His article was careful to point out that CAA did *not* control a preponderance of talent in Hollywood, contrary to myth; and indeed, three out of five recent Oscar nominees for Best Actress (Sigourney Weaver, Meryl Streep, and winner Jodie Foster) were represented by the rival International Creative Management. And yet, "CAA is stronger than its competitors, and probably stronger than any studio, because of the peculiar ferocity with which the 42-year-old Ovitz and his two co-owners— actors' agent Ron Meyer, 44, and TV agent Bill Haber, 47—patrol the wide swatch of Hollywood they have claimed as their territory." *The New York Times* article noted that Ovitz "has the hottest client list in the movies."

Of all the criticisms Ovitz heard voiced against CAA and its agents, one in particular aggravated him like no other: that he had turned out nothing but a group of robotlike drones who marched obediently to his orders. Near the end of his three-hour interview with the *Los Angeles Times,* he noted: "We have been accused of being everything under the sun. I read the other day that people say there are 'Moonies' here. The reality is that people here are as individual as any human being you'll ever meet, and they are more interesting than most people you might meet in our business.

"They are really well-rounded people. They are good people. They are people you could have a meal with and whose company you would enjoy. These are people you can trust. They are people if, God forbid, your child was sick, you could call in the middle of the night and they would be there.

"Now, if you were a studio executive, and you had a relationship with somebody like that, I can give you ten people who will tell you that is a bad thing for a studio executive to call one of the agents in this company because his kid is sick. But you can't *not* have relationships with people. That is what this business is about. And you cannot have relationships with people [only] when everything is fair weather and great.

"It's like a marriage. And that is what we encourage here. We encourage long-term thinking."

He then launched into an impassioned defense of CAA's attitude toward secrecy:

"All of the conversations that take place externally about us, in my opinion, are predicated on the fact that we do not give out information. Yes, we do keep information very quiet. We have such delicate information, and it is not anyone's business. We do not share our client's business. We just do not. Even between clients we do not share it, unless the client says, 'We want you to tell so and so.'

"We function very similarly to a law firm. We have very strong fiduciary obligations. And that makes us very unpopular with the press community. Because they feel we are withholding information. It is not about withholding information, it is about doing what is right.

"One of the pillars of this company is that we like to do what we feel is right and proper. That does not mean that everyone is going to agree with it. The reality is that most people will not, because it is going to get in their way. That is not our intention. Our intention is to service our clients. The clients really are in the limelight of what we do. Therefore, just by deductive reasoning, *we* should not be.

"All the credit we get for all the other things that we *don't* do, and all the criticism we get for all the things we do, is a byproduct of the nonsense that permeates this community, which is a gossip-oriented community. We run a company that is authentically opposed to gossip-mongering, so we have a built-in conflict going in the door. We are opposed to that whole nature of chatting up people's lives, whispering in people's ears about somebody's problems, or gloating over someone's failures.

"We feel strongly that if people in the entertainment business worked toward each other's success rather than each other's demise, it would be a much better environment for all of us.

"From the day we started in the business, we have never understood this negative philosophy. We have never been able to figure it out, except that I guess it goes to the basic insecurity of everybody. If everyone rooted for each other, and collaborated more with each other, we would make better projects, there would be a wider marketplace."

Those remarks are not only heartfelt and plaintive but unique, in that nowhere else in print, up to that date, had Michael Ovitz spoken out at such length.

13

Foot Soldiers

CAA NOW WAS the unofficial king of the Hollywood talent agencies. If a project was important, whether a film or a television show, it probably bore Michael Ovitz's stamp on it somewhere. The majority of nominees for both the Emmy and the Academy Awards tended to be CAA clients. (Indeed, in 1990, every one of the Best Actor and Best Director nominees was represented by Ovitz's agency.) Yet Michael Ovitz still felt unsettled. He knew all too well that just as numerous talent agencies had risen, so too had they fallen. There were no guarantees in this business. Major talent could walk out of CAA's door at any time. The whole business seemed so impermanent and ephemeral. Therefore Ovitz wanted to let the world know that CAA was going to fight hard to become a permanent fixture, to stick around for a long, long time. The best way to do that, he thought, was to build a temple.

In 1985, Michael Ovitz looked around the offices at 1888 Century Park East and decided it was time to expand. But this time he didn't just want larger offices, he wanted CAA to build and design its own office building. And not just any office building, but the very best. He wanted it to be noticed, and he wanted it to be at the very vortex of all of Hollywood. With CAA now the preeminent institution in Hollywood, the most powerful, the most talked-about, the most exciting, it seemed only fitting that the building should reflect CAA's supremacy.

Ovitz began to plan the new building in the spring of 1985. "Mike drove me crazy to find a unique, prime piece of land to build a building," says Bob Goldman, CAA's chief financial officer. When Goldman finally had come up with the perfect site—the corner of Wilshire and Little Santa Monica Boulevards—he negotiated the purchase and arranged for financing. Ovitz insisted upon selecting the architect personally. Most of the well-known architects were in New York, and Ovitz traveled there to interview them. "He wanted nothing less than the best," says Goldman. High on Ovitz's list was the renowned architect I. M. Pei, who had designed the East Building of the National Gallery of Art in Washington, the John F. Kennedy Library in Boston, and the Grand Louvre in Paris.

Ovitz relayed his interest in Pei to the architect through Arne Glimcher. Glimcher told Pei very little about Ovitz, of whom Pei knew nothing whatever. Even when Ovitz visited Pei in his New York office, the architect still was not aware of the major impact Ovitz was having upon Hollywood. "I'm from the East Coast," Pei notes. "His fame had not reached me."

From the moment the two men met, Pei was impressed with Ovitz. He found him to be modest ("He never said, 'Guess who I am?' "), simple, low-keyed, and well prepared ("He knew me better than almost I do."). Ovitz's decision to hire Pei was in keeping with his insistence on adhering to the highest standards. Pei is widely regarded as one of the greatest architects of our time. And once he became known to those at CAA, he easily won their approval. "I. M. Pei," Bob Goldman enthuses, "is the most impressive person I've ever met in my life."

After explaining to Pei that he wanted to create a new office building for CAA, Ovitz had little to say about the specifics of its design. Instead he spoke of CAA's corporate culture, especially of how its agents are closely-knit and creative. Getting the Canton-born Pei to agree to design his first building in Los Angeles was no small achievement for Ovitz. Pei visited Ovitz's Los Angeles office and found it to be small, not showy. The architect encouraged Ovitz, as head of CAA, to take a larger office in the new building. Ovitz declined, suggesting that size was less important than making sure he had easy access to his colleagues. Only when Pei lunched with Ovitz one day did Pei get a sense of this talent agent's extraordinary reach. "Everybody came up to him," the architect recalls.

Finally, Ovitz got around to discussing just what kind of a building he was envisioning. He wanted it to be functional, but of high architectural quality. He wanted classical lines, to create a perception of power. Pei was excited and intrigued: "I had never done anything in that part of the world, simply because there was no permanence in Hollywood. Things seem to come and go. It worried me a little bit." Pei related his concerns to Ovitz, who told the architect: "That's precisely why I came to you." Pei liked Ovitz's high standards: "Michael Ovitz wanted to make a conscious attempt to try to do something good. That was the kind of compliment very few people had paid to me."

Ground-breaking for the new CAA building occurred in December 1987. Ovitz closed CAA for the day, and invited all 300 staff members to attend the event. At the ceremony a Chinese *feng shui* master blessed the building, sprinkling rice and wine on the site. The goal of *feng shui* (pronounced *fung-shway*) is the creation of harmony and balance, and its devotees believe that positioning temples, homes, and businesses in such a way as to be in harmony with the energy of the land can bring good luck, health, and fortune. Ovitz had of course been inspired to invite the *feng shui* master by the fact that I. M. Pei hails from China, and also simply because "I wanted to do something that was cool, that was different." Bob Goldman, who watched the ceremony with some amusement, thought that the others at the ceremony shared his view of the proceedings. Prior to the dedication, the priest had advised changing the locations of offices and the focus of the building. "It wasn't very constructive," a CAA executive recalls. "We didn't follow many of the suggested recommendations." One recommendation was to have the front door in a different location. But the building's design was nearly complete, and Ovitz didn't want to bother Pei with the change. Another recommendation was to have water fall over the walls at the entrance. Ovitz was against this, so instead a hose was run over the top of the building and down the wall, a prop that was displayed for just one day soon after the building opened.

Most of Pei's projects take from 10 to 15 years to complete. He took only four and a half years to build the CAA offices, attributing that speed to the ease with which Ovitz and Bob Goldman made decisions. Money, Ovitz told Pei, was a consideration, but not a major one. Accordingly, Pei used stone from Italy rather than the stucco that often was used in Hollywood. Although newspaper reports had estimated the cost of the building at a much higher figure, the building, according to Ovitz, came in at around $12 million.

At CAA's previous premises, almost all of its personnel were on one floor. This made for an easy camaraderie, with agents often dropping in on one another. Ovitz wanted to retain that ease of access even though CAA now would be spread over three floors. Most office buildings are box-shaped, and convey little sense of open space; Ovitz therefore asked Pei to design in ample non-office space, despite the higher cost. He wanted anyone entering the atrium to feel mesmerized by its spaciousness, its beauty, its "spirituality." The atrium, with its wide-open space, was meant to convey a feeling of the outdoors; off to one side of the atrium is a large tree and a cast-bronze sculpture by Joel Shapiro. A huge Lichtenstein painting covers the wall across from the front entrance. At

Ovitz's suggestion, Pei designed a bridge to connect two distant parts of the building along the top floor, to facilitate people's movement.

Anyone in the atrium gazing up at the bridge gets a sense of frenzied activity: clients heading for offices, agents scurrying back and forth. Peering up at the top-floor offices near the bridge, one sees CAA staffers wearing headsets, talking on the phones. All this was part of a conscious attempt to convey the idea that the place was humming. While there were around 500 people working in the building, of whom around 130 were agents, Ovitz wanted someone to feel that 1000 people were around, giving "this New York sense of being on Fifth Avenue," as he puts it. "We didn't want to have a building that was in effect dead," Bob Goldman notes. CAA was receiving about 1000 phone calls an hour, and Ovitz wanted the energy that flowed from those calls to reach down to the visitors in the atrium.

The building was designed so that one had to walk through the atrium in order to reach someone's office. Visitors drove to a parking garage underneath the building, where valets parked their cars next to an assortment of Porsches, BMWs, and Mercedes. An elevator took the guests to the atrium, where receptionists sat behind a counter waiting to arrange meetings. This was in notable contrast to other buildings, where a visitor walks through a small lobby, rides an elevator, and then reaches the office. "We didn't want to fall into that trap," says Bob Goldman. "The whole idea was to force people to spend some time in the atrium, where they could feel the grandeur and openness and excitement of the place." And above all, the sense that CAA was the hub of Hollywood deal-making.

Visiting Roy Lichtenstein's studio on one occasion, Ovitz asked him to paint a mural for the atrium. Ovitz had brought with him a miniature model of the building's interior, but he had no idea what he wanted Lichtenstein to paint; all Ovitz knew was that the mural should be large. Lichtenstein proposed that he do something based on Oscar Shlemmer's "Bauhaus Stair," which used to hang in the main stairway of the Museum of Modern Art. It reminded the artist of people going to the movies, which he thought would be appropriate for the CAA atrium. Ovitz liked the idea. Lichtenstein decided to make the mural 26 feet tall and 18 feet wide. After three months of preparation, Lichtenstein and three assistants began to paint the mural, standing on scaffolding and working even after the building had opened.

When the building opened for business on Monday, August 28, 1989, it immediately became one of the landmarks of the Hollywood business community. As Bob Goldman puts it: "It established us as more of an institution, rather than just a bunch of guys working in an office who maybe are here today but gone tomorrow. There's been a history of a great deal of instability in the agency business. This building clearly established us as a company that would—at least in the entertainment indus-try—be considered an institution."

On the morning of the opening, Ovitz called the staff together for a meeting in the ground-floor movie theater. As he walked down the the-ater's aisle, the audience burst into spontaneous applause. "Everyone felt that the momentum of the agency was hitting its full stride," says Michael Rosenfeld Jr., a CAA agent at that time. "Moving into that building was the agency at its greatest moment of triumph."

In the hallway of the same third floor as Ovitz's office, there stood a bronze bust of Phil Weltman. On it was inscribed: "To Phil Weltman, who taught us the meaning of integrity and self-respect. We dedicate this agency." It was signed: "Bill Haber, Ron Meyer, Michael Ovitz, Rowland Perkins, and Michael Rosenfeld. January 20, 1975."

The building marked a turning point for Ovitz and CAA. After all those years spent in creating the illusion of power, Ovitz now felt strong enough, confident enough to put together an institution that stood for power itself. If the outside world wanted to get at the inner workings of the talent agency, it could now confront CAA in all its might, as embod-ied in Michael Ovitz's temple. The building was no illusion. Nor was it meant to be.

THE QUESTION FACING Ovitz no longer was whether he *would* be sub-jected to public scrutiny, but whether he could find a way to sail through these uncharted waters smoothly. Even in the wake of the major newspaper profiles that had come out earlier in 1989, no one outside of CAA *really* knew how Ovitz functioned: How did he handle clients? How did he man-age to package one movie after another? Exactly how much money had he and the agency amassed? The one verity that everyone could touch and feel was I. M. Pei's modernistic assertion of power and influence, as it dom-inated the corner of Wilshire and Little Santa Monica. Thus the creation of the building only seemed to heighten the public's hunger for the answers to even more burning questions: What are the real means that Michael Ovitz has employed in order to gain success? Was his magic formula actually comprised of nothing more complicated or abstruse than teamwork, disci-pline, loyalty, and hard work? Or buried under such homilies, was there a darker truth? Had he acted brutally or benignly in acquiring and keeping clients, and in finding projects for them? Why was it that CAA had become a powerhouse, when other agencies had not? The fact that no one had even a clue to the answers to these questions was yet another tribute to the Ovitz genius for staying out of the limelight.

But then along came a man with a bushy beard, a marvelous ability to write action-packed, erotic, and sellable screenplays, and a pungent personality. His name was Joe Eszterhas. And he was about to help the public to learn some things about Michael Ovitz that seemed to provide at least partial answers to all of those questions.

Eszterhas began his career in journalism, first with the *Cleveland Plain-Dealer,* then with *Rolling Stone* magazine as its star investigative reporter. After his first screenplay, a melodrama called *F.I.S.T.* (1978), was turned into a motion picture starring Sylvester Stallone, he left the magazine. He then wrote the screenplays for the films *Flashdance* (1983) and *Jagged Edge* (1985), receiving $1.25 million a script and thereby becoming the highest-paid scriptwriter in town. He also was one of CAA's prized clients, and the agency took pride in the role it had played in accelerating Eszterhas's career. Everyone was happy: Eszterhas, Ovitz, and all the CAA agents who were benefiting from the screenwriter's talents.

And then one day, Joe Eszterhas decided to leave the agency. That was something Michael Ovitz could not tolerate. After all, the screenwriter was one of his biggest rainmakers. But Eszterhas had a problem. He had once had an agent, Guy McElwaine, who had been at International Creative Management and then moved on to head Columbia Pictures. Eszterhas felt very loyal to McElwaine, and when Guy decided to return to the agency business in August 1989, going back to ICM, the screenwriter felt that he should leave CAA and rejoin his old agent at ICM. Eszterhas paid a personal visit to Michael Ovitz on September 19, to break the news to him. He assumed, rather naively, that Ovitz would be very sympathetic, and would understand the screenwriter's need to join his friend at another agency.

Eszterhas walked into Ovitz's office feeling a little tense, but hoping that the meeting would go smoothly. He started to explain his situation to Ovitz, but before he was that far into the story, the talent agent went ballistic. Eszterhas had missed the point completely: You just don't cross Michael Ovitz. For Ovitz, only one thing mattered: One of his biggest clients had just announced that he was walking out the door, taking with him those million-dollar screenwriting fees.

Precisely what the two men said to each other has been the subject of wild speculation and heated, furious debate throughout Hollywood. According to Eszterhas, Ovitz threatened to ruin his career. At that time Ovitz denied that he ever made such a threat.

At any rate, Eszterhas was deeply offended and upset that Ovitz had been so withering in his verbal attack upon him, and he told Ovitz so in a lengthy letter dated October 3. He had decided to leave CAA, Eszterhas wrote in the letter, not because of any problems he had experienced with CAA, but simply out of loyalty to McElwaine. He had been certain that Ovitz wouldn't be happy about his departure, Eszterhas wrote, if only because no other CAA screenwriter was making $1.25 million a screenplay, "but I was unprepared for the crudity and severity of your response.

"You told me that if I left, 'My foot soldiers who go up and down Wilshire Boulevard each day will blow your brains out.' You said that you would sue me. 'I don't care if I win or lose,' you said, 'but I'm going to tie you up with depositions and court dates so that you won't be able to spend any time at your typewriter.' You said: 'If you make me eat shit, I'm going to make you eat shit.' When I said to you that I had no interest in being involved in a public spectacle, you said: 'I don't care if everybody in town knows. I want them to know. I'm not worried about the press. All those guys want is to write screenplays for Robert Redford.' You said: 'If somebody came into the building and took my Lichtenstein off the wall, I'd go after them. I'm going to go after you the same way. You're one of this agency's biggest assets.' You said: 'This town is like a chess game. ICM isn't going after a pawn or a knight, they're going after a king. If the king goes, the knights and pawns will follow.' "

Accusing Ovitz of blackmail, and extortion, Eszterhas wrote that he was horrified by the language that Ovitz allegedly had employed, "which sounded like something out of bad gangster movies. You are agents. Your role is to help and encourage my career and creativity. Your role is not to place me in personal emotional turmoil. Your role is not to threaten to destroy my family livelihood if I don't do your bidding. I am not an asset; I am a human being. I am not a painting hung on a wall; I am not part of a chess set. I am not a piece of meat to be 'traded' for other pieces of meat. . . . This isn't a game. It's my life."

The screenwriter acknowledged that he was taking a risk in fighting back against Ovitz: "Yes, you might very well be able to hurt me with your stars, your directors, and your friends on the executive level. . . ." And, yes, Eszterhas wrote, he took Ovitz's threats very seriously indeed. He had just purchased a new house, but faced with these threats, he and his family had decided to put the new house up for sale and remain in the old one. "Do you have any idea," he added, "how much pain and turmoil you've caused [my family]?"

Only four people apart from Ovitz were given a copy of the letter: Rand Holston, a CAA agent who had provided service for Eszterhas; Barry Hirsch, Eszterhas's attorney; Irwin Winkler, who had produced some of Eszterhas's films; and Guy McElwaine. Yet the letter was leaked to the media. Both Eszterhas and McElwaine denied that they had leaked the letter's contents, but that hardly mattered to an entertainment industry voraciously hungry for every tidbit about the mysterious Ovitz.

The result of the leak was a firestorm of publicity, one that turned "the Eszterhas Affair," as the press quickly dubbed it, into the number-one story in town. In general, squabbles between an agent and a client seldom rated more than a few lines in *Daily Variety* or *The Hollywood Reporter.* But now, when a major client of the all-but-mythical and omnipotent Mr. Ovitz seemed ready to take him on, the incident became national news. Articles appeared everywhere, and the pundits went into high gear as they scrambled to sort out the implications of the episode. The affair wrought important changes in the perception of Michael Ovitz. Until then he had largely succeeded in creating an image of himself as being all-powerful; half-genius, half-magician; aggressive and persistent; highly disciplined and hardworking. If some had believed that he was not so much aggressive as belligerent, persistent as intrusive, hardworking as manipulative, then at last they seemed to have been provided with some evidence in support of their conjectures. In the past, Ovitz had cleverly orchestrated the media, making certain that no such evidence, if it was there, ever got out. Hence, the major waves set in motion by the Eszterhas Affair.

In an attempt to calm the waters, Ovitz replied to Eszterhas's letter, a response penned on the same day as the screenwriter's letter arrived:

"When I received your letter this morning I was totally shocked, since my recollection of our conversation bore no relationship to your recollection. Truly this appears to be one of those *Rashomon* situations, and your letter simply makes little or no sense to me.

"As I explained to you when we were together, you are an important client of this company, and all that I was trying to do was to keep you as a client. There was no other agenda. If you have to leave, you have to leave and so be it. I have talked to Guy [McElwaine] and I have told him that whatever we can do to be helpful in this transition we will do. Of course, as you assured me, I am expecting that you will pay us whatever you owe us.

"I am particularly sensitive when people bring families and children into business discussions. If someone said to me what you think I said to you, I would feel the same way as you expressed in your letter. I think that your letter was unfair and unfounded, but it does not change my respect for your talent. I only hope that in time you will reflect on the true spirit of what I was trying to communicate to you.

"I want to make it eminently clear that in no way will I . . . or anyone else in this agency, stand in the way of your pursuing your career. So please, erase from your mind any of your erroneous anxieties or thoughts you may have to the contrary.

"Best wishes and continued success."

Ovitz won support from his friends.

Bill Carruthers, the daytime television producer and an Ovitz client both at William Morris and CAA, sought to soothe Ovitz by sending a note: "It hurts me that people are doing this to you. I can't believe what I'm reading is true. For what it's worth I'm here, and I'll discount all these rabid rumors about the way you do business and the kind of business person you are." When the *Los Angeles Times* approached director Sydney Pollack for comment on the Eszterhas–Ovitz flare-up, the director became irate. Pollack says, "They wanted to nail Michael to the cross. I said, 'I don't believe Eszterhas's story. That letter was terribly self-serving.' Nobody wanted to write anything good about Ovitz."

Two days after Ovitz's letter arrived, Eszterhas wrote back, indicating that he did not believe Ovitz for a second. In this letter, Eszterhas made a five-point reply:

"1. You can quote *Rashomon* as much as you like, but words like 'my foot soldiers will blow your brains out' . . . leave little room for ambiguity.

2. I am particularly sensitive when people bring their families and children into business discussions, too—and I hope that in the future you will reflect that keeping important clients isn't worth haunting families and children the way you haunt mine.

3. I understand very well 'the true spirit' of what you were trying to communicate to me in the meeting, and will live my life accordingly.

4. My 'erroneous anxieties' notwithstanding, we are selling our new house anyway.

5. Please understand that after the things you and Rand [Holston, the CAA agent who also talked to Eszterhas, trying to talk him out of leaving CAA] said to me, I can hardly take your 'best wishes' for my 'continued success' seriously."

It was taken for granted, in the weeks following the incident, that no one was ever going to discover who was telling the truth, Eszterhas or Ovitz. Yet as far as Ovitz's image was concerned, solving the mystery was virtually beside the point. The very fact that the affair had been given so much attention in the media made many believe that Eszterhas was telling the truth. Had Ovitz been less private, less enigmatic until then, he might have built up a backlog of goodwill that would have kept the public from rushing to judgment.

As things then stood, Ovitz could do little to make the incident go away. Old habits die hard, and he continued to maintain that the best way to handle such a controversy was to avoid talking to the press. Although one might have expected him to turn to Howard J. Rubenstein Associates, Inc., the public relations firm he had hired a year earlier, Ovitz found the Eszterhas matter to be so sensitive that he wanted to handle it entirely in-house. Therefore he asked Ray Kurtzman, the head of business affairs at CAA, to deal with the expected press requests. And although Kurtzman was expected to merely repeat over and over again a few pat phrases extracted from Ovitz's letter to Eszterhas, the business-affairs man still found the challenge daunting: "I had no idea how to handle the press," Kurtzman asserts. "At first I thought 'What's so hard about it? I've negotiated deals before. It's the same thing.' But it was literally the worst experience of my life, in terms of how to deal with people. All those questions of using quotes, going off the record, being on background only, I didn't know any of it. I felt like I was a lamb led to slaughter."

Some odd footnotes to the Eszterhas episode would crop up later. Within a few months of informing Ovitz that he was ending his relationship with CAA, Joe Eszterhas was paid a record $3 million for writing the screenplay for the hit film *Basic Instinct*. CAA agents were less annoyed by the unfavorable publicity over the Eszterhas affair than by the fact that they now had to explain to other CAA screenwriters why *they* were not being paid huge sums for their scripts.

However upset Ovitz may have been at the time of the Eszterhas affair, he had cooled down enough in three and a half years to poke some fun at himself.

He did so in March 1993, when he and Ron Meyer appeared in the 45-minute film called *TSS*, spoofing the Warner Brothers film *JFK*. It was made as a fiftieth birthday present for Warner Brothers chairman and co-CEO Terry Semel, by Semel's wife Jane and producer Joel Silver. While numerous Hollywood actors, directors, and producers appeared in the film, the Ovitz scene was the most talked-about—and with good reason. Filmed on the Warner Brothers lot, the scene begins with the Batmobile racing noisily down a dark street. A man then runs in front of the car and dashes to the other side of the street, where he knocks over some garbage cans. Batman (played by Ovitz), wearing a CAA logo on the front of his outfit, emerges from the Batmobile. Nearby is his sidekick Robin, played by Ron Meyer. Batman approaches a man lying on the ground, who by now has a petrified look on his face, and grabs him by the throat.

"Who are you?" the man asks in a frightened voice.

Panning to the front of Batman's uniform, the camera shows the CAA logo, then moves to his face.

"I'm Mike Ovitz," says Batman, his tone deadly-serious. "Don't ever talk to any of our clients again, or I'm going to march our foot soldiers down Wilshire Boulevard looking for you."

AFTER ALL THAT had "gone down" between Joe Eszterhas and Michael Ovitz, it was truly incredible that, in 1995, Joe Eszterhas practically begged to be admitted back to CAA—one of the more amazing acts of contrition in Hollywood history.

That summer, Eszterhas put out feelers to CAA agents, and heard back that they would be delighted to forget all about the past and have him return to the agency. CAA agent Bob Bookman was all set to take Eszterhas on as a client, once Ovitz's approval came. All that was required was for Ovitz and Eszterhas to work out the formal language of the letters they planned to release to the press, expressing their mutual joy and glee over this startling reconciliation.

Indeed, Eszterhas was so concerned to ensure that the reconciliation would indeed take place without a hitch, that he not only wrote his own letter but drafted one for Ovitz to sign!

"Dear Mike," began Eszterhas's proposed draft. "I was so happy to hear from Bob Bookman that there was no animosity on your part or on the part of CAA concerning events that took place six years ago."

In reply, Ovitz was supposed to say: "Dear Joe: Welcome back. I was happy to hear we could put the past behind us. We too look forward to working with you in the same spirit of friendship and mutual respect."

All seemed fine and good, and the two men apparently were ready to lose themselves, and the past, in a big warm embrace. But then, Ovitz got cold feet. The language in the letters may have been acceptable to him, but Ovitz still couldn't forgive and forget.

Eszterhas then inadvertently provided the talent agent with a way out of the deal, when he insisted that Ovitz add a line to Ovitz's already agreed-upon letter: "You know how much I've always admired your talent." Exactly why Eszterhas needed that reassurance is not clear. But as it turned out, demanding a change in the final draft of that letter only played into Ovitz's hands. In effect he said, *Forget the deal.*

But still the screenwriter did not abandon his efforts to try to insinuate himself back into Ovitz's good graces. In the winter of 1996, Eszterhas invited Ovitz to play a role in a movie for which he had written the screenplay. Ovitz declined.

In speaking to the author about his relationship with Joe Eszterhas, Ovitz dwelt on how unpleasant and ungrateful Eszterhas had been to him and CAA: "He was an important client at CAA, and I'm the most competitive guy in the world. He was unkind to four agents. He abused one of them." Ovitz didn't stop there. To back up his assertion that Eszterhas had been ungrateful to him, Ovitz noted that when the screenwriter had had a chronic back pain, Ovitz had arranged for doctors to try to treat him.

In recalling his fateful meeting with Eszterhas, Ovitz was careful to describe the session in such a way as to make it sound as if he and Eszterhas had gotten along fabulously, and there had been no rancor whatsoever. As Ovitz tells it, the screenwriter began the conversation by expressing his regret that, despite his link to CAA, he had gone ahead and taken on a new agent, McElwaine. According to Ovitz, Eszterhas was looking for a way to back out of the deal that he had made with McElwaine, so that he could stay with CAA.

"Tell him I'm going to sue you," Ovitz suggested. Presumably the threat of an Ovitz lawsuit against Eszterhas would scare McElwaine into submission. (Neither the screenwriter's supposed wish to get out of the McElwaine arrangement, nor Ovitz's advice to him with regard to the threat of a lawsuit, were mentioned in their exchange of letters.)

The question that was on the minds of everyone connected to the Eszterhas Affair, and that certainly was uppermost in the author's mind as he talked with Ovitz, was this: Had he or had he not made the notorious threat to march his foot soldiers down Wilshire Boulevard and blow the screenwriter's brains out?

The question was posed: What in fact had he said to Eszterhas in that regard?

Then came Ovitz's startling response:

"Eszterhas and I were joking with each other when I said: 'You don't want our foot soldiers going up the street gunning for you, do you?' "

Until that moment, Ovitz always had denied ever making any "foot soldiers" remark of any kind. Was this the first time he had admitted to making the infamous remark?

Yes, said Ovitz, it was.

He also said that he was shocked to receive Eszterhas's letter, because he had been under the impression that they had had a great meeting. Ovitz immediately sensed that the Eszterhas letter would get leaked, as of course it was. He blames ICM agent Sue Mengers: "I saw she was copied on the letter. It's my assumption that she leaked it. We were creaming ICM at the time. That's why she leaked it."

14

The Über-Agent

DESPITE THE JOE ESZTERHAS setback, Michael Ovitz's star continued
to rise. In 1989, CAA's influence had reached a new high, and he personally was earning well over $1 million a year. Yet at the same time, Ovitz
sensed that the institution he had built into the most powerful force in
Hollywood was becoming too confining for him. Still, he wasn't prepared
to take the company public or to sell it, steps that certainly would have
made him a fortune. Had he been less ambitious, less restless, he might
have chosen to stay put, to keep his eye on the core business and try to
make CAA even larger and more powerful. There were certainly enough
challenges facing the agency business; for one thing, the country was in
the throes of a recession, which meant that the movie business was in its
worst financial shape of the past two decades. Thus it was that CAA
began to seek out new revenue streams. Now that Ovitz had launched
Magic Johnson's business career, perhaps he could do the same for that of
other star athletes. He toyed with the idea of opening a sports division,
but shelved it as soon as he realized that the country already was over-
flowing with sports agents.

Still, staying put seemed boring. His friends began noticing that Ovitz
did not seem to be enjoying the talent-agency business as much as in the
past. Dustin Hoffman had gone off to London for a year after doing *Rain
Man* and had returned to Hollywood to find Ovitz a changed man. "How
long are you going to do this?" Hoffman asked him. "You clearly don't relish it."

Ovitz replied that his greatest satisfaction had been doing *Rain Man*, as
if to acknowledge that he had accomplished all he ever wanted as a talent
agent.

"That was his greatest experience," Hoffman said. "He felt he couldn't repeat it. That's why he wanted to move into other areas."

Indeed, Ovitz wanted to play in a bigger league. He wanted to be more than just a talent agent. The idea of doing more than one thing had always been in his blood. "I didn't want to die having one career," he explains, but no one has ever found it easy to switch careers in mid-life. (Ovitz would turn 43 in December of 1989.) Ovitz first explored the idea of setting up his own film company, with the help of a few trusted clients. He broached the notion to director Ivan Reitman on a number of occasions, but he never followed through. Perhaps, Reitman surmises, this was because Ovitz feared that such a company, with its limited assets, would be too small a player to satisfy his ambitions. Ovitz's greatest dream was to head an entertainment empire. He had taken the agency as far as he could and, for all its clout, CAA still was dwarfed both in size and resources by a number of the mighty entertainment conglomerates of the day. He couldn't help but dwell on what it would be like to run one of those giants.

Ovitz also understood that, ever since Saul Steinberg had threatened The Walt Disney Company with a takeover attempt in 1984, there was a growing interest on the part of major corporations to acquire Hollywood studios. Ovitz liked to believe that no one in Hollywood had a better grasp of the entertainment industry than he did. Why not put that knowledge to work on behalf of these corporations? He had no game plan, no long-term strategy in terms of encouraging these corporations to solicit his advice with regard to such deal-making. But if and when opportunities arose, Ovitz wanted to seize them: "I wanted CAA not to be just a talent agency, but a resource for its clients, to be a repository of information and to have an ability to move things around."

His entry into the arena of corporate consulting wasn't exactly a triumphant one. In 1988, CAA entered into a consulting relationship with Archer Communications, which hoped that its Qsound technology would become the new standard for the audio industry. But the technology turned out to have been ill conceived, and Ovitz was forced to beat a retreat. The experience may have slowed him down a bit, but it did little to dissipate his enthusiasm.

What Ovitz was contemplating was unique within the world of the Hollywood talent agency. Other agencies were all too happy to stick to their core business, not only because they lacked Ovitz's broad-ranging business contacts and sophistication, but also out of an understandable belief that talent agencies ought to stick to finding work for Hollywood talent. And yet the fact was that a number of major corporations, including foreign ones, were seeking to gain a foothold in Hollywood, and they needed someone to guide them through the town's corporate maze. Who better than Michael Ovitz? No one was better suited than he to help these executives assess Hollywood properties and personnel. "It wasn't that they liked us," says Ovitz, speaking of these executives. "We weren't out to win a popularity contest. It was because we were effective."

Ovitz's first major foray into the field of corporate consulting came when electronic giant Sony attempted to buy into Hollywood, in order to market its ever-expanding video technologies.

In 1988 Sony hired Ovitz as its Hollywood consultant, as it sought to acquire a major studio. Walter Yetnikoff, then head of Sony Records and an Ovitz client, had introduced him to Sony's president, Norio Ohga, a one-time opera singer.

Sony's goal was to gain a major stake in a Hollywood studio by means of either a partnership or an outright buyout; it wasn't interested in conducting a hostile takeover. In 1987 it had purchased CBS Records, as part of its strategy to market American pop culture by means of cutting-edge Japanese technologies in music, television, and film.

Ovitz sought to steer Sony to MCA, a company he felt possessed an array of riches: a strong film library, significant real-estate holdings, several theme parks, a publishing house, and a group of executives whom he thought of as the best in Hollywood. At the time, the 77-year-old Lew Wasserman and his board were hoping to get $8 billion for the company, but others thought that was an exaggerated figure. Despite Ovitz's enthusiasm for the company, Sony thought MCA too expensive even at $5 billion. He then sought to interest Sony in purchasing MGM/UA. Sony asked Ovitz to assess the studio's assets, which he did. But terms for the deal couldn't be worked out.

Sony began then to take a serious look at Columbia Pictures Entertainment, and Ovitz was asked to assess Columbia's overall value. Sony (itself worth $16 billion) finalized the deal in October 1989, purchasing Columbia Pictures Entertainment for $3.4 billion and thereby making the transaction the largest Japanese takeover of an American company to date. By no means was Ovitz the key figure in Sony's corporate foray into Hollywood; he was, however, an important member of a team led by Peter Peterson, chairman of the Blackstone Group, an investment-banking firm, and a longtime Sony adviser.

Sony wanted Ovitz to run Columbia. In the course of the negotiations for Columbia he had impressed quite a number of people, including

Michael Schulhof, the vice chairman of Sony USA, as well as the Blackstone bankers. Sony's executives had learned of the dispute between Ovitz and MGM over how many theaters the film *Rain Man* should play in, and were struck by his prescience about how well the film would do. The Sony attorneys spent a month working up an offer to Ovitz, even devising a code name for him: Superman! Sony was proposing that Ovitz run Columbia Pictures; that CAA would be bought out (which would allow Ovitz to cash-out his majority share); and that the agency then would be sold back to CAA agents on good terms. Ovitz would have earned a cool $100 million from this arrangement, but he sought an even richer deal. In his counter-offer, he insisted upon running not only Columbia Pictures but Sony's record division as well—the latter being the mainstay of Sony's American entertainment empire. He was to enjoy virtual autonomy, and net $200 million. Sony didn't respond to the proposal, but Ovitz believed that ultimately its executives would come around, so confident was he that there was simply no one else as capable as he when it came to running Sony's American operations. Later, according to Ovitz confidants, Ovitz sought to dispel the notion that Sony had rejected him; it was, Ovitz insisted, the other way around. And Ovitz now suggests that he never really considered going to Sony under any circumstances, but was flattered to have been approached for the Sony position. Since Sony executives aren't talking about the Ovitz negotiation, and since Ovitz has every reason to want the world to think that he rejected Sony and not the other way around, it's hard to get at the full truth. And yet there is enough on the public record to indicate that Ovitz wasn't ready to move away from the agency at this point. He obviously enjoyed being asked to help run a multibillion-dollar business, and loved the idea of being paid millions of dollars to do so. And that's why he negotiated with Sony.

At any rate, Ovitz had little reason to brood about the offer and/or rejection: Simply for helping to broker Sony's acquisition of Columbia Pictures, Michael Ovitz was paid some $8 million.

In light of the three major newspaper profiles, the Eszterhas Affair, and now the Sony deal, Michael Ovitz believed that the time was right for CAA to have its own in-house spokesperson. He learned that Stephen Rivers, who had been an aide to Jane Fonda and Tom Hayden, was available. They met on several occasions in December 1989 to discuss the job. Ovitz told him that he now understood that there should be someone at CAA to answer journalists' phone calls; he gave Rivers the mandate of trying to build up good relations with entertainment-industry reporters. While Ovitz didn't say as much to Rivers, it was his hope that in appointing a full-time spokesperson, he could alter the image of CAA as a cloak-and-dagger operation.

Only a few Ovitz confidants knew of the machinations of his corporate consulting. One of these was Sandy Climan. He began his career at MGM, at first in the area of pay television and later in that of international distribution, and then shifted to feature-film production. He studied at Harvard as an undergraduate, then obtained an MBA from the Harvard Business School. Climan was a superb numbers-cruncher and financial analyst, and he and Ovitz got along very well.

In the summer of 1989, Climan prepared a memo in which he noted the top-ten Japanese firms that were eager to acquire a Hollywood studio. Both Ovitz and Climan began to focus on Matsushita, especially since its 94-year-old patriarch, Konosuke Matsushita, had died that April. The hardware firm, considered conservative while under Matsushita's leadership, was seen as perhaps ripe for innovation in the wake of the patriarch's death.

Ovitz had wanted to find a buyer of MCA for two and a half years. In 1987 he had watched the company's stock fluctuate when Lew Wasserman was hospitalized. Then he had pushed MCA when Sony was in the market for a Hollywood studio. Finally, in the fall of 1989, Matsushita contacted Ovitz, and he was all ready for them. By this time he had put together a small group at CAA whose mandate was to search for new corporate clients (such as Sony) that wanted to acquire Hollywood companies and to use Michael Ovitz as their middle-man. As soon as Matsushita's approach to Ovitz came, he ordered the CAA team to run a computer check on the Japanese firm in order to come up with a more detailed breakdown of the company. The most interesting fact gleaned from the search was that Matsushita had a great deal of money in its acquisition war-chest: $12 billion in cash, plus $13 billion in securities.

Matsushita's executives wanted to meet Ovitz personally. It was the common practice for a Japanese company to send lower-level executives to an exploratory meeting, but the executives sent word to Ovitz that Masahito Hirata, the executive vice president of Matsushita who happened to serve as the top aide to Ako Tamii, the company's president, would attend. Ovitz was pleased that the firm seemed to be taking matters so seriously. Since secrecy had to be preserved, the site of the meeting was important. Japan was too risky, for the Japanese press followed the moves of senior Matsushita executives doggedly, and all the more so in the wake of the Sony–Columbia deal. Honolulu finally was arrived at as the safest site. The Matsushita executives set the timetable: The meeting would take place at the end of November.

In order to prepare for it, Ovitz read several of Konosuke Matsushita's books. He took with him the man who would play a major role in these deals, Sandy Climan. During those two days of meetings, no one spoke openly about a deal. Instead the topics included the Matsushita firm, CAA, martial arts, children, art, music, and life in general. One Matsushita executive finally asked Ovitz how much he wanted to be paid to be a consultant. Ovitz shrewdly deferred the matter to a later date. He suggested that they talk about money only after he had done something for Matsushita. But he did ask that Matsushita appoint him lead consultant. He had no interest in playing just a minor consulting role, as had been the case in the Sony deal; this time he wanted to be in control.

Meanwhile Ovitz stayed in touch with the Matsushita executives, providing them with the equivalent of a continuing seminar on the entertainment industry. He traveled to Japan at least once every two months. He and Climan flew to San Francisco and left for Japan from there, to avoid being spotted leaving on an international flight from the Los Angeles International Airport. Ovitz and Climan even went so far as to use fictitious names in their correspondence with the Matsushita executives: They became the Nelson family; Ovitz was Mike Nelson, Climan, Sandy Nelson! (These were characters in the popular television program of the 1950s, *Sea Hunt.*)

On one occasion, Ovitz and Climan told their wives and children that they were going to England. When he purchased a kimono for his wife, Climan decided not to tell her where he had bought it; instead he informed her that kimonos were all the rage in London! She gave him a puzzled look, but asked no questions. Climan tried to fool his secretary as well. He made a point of calling her from Osaka just when CNN was presenting its international weather report, making sure to turn up the sound when the weather person talked about waves lashing at the English coast. (Climan's secretary was skeptical.) Around the office, in order to keep anyone from learning about the Matsushita deal, Climan did all of the faxing and photocopying himself.

Ovitz, Climan, Bob Goldman, and Ray Kurtzman did their best to disguise the fact that they were engaged in any efforts outside the sphere of the agency's core business. "I never wanted anyone to know I was out of town," Ovitz says. "I didn't want them to know I wasn't running the agency." Working in his favor was the time difference between Los Angeles and Osaka. Ovitz sometimes would leave for Japan on a Sunday and arrive on a late Monday afternoon, Japan time, when it was still only 12 midnight Sunday in Los Angeles. He would have a dinner meeting, return to his hotel room for a few hours of sleep, then arise at 3 a.m. in order to return phone calls to L.A. and thereby keep anyone from discovering his true whereabouts.

Once, however, all efforts to maintain secrecy went out the window, as Ovitz and his three colleagues (Goldman, Kurtzman, and Climan) boarded an airplane in Osaka for the long trip back to California. They were just storing their briefing books in the overhead compartment when into the plane walked actor Charlie Sheen and his publicist. Though Sheen wasn't a CAA client he immediately identified Ovitz, said hello, and asked him what he was doing in Japan. "Just business," was the curt response. Soon word spread throughout the entertainment industry that Ovitz had been in Japan, although no one knew why.

Ovitz insisted that all memos with regard to the Matsushita dealings be handwritten. He wanted nothing to be on computer disks. It was too easy to misplace them, and they could fall into the wrong hands. Even the Matsushita executives, in listening to his ongoing seminars, had to take notes in longhand, for tape recorders were forbidden. Unable to restrain his old gift-buying impulse, Ovitz gave the task of purchasing them for his Matsushita colleagues to his long-time assistant and to no one else. He demanded the right to approve the recruitment of anyone connected to the deal: There would be no young law-firm clerks or investment-banking aides who might learn some details of the deal, switch firms, and divulge those details to the media. Yet despite all of these melodramatic steps, or perhaps because of them, the Matsushita executives were mesmerized by Ovitz, and placed their entire trust in him.

THE REST OF Hollywood, if not exactly mesmerized, certainly did feel respect for Michael Ovitz's tremendous clout. In the past this town had had more than its share of powerful people, but it was only early in 1990 that the entertainment media got around to ranking the high and mighty. That such rankings were coming into fashion was a boon for Michael Ovitz. Having his name appear at the head of most of these lists substantiated what many had already believed: that Michael Ovitz really was the most powerful figure in Hollywood. In March of this year he was promoted to chairman of CAA, with Ron Meyer taking over the presidency.

It was in early 1990 that *Premiere*'s editors dreamed up the idea of creating a Power List of the one hundred most powerful figures in the movie business, a list that would appear in May of that year. Editor-in-Chief

Susan Lyne assigned the magazine's editor, Chris Connelly, to oversee the project; he in turn assigned four reporters to canvass people in the industry (both candidates for the list and non-candidates), asking them who should be on the list and why. On the wall in his office, Connelly pinned index cards bearing the names of possible candidates for the Power List. Over the next three months, as reporters returned from interviews, the editor shuffled the order of the cards up and down the wall as his perception of their ranking changed. Guided by intuition rather than any rigid formula, he and his reporters traveled to New York City, where they spent many hours finalizing their choices with Susan Lyne. Although Susan could veto any of the choices, she made a point of helping her group to reach a consensus.

When the list appeared in the May issue, Michael Ovitz topped it. "Despite recent defections," *Premiere* wrote, "and *l'affaire Eszterhas,* the CAA uber-agent still has more A-list talent at his fingertips than anyone else in town and can package pricey projects at the studio of his choice. Notable projects include *Ghostbusters I* and *II, Twins, Out of Africa,* and *Rain Man.* A martial-arts aficionado who takes the Japanese way of doing business very, very seriously. Well-connected politically (he recently co-sponsored a $1,000-a-plate dinner for Bill Bradley) and journalistically (he counts *L.A. Times* honcho Shelby Coffey among his friends). May be feeling restless, tough; why settle for the agent's ten percent, when that other Michael at Disney makes so much more?"

Lew Wasserman was listed as number two on the power list, followed by Michael Eisner, Barry Diller, Warner Brothers' Steve Ross, Steven Spielberg, Jeffrey Katzenberg, Warner Brothers' Bob Daly, Tom Pollock, and Frank Mancuso.

Even as the scuttlebutt over the *Premiere* power list was spreading all over town, CAA specialists were trying to determine which studios represented the prime targets for Matsushita's executives. Orion was one, but it seemed too small; Paramount was another, but its holdings were diverse (the publisher Simon & Schuster, the NBA team, the New York Knickerbockers) and it didn't seem to accord well with Matsushita's business strategy. The one company that had the kind of show-biz operations that Matsushita was looking for was MCA. Ovitz had always liked Lew Wasserman's company, and if MCA had been too pricey for Sony's blood, Matsushita might be willing to pay the price. Also, MCA and Matsushita seemed such a good fit, given their conservative management styles and paternalistic cultures. Best of all, MCA actually was hunting for a buyer.

Thus it was that in the spring of 1990, Ovitz urged Hirata to take a serious look at MCA. Then in June, Stephen Rivers met with Ovitz, Sandy Climan, and Bob Goldman, and Ovitz told the CAA spokesman: "We can't talk about this, but there's something big that's going to happen down the road. Keep your ears open. Make sure you have the right assistant; it's going to get crazy at some point."

In late August, Ovitz contacted Felix Rohatyn, the investment banker at Lazard Frères who happened to be a member of the MCA board, asking Rohatyn to convey Matsushita's interest to MCA. Hirata and Wasserman then met at Wasserman's home, got along well, and the deal was moving ahead. By this time, swearing everyone to secrecy, Ovitz had organized a team of 125 people on behalf of Matsushita, among whom were staffers from CAA, including Stephen Rivers; a group from the public relations firm of Adams & Rinehart; and a law firm in New York, Simpson Thacher & Bartlett. Ovitz turned to his friend Herb Allen to handle the investment-banking side for Matsushita. Allen recalls that "we probably had a more conservative viewpoint on the price to be paid than others in the deal. While the Japanese would have paid a lot more money, we didn't think it was worth it, so we helped out there."

Problems developed soon after Ovitz had assembled the team. Sidney Sheinberg, the President of MCA, learned of the secret efforts to sell MCA, and informed the MCA board. He also informed David Geffen, who only recently had become MCA's largest shareholder with his 10 million shares. Early in September, eager to conclude the deal quickly, Ovitz met a number of times with Wasserman and Sheinberg. He didn't mention the price Matsushita would be willing to pay for MCA. Then on September 19, in session this time with Sheinberg and Rohatyn at Lazard Frères, Ovitz indicated that Matsushita was thinking of paying between $75 and $90 a share. But Iraqi leader Saddam Hussein had invaded Kuwait the previous August 2, causing the stock market to plunge. Thus MCA's stock was trading in mid-September at a mere $36 a share, and Rohatyn's response to Ovitz was that MCA would not bargain on the basis of the stock's present depressed value. Then on September 25, *The Wall Street Journal* broke the story of Matsushita's interest in MCA, and MCA's stock soared from $34.50 to $54.25 overnight. Though Matsushita was distraught over the leak, blaming MCA, its executives did schedule a New York meeting for late November, to work out the final details of the deal. Matsushita, however, told the Japanese press that the deal might not come off, arguing that MCA was trying to make itself more valuable by leaking details of the proposed merger. Lew Wasserman became infuriated and, as the meeting neared, tensions rose dramatically.

Once the news of the possible deal had leaked, reports began to surface that Ovitz wanted to run the MCA studio. Ovitz denied the report.

In late November, Wasserman and Sheinberg had dinner with Hirata and Keiya Toyonaga, another Matsushita executive, at the Plaza Athenee in New York. Accompanying them were Michael Ovitz, Felix Rohatyn, and Bob Strauss, a power broker in the Democratic Party and an MCA board member who was serving as a paid adviser to Matsushita. The next morning, both sides met in Sheinberg's apartment in the Trump Tower to finalize the deal. Trouble arose when they tried to agree on the price of the buyout. Wasserman seemed to be content with $75 a share, the price that Ovitz had broached in earlier talks. But the Matsushita men now offered only $64 a share, and to their great disappointment, Wasserman pronounced the deal dead on arrival. Ovitz told the Japanese that he believed Wasserman was serious, and wouldn't budge; Ovitz hoped that Hirata was bluffing, but the Matsushita executive stood firm at the $64-a-share figure. Wasserman was in a real bind now, for he knew that if he walked away from the deal, the MCA stock would plummet just as fast as it had risen upon the news of the proposed deal.

By now more negotiator than consultant, Michael Ovitz put his own kind of pressure on the players by declaring, on Thanksgiving eve, that the deal was dead and that he had had enough: He was boarding a plane to join his family in Los Angeles for the holiday. Was this flight a negotiating ploy on Ovitz's part? It seems unlikely, since most of the others also thought that the deal was finished: The two sides were too far apart on price and the Japanese wouldn't budge. But some of the negotiators were mindful of the possibility that Ovitz might be leaving the bargaining table only to jolt the participants into changing their minds.

That same Thanksgiving eve, Bob Strauss dined with Lew Wasserman. Wasserman indicated that if the price were just a few dollars higher, he might reconsider. Just as they were concluding their conversation, Ovitz's plane was landing in Los Angeles. Three and a half hours later, at 5:30 a.m. Los Angeles time, Strauss and Rohatyn were on the phone to Ovitz, suggesting that a deal might still be possible. Ovitz phoned Hirata and convinced him to raise the offer by $3 a share; he then arranged for Hirata and Toyonaga to meet again with Wasserman and Sheinberg. When the four men did meet again back in New York, it took them all of 45 minutes to conclude the deal, which called for Matsushita to pay $66 a share, or $6.59 billion.

Few deals were being made at that sluggish time on Wall Street, so the transaction was even bigger news than usual. Critics assailed the deal as representing one more piece of America being sold off to the Japanese, but

David Geffen certainly wasn't complaining: The deal made him an even wealthier man. And Wasserman and Sheinberg could take solace from the fact that MCA was likely to remain in one piece.

Ovitz's business friends love to point out how much he contributed to the deal. Says Herb Allen: "The complicated part that Mike did was selling the Japanese on the concept, and then bringing Wasserman to the bargaining table. The greatest achievement was moving the Japanese, and getting Wasserman to agree. Mike brought the deal from his own goal line to about the one-yard line of the other side. For the actual closing of the deal, he had assistance." (Allen credits himself and Bob Strauss for providing that assistance.)

In fact, this had been Herb Allen's first chance to get to know Michael Ovitz, and he liked what he saw: "He was very effective, very determined. He was participating in an arena [investment banking] where he had no experience, but he absorbed the information and made the deal happen. This was a major financial transaction, very different from signing a star. I admired his desire for the success of the deal, and his willingness to accept advice from people who had done these things before."

As for the members of CAA's deal-making team, the experience of working with Ovitz on this one was harrowing. Ray Kurtzman thought the deal had died at least a dozen times. Each time, when he asked Ovitz how he was going to overcome the latest obstacle, Ovitz's response was "Never let up."

The deal had its modest advantages for Ovitz himself: For one thing, he took in $40 million in consulting fees. The high fee aroused much envy on the part not just of other Hollywood talent agents but also of investment bankers on Wall Street, who were all too aware that in recent days there had been fewer and fewer deals to broker. And it only rubbed salt in the wounds of the Wall Street crowd that a mere Hollywood talent agent had pulled off this huge deal.

According to Ovitz, his fees went into a separate company that had nothing formally to do with CAA. Only those agents who worked directly on the deals with him were compensated.

The Sony and Matsushita deals provided Ovitz with close relationships to the owners of two major Hollywood studios. But far more importantly, it was now clear that Michael Ovitz had become a full-fledged member of the elite fraternity of corporate deal-makers. No other Hollywood person had ever dared to step within that rarified circle.

But Ovitz had still bigger things in mind for himself. When journalist Connie Bruck, interviewing him for a piece she was writing in *The New Yorker*, noted that the MCA deal had been an incredibly apt culmination

of his longtime interests and labors, Ovitz snapped: "I don't see it as a culmination. I see it as a plateau." In the past Ovitz had limited himself to
signing up movie and television clients and then finding work for them.
Now he was engaged in the delicate task of brokering corporate deals
between the Hollywood studios and some of the most powerful corporations in the world. In so doing he had redefined and reshaped the job of
"talent agent" into one that made him one-part corporate consultant, one-
part investment banker. And in time, he believed, those new roles might
suit him perfectly.

Excited and even emboldened as he may have been by his adventures outside CAA's traditional core business, Michael Ovitz still was
determined not to let his own outside work interfere with his agency's central mission: the acquiring and nurturing of show-business clients. In the
winter of 1991 he had his eye on a young director, Tim Burton, who had
been lighting up Hollywood with some brilliant films, including *Beetlejuice*
(1988), *Batman* (1989), and *Edward Scissorhands* (1990). Ovitz had
become a big fan of Burton's. "I loved his work because it was very
painterly and artistic. You'd look at *Edward Scissorhands*. It was like an
oil painting, with the reds and blues of the tract houses." When Ovitz
learned that Burton was a student of art, he invited him to his Brentwood
home to see his art collection. Burton represented a special challenge to
Ovitz because the agent had never met the director before. Yet Ovitz felt
he could offer the director an agency that was putting together the best
deals in town, and whatever Ovitz said to him clearly proved effective:
Burton dropped William Morris, and signed on with CAA.

Needless to say, William Morris executives were furious. They contended that Ovitz had promised Burton the moon—including his own
theme park—but that nothing was delivered. "None of it happened," says
William Morris President Jerry Katzman bitterly. "There was no reason for
Burton to leave William Morris, and no reason for CAA to go after him,
except that was what CAA did. It was never happy until it had every
client." Ovitz contends that "I had high hopes for Burton, but he didn't
want to build the company we wanted to build for him."

Katzman has acknowledged that CAA is not the first agency to pursue
clients aggressively ("stealing clients," in Katzman's phrase), but CAA
went after Morris *agents* as well, hiring away Fred Spektor, Rick Nicita,
Kevin Huvane, Bryan Lourd, Beth Swofford, and Jane Sindell: "We were
not only looking over our shoulders at our clients, but our agents as well."

While at CAA, Burton co-produced *Tim Burton's The Nightmare Before Christmas* (1993) and *Cabin Boy* (1994). In the mid-1990s he also produced *James and the Giant Peach, Batman Returns,* and *Batman Forever.*

THE SECOND *PREMIERE* power list appeared in May 1991, and once again Michael Ovitz's name headed it. The rest of the top ten were: Michael Eisner; Fox Chairman Barry Diller; MCA President Sidney Sheinberg; Walt Disney Studios Chairman Jeffrey Katzenberg; Warner Brothers chiefs Bob Daly and Terry Semel; Universal Pictures Chairman Tom Pollock; Twentieth Century Fox Chairman Joe Roth; Paramount Communications President Stanley Jaffe; and Columbia Pictures Chairman Peter Guber.

Of Ovitz, *Premiere* wrote:

Rank last year: Take a guess.

Job title: CAA pooh-bah, godfather, shogun, whatever he wants.

Status report: Confirmed position as international wheeler-dealer with the Matsushita purchase of MCA; packaged *Hook* . . . and *Havana.*

Strengths: What a year! Everything from the big picture to the big deal. Added Coppola and Spielberg, after snaring Costner in 1989. With the waning of the truly bankable star, the power of the agencies may not be quite what it was. But calling Ovitz an 'agent' is like calling Howard Hughes 'a movie producer.' And while rivals try to build dynasties, Ovitz has entered the next generation.

Weakness: What do you do as an encore when you're Ovitz? Maybe even he's not sure. Does he want to run MCA? Technically, he never made a movie, but that won't stop him (nor should it). He's not the most personable guy in the world, but that hasn't hurt him either. As Jesse Jackson might say, if he can conceive it, he can achieve it. Maybe someone will figure an antitrust angle.

What to watch for: Whatever he wants you to watch for.

WHEN SOMETHING NEGATIVE happened to Ovitz—and certainly federal legal action taken against him was just that—the man was so powerful, the media so in awe of him, that it tended to get downplayed.

Thus although an item appeared in the *Los Angeles Times* of August 31, 1991, telling of Ovitz's alleged involvement in some wrongdoing, the newspaper gave scant attention to the event. Ovitz and six other pension-plan trustees had settled three Labor Department lawsuits that had accused them of conflict-of-interest. More specifically, what Ovitz and the other trustees were accused of was investing money from three pension funds, two of which were separate from CAA, into Toluca Investments, a limited partnership in which the CAA pension fund had invested.

According to the government, the trustees slowly started to put their own money into the partnership, which came back to them in the form of interest payments to their companies' pension funds. The transaction turned up as part of a routine Labor Department audit in 1988. The government argued that the partnership had violated prohibitions with regard to trustees transferring plan assets with an eye to their own benefit, while acting on behalf of parties whose interests were in fact not well served by the plan.

Bob Goldman, CAA's chief financial officer, and Bill Haber, one of the five CAA co-founders, were named as the other CAA trustees involved.

None of the trustees, including Ovitz, admitted to guilt. A consent decree was agreed upon that settled the Labor Department suits. The decree indicated that Ovitz, Goldman, and Haber, along with four others, received $546,452 from the partnership in exchange for their interests in the partnership. As a result of the consent decree, Ovitz, Goldman, and Haber were required to divest themselves of their interest in the partnership. When asked about the pension fund case in the spring of 1997, Ovitz said he believed that the media had paid too much attention to the matter: "We didn't think we did anything wrong. There was nothing heinous about what we did."

What seems most significant about this matter is that Michael Ovitz's need to settle a series of lawsuits brought by the federal government caused not a ripple of controversy. Despite Michael Ovitz's contention that the press had overplayed the incident, in fact the media treated the incident as being just that, an incident. The consent decree, as filed in Los Angeles Federal District Court, was a matter of public record, and the U.S. Labor Department even issued a press release, due to Ovitz's involvement in the case. Yet very few news organizations ran a story. *The Hollywood Reporter* ran a brief item referring to the Labor Department news release, and citing CAA spokesperson Stephen Rivers as saying: "This is at most a technical violation of the ERISA (Employment Retirement Income Security Act) regulations."

Buoyed by the Sony and Matsushita deals, Michael Ovitz began to believe that he had found a new role for CAA. He could now take the agency in a host of new directions, ones that would open up new revenue streams while at the same time giving him a heightened sense of personal satisfaction. Soon, "branching out" had become the main focus of his activities. On September 4, 1991, he brought the world fresh evidence that the Matsushita deal was no fluke. It was announced on that day that the Creative Artists Agency was entering the field of advertising, an unprecedented move that would blur the line between Hollywood and Madison Avenue. The Coca-Cola Company, trying to regain the market-share edge it had lost to rival Pepsico, had hired CAA as its media and communications consultant for its advertising strategy. The CAA deal brought a stinging slap in the face to Coca-Cola's two huge, New York–based advertising agencies: McCann-Erickson Worldwide, which handled the Coke brand, and Lintas:Worldwide, which created advertising for Diet Coke.

Ovitz was exploiting relationships he had cultivated in earlier deals. He had a strong friendship with Coca-Cola President Donald Keough, forged when Coca-Cola had purchased Columbia Pictures and later sold it to the Sony Corporation. He had an important link with Herb Allen, the investment banker who happened to be a member of the Coca-Cola board; and he also had a connection with Peter Sealey, Coca-Cola's Senior Vice President for Marketing, whom Ovitz had known when Sealey ran the marketing department at Columbia. Ovitz suggested to these friends that CAA could produce commercials as well as, if not better than, the Madison Avenue shops. He didn't envision turning CAA into a full-fledged advertising agency, but rather turning loose CAA's imaginative clients and staff to come up with some great new advertising ideas.

Thus, even as he expanded his influence into one of the most important sectors of American business, Ovitz also, in making this deal, was putting CAA's talent list at the disposal of Coca-Cola to promote its products. This wasn't really so unusual, since Paula Abdul and Elton John already had appeared in Coke commercials, and Michael Jackson was a Pepsi-Cola pitchman. But it was not only Ovitz's access to the stars that had drawn the executives at Coca-Cola to him. It was also the belief that CAA had its finger on the pulse of American culture, and that that could prove highly useful.

In 1991, Coca-Cola controlled nearly half of the $47-billion-a-year worldwide soft-drink market, way ahead of Pepsi, which controlled only 15 percent of it. But domestically, the Atlanta firm had been hunkered down in a drawn-out battle with Pepsico: Pepsi had 33.2 percent of the American market, compared to Coke's 40.9 percent. Both companies spent about $200 million each year on their American advertising, but one survey had indicated that America's television viewers preferred Pepsi's commercial.

SHELLY HOCHRON RAN the marketing department at Paramount Pictures, and then its counterpart at Columbia Pictures. Now, in the fall of 1991, she was a production executive at Tri-Star Pictures. She had met Michael Ovitz a few times, and she still remembers the first time vividly. It was at Tri-Star, and Ovitz had come to the studio on behalf of Warren Beatty to discuss the marketing campaign for the film *Bugsy*. She recalls him entering the room: "Michael enters a room either blessed or cursed with a certain mystique about him which either alienates or attracts people. He is preceded by his reputation, so you have an anticipation of someone important. He lived up to that reputation. He was perfectly dressed, extremely neat, physically elegant. His posture was straight. All very deliberate, but it seemed natural for him. He's renowned for his eye contact. When you speak to him, you feel like you're the center of the universe."

Shelly had read in the newspaper that Michael Ovitz had concluded the deal with Coca-Cola. She was sitting at her desk one afternoon a week later, when Ovitz phoned her. After they had exchanged pleasantries, he said, "Let me just ask you something."

"What's that?"

"Are you happy?"

"I assume you're speaking professionally." She paused. "I think I could be happier."

"How would you like to come and talk to me?"

She said she would love to, and felt no need to ask him what he had in mind: "It didn't matter. It was like a summoning."

She then congratulated him on the Coke deal. "This sounds very exciting."

"You have no idea."

She felt thrilled, though she couldn't have said why.

Hochron's impression on first arriving at CAA: "It was very impressive. Everything Michael does is. They parked my car. I felt very important. There was someone waiting for me in this massive, cathedral-like lobby. I was made to feel very special. He must really want me to do something for him, I thought."

When she walked into the office, Ovitz rose from his chair, gave her a big, friendly handshake and had her sit down on a couch. *What a wonderful way there is about him,* she thought, *how successful he is at making me feel valued.* She felt good.

They talked for an hour, and Hochron still remembers every detail. "He always had three white gardenias floating in a round crystal ball. His office was very fragrant, and everything was very meticulous. A sculpture was perfectly placed by the window. The room was very austere. I remember thinking: 'Something very important goes on here.' "

Michael Ovitz then asked Shelly Hochron to leave Tri-Star in order to work on the Coca-Cola account for him.

"It sounds interesting," she answered, then asked all sorts of questions. *Are you going to make commercials? What will you be consulting on? With whom will you be dealing? Do you have any concept of the extent of your role? What do you see as my role? Basically, what are we going to do with this?* Ovitz answered all of her questions briefly: "We have an agreement. The agreement is to begin a relationship. To formalize some kind of relationship, and see how this develops. Why don't you just come and work with me? We'll have fun."

Her proposed job sounded amorphous to her, and Hochron wasn't at all sure what she was supposed to do. But she also wasn't all that happy at Tri-Star, so she asked Ovitz to give her some time to think about what he was proposing.

Fine. When would he hear from her? He suggested that she call him on the following Monday morning. Then, evidently bothered that Hochron was having any hesitation at all about joining him, Ovitz asked: "What would prevent you from doing this?"

She thought for a moment, then answered: "I'd like to stay in the movie business. I want to make movies. I'm not an agent. I don't want to go back to marketing per se."

There had been no mention of money, but Hochron simply assumed that Ovitz would pay her as much as, if not more than, she had been making at Tri-Star.

Early Monday morning she called Ovitz, knowing that he was eager to hear from her. He wasn't in, but at 1:00 p.m. she heard from him: "I don't understand why you didn't call me, as you promised." She explained that she had phoned earlier. Ovitz then became upset that he hadn't been given the message. Once he had calmed down, she told him that she had decided to take the job: "I don't know what it is, but quite honestly it sounds new enough and exciting enough and *it's you,* so I'll do it." But when Hochron informed her Tri-Star boss, Mike Medavoy, that she planned to leave a year before her contract expired, he wrote her a note telling her that he refused to let her out of her contract. He even threatened to sue CAA and Coca-Cola if she left Tri-Star. Confused and distressed, Hochron showed the note to Ovitz. He assured her that Medavoy was bluffing, that he wouldn't insist that she stay if she wasn't happy or productive. She felt comforted: "No matter what, I felt Michael would take care of me." And Ovitz did just that. She came to work for him, and nothing further was heard from Medavoy.

As it turned out, it was the advertising firm of McCann and Erickson, rather than Mike Medavoy, who became the thorn in Hochron's side. McCann and Erickson had worked with Coca-Cola for forty years, Coke was McCann's most important worldwide account, and the CAA deal posed a serious threat to that relationship, raising the prospect that McCann would lose a good deal of money. For the first few months, Shelly Hochron tried to work with McCann, in effect to serve as an adviser to them. But it soon became clear to her that it was the relationship between Coke and McCann that was in need of an overhaul. Fearing that the material was too volatile for any secretary to see, Hochron wrote Ovitz a handwritten letter and entitled it "Random Thoughts." In essence she blamed McCann for being uninspired, and she thought that the practice of having CAA report to McCann should come to an end, as it would lead eventually to sabotage. Instead, McCann should report to CAA, and obtain the agency's endorsement of its plans. CAA, she wrote, "should be a partner in strategizing the future, not vendor to a client." Ovitz agreed, and then surprised Hochron by asking her if she was prepared to take over the account. She said yes.

The Ovitz link to Coke was unpopular in some quarters on Madison Avenue, since a major company seemed to be saying: "We don't need a full-service advertising agency; we just need creativity, and for that we're going to Hollywood." It was a shot across the industry's bow. Many on Madison Avenue wanted Ovitz to fail, or at least to move on quickly to his next project.

Now THAT POWER levels in Hollywood were being carefully calibrated by *Premiere* magazine, candidates for its power list waited anxiously each May to learn whether they would be on it—and if so, in what place. Great excitement and tension preceded the big event. In the days leading up to the list's publication, aides to the titans phoned *Premiere:* either they got their hands on a copy of the list as soon as it was compiled or, as some said, "I'm going to lose my job."

In May 1992, when the *Premiere* power list was published, the name "Michael Ovitz" headed it for the third straight year. The magazine explained why:

> *Status:* . . . Terrified Madison Avenue with Coca-Cola "macrovision" deal; also consulting with twenty-five or so other companies from Topps baseball cards to . . . Apple? Sought foreign monies for Orion. Continuing to consult with Matsushita. Trying on Lew Wasserman's shoes, brokering reconciliation between Diller and Eisner (or did Geffen do that?), settling Frank Mancuso–Paramount suit, and smoothing messy Frank Price–Mark Canton transition at Columbia. Signed Stanley Kubrick. Wooed Tim Burton away from William Morris. Eleven-year-old son teaching him how to use a computer.
>
> *Strengths:* Tenacious, smart, methodical, with a surprising sense of humor. Much feared. After a year of major deal-making, he's back in the day-to-day swing of things; going to Monday general meetings and Wednesday movie-project meetings, walking the halls, offering encouragement, and pressing for follow-up. Not afraid to make mistakes (and he does); one of the few Hollywood powers with enough job security to think and act long-term. Says he has a master plan. . . .
>
> *Weaknesses:* So what is it? Likes to talk ruefully about bad things that are destroying Hollywood (e.g., the big, greedy deal) while perpetuating same. Foray into hardware with Qsound was an embarrassing failure. Connie Bruck's *New Yorker* story lampooned his mania for secrecy and said he was out of the loop when the MCA–Matsushita deal finally went down, a point he takes *great* exception to. Still star-dependent, though note that three of today's biggest stars aren't his: Arnold, Eddie, and Julia. Note also that recent major hits (*The Hand That Rocks the Cradle, The Addams Family, Wayne's World*) don't have big-ticket talent.
>
> *What to watch for:* Outgrowing CAA. Does he want to run a studio? No—he wants to *own* a studio. Might a post-Matsushita Universal appeal to his synergistic side? Paramount après—Martin Davis?

Thus for three straight years, Michael Ovitz had been hailed as the King of Hollywood. As they say in that town, "What are you going to do for an encore?"

15

I've Been to See the Godfather!

THE MEDIA COULDN'T help but take notice of the heights to which Michael Ovitz had risen. With increasing frequency it reported on him, while taking it for granted that he was indeed the most powerful business figure in Hollywood. Encouraged to do so by his new spokesperson Stephen Rivers, Ovitz grudgingly agreed to see reporters from time to time. Almost always the conversations were off the record. This gave him a decided advantage, in that if a reporter asked him to verify a certain set of events, Ovitz could provide his own assessment while then remaining aloof from any news stories that arose on that subject.

In 1990, Alan Citron had become the entertainment reporter for the *Los Angeles Times*. Asking around who might be good sources, he was told *not* to rely on Michael Ovitz. He was too distant, too unapproachable. But Citron had been friendly with Stephen Rivers, and thus Rivers did arrange for the *L.A. Times* reporter to meet Ovitz for a 15-minute courtesy call. Ovitz gave Citron some advice about Hollywood—"Be careful what you hear. There are a lot of false rumors. People like to kill each other"—then promised to help the reporter.

In time, Ovitz became one of a dozen or so sources whom Citron felt he could rely upon for guidance with regard to Hollywood business stories. And the very fact that Ovitz continued to make himself available to Citron shows that he deemed the reporter to be trustworthy. (Those reporters whom he mistrusted, he refused to see; the tactic seemed flawed, however, in that those were the very reporters who then tended to pen the few negative news stories that got into the newspapers.) Citron's conversations with the talent agent were almost always off the record. "There was a time," recalls Citron, "when Ovitz was so 'underground,' just having a quote from him was a journalistic achievement."

Ovitz cultivated editors as well as reporters. Tina Brown had become the editor of *Vanity Fair* in 1984. Six months later, Michael Ovitz invited her to lunch. Not many people believed in *Vanity Fair* at that time, but Brown hoped to turn the magazine around. When Ovitz met Brown for lunch he asked to represent *Vanity Fair,* and talked excitedly about creating other related ventures for the magazine, including a TV show. No one had talked to her in such terms before, and therefore Tina Brown listened carefully. She recalls that "Ovitz wasn't the mythic, highly-charged figure he became. He was a coming agent; but not a household name. I liked him enormously. He was enthusiastic, creative, and supportive. He saw what I was trying to do." Nothing came of Ovitz's business proposals, but the relationship deepened. Whenever Brown came to Hollywood, she sought Ovitz out. He became a valuable asset for her, in that he allowed her to hold brainstorming sessions with the CAA agents, all of them off the record of course. These were the best and the brightest agents in town, and Brown loved to drink in what they had to say about the Hollywood scene: "I always found CAA the most dynamic shop by far." Yet she knew that Ovitz's new openness toward the media wasn't really his cup of tea. He liked it better when he had simply stonewalled the media. Still, Brown advised him to get over his hang-up about the press. Simply sidestepping all queries might have been possible in earlier days, but not in the early 1990s.

In cultivating relationships with leading figures in the media, Ovitz accrued another benefit: He could always pick up the telephone to one of them and ask that a story *not* be run. He rarely did this, however, simply because he didn't have to: Few in the media wanted to get on the bad side of Michael Ovitz. Susan Lyne, founder of *Premiere* magazine, tried never to let Ovitz get the upper hand with her over whether a news story would run. But that was no easy task. In the early days of the magazine, Ovitz asked Lyne not to run certain items; her routine response was: "If you're asking me not to run this item as a favor, I can't do that. But tell me why the item is wrong, and I won't run it." If Ovitz proved to be convincing, she wouldn't run the item. On a few occasions Ovitz said: "This story is wrong and I'll tell you why it's wrong, but I don't want to see that in the magazine." But he rarely intruded, and that is why those who were involved in one Sean Connery incident remember it so vividly.

It happened in 1992. *Premiere* had run an item revealing that Sean Connery had walked off the set of the film *Medicine Man* in order to play golf. With millions of dollars invested in Hollywood movies, producers usually are reluctant to grant even their superstars, like Connery, a day off at the links. Connery may have considered his jaunt to be fairly innocent, but a few days later someone informed him that the magazine had singled him out as being a delinquent actor. Even a star of his stature could scarcely afford such damning publicity. Thus Connery got on the phone to his agent and close friend, Michael Ovitz, who in turn gave an earful to the *Premiere* magazine editor. Ovitz told her how upset his client was over the article, and insisted that Connery never would walk off a movie set. Ovitz insisted upon a retraction.

The editor refused to retract, arguing that the magazine's source was reliable. But she knew that she still had Michael Ovitz and his fury to contend with, so she offered a kind of compromise. If Ovitz could produce someone to write a letter to the editor, saying that Connery would never leave a set, she would agree to publish it along with an Editor's Note stating that the magazine was fully aware of Mr. Connery's fine reputation for being a hard worker. Ovitz went ahead and found a letter-writer, and the editor fulfilled her part of the bargain by publishing the letter along with the Editor's Note.

Meanwhile, the *Los Angeles Times*'s Alan Citron had chosen to stop using Ovitz as a background source, finding it too complicated to interview him: "It could be a tiring experience, because he was such a perfectionist about every word that came out of his mouth." Of the hundreds of Hollywood executives and celebrities whom Citron was in the habit of interviewing, Ovitz was among the very few who seemed to derive genuine pain from being interviewed. Worrying that he might later regret making some utterance, he insisted upon knowing in advance precisely which quote a reporter planned to use. Sometimes he would ask Alan Citron to read back notes from their interview, and Ovitz would say, "I can say that better." He was, Citron noted, "like an over-eager student."

When the *Los Angeles Times* decided to do a major profile of Ovitz in the spring of 1992, Alan Citron asked Stephen Rivers if Ovitz would cooperate.

"Absolutely not," replied Rivers, and in subsequent days he phoned the reporter several times to urge him not to pursue the story.

Ignoring the advice, Citron began to interview Ovitz acquaintances. Two months later, Ovitz had decided that it was time to start cooperating with Citron. "From that point on he was almost *too* accessible," says Citron. Ovitz invited him to dinners lasting as long as four hours; lined up celebrity interviews—"so many," Citron remembers, "that I didn't have time to see them all"; and held frequent if brief phone conversations with the reporter. But only at their final meeting did Ovitz agree to speak on the record. It often was said in the media that Ovitz diabolically threatened to deny reporters access to celebrities if they wrote negatively about him or CAA, but he was far more subtle than that: Ovitz simply selected a few reporters like Citron and provided them with a good bit of access to the film stars. In so doing, he sent a clear message to other journalists: *If you want this kind of access, too, you had better play ball with me.*

When Citron asked Ovitz if he would pose for a photograph for the story, he declined, unwilling to become so visibly identified with a story that might turn out to be negative. The reporter then warned him that without a posed photograph, the *Times*'s photo editor would simply make use of some old photo of Ovitz provided by one of the photo agencies. But that prospect held no terror for Ovitz, since he held the rights to all of those photos and had no intention of approving their use. Thus, with no decent photograph of Ovitz available for the newspaper's magazine cover, the *Times* decided to run his caricature, with celebrities popping out of his forehead, mouth, and ears.

Appearing on July 26, 1992, the magazine profile was entitled "Eating Hollywood Alive: The Insatiable Appetite and Other Deadly Sins of Mike Ovitz." It began by recounting Ovitz's coup in snaring Tim Burton, suggesting that the coup was classic Ovitz, "incisive and inflammatory." Describing Ovitz as "awesomely respected and feared" in Hollywood, Alan Citron suggested that for all of the talent agent's success, the more he turned from agenting to corporate consulting, the higher was the resistance rising to his way of doing business—"especially from a fluid anti-Ovitz cabal" that at various times consisted of Walt Disney Studios Chairman Jeffrey Katzenberg, entertainment mogul David Geffen, and producer Ray Stark. Citron acknowledged that Ovitz generally was identified as being the most powerful figure in Hollywood, but cited Stark as suggesting that CAA's power-grabbing, and its closely-guarded management style, were insidious influences upon the industry. "It's not agents," Stark said. "It's *secret* agents."

That Stark quote marked one of the very first occasions on which a major Hollywood figure had dared to publicly vent his wrath against Michael Ovitz and his agency. David Geffen also was cited in the article, as blaming Ovitz for throwing the entire Hollywood economy out of whack. Just as Stark's comments were terse, so too were Geffen's. Joe Smith and Barry Diller, in contrast, provided sympathetic comments about Ovitz.

While some thought that Alan Citron had been too gentle in his treatment of Ovitz, Ovitz himself was irate after reading the profile, not at his critics so much as at himself. "If that's who I am," he told one colleague, "I have a lot of reevaluating to do about myself." Other than during the

Joe Eszterhas episode, the media had fired no heavy artillery at Ovitz, and now that a few shells had crossed the perimeter and landed more or less on target, Ovitz took the attack very personally indeed.

It's easy to identify Ovitz's basic problem with the media: He simply cares too deeply about what is written about him. Had he been the head of a meat-packing firm in Chicago, or an auto supply company in Minneapolis, the media would have been glad to ignore him. As it was, he operated the most powerful talent agency in Hollywood, and that was all it took to tantalize the press. But would Ovitz have received better treatment from the media if he hadn't cared so much about what was written about him? Not necessarily. Still, once it became clear to journalists that Ovitz wanted to keep as low a profile as possible, even as he engineered some of Hollywood's most glamorous deals, he became an even more favored subject of scrutiny. Had Ovitz decided to explain himself to the media for say, a year, and not worry about what journalists had to say about him during that period, he might well have been better off. For after that year the media might have grown tired of him, and he would have become far less fascinating to them. *Too* accessible, *too* conspicuous, he would have become commonplace. But Ovitz never afforded the media that chance to get bored with him. By remaining "underground" while dealing with the media only very selectively and on a "need-to-know" basis, Ovitz helped to feed the media frenzy about him. He never really seemed to understand *why* the media was so fascinated with him, and that made it all the more difficult for him to come up with an optimal strategy for deflating that fascination. At any rate, Michael Ovitz was simply too inscrutable, too controversial, too inaccessible, for the media to ignore. Ironically, he had it in his power to change all that; but for as long as he failed to exercise that power wisely, he remained a damn good news story.

0CTOBER 15, 1992. CAA executives were making their first presentation to Coca-Cola's senior executives in a very crucial meeting held in a windowless conference room at Coca-Cola headquarters in Atlanta. Michael Ovitz and his aides, Shelly Hochron and Len Fink, walked into the room and seated themselves around a U-shaped table. Fink had been hired by Ovitz to help Hochron with the Coca-Cola account; he had been associate creative director at the Chiat/Day Advertising Agency in New York. Also attending were Phil Geier, head of the McCann-Erickson parent firm Interpublic; John Bergin, a McCann-Erickson executive; and Coca-Cola executives Donald Keough, Douglas Ivester, and Peter Sealey.

Ovitz spoke for a few minutes, then asked his aides to continue. Hochron and Fink threw out nearly 50 ideas as "possibles" for Coca-Cola's future advertising campaigns. Among them: A dog digs up an old Coke bottle; "Renoir throws a party"; polar bears observe the Aurora Borealis, with the punch line being: "Always cool . . . always Coke." A Star Trek–like crew ferrets out a man-eating alien in their midst, by testing everyone's knowledge of Coca-Cola trivia. Hochron also mentioned that famed directors Francis Ford Coppola and Rob Reiner, both CAA clients, might be available to direct some of these ads.

It took about five seconds for the people around the table to realize that Michael Ovitz and his team really did know something about advertising.

Even a rival advertising executive, John Bergin, was impressed. He passed a note to a colleague on which was scribbled the two simple words, "We're dead." Bergin later would tell a reporter that Ovitz was "so goddamn charming, I almost caught myself cheering for his f—in' stuff." Another McCann executive would describe the CAA team's performance as having constituted "one of the power plays of the century."

On September 21, after she had returned to Los Angeles, Shelly Hochron received a huge bouquet of flowers and a note from Ovitz:

> Dear Shelly,
>
> Best picture, best screenplay, best actress, best mind . . . incredible job as always.
>
> Love, Michael

MEANWHILE, THE CORPORATE consultant was keeping his hand in all that old Hollywood maneuvering. In the fall of 1992, Michael Ovitz took on the ticklish assignment of trying to further the career of Hollywood's most influential businesswoman, Sherry Lansing. She had been a CAA client dating back to 1983, when Lansing and Stanley Jaffe put together a production company to produce such films as *Black Rain, The Accused, Racing with the Moon,* and *Fatal Attraction.* Jaffe, known for his confrontational style, became president of Paramount Communications in the early 1990s, and soon asked Lansing to join him as studio chief. She was ambivalent, eager to spend more time with her family and to travel less. Over breakfast one day, she asked Michael Ovitz to help her make this difficult decision.

Ovitz asked Lansing a set of questions, among them these two: *How would she feel reporting to Stanley Jaffe? How did her new husband, direc-*

tor William Friedkin, feel about all this? That last question surprised her. It was personal. Few others would have dared to pose such a query, and she liked that about Ovitz. Her husband, she replied, was neutral on this one. *How did little Jack feel about the job?* Ovitz asked, referring to Lansing's son. Another personal question, but still Lansing wasn't put off. She said she really didn't know how her son felt, but Michael Ovitz really did seem to understand, as few others did, what the actual influences impacting her decision were. Ovitz then summed it all up for her: Her decision had nothing to do with money, or with proving herself. It came down to what sort of lifestyle she wanted to have over the next few years. *What a wonderful person Ovitz is,* she thought, *so caring.*

Lansing decided to join Jaffe at Paramount, and asked Ovitz if he would negotiate on her behalf.

Ovitz had one concern: Sherry Lansing and Stanley Jaffe had been close friends for so long that Lansing easily could undermine Ovitz's efforts by conversing too candidly with Jaffe. Thus, for as long as the terms weren't settled, "You can never talk to him, you hear me?" Ovitz insisted, and Lansing reluctantly agreed. Ovitz told Jaffe the same thing. Lansing tried her best to live up to the agreement, but not always with total success.

"Did he try to bring up the negotiation?" Ovitz asked, when he heard that Lansing and Jaffe had indeed been conversing.

"No," Lansing said, although she knew differently. Nonetheless, Ovitz wrapped up the negotiations successfully, and Lansing became the chief of studio at Paramount Communications on November 4, 1992.

Once Sherry Lansing had become a studio chief, Michael Ovitz ceased to be her agent. But with so many of Ovitz's clients working for Paramount, they did talk frequently. Ovitz occasionally phoned Lansing and asked if she was feeling all right. "Sure," she replied, "why do you ask?" "I'm worried about you. You must be overtired or stressed, because if you weren't, you could never have made the mistake of not paying my client what we asked for." Sometimes the ploy worked, sometimes not.

Ovitz never showed her his tough side. When he wanted something of her he worked hard to win her over, but always using his charm, nothing else. "He is brilliant," Lansing says, eager to dispel the notion that Ovitz always bullies his way into getting things. "Mike Ovitz never threatened. He was never threatening; he was persuasive; he had an opinion. There was never any implied threat. CAA would decide on a director, and they would come at me on all fronts to try to convince me to take the director. They didn't always convince me, but there were no mixed signals. The camaraderie there was incredible. Ovitz has an incredible genius for business. I just love the guy. I don't have one negative thing to say about him."

So MUCH POWER, so much influence. The truth was, however, that Michael Ovitz was getting bored handling even such interesting and powerful show-business clients as Sherry Lansing. He wanted to ascend to even greater heights. CAA was a tiny operation, compared to many other corporate giants. Its revenues were moving steadily upward, but they were still "only" between $100 and $200 million a year, dwarfed by the billion-dollar firms with whom Ovitz had been dealing. How he would have loved to build CAA into one of those giants! But he knew that to be impossible. He would never take the agency public, and he would never sell it. And even if he did, where would *that* leave him? Exceedingly wealthy, but out of work. On occasion he toyed—sometimes quite seriously—with the idea of leaving CAA in order to become part of a much larger operation. He turned to business friends from time to time as potential partners, working especially closely with Gary Wilson, whom he had gotten to know when Wilson arrived in Los Angeles in 1985 to join the senior management team at The Walt Disney Company. Wilson and Frank Wells helped to run the business for the next four years, and then in 1989 Wilson left the company and, along with Al Checchi, purchased Northwest Airlines. It was Checchi who had introduced Ovitz to Wilson. Ovitz and Wilson never became close personal friends, but Ovitz had always admired his deal-making skills and the fact that he had managed to take over a major company. Thus when Ovitz decided that the time had come for him to extend his reach beyond CAA, he turned to Gary Wilson. He began to talk to him about buying, along with other partners, a large-sized entertainment company, with it being understood that Ovitz would become the chief executive officer of the firm. But although these men seriously looked into the purchase of various companies, they couldn't find one that seemed like a good buy. And there were two other problems as well. First, Ovitz found that, as an agent, it was very difficult to try to buy companies to whom he was selling clients and projects; and second, a great deal of cash was required.

Meanwhile, corporate consulting was beginning to take up more and more of Ovitz's time. On February 10, 1993, CAA unveiled its first set of advertising ideas for the new Coca-Cola campaign, at New York's Museum of Television and Radio. The *Los Angeles Times* noted that the advertisements "evoke everything from the staccato rhythms of MTV to the wistfulness of Steven Spielberg films." The company's new motto would be "Always Coca-Cola," replacing the "You can't beat the real thing" phrase introduced by Coke four years earlier. Of the 26 ads produced, CAA had done 24, McCann-Erickson only two. The 45 minutes of "Always Coke" commercials featured no single personality, like Max Headroom. Instead, they ranged from 15-second "real-life" snippets to "high-concept" pieces—some whimsical, some romantic, all hipper than Coke's traditional image; in short, more Hollywood. While no CAA clients appeared in the ads, two directors, Richard Donner and Rob Reiner, made spots.

Among the ads was a minute-long one called "Glassblower," filmed in Tuscany by the *Northern Exposure* team of Joshua Brand and John Falsey: A beautiful woman spies on a male glassblower, who is artfully fashioning a Coke bottle. Richard Donner directed an elaborate sci-fi ad called "Spaceship," depicting a dangerous alien whose identity is humorously discovered when it is revealed that the creature does not know the name of earth's most popular beverage. But it was the "polar bears" ad that really captured everyone's imagination, with its clan of animated white beasts enjoying the Northern Lights with Cokes in hand. Coca-Cola executives seemed quite pleased with CAA's efforts, and over the coming years kept asking Shelly Hochron and her team to provide them with more material.

Ovitz was proud of the ads, and gave an advance look at them to some business friends including publishers Mort Zuckerman and S. I. Newhouse. "Enormously creative," Newhouse told Ovitz. Robert Wright, the president of NBC, couldn't get over what Ovitz had done: "The whole idea that Michael Ovitz, an agent, could come out of the woodwork and have such a prominent role in the advertising and marketing of Coca-Cola is really extraordinary, and is an accomplishment that defied great odds. Having that much involvement in the production of advertising is incredible."

Despite all of his "extracurricular" activities, Michael Ovitz made a special effort not to ignore CAA's core business. His making deals for Sony, Matsushita, and Coca-Cola would mean little if film stars began to walk out the agency's door, or if CAA failed to pull in new top-bill clients. For that reason, Ovitz was thrilled when he learned that one of television's biggest personalities was seeking his help.

David Letterman had wanted to host NBC's *Tonight* show on late-night television for as long as he could remember. He had been the increasingly popular host of *Late Night with David Letterman* in the 12:30 a.m. slot since February 1, 1982, and assumed that he had a good chance of being chosen to succeed Johnny Carson, host of the *Tonight* show, when Carson retired. But when NBC announced in June 1991 that Jay Leno would succeed Carson in May 1992, Letterman was crushed, and embittered that his long-standing ambition seemed to have been permanently derailed. He even feared that his television career might be over for good. Although Letterman's contract expired only in April of 1993, NBC's choice of Leno drained Letterman of the desire to work any longer for NBC. Letterman's executive producer, Peter Lassally, suggested to Letterman that he consider embarking on a film career, but the talk-show host hated the idea. He was a television personality, period.

Up until then Letterman had had little use for agents, but that July, when Lassally proposed that he consider asking Michael Ovitz to take him on, the talk-show host listened carefully. "That kind of intrigues me," he said. Peter Lassally doubted whether he could just call up Michael Ovitz and ask to set up a meeting for Letterman. Ovitz seemed too big for that. Then Lassally remembered that his son Tom, who was an executive vice president at Warner Brothers, had a close friend at CAA, Jay Moloney. Tom called Jay, to ask if he would be willing to talk to his (Tom's) father. Moloney agreed, and therefore Peter Lassally phoned Moloney and asked the agent if Michael Ovitz might be interested in talking to David Letterman. Moloney sent word back to Lassally that Michael Ovitz was very interested indeed.

Back when Letterman was a stand-up comedian working out of L.A., he had met Michael when Ovitz was an agent at William Morris. Letterman had been appearing as a guest on The Jackson Five's summer TV show, which Ovitz had arranged for his clients, The Jackson Five. Letterman recalls little of note about that first meeting beyond the fact that Ovitz seemed like another of those "young, bright-faced agents, and there was no shortage of those in California." Over the years, however, he had followed Ovitz's career, and knew him to be far more serious-minded than the average talent agent.

Thus it was that on a late summer morning in Los Angeles, talk-show host David Letterman, still a bit skeptical, and TV producer Peter Lassally entered the CAA atrium and were escorted to Ovitz's long, narrow office on the third floor. There a warm, bubbly man delivered a rapid-fire pitch that kept Letterman rapt. Ovitz began by saying that he saw Letterman as a huge star "with geometric possibilities," whatever that meant. He had drawn up a plan for the talk-show host's future, and CAA was prepared to deliver on everything he wanted, including Letterman's long-time dream of being offered the *Tonight* show. Indeed, Ovitz promised, not only would Letterman be offered that show, but the other two networks would make similar offers. And still Ovitz wasn't through: Letterman, in his capable hands, would arouse great interest among the Hollywood studios. Letterman left the meeting after an hour, feeling giddy. He and Lassally drove back to the executive producer's beach house, so stunned by Ovitz's performance that they didn't say a word. Upon their arrival at the house, Letterman finally blurted out: "That was too much." Spotting Lassally's wife, Alice, he shouted: "I've been to see the godfather! I had a meeting with the godfather!" Letterman later would recall that "a lot of what Ovitz said to me was enigmatic. But here was a man of great intelligence, of great power. He had a very, very strong energy. I liked him immediately."

Sitting down with Lassally at the beach house, Letterman asked him for his impressions of Ovitz: Should they go with him? Lassally was of two minds: On the one hand, he was doubtful that Ovitz could deliver on all that he had promised; but on the other hand, he liked the idea of having him on their side. It would be a signal to the industry that Letterman should not be counted out. Finally, Lassally simply urged the talk-show host to think carefully about whether to take on Ovitz. A few days later, Letterman excitedly informed Lassally that he was ready to sign with CAA. "I couldn't wait to begin that association," Letterman remembers.

Ovitz certainly had his work cut out for him. He had to figure out a way to get Letterman out of his NBC contract, which would be no small task in and of itself. NBC retained "first negotiating position," meaning that Letterman couldn't negotiate with anyone else until NBC's initial negotiating period came to an end in February of 1993. In early 1992, Ovitz began to talk to NBC executives, searching for a way to release Letterman from his contractual restraints.

Jay Moloney recalls how skeptical he was about the likelihood that Ovitz would be able to get Letterman out of his NBC contract. But Ovitz always told him: "Don't worry." And whenever Moloney tried to suggest to Ovitz that it was more complicated than that, that it was virtually impossible to free Letterman from his contractual obligations, Ovitz just smiled.

Ovitz employed a gentle approach with the network brass at first, suggesting that NBC would foster a great deal of goodwill with Letterman by being conciliatory about the contract. NBC's executives, however, felt that they would get nothing in return for their goodwill. Nonetheless, they did want to remain on good terms with Letterman, a factor that Ovitz was able to exploit. After a bit of the Ovitz magic had been applied, NBC caved in a little by permitting Letterman to negotiate freely; in return for that consideration, he agreed to extend his NBC contract from April 2, 1993 to

June 3, 1993, thereby providing the network with an additional three months of advertising revenue. Ovitz then invited CBS and ABC, as well as the studios and syndicators, to make their pitches to Letterman.

With CBS, Ovitz struck gold. He enticed the network into offering Letterman an incredible deal: a three-year contract worth $42 million, calling for him to be the first host of a late-night talk show on CBS to make a serious challenge against the *Tonight* show in a generation.

But Letterman still was hoping for a miracle: that he would be named host of the *Tonight* show.

One evening in early January 1993, Letterman was in his office after taping a show. Ovitz phoned from Los Angeles to say that NBC had asked him to host the *Tonight* show. It was the news Letterman had been hoping to hear ever since he became a television broadcaster. And now it seemed within his reach. But alas, there was a catch. What NBC actually was offering was for Letterman to replace Jay Leno, and not immediately but only in 17 months, when Leno's contract expired. Allowing Leno to host the *Tonight* show through the length of his contract would save NBC $18 million in severance pay.

Concentrating on the offer and not on the catch, Letterman greeted Ovitz's news with delirious joy. "That was an amazing accomplishment," Letterman would say later, "as was the fact that Ovitz could get me a job anywhere."

But Letterman's glee turned to gloom when he listened to Ovitz explain NBC's terms: Not only would Letterman have to wait those 17 months, but the NBC offer wasn't as attractive financially as the CBS one: He would get a higher salary than his current $7 million, but NBC would not commit itself at this stage to how much more and the show's budget would be no higher than 5 percent above Leno's current one. Ovitz thought it a bad deal, and recommended that Letterman go with CBS. But Letterman found that he couldn't give up on his old dream that easily: "I can't make this decision. It's every race driver's dream to drive a Ferrari. You're asking me to give that up."

"Time is running out," Ovitz said, referring to the CBS offer.

"I appreciate what you're saying, and I understand. But I just can't make this decision. I need to see how my stomach is going to feel for a couple of days."

Ovitz agreed to try to stall NBC. He would encourage its executives to draw up a contract for Letterman, knowing that he could buy some time that way.

"Great idea!" Letterman declared. "I don't want to be the only one whose weekend is ruined."

Over that weekend Letterman phoned friends, and listened uncomfortably as they all urged him to take the CBS offer. Relaying what he was hearing to Ovitz, Letterman remained torn. "CBS is like a train coming out of the station," Ovitz said, and it was the right time to board it.

Finally, Letterman had an idea. One person, and one person only, could really know what he was going through: Johnny Carson. He would ask Johnny. Whatever Johnny told him to do, Letterman would do.

Getting Carson on the phone, Letterman asked him bluntly: "If you were in my shoes, what would you do?"

Carson replied that, given the way NBC had treated Letterman, "I'd walk."

Carson's words were enough to convince Letterman. He decided to take the CBS offer.

But the next morning, Letterman was feeling unsure yet again. He called Ovitz, who decided to work on Dave by telling him a personal story. Once, he said, he had gone out and bought a house—and he really couldn't afford the house, so he was miserable in it. For the first few months his entire family, his wife and his kids, were miserable. But then he got used to the place, and began to like it: "I'm still in that house. It's the best house I ever lived in. It's the best thing I ever did in my life. Don't look back, David. Just keep going."

Letterman relented at last: He would take the CBS job. "It was a lovely piece of work on Michael Ovitz's part," Letterman says.

What was Ovitz's secret? *Not clear,* Letterman says: "There were so many other levels that were not apparent to me, relationships with people that I wasn't aware of. Michael Ovitz was able to do things that to this day I don't fully understand. But I want to go on record as saying that I have great regard for this guy. He did something for me that changed my life and the life of about one hundred other people with whom I work. He kept me in the business. He put me in business. My relationship with him has been the most important aspect of my professional career.

"I get such a kick out of this guy. When I knew him he was a gunslinger. He was cocky. It was as if he were saying, 'Okay, who's beating up on the school marm? I'll take care of it.' He's one of the few people who looked me in the eyes and told me what he'd do and within six months he accomplished it. That doesn't happen in many walks of life."

In 1994, *New York Times* reporter Bill Carter wrote a book called *The Late Shift,* all about the Letterman–Leno late-night talk-show struggle. Two years later, a docudrama based on the book was aired on cable television. The actor Treat Williams, who had starred in the film version of the hit Broadway musical *Hair,* played Michael Ovitz, and won an Emmy nomination for that role. Though a fictionalized portrayal of Ovitz, this TV film does provide a rare glimpse of Michael Ovitz in action: pitching deals, taking charge, promising to save the day—and saving it.

THE EXPERIMENT OF having an in-house spokesperson had worked out well enough that Ovitz decided to continue the practice even when Stephen Rivers opted to leave CAA to set up his own public relations firm. George and Barbara Bush would be leaving the White House on January 20, 1993, and thus Anna Perez, Mrs. Bush's press secretary, was on the job market. Rivers knew of Perez, and told Ovitz about her. She began work as CAA's second official spokesperson on February 1. She was given no specific marching orders, but it was understood that her prime directive was to keep Michael Ovitz out of media trouble. Thus, preventing CAA from appearing in the news was her main task. In the two and a half years that she worked for CAA, she issued fewer than a dozen press releases, and 90 percent of those simply announced personnel changes within the firm. Other talent agencies routinely sent out news releases when they signed clients; but Ovitz always had been very chary of volunteering any information about clients. Besides, he believed that in simply signing a client, the agency had not yet performed any service worthy of note.

Although she certainly was accustomed to working in secretive places—the White House, for one—Anna Perez was astonished by how deeply engrained were the suspicions of CAA agents toward the media. Their implicit assumption was that the media existed in order to bring harm to others, especially to Hollywood talent agents. "With most of the major Hollywood talent already in our embrace, what more could the media do for CAA?" So the argument of these reticent agents went. When reports of CAA staff meetings reached "the trades," agents went ballistic, and demanded of Anna Perez that the loose-lipped employee be ferreted out. Perez's reply was to note that many a front-page story in the *Washington Post*, about matters considerably more weighty than the comings and goings of movie stars, were due to a leak, and many people disliked those leaks; but still no one tried to find out who was talking to the media, since it was considered to be a hopeless cause. Therefore she advised CAA agents not to get overly excited about the leaks.

Even when someone at CAA was about to be touted in the media for doing something exceptional, the gun-shy agents always headed for the bunkers. Perez recalls the time when a few CAA agents were selected by a local magazine to appear on a list of the Most Influential People in Hollywood under Thirty-Five Years Old: Those CAA agents selected for the honor refused to send in their photographs!

Early in 1993, as the editors and reporters of *Premiere* gathered together for their annual Power List deliberations, they knew they faced a difficult decision. For the past three years, Michael Ovitz's name had headed the list. But did he deserve the top slot for a fourth straight year? Some thought not. He was, after all, just an agent, they argued to Susan Lyne, and agents didn't wield the *real* power in Hollywood. Susan Lyne felt that Ovitz was a unique figure, someone who had a unique ability to take the entertainment industry in directions it had never gone before. But even she was resigned to the idea of dropping Ovitz down from number one. "Either we retired the Ovitz number, or it was time to make a change," she says. "We chose to make a change."

Lyne had lunched with Ovitz a week earlier, but hadn't mentioned anything to him about the forthcoming Power List rankings. So, rather than have him learn "the bad news" by reading it in the magazine, Lyne called him after the magazine had gone to press to inform him that this year he was going to be number three, not number one. Ovitz was not pleased. He voiced dismay that she had not informed him at their lunch the week previous, while he still had time to argue on his own behalf.

Warner chiefs Terry Semel and Bob Daly were a joint number one; Disney Chairman Michael Eisner, number two. *Premiere* had chosen the two men because, in its view, "power in Hollywood has shifted from sellers to the few remaining big-time buyers." And Warner had grabbed the number-one spot in market share by releasing such major hit sequels as *Batman Returns* and *Lethal Weapon 3*, as well as the low-cost hits *Under Siege, Passenger 57,* and *The Bodyguard.*

With his efforts on behalf of Sony, MCA, and Coca-Cola, Michael Ovitz had plunged his talent agency into spheres of American business life that no one in Hollywood had entered, thereby winning many plaudits for stealing the thunder of Wall Street and Madison Avenue. But his next turn at corporate deal-making turned out to be far messier, more complicated, and more controversial than anything he had attempted before.

This time, the world's seventh largest bank, Credit Lyonnais, had asked CAA to help it manage its assets. Never before had the secretive, state-owned French bank sought outside counsel in the management of any part of its troubled $3 billion portfolio of entertainment and media loans. The talent agency also would advise on future investments. The bank's arrangement with Ovitz was announced on March 25, 1993.

Ovitz was stepping in to help the bank after it had been widely criticized in the investment community for the entertainment loans it had granted—especially to financially-strapped MGM and its dominant partner United Artists, and to Carolco Pictures. Credit Lyonnais, in effect, now controlled MGM, with a 98.5 percent share, because it had been forced to take over the studio after Giancarlo Paretti, the Italian financier who borrowed money in order to acquire the company, defaulted. The bank had invested $1.3 billion in MGM and was losing an estimated $1 million a day.

With a number of Hollywood studios going bankrupt or drastically scaling back the number of films they produced, Ovitz had a compelling reason for keeping MGM alive: Nothing was more vital to his talent agency's well-being than the existence of as many studios as possible, hiring as many clients as possible. Yet Ovitz had little time to help revive the studio so that it could be sold to a buyer, for Credit Lyonnais had to sell MGM by 1997: An American law stipulated that a foreign bank which controlled an American firm had to divest itself of the property within five years. At first, the media seemed inclined to accept Ovitz's latest project as representing another major achievement for the talent agent. "Mr. Ovitz," wrote *The New York Times*, "was leapfrogging over his competitors. In fact, he was no longer just an agent but a powerful fixer whose worlds reached far beyond Hollywood."

Yet Ovitz's consulting deal with the bank soon began to stir up controversy in Hollywood. Critics charged Ovitz with a conflict-of-interest, arguing that he was about to become both the buyer and the seller of talent. MGM, after all, hired actors, directors, and writers who might well be represented by Ovitz's CAA, yet here was CAA planning to help run a studio, which could then feel obligated to show favor to CAA clients. The major talent guilds representing Hollywood's actors, writers, and directors were sure to scrutinize the projected deal vigorously, since the guilds had agreements with the talent agencies that barred those agencies from representing studios in business dealings. What bothered them was the possibility that Ovitz might try to "play both sides of the fence," as in this hypothetical scenario: Julia Roberts (then a client at ICM), wants $10 million to do an MGM film, but CAA is now in a position to say that she isn't worth that much, and to get one of its own clients hired for less money.

In defending himself against such claims, Ovitz told *The New York Times:* "I am not dealing with MGM. I am dealing with the bank in Paris. Alan Ladd Jr. (chairman and chief executive officer of MGM) makes these decisions, as well as the marketplace. We are not telling him how to run his company."

But Ovitz's comment allayed no fears at the other Hollywood talent agencies. Indeed, Jeff Berg, chairman and chief executive officer at ICM, was fuming. He wanted to speak out publicly against Ovitz's arrangement, and hoped that Jerry Katzman, president of William Morris, would join him. But Katzman preferred to deal with the issue privately. He didn't want to be perceived as engaging in a public vendetta against Michael Ovitz and CAA. Rather, he sought to engage in some quiet diplomacy with Ovitz, to ensure that William Morris would not be operating from a position of weakness when negotiating deals with MGM for its clients.

Thus it was that Jerry Katzman and Walt Zifkin of William Morris asked Michael Ovitz to meet with them, and were invited to CAA's offices. At the highly-secret session, attended also by Ray Kurtzman, Katzman and Zifkin sought assurances from Ovitz that he would not take unfair advantage of his prospective special relationship with MGM. All that he was trying to do, Ovitz assured them, was something good for the industry; although he admitted that if it was good for the industry, it would be good for his own talent agency as well. It was better to revive MGM, he argued, so that all Hollywood talent agencies could find work for their clients, rather than have the studio become incapable of generating work. Katzman indicated that he liked what he was hearing, but only as long as William Morris could be certain that the competition among talent agencies would remain open. Ovitz assured them that it would. The meeting, which mollified the William Morris executives, was never made public.

Once ICM's Jeff Berg had realized that William Morris wasn't going to be joining him in his public campaign against Ovitz, he decided to lash out against CAA on his own. "The question," Berg told *Newsweek,* "is, 'What powers of suggestion or influence will exist (for CAA) that we won't have access to?' We think it's not a level playing field." Ovitz was being assailed by Wall Street as well. Investment bankers, their pride still piqued by the seemingly effortless way in which a mere *talent agent* had brokered the giant Matsushita–MCA deal, were wondering yet again why Credit Lyonnais hadn't hired a large, New York–based investment-banking firm.

Ovitz felt obligated to answer the various charges in public, and did so in an interview published in *Time* on April 19, 1993.

"I'm not advising MGM," Ovitz insisted. "I'm advising a bank that holds a major stake in MGM, that has loaned $1.3 billion to various entertainment companies and wants to rethink its entertainment investment strategy." He argued that his arrangement with Credit Lyonnais was "perfectly legal." Asked how he could separate his responsibility to represent a client's interests from his responsibility to advise a company that might conceivably employ that client, he seemed to suggest that what he was doing should be seen as being above criticism, simply because others in Hollywood habitually behaved in the same way: "Look, this industry *invented* conflicts of interest. In what other business would you have a lawyer who represents the chairman of a major film studio and also represents an important actor, be the guy who makes the deal between the actor and the studio chief? Hollywood is a small, familiar place. Everyone does business with everybody else. The same complications occur in investment banking, but just as they build a Chinese Wall to separate the parts of their companies that have competing or conflicting interests, we have built a Chinese Wall at CAA. It's all about ethics and how you do business."

One thing was certain: Ovitz's conflict-of-interest problems with regard to the MGM deal would be resolved by the talent guilds. If they found Ovitz guilty of a conflict of interest, he would quite certainly be forced to rethink his whole agreement with Credit Lyonnais. Yet so powerful was Ovitz, that numerous studio executives and rival agents phoned the guilds simply to voice their support for him.

In early May, in a major triumph for Ovitz, the guilds gave their qualified approval to the arrangement, expressing confidence that CAA would not interfere in creative decisions at MGM and would not acquire confidential information about the clients of other agencies who were working on MGM films. With the guilds thus providing a certain degree of closure for this issue, Ovitz felt more certain that he would face no lawsuits, and that eventually the industry-wide clamor would die down. That is in fact what happened, yet the Credit Lyonnais flap still left a bitter taste in the mouths of rival talent agents. "There was no love lost between Morris and CAA," acknowledges Jerry Katzman. "We didn't like their tactics. We were forced to spend more time looking over our shoulders and having to protect our flank than going out and getting jobs for our clients. That became the legacy that they've left us. Because of that, everyone became the aggressive kind of agents that CAA has bred."

Meanwhile, Michael Ovitz was gaining a reputation as a guy with a knack for finding senior studio jobs for the small clique of unemployed

Hollywood executives. It was a reputation he deserved, though he and some of his acquaintances downplayed the significance of his headhunting by contending that lots of talent agents did the same thing. In newspaper articles focusing on Ovitz's "Hollywood headhunting," the suggestion often was made, implicitly at least, that Ovitz somehow was doing something nefarious in installing these people in studio positions; in other words, that he cared less about being altruistic than about guaranteeing a friendly studio response for his proposed client deals. This was in fact the old conflict-of-interest charge dressed up in new clothing. But Ovitz didn't need friendly studio chiefs in order to secure jobs for his clients; all he had to do, to make the studio chiefs turn their heads, was to wave around his impressive client list. Yet whenever Ovitz worked behind the scenes in order to secure a studio position for someone, he always seemed to be "maneuvering" and "manipulating," and thus it was assumed that he had some sinister motive. In reality, his motive was simply to ensure stability at the studios, so that the jobs would continue to flow in to his agency and its clients.

Ovitz seemed to be up to his old ways in July of 1993, when MGM dismissed Alan Ladd Jr. as chairman and chief executive officer and turned to Frank G. Mancuso, the former chairman of Paramount Pictures, to rescue the crippled studio. At the same time Credit Lyonnais announced that it planned to revive MGM's companion studio, United Artists, which hadn't been producing movies for many years. Michael Ovitz was credited with putting together the deal that placed Mancuso in charge of MGM.

Ovitz also played a pivotal role in finding a boss for United Artists. Ovitz had known John Calley for years. Calley had helped run Warner Brothers from 1960 to 1980, along with Ted Ashley and Frank Wells. They had turned out such hits as *The Exorcist, A Clockwork Orange, Mean Streets,* and *All the President's Men.* In 1980, Calley left Warner. He proceeded to drop out of Hollywood for the next decade, moving into a large mansion on Fishers Island in Long Island Sound. He then moved to Washington, Connecticut, still doing little. While he produced a few pictures, notably *Postcards from the Edge* and the critically-acclaimed *Remains of the Day,* he visited Hollywood only three times in all of the 1980s.

Then one day, early in 1993, he received a call from Michael Ovitz. Ovitz planned to be in New York and wanted to get together. Calley and Mike Nichols were close friends, and so they met at Nichols's office on 57th Street.

"How's your life?" Ovitz asked, a question he often posed when he was hoping to make a major change in that life.

"I'm enjoying it," said Calley. "I made the right choice."

"Do you ever think of wanting to do something else?" asked Ovitz.

Calley smiled and responded: "I think I'm doing too much recreational sleeping." He was in fact sleeping 16 hours a day at times. He then expressed a desire to return to Hollywood and help run a studio, but at the age of 63, he felt some understandable anxiety about a possible comeback.

Six months later, as the summer was beginning, Ovitz called again. "Something's coming up with MGM and Frank Mancuso. Are you going to be out here?"

Calley had just produced *Remains of the Day*. He said he planned to be in Hollywood to screen the film for Columbia Pictures, which had financed the movie.

"I think you should meet Frank Mancuso," said Ovitz. "He's exceptional. He's going to take over MGM." Ovitz made no mention of the fact that he personally had arranged that takeover.

Calley was interested. Ovitz arranged the meeting. Calley and Mancuso got along, and Mancuso offered Calley the job of trying to reinvigorate United Artists.

Having accepted the job, Calley tried to sleep that night but was restless and awoke at 3:00 a.m. He walked around the block near his Westwood hotel several times, telling himself over and over again that he liked his present life, that he felt comfortable and safe. The next morning he called Mancuso to apologize and to say that he couldn't take the job after all: "I don't want to change my life."

He returned to Connecticut. Ten days later Ovitz was again on the phone to him: "I've talked to Frank, and I think we've figured out a way that will get you back. We've structured a deal that is irresistible." Ovitz had arranged for the insertion of options in Calley's contract that would allow him to leave the job if he became uncomfortable. It had been nearly impossible to structure the deal with those options, but Ovitz had managed it. Calley still had a slight itch to run a studio. Ovitz made it clear that he wasn't pressuring him, just letting him know that the conditions would be ideal if he decided to take the job.

Like so many before him who had acceded to a Michael Ovitz wish, Calley relented at last, and began the long, sustained, and ultimately successful effort to revive United Artists. He gives full credit for all that transpired to Michael Ovitz: "I wanted to change my life and couldn't face it myself. Yet somehow he knew it and helped me attack it, not by lecturing me, or haranguing me, but rather by creating a situation in which there was an alternative to the life I was leading. He goes beyond normal representation. He's a life-counselor."

Over the next few years, John Calley would make the best possible use of a tiny staff and a cost-conscious strategy to bring success to United

Artists with such hits as *The Bird Cage,* which grossed $100 million, and the latest James Bond thriller, *Goldeneye,* which grossed $92 million. In 1996, Calley accepted an even bigger job as the president and chief executive officer of Sony Pictures Entertainment. And his achievements at United Artists paved the way for the sale of MGM/UA on October 10, 1996, to billionaire Kirk Kerkorian, MGM chairman Frank Mancuso, and Australian media company Seven Network Ltd., for $1.3 billion.

ALTHOUGH NOT APPARENT, given all of his CAA and other activities, the most powerful figure in Hollywood, the man whom David Letterman had affectionately called "the godfather," was still restless, looking for yet more worlds to explore. And there were so many opportunities out there, so many people who would just love to exploit Michael Ovitz's skill and talent, his passion and drive. He was now 47 years old, with lots of living still left to do. But one thing he knew for sure: He didn't want to die an agent. He had a vivid image before his eyes of a very crusty Abe Lastfogel, plodding down the corridors of William Morris. That was not going to be Michael Ovitz's fate.

16

I Have a '95 Ovitz

Ovitz loved sports. He had been a fairly decent gymnast as a youth, and trained daily in the martial arts as an adult. To watch a basketball game with one of his children was something that gave him enormous pleasure. Yet he was reluctant to involve himself in the business side of sports. His advisory role in Magic Johnson's career had been the only exception to his rule of never dealing with athletes. But he admired Nike, the world's largest athletic-shoe firm, and its boss, Phil Knight. Interested in finding out more about the world of television and television advertising, Knight got in touch with CAA's Sandy Climan. By October 1992, Climan had arranged for Ovitz to visit Knight at Nike's headquarters in Portland, Oregon. Ovitz offered Knight a number of insights into how Nike could draw upon the entertainment world for its advertising campaigns. "He makes a terrific impression," Knight recalls. After a few more sessions like that one with Knight, Ovitz was ready to do business with Knight's company.

On January 19, 1993, it was announced that Nike had entered into a joint venture with CAA to produce a series of special sporting events and programs. That summer Ovitz and Knight tried their hands at a project that, on the surface, sounded promising. For years, college football had been feeling a mounting frustration that unlike other sports, no single game was played to determine the college football national champion. Instead, unofficial newspaper surveys had been used to determine which team became the national champion at the end of the season. But the fans would have preferred to have the championship be determined in a game at the season's end that pitted the two top teams against one another.

Thus it was that in the summer of 1993, Charles Young, the chancellor of UCLA working on behalf of the NCAA, was trying to develop an end-of-the-season playoff arrangement, complete with quarterfinals, semifinals, and a final national championship game. Young chaired a special NCAA committee mandated to study the feasibility of creating a genuine national championship for college football. He was a great admirer of UCLA graduate Michael Ovitz, and quite familiar with Ovitz's ability to take the talent-agency business into all sorts of other worlds, including sports. Perhaps, Young thought, Ovitz has some ideas on how we might establish a college football championship game that would be commercially viable. Therefore Young asked Ovitz if CAA might be interested in serving as a consultant, or even in managing such an event. Ovitz jumped at the chance, even though he had largely kept CAA out of the sporting arena. He simply liked the idea of being a part of college football's top game. Young asked Ovitz to have his CAA team make a presentation to the NCAA.

Eager to see the proposal succeed, Young tried to give Ovitz advice on how to make the presentation, but Ovitz politely brushed him off, saying he knew more about such presentations than Young did. But when Ovitz's CAA group appeared in a Kansas City hotel conference room, before an NCAA leadership comprising 50 university presidents, it made the mistake of employing hard-rock music and video images projected onto a screen. This gave the rather stodgy NCAA representatives the unsettling feeling that they were at a rock concert. What was more, although the proposal was supposed to concern college *football*, images of *basketball* players floated across the screen!

Any chance for the CAA proposal to win over this group died with the loud music and the last flickering images cast on the screen. Afterward, Young told Ovitz that he had misjudged his audience: "I know this audience better than you, Mike, and you turned them off."

"Why?" Ovitz asked. He was baffled. In other places, in other times, such presentations had dazzled audiences.

"This is not a hard-sell, slick group of people," Young said, pointing out that of the 50 college presidents on hand, 49 surely hated rock. And all 50 quite certainly believed that all Hollywood people are slick hucksters.

When he recounts the story of that sad hour that he and Michael Ovitz spent together in that Kansas City conference room, Young has a hard time explaining what went wrong, given the fact that Ovitz and his CAA staff had performed so well on so many other occasions: "It was one of the few unsuccessful things I've seen Michael involved in," Young says, disheartened to be the source of seeming criticism of Michael Ovitz.

In time the NCAA would drop the idea of holding a series of play-off games leading to a single national championship game. Instead it would adopt a plan that seeks to pit the highest-ranking teams against one another for the national college football championship. Each year, one of the major bowls is selected as being in essence the championship game.

In the wake of their failed attempt to launch a Super Bowl of college football, Ovitz and Knight talked about sponsoring other events, including a track-and-field meet and a tennis match, but nothing ever materialized. "Those kind of projects required a lot of work," Knight notes.

LONG BEFORE ANYONE else in the Hollywood talent-agency business had come alive to the vast potential of the new technological wonders, Michael Ovitz was studying the subject and searching for ways to exploit their potential—as in the meeting with Bill Gates. Ovitz understood that the odds were against his being able to turn these technologies into commercially viable projects, but he wasn't put off by that. He liked the idea that CAA was offering its clients an agency busy exploring the new technologies, in much the same way as a "think tank" analyzes the latest sociopolitical trends.

Indeed, he had groomed one of his agents, Dan Adler, to help him in this area in particular, by having Adler devote all of his time to visiting electronic laboratories and firms. Dan's mission was to learn all that he could about where the new technologies were heading, and to report back to Ovitz. It was the kind of entrepreneurial step that other talent agencies considered way beyond their purview—too far from the core business, too wasteful of precious human resources. But it was exactly the kind of adventure that Ovitz loved to see CAA embark upon: uncertain at first, but with potentially high payoffs down the road. So Dan Adler spent time at places like the MIT media lab in Cambridge, Massachusetts, and hung out in Silicon Valley, developing relationships with computer specialists and then alerting CAA clients about the new cutting-edge technologies.

For Ovitz and Adler, their explorations into the high-tech world were all very preliminary and tentative, and neither really knew what might come of their efforts. But they both sensed that being in on the ground floor had to give CAA a competitive advantage over other talent agencies, even if it would be some time before their efforts had any effect upon the agency's bottom line. One of the new technologies that did seem promising was related to the telephone networks. Ever since the telephone's invention, consumers had employed the instrument in order to communicate by voice. Then, beginning in the 1980s, written transmissions also became possible: the telephone as fax machine. But in the early 1990s, researchers were looking for ways to turn telephone networks into machines that could broadcast and transmit video images as forms of entertainment into people's homes. The research was in its infancy, but it provided Michael Ovitz with yet another opportunity to engage in corporate deal-making in a field far removed from the world of Hollywood.

Telephone executives around the country knew that they were on the verge of some important breakthroughs in technology, and that soon it would be possible for Americans to bring entertainment and culture into their homes through telephone networks. As their specialists worked to make the technology feasible, they realized that they had to find someone who could help them to tap into Hollywood and to bring its films and performers into people's homes. Ivan Seidenberg was the chairman and chief executive officer of the New York–based telephone company Nynex, one of the seven regional telephone firms known as "the Baby Bells." Nynex had been moving toward wireless communication, and Seidenberg was eager for Nynex to get into the distribution of content. He too had been following Michael Ovitz's career of late, and sensed that Ovitz was the man who could help Nynex develop its "content strategy."

In early 1993 Ovitz arrived at his first meeting at Nynex in New York, along with Sandy Climan and a few other CAA staffers. Seidenberg and Ovitz hit it off immediately. The two men found that they had much in common: Both had been married in the same year, 1969; both had birthdays in mid-December (Seidenberg's was December 10; Ovitz's, December 14); and both were aficionados of the new technologies and eager to exploit them. "I was the techie freak," Seidenberg says. "Michael was the consumer-entertainment maven. Together we were connecting points, building perspective." Over the next 18 months, Ovitz and Seidenberg looked into possible cooperative ventures between CAA and the telephone companies, and Ovitz began to meet with telephone executives from the other Baby Bells as well. On several occasions, at Ovitz's initiative, Seidenberg traveled to Los Angeles, to swap ideas with several CAA clients including Michael Crichton, Ivan Reitman, Aaron Spelling, and Warren Beatty. Hoping to bridge the gap between the worlds of technology and entertainment, Ovitz was looking for answers to this question: *If a telephone technology existed that could bring consumer entertainment into millions of American homes, how would the telephone companies exploit that technology?* Still, the ideas that were tossed around by all concerned weren't nearly as important as Seidenberg's growing sense of confidence that he and Ovitz could do business together: "If we could get the technology out there, there would be people who could use it."

WHILE OVITZ WAS busy drumming up business on Madison Avenue, in Japan, in Silicon Valley, at Nike headquarters, and among the Baby Bells, the edifice he had erected on the corner of Wilshire and Little Santa Monica was fast becoming Hollywood's most powerful employment magnet: Many young people wanted to find work there. Only a select few actually did—1 out of every 25 applicants, to be exact. For a young person just out of college, a job in the mail room at Creative Artists Agency was simply the most prized in all of Hollywood. CAA was bustling with energy in the early 1990s, and thanks to Michael Ovitz's achievements and the positive media coverage he was receiving, the world of the talent agent was looking every bit as glamorous as the world of investment banking a decade earlier.

Although some agents-in-training at CAA even possessed law degrees, the trainees were paid $300 a week, and for that relative pittance they were expected to put in 100 hours a week, including weekends. But few complained. After all, hadn't their intrepid leader, Michael Ovitz himself, gone through the same experience in William Morris's mail room?

CAA agent trainees arrived at work between 7:30 and 8:00 a.m. each day. Three times a day they ventured around town on errands, dropping off scripts at various places and learning the lay of the land as they maneuvered around town. They helped to sort the thousands of items of mail, some of these being fan letters. Below each agent's mailbox was a large box that had written on them "Tom Cruise" or "Luke Perry," or the names of whatever other CAA stars that agent was handling. Agents then turned this fan mail over to the stars.

Whenever any trainee found the work too taxing, all he or she had to do was look up at many of the senior CAA agents: They all had started in the mail room, and some of them had become millionaires.

THE GREAT HOLLYWOOD studios had become increasingly passive when it came to finding stories to be made into movies. No longer did they have story departments, as in the old days, and CAA sought to exploit that opportunity. Eager to package as many stars as possible into a project, CAA agents spent hours poring through books and magazines in search of viable movie ideas. Mort Janklow, the New York literary agent, had strong ties to Michael Ovitz. Janklow's partner Lyn Nesbitt was literary agent to Michael Crichton, and Nesbitt and Crichton knew that CAA always was looking to mesh its clients with good story ideas. "It was the only place in town where I saw that kind of combing the world for ideas and possibilities," Crichton notes.

For five years now, Michael Crichton had been working on a book about dinosaurs, but he still hadn't finished it. He decided to talk to the people at CAA about his latest idea, and the reaction there was enthusiastic. They urged him to finish the book, so that they could go about making a movie out of it. The book, *Jurassic Park*, was published in 1991, and became a huge best-seller. Some time later, Crichton got back in touch with CAA, to find out the status of the movie deal. That was when the trouble began.

"With an agency so large and with this kind of Machiavellian nature," Crichton notes, "you never know how your project fits into other agendas, and that gets to be a big problem. Eventually I began to feel CAA was too much like the CIA, and I needed some inside information about what was happening. You can't go to Ovitz on that. Mike is Mike." The movie business, in Crichton's view, was "very short on honesty," and this was what he was experiencing now. "This is the other side of that CAA power. I was very naive about it when *Jurassic Park* was being sold."

Finally director Steven Spielberg, who appeared set to direct *Jurassic Park*, phoned Michael Crichton to ask whether they were going to make the movie.

"Probably," Crichton replied. "I don't know why not."

Spielberg, as far as Crichton could figure out, was annoyed at Ovitz for insisting that Spielberg must become a CAA client *first*, before the talent agent would make him part of the *Jurassic Park* package that CAA would sell to a studio. As Ovitz saw the world, Spielberg's signing-on as a client was a mere given. Ovitz sensed that *Jurassic Park* would become a blockbuster, and he saw no reason why Spielberg should hesitate to join Ovitz's agency.

At any rate, Crichton had begun to understand why the movie project was being held up, and why no one was willing to tell him the truth about the delay. He was amazed that Ovitz would allow a potential blockbuster of a movie to drift around in Hollywood purgatory over such a seemingly minor issue such as Steven Spielberg's joining CAA.

Ovitz admits that he expected Spielberg to become a CAA client before he was added to the *Jurassic Park* package. Ovitz had been pursuing Spielberg for two years, and as part of his lure had spoken of helping

Spielberg to launch his own film studio. But Steven's wife, actress Kate Capshaw, had quashed the idea, because she felt it would be too much work for her husband. Ovitz notes: "It was pretty much understood that if I was going to give Spielberg the book (*Jurassic Park*), he should become a client. I didn't come in and say, 'if you do this movie, you have to be a client.' But it was pretty clear."

Spielberg did become a CAA client, however, and Crichton confessed to being "naive that CAA was running such explicit agendas with my material."

The movie *Jurassic Park* appeared in 1993. It went on to become the second-highest box-office earner in movie history, earning, as of 1996, nearly $360 million. That makes it second only to another Steven Spielberg super-hit, *E.T.: The Extraterrestrial,* which as of 1996 had grossed nearly $400 million.

Jerry Seinfeld, the stand-up comedian who put together the most successful television comedy show of the Nineties, had to face none of the crises and dilemmas that David Letterman had faced. Within a few years after his show, *Seinfeld,* debuted on NBC television in 1989, it was sitting near the top of the ratings. Seinfeld had worked with some agents in the past, but none of his experiences had been much to his liking. Over the previous few years he had been represented by a small agency, but it had gone out of business and for the time being he was without an agent. Toward the end of 1993, when the show nudged aside *Cheers* to become the highest-rated program for the first time, Seinfeld stepped up his search for representation. He was looking for someone who could keep him on top on TV, but also someone who could develop a movie career for him. He was introduced to agents at William Morris and then, thanks to Howard West and George Shapiro, co-producers of *Seinfeld* and long-time acquaintances of Michael Ovitz, to Ovitz and Ron Meyer at CAA.

"We don't make stars," Ovitz explained to Seinfeld. "If you're a star, we can help you. If you already have your house in order, we have our house in order, and we can maximize what you've already achieved." Seinfeld liked the agent's honesty. Ovitz and Seinfeld bantered easily. "Lots of joking, lots of fun," Howard West would report later. Ovitz and Meyer betrayed no urgency or desperation about signing Seinfeld as a client; they were, West suggests, "too strong, too powerful" for that. As opposed to Ovitz's pitch to Letterman, in which content had mattered a great deal, the content of Ovitz's promises in particular, the meeting with Jerry Seinfeld was devoid of much substance. Ovitz simply spoke in generalities, and Seinfeld reacted positively: "In agenting," Seinfeld notes, "as in all sales, it's not what you're selling but how you sell it that impresses the buyer. What I liked was Ovitz and Meyer's expertise, and their subtlety. It wasn't a hard sell. It was just my speed. They said they would be ashamed of themselves if they could not develop a good movie career for me."

Seinfeld finds it hard to explain just why he did choose to have CAA represent him: "I thought the guys at CAA's suits fit better," Seinfeld says half-jokingly, though his voice is serious. "They had a nice little snack tray set up," he adds, perhaps his comical way of saying how difficult it is to choose any agent on the basis of just one meeting.

Seinfeld remained the top-rated show during the 1994–1995 season, but fell to number two in 1995–1996.

In 1995, Ovitz helped Seinfeld to renegotiate his contract with NBC. He called New York and spoke to Robert Wright, the president of NBC, trying to make it clear that Seinfeld wasn't in the network's pocket, that the comedy star might not be willing to do the show the next season. For one thing, there was a chance that Seinfeld's close friend, and the person who helped to mold the show, Larry David, would leave the show, and Seinfeld had been muttering that he didn't want to do the show without David.

The agent and the comedian became friends. It was through Ovitz that Seinfeld became interested in the Japanese martial art aikido, which, Seinfeld notes, "is very much about the moment that conflict begins, and the idea is, to end it at the same moment. Ovitz is very much about that moment." Seinfeld remembers Ovitz telling him that he had a very limited time frame in mind for how long it would take to wrap up the negotiations with NBC. "Very aikido," Seinfeld recalls. "It was not going to be a long fight." Unwilling to give NBC too much time to think about the situation, Ovitz hoped to wrap up negotiations within 10 days, just before the winter holidays.

Thus, the time was right for Ovitz and Wright to get together. They met for lunch in Beverly Hills, and by the time they got around to the kind of deal Ovitz had in mind for Seinfeld, Wright was ready to buy—he wanted the show very badly for next season. And so, Ovitz closed the Seinfeld deal well within his allotted time frame.

Seinfeld likes the way Ovitz operated on his behalf: "His understanding of 'the negotiation' was very deep and fascinating to me, the way he prepared for it, his philosophy of it, and the way he executed it exactly according to plan. His philosophy was that when a guy like me renegotiates, it's like a guy coming into the room with a big sword. And the idea is to never touch the sword. That's a successful negotiation. I've always been a sucker for that agent stuff."

For Seinfeld, having Ovitz as his agent has been an effortless experience: "He's got so much experience and he's so skilled at it you just say, 'Do your thing.' There's nothing you have to tell him." As it turned out, the Seinfeld contract talks became one of the last deals that Ovitz ever finalized at CAA. "I like to brag I got one of the last Ovitzes," Jerry Seinfeld says with a smile. "I have a '95 Ovitz. They don't make them anymore."

Yet again, Susan Lyne and her *Premiere* staff were preparing the Power List, this one due to come out in May 1994. But she had a problem. Michael Ovitz had brought her into his confidence, divulging that he was engaged in still-secret negotiations with the telephone companies and that something awfully important was going to happen soon, he couldn't say when. But when it did, once again he would have changed Hollywood irrevocably. As Lyne sat through meeting after meeting with magazine staffers, trying to come up with the power list, she was dying to tell her colleagues what she knew of Ovitz's plans. But she felt that under no circumstances could she betray Ovitz's confidence. All she felt able to say to them was that Ovitz was involved in something very secret and potentially very significant for Hollywood, and that the magazine would look silly if it didn't put Ovitz's name atop its May power list, and Ovitz then pulled off another of his corporate coups a few months later. As always, however, Lyne refused to exercise the veto power she had over the staff's decision, and a majority of the reporters felt that Ovitz didn't deserve to be number one. Thus when the list came out, Steven Spielberg led it for having done something that no one else in film history had done: He not only had put together the second-greatest box-office champion of all time (*Jurassic Park*), but also had filmed and edited the most critically-acclaimed film of 1994, *Schindler's List*. Number two on the list, down from number one the year before, was the Warner Brothers leadership team of Bob Daly and Terry Semel. Ovitz retained his number-three position, but Susan Lyne still was afraid that the magazine might have made a mistake by not positioning Ovitz in the top spot.

All of Michael Ovitz's careful planning came to a peak in October 1994, when he and the Baby Bells announced that CAA and the phone companies would be entering into a joint venture with the Nynex Corporation, Bell Atlantic Corporation, and Pacific Telesis Group, to buy or invest in programs that the existing Hollywood studios would turn out. The telephone firms planned to distribute these programs over their improved, sophisticated telephone networks. Explaining the goal, Seidenberg said: "We'll bring technology to your home, but you'll have a twenty-five-inch pipe instead of a two-inch pipe." Ovitz had persuaded former CBS executive Howard Stringer to run the venture. According to *The Wall Street Journal,* Ovitz himself was getting $50 million for the good advice and counsel he had rendered.

This "telephone deal" brought Ovitz yet more praise. "Michael Ovitz is sort of the corporate equivalent of a world-class watchmaker," said NBA Commissioner David Stern. "He understands how things run, and what connects them. Once you begin to get that kind of understanding, you begin to see connections between seemingly unconnected businesses or phenomena. So it didn't surprise me that someone like Michael would understand that entertainment and movies are content for a broader audience; and that he was led to focus on the content-providers like the telephone companies. He understood the potential for a variety of changes that were coming."

Ovitz of course was thrilled with this telephone venture, but Susan Lyne was bemused. Now she was *sure* that *Premiere* had made a mistake.

MICHAEL OVITZ'S REACH seemed just plain incredible to many. "After a time," says CAA agent Richard Lovett, "it became clear and assumed that if something big was happening in town, Michael was at the center of it." Working as he had to transform so many different areas of American business life, Ovitz had gradually but deftly turned his agency into a place that now only partially resembled a talent agency. Still, most agents were thrilled that CAA was casting such a wide net. The heightened amount of admiration felt by the public and the industry for CAA made it that much easier to bring in new clients and to service existing ones. But the joy that Lovett and other agents felt at CAA's rising revenue stream was tempered by their belief that Ovitz's corporate consulting really had caused the core business to suffer. No one could point to any specific case of a client lost, or a film package that had slipped away, but as Ovitz's closest associate, Ron Meyer, argues, "It was important to hold the reins on the agency business, not to lose sight, or let the community lose sight, that we are still agents. Once clients had the feeling that we were more interested in building other businesses than talent, that would be the disintegration of the talent business."

Ovitz has little time for such concerns, contending that he still spent 85 percent of his time at CAA in handling Hollywood clients. And yet Ron Meyer, as he watched Ovitz pay more and more attention to the corporate deal-making, stepped up his own efforts on behalf of the core business, in order to compensate for what he perceived to be Ovitz's diminished role in handling talent. Bob Goldman, CAA's chief financial officer, shared Meyer's discomfort, suggesting that in some ways Ovitz's corporate consulting was detrimental to the agency: "The publicity was very helpful; the notoriety was something that all the other agents could capitalize on. It showed how powerful the agency was; the negative side was that we could be criticized for lacking focus; and it was a valid criticism, because Mike was up to that point so singularly focused on the agency business that we always maintained our position. If he was going to be looking into those other areas, he wouldn't be as attentive to the agency business."

On Wall Street, the men and women of high finance looked down upon Ovitz as a mere intruder, a man who had risen to no higher level than that of a Hollywood talent agent and therefore should have been deemed ineligible to carry out corporate deal-making. Veteran financial analyst Harold Vogel acknowledges that "a lot of people on Wall Street thought he was poaching on their business, on their bread and butter." How would a talent agent like it, the argument went, if an investment banker started to make deals with film and television stars?

Meanwhile, rival Hollywood talent agents were giving mixed reviews to Ovitz's corporate consulting. At William Morris, Jerry Katzman praised Ovitz for refining the talent-agency field by exploring new areas of business, but he still thought that talent agencies had no reason to get into the advertising field. At ICM, Jeff Berg was more sharply critical of Ovitz's forays. He recalls: "We didn't try to emulate Ovitz. Mike saw himself as a kind of investment banker. I see myself as a deal guy. If I'm working on a deal, I'll bring in an investment banker. Ovitz saw himself as an advertising guy. That's the last thing we wanted to do. We didn't want to make Coke commercials. It's a complete waste of our time." Yet Marvin Josephson, the founder of ICM, commented favorably on the fact that Ovitz had broadened the concept of "talent agent," and had made it respectable for ambitious corporations to turn to a senior Hollywood agent rather than to a Wall Street investment banker.

Ovitz rarely commented publicly on his corporate consulting; when he did, he sought to knock down reports that he was guided by some personal, secret agenda: "Every time we get involved in consulting for a company from Sony to Matsushita to Credit Lyonnais," he told *The New York*

Times, "there are accompanying rumors that we are going to run the acquired companies. The past is prologue here. Look at the history of this. It speaks for itself. I'm not running Columbia. I'm not running Universal. I'm not running MGM."

H E WAS, HOWEVER, running Hollywood.

Throughout the late Eighties and early Nineties, the media had described Michael Ovitz in various ways: *perhaps* the most powerful figure in Hollywood; *said to be* Hollywood's most powerful broker; *considered to be* the most powerful talent agent in town.

Almost always there was the qualifier attached. Rarely was anyone prepared to call him outright "the most powerful figure in Hollywood." By the mid-1990s, however, all that had changed: Michael Ovitz was routinely described as the most powerful figure in Hollywood.

One actor who benefited from Ovitz's reach was Dustin Hoffman. He recalled the kind of power Ovitz wielded: "If Michael picked up the phone and called the (Terry) Semels, or the (Sydney) Pollacks, or the (Sherry) Lansings, they took that call. And they listened. And the chances are that Mike would persuade them to do what he wanted. He would get his way. He would make whatever it was he was after, happen. There was no one else in Hollywood who had that kind of respect."

"If you wanted to do business," says Graydon Carter, the editor of *Vanity Fair,* "you had to do it with him. That's pretty much the definition of power." And if you wanted to try to take on Michael Ovitz, he always seemed to hold all the cards, and to know how to come up with a winning hand. In February of 1995, *Forbes* had the temerity to undertake six weeks of research for a profile it planned to do on Ovitz, apparently to be critical in tone. As soon as he found out about the planned article, Ovitz got on the phone to *Forbes* publisher Steve Forbes. He told him that he had heard about the story, and he pointed out that because CAA was consulting for the magazine on the new technologies, the magazine had a conflict-of-interest in doing the story. Forbes agreed, and spiked the story. Such was Ovitz's power that Forbes never seemed to have contemplated the alternative option: canceling the consulting contract with CAA, rather than drop the story.

Ovitz certainly relished his power. He certainly would rather be number one on the *Premiere* power list than number two or number three. He liked the idea that when he walked into a room, people cast their eyes his way. But just how desirable was it to be that powerful? Most people, having heard about Michael Ovitz but knowing very little about him, assumed that having all that power must be intoxicating, exciting, and a good deal of fun. But for Ovitz, power always had been a double-edged sword.

During his first decade, as he tried to build up the greatest talent agency in Hollywood, it took him some time to adjust to the fact that the power he possessed had its limits. He assumed that his increasing influence, his ability to woo major movie stars away from other talent agencies, meant that he could wield his power without having to worry too much about what others were feeling and saying about him. Accordingly, the more things went his way, the more controlling he became. Hence his continuing efforts to keep the media at bay (few interviews and photographs) and his selective efforts to engage in damage-control whenever others appeared to be tampering with his positive image (as in the plan to quash the movie *Wired*).

Refusing to believe that there could be any real limitations to his power, he came to love being on top. And if, during the Eighties, he had obtained much satisfaction from his struggle to build CAA, by the early Nineties Ovitz had begun to feel that, with each new world he conquered, power itself became less important to him. What he really craved now was the respect and the recognition of his peers.

Seeing his name near the top of the various power lists always would please him, as it was a remarkable tribute to the influence he had amassed. But as each new list appeared, he realized anew that all of that power had brought many jealousies and resentments along with it. He also came to understand that his power was limited and probably ephemeral, and to feel somewhat embarrassed by how aggressively he had acted back in the early days. He frequently suggests that he was naive back then. And while others might think him omnipotent, Michael Ovitz himself knew that he was not. He knew that the people wielding the real power in Hollywood were the studio chiefs, and he had great respect for them, for people like Barry Diller, Michael Eisner, and Terry Semel. He tried to tell anyone who would lend an ear that he had never been after power. Sure, he had spent much of the early years trying—and succeeding—to look and indeed to be powerful, but all of that effort had been expended to a very specific end, that of lengthening CAA's shadow.

No, he argues vociferously, it was never power that he was after, but something else: "Everyone said all I wanted was power. But I only wanted to be respected. That was why I made people at CAA wear suits and why I built the building. It's true that I was out to make money. I certainly didn't want to work pro bono. But you want more than money. You want respect."

In the many conversations that Ovitz held with the author, rarely did he seem to show any great degree of relish for all the power he had acquired, but frequently mentioned that his failure to earn widespread positive recognition from the Hollywood community was a constant source of frustration to him. He contended that although he packaged 170 films over the course of his agenting career, only three times was he singled out for praise by his industry. First when Dustin Hoffman lauded him at the 1989 Oscar awards ceremony, for being the catalyst behind *Rain Man;* again on Christmas eve of 1993, when David Letterman phoned to thank him for having salvaged his career as a late-night talk-show host; and yet again in 1996, when Tom Cruise sent him a bound book of still photographs from the film *Mission Impossible,* with the inscription: "Look what you made happen." On the surface, it might seem odd that Michael Ovitz could feel that he has failed to win much respect over the course of his career. How could he think that people don't respect him? Doesn't the mere fact that he became Hollywood's most powerful figure constitute sufficient proof of his industry's respect for him? No, to Michael Ovitz it does not.

For he is careful to distinguish between *power* and *respect.* Being powerful, however heady and useful it may have been at first, had become little more than a burden, for it meant that some of those who held him in such awe could quickly turn against him. And some did, accusing him of being manipulative, ruthless, greedy, arrogant, for they had witnessed firsthand Michael Ovitz "the bad cop." "In a town that occasionally requires people to play hardball," notes Sydney Pollack, a great admirer of Ovitz, "there is no tougher hardballer than Mike Ovitz." Echoing the sentiment, another admirer, David Letterman, says that he can understand why some people don't care for Michael Ovitz: "Because if he wasn't on your side, he could make your life very uncomfortable. Once he's established what's right and wrong, he's going to make it difficult for the people he believes to be wrong."

Power, therefore, seemed to Michael Ovitz to have many dangerous side-effects. Gaining the respect of others, on the other hand, was nothing but a blessing.

Hollywood Obsession

With EVERY NEW task that he performed in the early 1990s, Michael Ovitz seemed to be further distancing himself from the core business of CAA. He hated to admit that he had gotten bored with the talent-agency business, but the truth was that he had: "I wanted to do other things. . . . I just find a lot of things interesting. It's one of the reasons why I liked being an agent, because I got to do a little of everything; but when I did it for twenty-seven years, what else do you have?" Ovitz knew that he had boosted many a career:

Director Richard Donner: After he had signed with CAA and made the film *Inside Moves* in 1980, his career rose to new heights as he directed the three *Lethal Weapons* films (1987, 1989, and 1992); as well as *The Toy* (1982); *The Goonies* (1985); and *Scrooged* (1988).

Author/director Michael Crichton: His career grew into one of the most illustrious in Hollywood. His biggest year was 1993 when two of his best-selling books, *Jurassic Park* and *Rising Sun*, were released as major Hollywood films. He was a co-screenwriter of both films.

Sydney Pollack: Nominated for Best Director for *Tootsie* in 1982, and the recipient of an Oscar for best director for *Out of Africa* in 1985; he also directed *The Firm*, in 1993, which brought in over $77 million.

Sean Connery: In 1987, he had won an Oscar for Best Supporting Actor for *The Untouchables*. Connery seemed a natural to be cast as the seasoned mentor helping out a much younger hero and Ovitz aided him in landing such a role as the father of Indiana Jones (Harrison Ford) in *Indiana Jones and the Last Crusade* (1989).

Tom Cruise: After starring in *Rain Man*, in 1992 he and Paula Wagner formed Wagner-Cruise Productions. Their film, *Mission Impossible*, which was released in the summer of 1996, was the number-one-grossing film that year. Ovitz had delivered on his promise to the fresh-faced nineteen-year-old boy he met in his office years ago: Cruise had made films with Dustin Hoffman and Paul Newman and had worked with such outstanding directors as Martin Scorsese and Barry Levinson.

And Ovitz had turned CAA into Hollywood's most powerful institution. But there was no longer the fire in his belly to snare more big-name actors. What he hungered for now was the big corporate deal, and for that he needed to go beyond the confines of Hollywood. Many of his colleagues assumed that Ovitz simply felt resentful, though he never said so outright, of the huge sums of money being raked in by the Michael Eisners and Barry Dillers and David Geffens of the entertainment industry. To be sure, Ovitz was now a very wealthy individual. He owned 55 percent of CAA and had made millions of dollars over the years. Thus he may have been less interested in the huge sums he could hope to amass than in becoming a key player in a bigger league.

Had he been able to turn CAA into a business giant he might have been tempted to remain at the talent agency, but that was no longer possible. Business acquaintances like investor Ron Perelman understood that Ovitz felt frustrated at not being able to turn CAA into a larger financial asset: "Michael had reached the point where he had taken the talent-agency business as far as he could. He found that in the personal-service business it's difficult to create capital, because the business is tied to unique personal assets (the agents). So if he wanted to take CAA public, it would be hard to come up with an accurate market value for such a personal-service enterprise. For some time Michael had been looking to find a way to convert the business into a capital asset, but he just couldn't work it out."

Though he insisted to business friends that he would never leave Creative Artists, Ovitz was increasingly being sought after, and he found being pursued both flattering and exciting. He had long dreamed of running an entertainment empire along the lines of The Walt Disney Company or Time-Warner. He once told Susan Lyne that the business figure whom he admired the most was Rupert Murdoch, for Murdoch seemed to know how to put the pieces together in such a way as to build a truly global entertainment network. But to join a Disney or a Time-Warner would mean to subordinate himself to others, and Ovitz almost always had been the man in charge. He just wasn't a number two by nature.

At any rate, Ovitz clearly was getting restless. He told Nynex Chairman Ivan Seidenberg that he was planning a major life-change, but wasn't specific. Seidenberg encouraged him to move east, because that was where the action was. But Ovitz said nothing.

While Ovitz was mulling over his own future, other senior figures at CAA were growing increasingly frustrated. Rowland Perkins had left CAA in 1994 to start his own production firm, but three of the original five founders were still running the show. While Ovitz prized the fact that many CAA agents had come up through the ranks, the simple fact was that none of them had been given a piece of the partnership. Some CAA executives felt that, while Ovitz did deserve most of the credit for his corporate forays, others deserved some of it too, but the man-in-charge simply grabbed all the media attention. As one such executive's metaphor would have it, Ovitz and his partners had constructed a wonderful rocketship, and everyone had flown to the moon together, but now not everyone felt a part of the mission, not everyone felt that he/she had received sufficient recognition for helping CAA get to the moon. When it came time to celebrate CAA's twentieth anniversary, some of the senior managers at CAA felt subdued. The vaunted camaraderies seemed to be slipping away. Ovitz may have sensed a growing malaise, and that in turn may have contributed to his wish to part company with the agency. Still, most agents couldn't imagine a CAA that didn't have Michael Ovitz at the helm.

The media became obsessed with the question of what Ovitz would do next, but had to rely entirely on the speculations of a few largely uninformed sources. Ovitz never discussed the subject publicly; indeed, he hardly ever talked about it in private. But none of this stopped people from speculating about Michael Ovitz's next career move. He became Hollywood's favorite obsession.

Peter Bart, editor of *Daily Variety*, met with Michael Ovitz in the spring of 1995 and quickly realized that he was someone about to abandon ship. As the two men began to discuss the increasing competitiveness of the talent-agency business, Ovitz's eyes suddenly glazed over, and he quickly changed the subject: "It's all going to change—the whole game."

"What are you talking about, Mike?"

"By the end of this year, everything in this town will be changed," he repeated. "Every company will have to adopt a new strategy. Virtually every top executive will be swept aside."

"That's a rather apocalyptic vision," Bart said, perhaps a bit dismissively. "If everything is going to change, where does that leave *you*?"

Ovitz's expression revealed little. "I'll still be here, doing what I do," he replied, but even as he said those words, Bart noticed that he was rubbing his hands together nervously. Bart read that body language as suggesting that the talent agent already had plans to leave CAA. Meeting with Ovitz often during those next few weeks, Peter Bart began to notice how different he had become. He rarely made eye contact and his voice tended to trail off, indicating that he was having a hard time concentrating on routine matters.

THE TRIGGER FOR Ovitz was Edgar Bronfman Jr.'s decision on April 9, 1995, to acquire 80 percent of MCA for $5.7 billion. Two days later *The New York Times* reported that Bronfman was considering asking Michael Ovitz to become chairman and CEO of MCA, replacing the 82-year-old Lew Wasserman. Yet at a meeting with his agents at CAA that same morning, Ovitz said tersely: "You've read the papers. I've read the papers. Now let's move on." But while Ovitz could deny it all he liked, the newspapers continued to report that he was secretly negotiating with Bronfman. Thus his seemingly reassuring words to his agents brought them no relief. "We were extremely nervous about the negotiations," Bryan Lourd notes. "And we were unsure of what our futures would be, even whether there would be a CAA."

There were indeed rumors to that latter effect, as well as ones suggesting that the Young Turks would be gone before Ovitz was. As the atmosphere at CAA grew increasingly turbid, the Young Turks feared that they might begin to lose clients. Thus they began to meet more frequently, "mainly," observes Jay Moloney, "because we were dealing with a lot of uncomfortable clients, but also out of a sense of self-preservation." The workload increased, and phone calls with clients tended to double in length. Clients who dealt directly with Ovitz, such as Dustin Hoffman, were feeling especially nervous. "It was more information management than crisis management," Jay Moloney recalls.

Nor were CAA's agents the only ones to find the rumored Ovitz–Bronfman talks unsettling. Many were concerned that Ovitz's departure from CAA would set off a virtual earthquake in the business, one far exceeding the mere tremor created by Stan Kamen's death in February 1986. Ovitz's leaving CAA would mean that the agency's entire client list would be up for grabs, and that in turn might well serve to level the playing field in a talent-agency business thoroughly dominated by Ovitz for 15 years.

Newspaper reports suggested that both Ron Meyer and Bill Haber might join Ovitz at MCA, and Ovitz was indeed talking to some CAA staffers about joining him at MCA. When the MCA talks appeared to be moving toward a successful conclusion, Jay Moloney popped into Ovitz's office and asked him what plans he had for him, if any. Moloney said that he would prefer to remain at CAA, but Ovitz replied that he would like

Moloney to join him in whatever venture he might undertake. Still, he couldn't tell Moloney exactly what kind of work he had in mind for him.

Once the media found out that Ovitz was "in play," "Hollywood's most closely-watched deal," as *The New York Times* called it, was tracked relentlessly by the media. This had some discomfiting side-effects for Ovitz. Required as he was to keep his talks with Bronfman a secret, Ovitz was forced to deceive many people, including some close acquaintances at MCA itself. "Mike would never betray me, he'd never do this to me," said Sidney Sheinberg, MCA's president, unable to believe that Michael Ovitz could have entered into negotiations for a senior job at MCA without informing him. David Geffen tried to tell Sheinberg that he was being naive. Ovitz wanted nothing more than to inform Sheinberg, but for as long as the negotiations went on, he had no choice but to keep them confidential.

Ovitz found the whole experience tortuous, but nonetheless he kept his guard up even when interacting with clients whom he greatly liked and respected. Author/director Michael Crichton met Ovitz at a time when the talent agent was still in the midst of the negotiations. Crichton was eager to hear Ovitz speak about his corporate consulting, especially about his dealings with the Japanese and his advertising efforts for Coca-Cola. And assuming that Ovitz wasn't long for CAA, Crichton hoped to discover what he was planning to do next. "I enjoyed speculating on where he would go," said Crichton, "and trying in conversation to find out. We were talking more often now that I was this big important client. I wanted to get a sense of what he was thinking, which of course you can't get. He'll look you in the face and lie. I don't know how else to put it. If he's not going to tell you, he's not going to tell you. If he has to tell you something, he'll tell you something. After all this time, I'm not offended. He'll tell me something and I would say, 'That's not true.' Then he would smile. It was always an elaborate game, talking with him, to see if something would slip out. But usually it didn't."

In the midst of Ovitz's negotiations with MCA, the *Premiere* Power List for 1995 was published. Ovitz had moved up a notch from the previous year, to the number-two spot, behind Steven Spielberg. The magazine credited Ovitz for having picked up such formidable clients as Adrian Lyne (director of such hit films as *Fatal Attraction* and *Indecent Proposal*), and actors Eddie Murphy, Hugh Grant, and Billy Crystal. It also cited the new consulting arrangement he had forged with the Baby Bells as yet another reason for moving him up a notch. The editors wrote that Ovitz was the only Hollywood power player "who can truly punish his enemies." And yet it did fault Ovitz for not being an inside player in the new

DreamWorks studio being put together by Steven Spielberg, David Geffen, and Jeffrey Katzenberg.

On May 18, news reports mentioned that Ovitz was seeking $200 million in equity, or a 2.8 percent stake in MCA. Ten days later Ovitz's price tag, according to those reports, had been marked up to $250 million. And then on June 1, Ovitz and Bronfman were reported to have reached a preliminary agreement. When a *Newsweek* reporter asked Ovitz if the magazine would be embarrassed if it ran a cover story saying that he was going to take the MCA job, Ovitz told the reporter that that would be fine. But on the record, Ovitz hinted to the magazine that he was exploring more than just the MCA possibility. Then he added: "I can't predict the future, but the only thing that is for sure is that I love my life at CAA."

Suddenly, the negotiations with Bronfman hit a snag, and they collapsed altogether on Monday morning, June 5, 1995. At 6:30 a.m. Ovitz called Bronfman and told him that he didn't want to conclude the deal. He offered no reason. But in his discussions of the matter with close friends at the time, Ovitz was telling them that he had become concerned that Bronfman had fallen in love with Hollywood, and thus would want to run the company rather than let Ovitz truly be in charge.

On the other hand, many of Ovitz's business friends believe that Ovitz simply priced himself out of the market. Publisher Mort Zuckerman suggests that "Somehow Michael didn't have as full a grasp of what he intuitively does have: a sense of pragmatism. Part of it was getting along with Bronfman. He had too grand a sense of what was possible. Seagrams is still a public company. One of the real sticking points at MCA was bringing in a number of people from CAA, and on what terms he would bring them in. He could have used a Mike Ovitz to negotiate when he dealt with MCA."

But speaking 20 months after the talks collapsed, in an interview with the author, Ovitz suggested that he simply didn't have the heart to leave CAA, and that that was the main reason the talks collapsed: "I carried the negotiations on too long. I just didn't want to do it, and I carried it on too long. I overplayed it. It was a mistake to carry it out for so long, when I knew I wasn't going to leave CAA." Had he asked for too much money? Wasn't that the real reason for the collapse? No, he said, "it was never a mistake to ask for too much money," and he hadn't asked for too much on the MCA deal. But he was distraught that the negotiations had gotten into the press: "It destroyed the fabric of our company. It created instability, and for twenty years CAA was like a rock. There had been no instability. If you were a client or an agent, you had been protected. We had stable management. People made a lot of money. That was the image. In three months that started to erode. That was my fault. I was wildly flattered [to be asked to run MCA]. It's fantastic when people tell you everything you want to hear. I didn't want to leave my business, but I wanted to leave the agency business."

On the face of it that last comment sounds like a contradiction, but apparently what Ovitz means is that he was bored with the *agency* business but still enjoyed running his *own* business. The fact was, that MCA held little appeal for him either: "MCA was a challenge, but it was a company similar to CAA in that it was about making movies, and I wasn't going to be in charge. I'd be under a guy [Bronfman]. I don't function well as second-in-command. I don't want to go back to someone and ask 'Should I do this?' When I feel that something is in my stomach and in my heart, then I make a decision. I'm incredibly decisive. I just couldn't see working for the Bronfmans."

Nonetheless, Ovitz's disappointment had to be enormous. As ICM's veteran talent agent Sam Cohen observes: "Not to be able to consummate the biggest deal of your career, when you are essentially a deal-maker, must have been a tough thing to deal with." Ovitz contends that those negotiations represented the only time in his career when he had seriously contemplated leaving CAA: "What no one understands is that it was really fun to get asked to take these jobs. I didn't discourage it; but I never had any interest in leaving CAA until Bronfman bought MCA. It wasn't that I was so interested in MCA. I really had lost interest in the agency business."

Bronfman never did confirm that he negotiated with Ovitz. All he said publicly was: "Seagrams is continuing to address the issue of management, and we are not going to discuss individual names."

Investors took the news of Ovitz's decision to stay on at CAA in stride. In New York Stock Exchange trading, Seagrams closed down 50 cents, or 1.6 percent, to $30 in heavy volume of more than 2.6 million shares.

Later that same Monday morning on which he called Bronfman and backed away from the impending deal, Ovitz had to face his own CAA agents and break the news that, despite what they had been reading in the newspapers, he was not going to leave the agency. Ordinarily, the agents would have been thrilled to hear such news. But ever since the media had begun to tell them that Ovitz was planning to leave CAA, these agents had been placed in a terrible position. Should they remain at CAA, or take up an offer to work at a studio or another agency? Many of them feared the worst: that if Ovitz left CAA, nothing would be left of the place; its clients would walk out, and its vaunted power would dissipate into thin air. None of them had a clue what to do. They would have preferred to remain at CAA, but only if the old order prevailed, not if the solidity of the place broke down all around them.

Hearing that Ovitz wanted to address the entire staff, the employees were frantic. If he announced that he was leaving, all hell would break loose. In the unlikely event that he announced he was going to stick around, the agents would still face uncertainty, because Ovitz clearly had put himself "in play" and it didn't take a genius to sense that he wasn't long for CAA, however you sliced it.

Ovitz walked onto the stage of the CAA screening room at the 9:30 a.m. staff meeting. Some 120 agents, executives, and assistants had gathered there to hear him, and those present still remember how eerily silent the crowd was. Ovitz began with a pep talk. Peering out at the crowd, he told them that they were the future of the company. Over the past few weeks, he and his partners had tried to keep speculation to a minimum and to remain focused on reality. "And the reality is: I'm not leaving. Ron [Meyer] is not leaving, and Bill [Haber] is not leaving."

Smiles appeared on many faces, and the crowd broke into a standing ovation. People began to hug one another. The relief was palpable. CAA was not going to disband at its most senior level. Shelly Hochron visited Ovitz in his office right after the speech, to express the joy she felt at his staying on. "He was really heartened by the response," she would say later.

The MCA talks had been too tumultuous, too public for the taste of the very private Mr. Ovitz. And the public nature of those negotiations had taken its toll on Ovitz. For a long time he had lived a secret life, deciding if and when he would let the public in on his activities. But as he and Bronfman had tried to come to terms on the biggest deal of his career, the media and a whole array of industry people in Hollywood had commented and kibitzed from the sidelines. And Ovitz had hated every minute of it. He vowed that he would do everything he could to keep his distance from such public scrutiny in the future. Yet Ovitz had indeed allowed himself to be put in play, and there seemed to be no turning back. He would remain an object of overwhelming public interest.

By seriously negotiating with MCA, Michael Ovitz was saying, at the least, that he wasn't content to remain at CAA. "My heart isn't really in this," Ovitz told one of his closest friends, Arne Glimcher, referring to Creative Artists. Ovitz recalled for Glimcher a recent moment when, upon returning from lunch, he gazed from across the street at the CAA building. Ovitz thought to himself: "CAA is really something. It really is something." Glimcher found that to be a very telling comment, for it showed that while Ovitz was proud of what he had built and knew that the agency had been an extraordinary achievement, "it didn't mean Michael had to be there the rest of his life."

Nor apparently did it mean that CAA's other founders had to remain there forever either. After the collapse of the Ovitz–Bronfman talks, Edgar Bronfman Jr. still had some leadership positions to fill at his newly-acquired MCA. He had gotten to know Ron Meyer during the negotiations, and was struck by his talents. Bronfman decided to offer him one of the top management jobs, that of president of Universal Studios, just below the position that Bronfman had had in mind for Ovitz. Meyer had been enthusiastic about the prospect of joining Ovitz at MCA, so when the offer from Bronfman came, he heartily accepted it.

Meanwhile, as Meyer, unbeknownst to Ovitz, was negotiating with MCA, Ovitz was trying to settle back into his old routine at CAA. But it was no good. He was pestered by a feeling that he had mishandled the negotiations with Bronfman, and he felt boxed in: eager to leave CAA, but unable to execute what he called a decent "exit plan." While he never publicly acknowledged that he was seeking a position elsewhere, CAA's agents believed the continuing newspaper reports, and Ovitz's presence at CAA during June and July proved to be awkward for them: They were sure that he was merely in a holding pattern until the next offer came along. And clearly, Ovitz found life disconcerting. He had gone through the pregnancy, but had no baby to show for it.

Matters grew darker when Ovitz, in Los Angeles, received a phone call from Ron Meyer in New York City to say that he had decided to leave—and to take a senior job at MCA, no less! On Sunday, July 9, Ovitz phoned business friends to alert them that something big was about to happen. Phoning Shelly Hochron, he said: "Tomorrow we're going to announce that Ronnie is going to be president of Universal." Hochron couldn't believe what she was hearing.

"Okay," she said. "Are *you* okay?" She didn't know why she had asked him that. It was an instinctive response.

"Yes, everything's going to be fine."

Somehow, Hochron felt that everything was *not* going to be fine.

Ovitz picked up the phone and rang Jay Moloney as well, to tell him that Meyer would be leaving. Moloney could tell just by the tone of Ovitz's voice that something dramatic had happened; not the collapse of the agency, but clearly something that Ovitz hadn't at all anticipated.

The next day, Ovitz announced to the CAA staff that Ron Meyer was leaving CAA. Edgar Bronfman had chosen him to become president and chief operating officer of MCA. Though Meyer's post wasn't as broad or autonomous or as lucrative as the one that Bronfman had broached to

Ovitz, Meyer would be replacing Sid Sheinberg and thus would have one of the most powerful positions in Hollywood. In his new job, Meyer would run MCA's television and film business, which meant overseeing Universal Studios; he would also be in charge of the company's theme parks and music division. Lew Wasserman was to remain on as MCA's chairman emeritus, with Bronfman holding the title of chairman and chief executive of MCA. (Bronfman eventually brought in Frank Biondi, who previously had been number two to Sumner Redstone at Viacom, to take the post for which Ovitz had been negotiating.) Ovitz told people that he was feeling both excited and sad about Ron Meyer's departure: "It's a bittersweet situation. We've been friends for twenty years. We've had a very successful partnership. He'll do fantastic where he's going." CAA would not be adversely affected, Ovitz said. Others at CAA wondered about that, for they knew that Meyer had been handling the agency's day-to-day operations for a long time now.

On the heels of the Meyer announcement, Ovitz lowered his profile around CAA. For one thing, agents noticed that he didn't seem to be personally supervising the transition to the post-Meyer period. In fact he took some time off, and other agents took on the responsibility of making sure that Meyer's clients, including Sylvester Stallone, Tom Cruise, and Michael Douglas, were kept happy and well fed. Meanwhile, all those who had been adversely affected by CAA's powerful hold on Hollywood—especially the agents at other talent agencies—were gleeful: Ron Meyer was leaving, and Michael Ovitz appeared to be on the way out the door as well. "They wanted the whole agency to break apart," David O'Connor says, and he and the other Young Turks were urged by many to leave CAA before Ovitz shut down the agency altogether. But the Young Turks felt too much a part of CAA to quit. Still, they felt that their loyalty entitled them to some assurance from Ovitz that, in the event of his departure from CAA, the mantle of leadership would descend upon their shoulders. Over the past few months they had talked to Ovitz and Meyer about the need to put together a succession plan, but the two partners gave only vague assurances that at some point, if and when it truly became necessary to do so, real negotiations on the subject would ensue. "It was clear," O'Connor says, "that if Ovitz wasn't going to leave immediately, he was going to leave pretty soon, and there was no plan here at this company for any succession; we were pressing him pretty hard."

Once Meyer had left, and the Turks raised the succession issue with Ovitz all the more intensively, all that he would do was to promise the five agents that he would negotiate exclusively with them, with regard to transferring ownership of the agency, should the need arise. Clearly, Ovitz was reluctant to set any succession plan in motion. No surprise there, given the fact that Ovitz had put all of his lifeblood into the agency. To put together a succession plan would have been to admit that one day he really would be leaving CAA behind him.

The Young Turks, however, felt compelled to take action. Moloney, ill at home, phoned famed attorney Martin Lipton in New York. He hoped that Lipton would represent the Turks, even though they would be small potatoes in the eyes of such a high-powered lawyer. Lipton did agree to take them on as clients.

Michael Ovitz felt pressured. His back was against the wall. He was losing all interest in the agency he had founded, was canceling lunches and making far fewer phone calls. His eyes often had a distant, vacant look, as if he wanted to be—or already was—somewhere else. When he attended meetings with studio executives, he displayed none of the old spark and drive. CAA seemed a different, and lonelier, place to him now that Ron Meyer had left the agency. "Once I had left," Meyer recalls, "I think Mike recognized that it was time to change; I'm not saying I was the reason that he left. He had a lot of opportunities to leave; but he didn't; he recognized that for the company's sake and his sake we probably stayed at CAA the right amount of time."

Ovitz wanted to go quietly—with a whimper, not a bang. He made a conscious decision that any further effort to find a new job would only be conducted far from the harsh glare of the spotlight. One thing he knew for sure: If he got into negotiations with another company, no one would hear about it until it was all over.

IRONICALLY, OVITZ WAS thinking about leaving CAA at a time when the agency was in the midst of a two-year stretch (May 1994 to June 1996) in which it dominated the feature-film, television, and pop-music worlds. Most of the top-ten draws at the box office included at least one major CAA client. *Forrest Gump* was filled with CAA clients, including actor Tom Hanks and director Robert Zemeckis. In 1994, CAA represented 10 of the 50 top-grossing music acts, including Barbra Streisand, Michael Bolton, Bette Midler, and Rod Stewart. Sixteen of the prime-time television shows that were to premiere in the fall of 1995 had been packaged by CAA, including Michael Crichton's top-rated *E.R.* All told, CAA had stars, writers, and writer/producers in 40 shows. Some one-third of all of the prime-time entertainment on network television was comprised of dramas and comedies packaged by CAA, including *Dangerous Minds, The Jeff Foxworthy Show, Melrose Place,* and *Savannah.*

Its television clients included some of the biggest stars of the day, including David Letterman; Jerry Seinfeld; Helen Hunt; Jennifer Aniston, Courteney Cox, and Lisa Kudrow of the smash hit *Friends;* Ted Danson; Michael J. Fox; Nancy Travis; Jeff Foxworthy; Ben Bratt; John Lithgow; Jimmy Smits; Jonathan Silverman; Grant Show and Andrew Shue of *Melrose Place;* Patrick Muldoon; Brad Johnson; Garry Shandling; and Bill Maher.

MICHAEL EISNER AND Michael Ovitz had long been friends. They first met when Ovitz was a young television agent at William Morris pitching a game-show pilot to Eisner, who then was running ABC's daytime television operation. Eisner recalls finding Ovitz "pleasantly aggressive," but perhaps the "pleasantly" represents the softening effect of memory. For at the time, Eisner found it to be a bit too pushy when Ovitz sent his wife Jane flowers as part of his wooing of Eisner. But Eisner forgave Ovitz, and the two men did a good deal of business together; frequently the Ovitzes and Eisners vacationed together as well.

Eisner had performed miracles at Disney since he took over the vast entertainment empire in 1985. Yet he found himself continually challenged by the need to create first-rate day-to-day management. He had asked Ovitz on several occasions to come and work with him, first when Eisner was at ABC, then at Paramount Pictures, and finally at Disney. According to Eisner, both he and Frank Wells, Disney's number two in the early 1990s, wanted Ovitz to come on-board. "Frank selflessly would say to me consistently, 'If you can get Michael Ovitz in this company, I'll move to a third position.' "

On the day before Eisner went in for quadruple-bypass heart surgery on July 16, 1994, the Disney chairman asked Ovitz yet again to leave CAA and join him at Disney. And in the days subsequent to the operation, Ovitz was at his friend's hospital bedside for long stretches, often taking the phone away from Eisner so that he couldn't transact business and thereby overtax himself. One newspaper report indicated that Eisner had mentioned to his wife Jane that Ovitz was on his short list to take over Disney, if he didn't pull through the surgery. And then, all throughout Ovitz's 10-day negotiations with MCA (May 27–June 5, 1995), Eisner had urged Ovitz not to take the MCA position, so that he would be free to come over to Disney.

On July 28, three days before Eisner planned to publicly announce Disney's acquisition of Cap Cities/ABC, he phoned Ovitz and asked him to drop by his home. Eisner knew that Ovitz might think he wasn't feeling well again, so he assured him: "It's nothing bad."

Ovitz came by, and Eisner proceeded to disclose to him the secret details of the Cap Cities acquisition. Noting that Disney had now become "this giant company," Eisner raised the idea—yet again—of having Ovitz join Disney. Ovitz told Eisner that he had never run a public company. Eisner tried to ease his concerns: "You'll make it work." But Ovitz, still not certain what he wanted to do, was noncommittal.

In fact, Ovitz was facing a complex decision. He had three very different kinds of career choices in front of him. He could take the job Eisner was offering him; he could take a year off in order to evaluate the various job offers that were being proposed to him; or he could take a job with a major conglomerate, the identity of which he has not divulged. When he laid out these options for his wife Judy, she discouraged him from taking the job with the conglomerate, concerned that he would only become preoccupied with and discouraged by the inter-office squabbling he was sure to be confronted by there. She also discouraged him from taking the year off: He would have four wonderful weeks with the family, then would immediately grow bored and restive. Thus it was that both Michael and Judy Ovitz came to believe that the Disney job represented his best bet.

Two weeks later, Eisner and Ovitz and their wives were vacationing together in Aspen. It was Friday, August 11, and the two men and their wives were hiking in 12,095-foot-high Independence Pass, a mountain pass 30 miles outside of Aspen. Eisner broached yet again the subject of Ovitz's leaving CAA to come to Disney. He knew the hell Ovitz was going through after the MCA negotiations had collapsed and he had been forced to return to CAA, a place for which he no longer had much enthusiasm. This time Eisner was more concrete about the role Ovitz would play in helping to lead The Walt Disney Company. He talked in terms that made Ovitz listen intently. He laid out a plan that had Eisner taking on a passive role as chairman, while Michael Ovitz would essentially run Disney on a day-to-day basis. In January 1997, speaking for the first time of his Disney experience, Ovitz said in an interview with the author that Eisner told him: "We are going to be partners. We're going to run the company together and grow it. I'll handle the ceremonial parts and you will handle the operational side. You will make the strategic decisions for the company." Eisner told Ovitz that within a few years, Ovitz would replace him as Disney chairman. "He brought me in as his successor," Ovitz says.

Eisner then asked Ovitz a question that he had asked many times before, feeling now that his chance of getting a positive response was better than ever.

"Is this the right time in your life?" Eisner asked, meaning, *Is it now time for you to help me run Disney?*

Ovitz felt that it was. His life had been a whirlwind for the past few months; now he had the chance to settle into a new challenge, that of helping to run the world's largest media conglomerate. It took Eisner and Ovitz less than a day to work out the details, finalizing most of the deal on the phone the next day, Saturday, after their return to Aspen.

EISNER THEN CALLED Disney's directors to inform them of his decision. Sid Bass, whose family owned 19 percent of The Walt Disney Company, met with Eisner and Ovitz that day. Joe Roth, the Disney studio chief, flew to Aspen from Martha's Vineyard, where he had been vacationing. He met with the two men on Sunday, his goal being to get assurances from both Eisner and Ovitz that he would be able to run his film division without any interference from Ovitz. Ovitz assured Roth that he wasn't interested in being in the film business anymore. The three men then flew together to Los Angeles that evening.

By midnight, Eisner and Ovitz had wrapped up the details of their agreement. Michael Ovitz was about to become the president of The Walt Disney Company. Later, Peter Bart, the editor of *Daily Variety* would ask Ovitz why had he agreed to take the number-two position at Disney, after insisting for so long that in any new corporate job he might take on, he would be number one. "Because Michael said 'Please' " was Ovitz's reply.

CAA AGENT DAVID O'Connor had been in Las Vegas that same weekend, playing in a hockey tournament. Fellow agent Bryan Lourd reached O'Connor to let him know that Ovitz had called a meeting of the entire staff for Monday morning, August 14. *He's telling us what he's going to do,* was O'Connor's first thought. *He's telling us that he's leaving.* Then a second thought quickly came to mind, a paranoid one: *Ovitz is going to fire the Young Turks!* Perhaps he had become convinced that the five agents were going to defect, or perhaps he was upset that the Turks were aggressively trying to negotiate with him about succeeding him.

By Sunday evening, word had begun to filter out that Ovitz was going to make a bombshell of an announcement. No one yet knew of its substance, only that Ovitz planned to address the agents at a staff meeting the next day. As for Ovitz he was again on the phone, alerting friends that life would change for them the next day. Exactly *how,* he didn't say. That evening he said to Shelly Hochron in a mysterious, solemn voice: "I'm going to be making an announcement tomorrow. I want you to know that. We'll always be together; and eventually this is going to be terrific for you."

He didn't say what the "this" was. Nor did he hint why his announcement would make Hochron happy.

"I trust your instincts," said Hochron. "I hope whatever it is, it's good. I'm ready to hear whatever you have to say."

Monday morning, August 14, 1995. David O'Connor showed up at CAA bright and early, at 7:30 a.m. On his desk was a memo announcing the general staff meeting at 10:00 a.m. Clearly, something important was about to happen. General staff meetings were unusual, called only when matters were pressing, and yet there had been a lot of general staff meetings lately. Another memo on O'Connor's desk summoned him to a more private meeting with Ovitz at 9:00 a.m.

Who would be at the 9:00 a.m. meeting? O'Connor guessed, the Young Turks for sure. But who else, and why? O'Connor walked into Bryan Lourd's office and asked him if he knew anything. Lourd was as perplexed as he was: "Either he's going to say he's leaving, or we are fired."

Lourd was trying to make a joke, but O'Connor didn't think that either prospect seemed very funny.

9:00 a.m. Twelve senior agents walked into the second-floor conference room. Their faces betrayed the tension that coursed through all of them. There were the five Young Turks—Richard Lovett, David O'Connor, Bryan Lourd, Kevin Huvane, and Jay Moloney—some CAA veteran executives—Ray Kurtzman, Bob Goldman, Sandy Climan, and Tom Ross—and some senior agents: Rick Nicita, Jack Rapke, and Lee Gabler. O'Connor felt surprise—and relief—when he saw Nicita and Rapke. He immediately concluded that this meeting hadn't been called in order to fire the Turks.

Ovitz entered the room. David O'Connor looked at his face and thought he seemed tense.

"Well, I'm glad you could all make it." He tried to make his voice sound cheerful, as if he were about to convey some good news, but then his tone grew deeper and far more ominous. He then delivered the startling news.

"I asked you guys to come in today to tell you that I'm going to leave the company to go join The Walt Disney Company as its president."

"The twelve of you," he said, "will become the transition committee, and everything will be fine."

Ovitz paused. He looked at the others, as if waiting for their response. Dead silence.

"Well, don't all speak at once," Ovitz said, hoping to lighten the mood.

He saw only frozen faces. They were stunned. As if there had been a loud explosion. They were reeling, still in shock.

Michael Ovitz had just changed their lives. Radically. Just *how* radically, none of them could know. None even dared to ask himself.

Richard Lovett tried to compose himself. He had felt it likely that Ovitz would leave CAA soon, but to hear him at last say the words was a real shock: "At that moment we went from certainty about the way the day, the week, the month would lay out ahead of us, to a state of unknown moving at a million miles an hour."

Some in the room had learned that Ovitz had been talking to Disney. But this was the first concrete proof anyone had been given that the talks had concluded on a positive note. David O'Connor thought of how long he had worked for Ovitz, of how crucial a figure he had been in his life. And suddenly he felt badly for his boss. He could sense how difficult it had been for Ovitz to reach such a decision, how difficult it must have been to inform the 12 of them. Perhaps, O'Connor thought for an instant, Ovitz was worrying that the 12 men might vilify him for having chosen to leave. Then the thought passed quickly. This was no time to try to get into Ovitz's head. O'Connor knew that he had to focus on the near-future: "The next couple of years were going to be hell, this decision of his was going to wreak havoc. And the enormity of the task hit me all at once."

For Bryan Lourd, Ovitz's announcement brought with it a sense of relief. How Ovitz must have struggled with this decision, and now it was over at last! From this moment on, the new team could start working on the basis of the new reality. But Lourd still felt a certain sadness "because I knew he was the best boss I'll ever have."

Around the table, the whispers began: *What about the transition? Who's going to run things? How much time do we have?*

New questions, questions that never had to be asked during Michael Ovitz's long tenure at Creative Artists Agency. One man decided to speak up, Richard Lovett. He knew there was a lot to do, but he also was feeling compassion for Michael Ovitz.

"Wait a second, wait a second! Michael, how do *you* feel about this?"

Ovitz didn't respond. He still wasn't sure how the people around the table had taken the news. Slowly he rose from his seat to leave. The meeting had taken just 20 minutes.

The 12 agents remained behind. They had much to say to one another, much to do. But no one tried to assert himself, to take over the meeting. Slowly the conversation began to pick up steam, and it centered on what had to be done immediately.

Clearly, the number-one priority was to talk to the agency's major clients before anyone else in town had a chance to get to them. Hollywood was about to suffer through an earthquake, and the 12 men had been given advance notice of it. They needed to exploit the little time they had.

David O'Connor returned to his office and looked out the window. He was slated to have lunch that day with a friend from college, a financial analyst at Disney by the name of Andrew Greenbaum.

"Andrew Greenbaum is on the phone," O'Connor's assistant announced.

O'Connor picked up, knowing that he had to keep the secret for a while longer.

"Do you still want to have lunch," Greenbaum asked. "So, big news, huh?"

What does he mean by that? O'Connor asked himself. *What "big news" is he referring to? Can he know? Impossible! Unthinkable!*

"Well, I guess your guy is becoming my guy."

"How do you know this?"

The news of Ovitz's departure already had gotten out.

"It was on the financial ticker at 9:00 a.m."

At that split-second, David O'Connor began to fathom just how major an event he had just witnessed in that second-floor conference room.

He apologized to his friend: "I'm canceling lunch on you. I'm going to be pretty busy."

By the time the staff meeting was over, O'Connor now realized, the entire town would know that Ovitz was leaving CAA. The task before him and the others whom Ovitz was leaving behind seemed huge. "If I had known *how* enormous," O'Connor would say later, "it would have paralyzed me."

10:00 A.M. MICHAEL Ovitz walked into the screening room on CAA's ground floor. Almost everyone connected with CAA sat on the gray-felt theater chairs, seven to a row: executives, agents, assistant agents, agent-trainees, secretaries.

Ovitz moved behind a lectern adorned with the CAA logo, and pulled some prepared notes out of his jacket pocket, rare for him. He kept his jacket on, which was *ominous* and highly unusual for Ovitz to do when addressing the staff, a few agents thought. To them, it looked as if Ovitz no longer belonged at CAA, that he had become an outsider.

For several minutes Ovitz commented on CAA's strengths, on its assets. He seemed shaken; his voice cracked. Finally he got around to the main topic: He announced that he was leaving CAA to become president of The Walt Disney Company. Some in the audience gasped, others began to cry, one of the latter group being Shelly Hochron. Despite Ovitz's assurance the night before that the two of them always would be together, she had her doubts. She had been so comfortable working for Ovitz, and now she feared that things would be changing forever. Another agent, Jane Sindell, broke into tears too.

Once the audience had calmed down, Ovitz began to tell his troops how the transition would work.

As they listened, many members of senior staff grew bitter. "Before," says Richard Lovett, "they believed that Michael would take them wherever he went, but Michael never made specific promises." Yet that lack of promises didn't keep many from feeling betrayed and abandoned.

A FEW DAYS later, Mike Rosenfeld, a CAA co-founder who had left the firm in 1982, phoned Ovitz at his beach house in Malibu. Ovitz had been disappointed with Rosenfeld for throwing in the towel and retiring so early. Rosenfeld had once predicted to Ovitz that "someday you'll sell out to someone." No, Ovitz had told him, he had no interest in working for anyone else, or being beholden to shareholders. Now, on the phone, Rosenfeld told Ovitz. "I never believed you would do this." To which Ovitz replied with a sigh, "I'm burned out."

To THE YOUNG agents, Ovitz was something of a father figure. He had been their boss, their mentor, their guide through the thickets of the Hollywood business world. Thus the agents not only had to cope with the shock of his leaving, but also had to figure out how to manage on their own, the way orphaned children are suddenly forced to do. They knew it wasn't going to be easy. The very idea that they now would be in charge of CAA, so long the bastion of Michael Ovitz and his partners, was a daunting and very unsettling one. They knew they had no choice but to roll up their sleeves and get to work, but the transition team also knew that, with Ovitz and Meyer gone, it lacked managerial experience. Had Bob Goldman and Ray Kurtzman also left CAA at that moment—and Kurtzman had indeed given it some serious thought—the committee would have been filled with a bunch of young kids who had never managed anything. But there was no time to dwell on their lack of experience. "The first thing we had to do," Richard Lovett recalls, "was—everything." The Young Turks had been thinking about this moment for months, and they were ready for it. "We just naturally kicked into overdrive," remembers Bryan Lourd. The first major decision the Turks had to make was whether to stay at CAA. That was easy: They were staying.

Next they had to engage in damage-control with regard to their top-ticket clients. Decisions were made about who would phone which clients. Whoever enjoyed the best relationship with a client got the nod. Rick Nicita, married to Paula Wagner (Tom Cruise's co-producer), was asked to call Cruise. Sandy Climan knew Kevin Costner well, so he called him. David O'Connor, who had had lots of contact with Robert Redford, phoned him. "Redford had a very complicated relationship with Michael Ovitz," O'Connor says, "in many ways contentious. He was always understanding and respectful of Ovitz's power, but he didn't like his influence in his life; so Ovitz didn't talk to him that much."

All told, David O'Connor placed calls to 30 clients. He got through to most of them right away. Most had heard the rumors that CAA was splitting up, and they wanted to know what O'Connor and the other Young Turks were going to do. "We're staying at CAA," was O'Connor's standard reply. Jay Moloney spoke to Martin Scorsese, who reacted calmly to the news of Ovitz's departure. He then spoke to Steven Spielberg and asked him to grant a grace period, so that the new leadership team could take the time to get itself together. Spielberg agreed to stay with the agency for at least a year. Moloney was thrilled: If Spielberg was being that generous, maybe this thing could work without Ovitz. Moloney then spoke to Tim Burton, who was indifferent about Ovitz's leaving. He was content to stay at CAA even without Ovitz at the helm.

The clients expressing the most concern were those who had been handled directly by Ovitz and Ron Meyer: Tom Hanks, Robert De Niro, Danny De Vito, Al Pacino, Michael Douglas, Sean Connery, and Robert Redford, among others. But thanks to the transition team's urgent efforts, CAA held on to the majority of Ovitz and Meyer's clients. Still, in the first few weeks a number of important clients did jump ship: Barbra Streisand, Sylvester Stallone, Whoopi Goldberg, Steven Seagal, Winona Ryder, Madonna, Chevy Chase, Liam Neeson, and Ben Stiller. The William Morris Agency grabbed Stallone and Whoopi Goldberg by pointing out that, with Ovitz and Meyer gone, it would take the agency at least six months to reorganize, leaving their careers up in the air in the meantime. And that argument worked. "There's no question," says Morris President Jerry Katzman, "that a number of clients felt a personal tie to Ovitz. He was the leader. You didn't have to talk to him on a daily basis, but if you had a problem, he could get it solved." Post-Ovitz, CAA would manage to sign actors Anthony Hopkins, Nick Nolte, and Matthew McConaughey.

Holding the agency together was another priority. Agents had to feel comfortable and secure, needed to hear that they would still have a congenial place in which to work, and even the valet-parking staff was assured that CAA would not be closing. For the most part, the staff stuck together: Only one television agent left, and he was asked to leave. Two months later, Mike Rosenfeld Jr., another television agent, did leave to work for Disney, and a few months after that, Rob Sheidlinger, a motion-picture agent, left to become a producer.

The transition team needed a spokesperson, and everyone settled on Richard Lovett. In time Lovett would be given the official title of president, making him in essence Michael Ovitz's successor. The choice of Lovett made much sense: He had a great list of clients, including Tom Hanks, Hugh Grant, Michael Douglas (shared with David O'Connor), and Michael Keaton. He was very articulate; and he knew how to manage people.

The financial arrangements between Ovitz and CAA still had to be worked out. To Richard Lovett, Ovitz said, "You can have everything but three things."

Lovett tried to guess what they were: "The building, the Lichtenstein, and the Shapiro."

"You got it," Ovitz told him.

Bryan Lourd picked up the phone to Martin Lipton, the well-known New York attorney. Filling him in on Ovitz's decision, he explained: "We have an interesting situation. I can't find any parallels that exist in the service-business world, and I need your advice." Lipton began to outline a possible ownership arrangement for the post-Ovitz CAA. (In time, Ovitz would sell his ownership of CAA, and that ownership would be shared out among many managing directors and agents, in notable contrast to the past, when only the partners had a piece of the agency.)

Lipton pressed the transition committee to come up with officers. Lovett formally was chosen as the agency's new president. Three of the veterans—Rick Nicita, Jack Rapke, and Lee Gabler—were elected chairmen. The remaining eight members of the transition team became managing directors.

All was not bleak. Not only had the Young Turks taken up leadership positions at CAA, but they could now work to boost morale throughout the ranks, which had suffered in recent years. "People at CAA were really removed from Michael Ovitz in the end," says Bryan Lourd, "because he was away a lot and doing things that were much different from what the average employee was doing."

As word got out that Ovitz was leaving CAA for Disney, the shock waves began to be felt in Hollywood. *Oh, my God,* thought David Letterman. *It's the end of show business!* Not really. But it certainly did represent one of the largest corporate upheavals that Hollywood had seen in many a year. The place had experienced milder tremors in recent years: when Barry Diller moved from Paramount to Twentieth Century Fox in 1984, and when Eisner and Katzenberg went to Disney a year later, and when Frank Wells was killed in a helicopter crash in 1994. But for all of their influence, neither Diller nor Wells wielded the kind of power Ovitz had.

Ovitz's departure raised all sorts of questions: *Would power now shift back to the studios? Would other talent agencies, perhaps William Morris and International Creative Management, now surpass CAA? Could CAA survive without Ovitz and Meyer?* And of course: *Why did Michael Ovitz choose to change jobs?*

Some of Ovitz's business friends found his decision to go to work for Disney strange: Had he gone to work for Edgar Bronfman Jr., he would have enjoyed far more autonomy than serving under Michael Eisner, and he would have been taking on a far more interesting and considerable challenge as well, for there seemed to be a lot more to repair at MCA than at Disney. In short, Ovitz appeared to have virtually volunteered to hold less power. Had he stayed at CAA, it would have been far easier for him to keep a low profile as well, to engage in his deal-making with only a few of his trusted aides being in the know. But now at Disney, a public company, his financial situation would be an open book—from his salary to the number of shares he owned.

Hollywood insiders, however, understood Ovitz's decision. Regardless of how powerful he had become, he was still "only" a talent agent. He might appear to some to be more powerful than the studio chiefs, but none of the studio chiefs themselves thought so: They remained convinced that the only real power in Hollywood lay with them. And the studios possessed the prestige and glamor in a way that the talent agencies simply did not. Thus Ovitz did not need to be convinced that helping to manage a studio represented a step up for him. Better to be a somewhat smaller fish in the far bigger pond at Disney—with the prospect of taking over for Michael Eisner sometime in the future—than to continue on as CAA's biggest fish. And the fact that Disney had just acquired ABC Television made the prospect of going to work for Michael Eisner a much more compelling one.

Thus, the reaction within the entertainment community was largely positive. "Ovitz and Eisner," said producer and CAA client Jerry Bruckheimer, "are the two strongest individuals in our town." Echoing that thought was Harvey Weinstein, head of the Disney-owned Miramax Films: "We've got the greatest lineup in the history of the entertainment industry." And Steve Tisch, producer of the film *Forrest Gump*, suggested that "this will reinvent the whole entertainment industry."

As for entertainment attorney Bert Fields, he had this to say: "Disney is a wonderful company in many ways, despite the fact that I sue them all the time!"

Even given all of the problems that had been created for CAA by the loss of Ovitz, Meyer, and Haber (who left in October 1995), the company did very well financially in 1995. "This place is thriving," says Bob Goldman, the chief financial officer. "If you looked at the financial statements of the fiscal year 1995, and you looked at the financial statement of 1996, you would conclude that this is exactly the same company from an agency perspective." According to published reports, as of August 1995 CAA had more revenues than any other talent agency: $175 million, and over $1 billion in billings deriving from its 1200-strong client list. That latter number had risen dramatically in the early 1990s after hovering between 600 and 700 from 1986 to 1991. As for the number of its agents, that too had reached a new peak at 120. By contrast, rival William Morris had revenues of $125 million and 200 agents, but had many more clients (2500) than CAA. International Creative Management had revenues of $110 million, with 150 agents, and 2200 clients.

And by the way, what had now become of Ovitz's many ventures in the arena of corporate consulting?

As soon as Ovitz announced that he was going to Disney, the television-programming consortium backed by Bell Atlantic, Pacific Telesis, and Nynex severed its relationship with CAA. For at Disney, Ovitz would have responsibility for a rival telephone venture that included Ameritech, Bell South, SBC Communications, and GTE.

As for the Coca-Cola deal, CAA tried to keep Shelly Hochron and Len Fink actively working for the agency on the Coke account. But Hochron felt that without Ovitz's involvement, she and Len Fink probably would find their role to be a diminished one. Moreover Sergio Zyman, the senior vice president and chief marketing officer for the Coca-Cola Company, wanted Ovitz to stay involved in the Coca-Cola advertising effort. And thus Hochron, Fink, and Hochron's husband Jack Harrower formed a new partnership that would handle the Coke account, with Disney acquiring a minority interest in it.

As the rest of the world absorbed the shocking news of Ovitz's move to Disney, he was contemplating life after CAA, as a number two, helping to run one of the world's great entertainment companies.

18

Disney Demons

THE DEPARTURE OF Michael Ovitz from CAA, and his appointment as president of The Walt Disney Company, should have given him good reason to celebrate. He was, after all, getting just what he had always wanted: the chance to help run one of America's major entertainment empires, and with a clear understanding that in the near future he would be running the enterprise all by himself.

And yet, as it was, the leave-taking from CAA was marred by bitterness. Senior agents said that they would like to honor him with a farewell party, but Ovitz understood the mood at CAA well enough to know that the toasts would ring hollow, the conversation would be awkward, and the rehashing of old war stories would be seen as simply a waste of time by those young agents who would far rather use the time to work the phones in order to keep clients from going elsewhere.

Meanwhile, at The Walt Disney Company, senior executives were disheartened by Eisner's selection of Ovitz as president. They felt that the $44 billion entertainment conglomerate was performing very nicely indeed, thank you, and that the leadership was sound and quite capable of taking over for Michael Eisner if that ever became necessary. They saw no reason why someone from the outside needed to be brought in to play heir-apparent to Eisner. Thus, when they learned of Eisner's decision to appoint Ovitz, Stephen Bollenbach, chief financial officer, Sanford Litvack, senior executive vice president and chief of corporate operations, and Irwin Russell, a veteran attorney and Disney board member, met with Eisner at his Bel Air home and denounced the decision.

When Bollenbach asked Eisner why he had decided on a course that inevitably would bring grave dissension within the ranks of Disney's leadership, the Disney chairman argued that, now that the Capital Cities/ABC merger was going forward, he simply couldn't run Disney all by himself. But Bollenbach countered by noting that Ovitz lacked the experience to manage a large public corporation. Eisner defended his choice by pointing out that Ovitz had much experience in business and had run a large company. CAA, Bollenbach shot back, was a *tiny* company. (CAA had around 500 employees; Disney, 117,000.)

It soon became clear to Bollenbach and the two other executives, however, that Eisner was not about to budge. At least, Bollenbach suggested, why not create an "office of the president," with Ovitz, Bollenbach, and Litvack as members? Eisner vetoed that idea as constituting a display of weakness on his part, a compromise making it seem as if the CEO couldn't put together a genuine chain of command. Piqued and perturbed, Bollenbach and Litvack said that they would refuse to report to Ovitz.

And then, right into the midst of this contentious discussion, walked Michael Ovitz. Eisner introduced him to the three Disney executives. By now understanding Eisner's degree of resolve on this matter, Bollenbach told Ovitz that he was prepared to work with him. Ovitz understood the implications of that statement, and he told Bollenbach and Litvack that neither of them would have to report to him. Thus it was that, in agreeing to let the two men report to Eisner, and not to him, Ovitz surrendered a good deal of his authority even before he began his new job.

It was against this dark backdrop that Michael Ovitz and Michael Eisner made themselves available on August 14 to field reporters' questions, presenting themselves to the world for the first time as Disney's new leadership team. "Looking toward the future," Ovitz said, "this is an extraordinary playing field. And in the last week, in the conversations that we've had, it has become eminently clear that this is an opportunity that I just couldn't refuse." Reporters noticed that Ovitz appeared subdued and tense, whereas Eisner, seated next to him, was relaxed and animated. Ovitz, wrote one journalist of that meeting, looked "like a man who just climbed off Disneyland's 'Indiana Jones' thrill ride." No surprise there. For after all, it was only on that very same morning that Ovitz had formally quit his post at CAA, leaving behind him an institution in turmoil. And now he was embarking upon a major adventure, one that might turn out to be more a minefield than the welcome opportunity he had longed for for so long.

It was a tough day for him, Ovitz admitted to the journalists. Leaving CAA hadn't been easy, and yet he did feel that it was time to begin a new chapter in his life. Now he had a chance to spend that next chapter at the side of "a close friend—maybe my best friend," to work for a company of unlimited possibilities, and to have some fun. Eisner then explained his reason for hiring Ovitz: The ABC acquisition had compelled him to confront the management crisis at Disney head-on. After Frank Wells met his tragic end on April 3, 1994, when a helicopter crashed into a Nevada mountainside, he made up his mind to run Disney on his own "until I found the perfect partner." Eisner disclosed that, upon Wells's death, he had sought out Michael Ovitz and offered him the present job, but Ovitz had declined. Then, when Ovitz began to negotiate with MCA, Eisner contacted him to say: "If it doesn't work out, we're still here." Now that Eisner had at last snared Ovitz, the Disney chairman seemed to be genuinely excited: "The playing field is changing rapidly. I have brought a new partner into this company who understands change and who also actually understands the entertainment business. I am absolutely thrilled."

Did Eisner consider Ovitz to be his successor? the Disney chairman was asked.

Eisner wasn't prepared to give a definite "Yes" in response to that question. All he would say was: "We haven't discussed succession at the company, but he's the number-two man and if something happens to me, he'd be a pretty good candidate." That was, at the very best, a lukewarm endorsement of Ovitz, and constituted the first public acknowledgment that Eisner was backing off on his private promise to Ovitz that Ovitz would indeed succeed him, and in the near future at that.

In fact, the lack of any "heir-apparent" had haunted Eisner and the whole Disney empire ever since Wells's death, and had been a growing concern to the investment community as well. As of the start of 1994, Disney's stock was at $48 a share. It dropped to $40 when Frank Wells died three months later on April 3, and it remained at that level until August 24, when Jeffrey Katzenberg resigned as studio chief at Disney. In the wake of Katzenberg's resignation, the stock dropped slightly, to $39 a share, but gradually rose over the next year to an all-time high of $60 a share on the eve of the Disney merger with Capital Cities/ABC on July 31, 1995. On the day of the Ovitz announcement, August 14, the stock was at $59 a share. But when investment banker Herb Allen heard that his friend Michael Ovitz was going to Disney, he doubled his stock position in the company. "I think it will be a better company in five years with Mike there," Allen observed.

Notwithstanding his lukewarm endorsement of Ovitz as heir-apparent, Eisner promised that the two men would be functioning as equal partners. "We will be totally interchangeable in everything we do," Eisner told a journalist. And yet Eisner had been careful not to give Ovitz the kind of power that Frank Wells had enjoyed. Wells had been the chief operating officer and had reported directly to the Disney board; Ovitz would not bear that exalted title, and he would not report to the board. Eisner remained chairman and chief executive officer, and it would have been difficult for him to give Ovitz the COO title without ruffling the feathers of Bollenbach and/or Litvack. But while it did look like Eisner was retaining most of the power himself, Ovitz felt he had nothing to worry about, since the chairman had personally promised him that he would be handling only ceremonial tasks, while Ovitz would run the daily show and make all of the key strategic decisions. Besides, only 13 months had elapsed since Eisner's open-heart surgery, and Eisner's wife Jane was begging her husband to take it easy.

Eisner certainly sounded upbeat about Ovitz's prospects of success at Disney, when he wrote in the company's 1995 Annual Report: "Not only will he be the perfect president of the company, but he is a trusted friend. I already have creative notes from his three children, notes about improving Disneyland and The Disney Channel and a full presentation on an interactive CD-ROM game from an eight-year-old point of view. Our new research department!"

Ovitz INSISTED THAT he had not made the switch to Disney for financial reasons; yet there was no denying that after signing his new Disney contract, he was far better off financially. Michael Eisner understood that if Disney wanted Michael Ovitz as its new president, it would have to pay generously for him. After all, it wasn't getting just *anybody*. It was getting the man perceived by many as being the most powerful figure in Hollywood, and this at a time when there were precious few other talented business executives available. At any rate, and however you sliced it, the man touted as being one of Hollywood's greatest deal-makers had made one of the sweetest financial deals the town had ever seen: While the amount that Michael Ovitz actually would receive from Disney would depend upon how its stock fared, compensation specialists estimated that the total package might bring him as much as $150 million!

Ovitz's five-year contract as president of The Walt Disney Company, when it was made public the following December, showed that his annual salary was $1 million a year, $250,000 more than Eisner's. No need to feel sorry for Mr. Eisner, however: His compensation for the year ending September 30, 1995, amounted to $14.8 million, when stocks and bonuses were added in. Indeed, since he had taken over Disney in 1984, Eisner had become the highest-paid executive in the United States: Over his 11 years at Disney, Michael Eisner's performance-based package had earned him, according to newspaper estimates, more than $600 million in pay, bonuses, and profit on stock options!

Although Ovitz's actual salary of $1 million was low by Hollywood standards, the overall contract was not, for the bulk of the package's value lay in the five million stock options incorporated into the deal. Those options gave Ovitz the right to purchase the stock at $57 a share. If the stock didn't rise, the options would be worthless; but if over the next 10 years the Disney stock rose only from $57 to $77 a share—a feeble 3.1 percent annual increase—Ovitz still would garner $100 million in the course of a decade. And should Disney decide not to renew Ovitz's contract, he would automatically receive $10 million. Also, Ovitz was to gain access to one million options per year, after three years on the job. (Even before he came to Disney, Ovitz owned 203,560 shares of Disney stock.)

Thus it was that Michael Ovitz became most likely the highest-paid second-in-command in the United States. Of course, the deal that he had negotiated for himself had no up-front bonus and no guaranteed future bonuses. But Ovitz need not have been concerned about that. Eisner had been averaging $5.7 million in bonuses per year over the past decade, and number-two executives typically receive 75 percent of the top man's bonus—which in Ovitz's case would mean another $4.3 million a year. Although Disney might have preferred to get Ovitz more cheaply, the company wasn't in a strong enough position to bargain aggressively: Eisner was eager for an heir-apparent and Ovitz, as the most powerful figure in Hollywood, could demand, and expect to receive, a huge pay package.

Ovitz was given responsibility for all three Disney divisions—theme parks, filmed entertainment, and consumer products—as well as for the new acquisition, Capital Cities/ABC Inc. Ovitz was eager to make his mark on the company early on, but that would be no small feat: There were few deals for him to make any time soon, since the big deal—the merger with ABC/Cap Cities—had just been made. What Disney needed now was merely good management, since there was little that needed to be fixed: ABC was the nation's most successful network; Walt Disney World was the number-one theme park; and within the filmed-entertainment division, Disney owned the top animation studio and the number-one sports channel (ESPN). The company ran film and television operations, as well as a merchandising business that was exceptionally profitable due to the franchising of such characters as Aladdin and Mickey Mouse.

In 1996, revenues reached $21.2 billion, with operating income at $3.7 billion. There was no other company in America with Disney's consumer reach: Any project it promoted had the potential of reaching 400 million consumers who visited its parks and stores; watched its films and television programs or videotapes; played its games; or heard its music. It was the ultimate packaging company, capable of creating a product and packaging it so that there were 100 different ways to derive commercial benefit. And every seven years a new generation of young children came of age, ready and eager to purchase Disney products. "Disney's a perfect company," said a close Ovitz acquaintance. "I don't like them, but they're perfect, and they don't need much. That company is rolling."

Yet Michael Eisner still believed that Michael Ovitz was the right man for the job—or at least he did at the time that Ovitz began to work at Disney. Eisner believed that Ovitz would be able to open up and develop new markets abroad for Disney through his wide-ranging contacts, and thought that his friend's enthusiasm for and knowledge of the cutting-edge technologies would help Disney exploit those technologies. Ovitz also brought a love of travel and a fascination with Asia, that were in marked and hopeful contrast to the stay-at-home Eisner, who was always in search of more time to deal with Disney's filmed-entertainment division. Even before he officially took over, Ovitz was on the road for Disney, flying in September to Japan, China, and Europe in order to acquaint himself with the company's overseas operations. He hoped to boost Disney's overseas revenues from 23 percent of overall revenues to 50 percent, within five years. Ovitz certainly did seem to complement Eisner in the skills department, and thus there seemed to be every reason to believe that Ovitz would succeed at his new post.

Michael Ovitz became president of The Walt Disney Company on October 1, 1995.

Peter Bart, editor-in-chief of *Daily Variety*, had coffee with Ovitz soon after that, and asked him how he felt about the new job. "It's going to require some adjustments," Ovitz said with a smile. "Disney isn't a company as much as it is a nation-state with its own ideas and attitudes, and you have to adjust to them." It was a telling comment. On the job for only a short period, and Ovitz already appeared to be daunted by the Disney bureaucracy and its high-powered senior executives. Throughout his career, he had always been the key decision maker. Now he felt the need to adapt himself to what others were doing and saying.

Nonetheless, Ovitz did seem to be having a great time in those first few months at Disney. He spent each new day learning about a different aspect of the business. Ever since his school days, as the kid raising his hand fast-and-furious in class, Michael Ovitz had been intensely curious about the world at large. He had announced when he took the Disney job that he would need a couple of years in which to learn the job, and he believed he was being given a kind of grace period to do just that. He also wanted to use the first three to six months at Disney not only to learn the new job, but to stay in touch with the hundreds of CAA clients whose lives and careers he had sought to improve over the years. He felt that he owed them that much, and as they did keep calling him for advice, he kept taking their phone calls. It was as if in some ways he had never left CAA at all. According to Ovitz, his continuing consultations with former CAA clients irritated Eisner, who had little respect for actors and actresses. Ovitz recalls that, while he wanted to be cordial to his former clients, "Eisner wanted me to cut them off. Eisner hates talent. When I took Cruise or Seinfeld to dinner, he criticized me. He didn't care about me winding down relationships."

To those non-Disney people who met with Ovitz in his early days at Disney, he seemed like a kid in a candy store. He was thrilled to discover that he now had far more resources and personnel at his command, excited that the playing field was so much broader than it had been at CAA. He was especially proud of the fact that a huge television network was reporting directly to him. To sculptor Joel Shapiro, the Ovitz of this period seemed "much more buoyant, less anxious, distressed, more open." Sean Connery, whom Ovitz signed up to make films at Disney as one of his first acts as president, noticed that the new Disney president seemed more content on this new job, and that the reason for that was clear: "He's learning much more now than he did in the last four years or so at the agency, because he's had to start a whole new regime and scheme of things."

To his great disappointment, however, Michael Ovitz began to sense that Michael Eisner was not adopting the expected passive stance. Far from performing only a ceremonial role, the chairman seemed to be giving up none of the critical decision making, and he continued to formulate the company's overall strategy. Worst of all for Ovitz, while on the surface he was in charge of Disney's operating division, everything required Eisner's approval, and Ovitz was given no formal responsibilities of his own.

Meanwhile, Disney's senior executives remained distant and unfriendly, as Ovitz tried to make his presence felt. Feeling that he would make the quickest impact if he acted entrepreneurially, Ovitz tried to take on projects that would earn the company quick rewards, such as purchasing the Los Angeles Lakers. Later Ovitz would say: "I was trying to learn the business, and winding down my business at the same time. I saw Eisner giving me no responsibilities, which meant I started to migrate to projects that I thought would make an additive." He tried to purchase the Los Angeles Lakers. "Michael could do the Angels and Ducks, but when I tried to do the Lakers, it wasn't okay for me to do." (Disney owns the major-league baseball team the California Angels, as well as the professional hockey team the Anaheim Ducks.) When the plan to buy the Lakers fell through, Disney executives privately blamed Ovitz for having taken on such a marginal project.

Next, Ovitz began to try to consolidate Disney's operations, starting in Europe and hoping to do the same in Asia, in order to give executives the benefit of seeing one another often and exchanging ideas. But Eisner and other Disney executives received the plan coolly, believing it to be far too costly and of no real benefit to the company. Even when Ovitz induced actors Sean Connery and Sally Field, and producers Frank Marshall and Kathy Kennedy to enter into production deals with Disney, his efforts didn't generate much enthusiasm among the other senior executives.

Ovitz also aided Disney Studio Chief Joe Roth in bringing director Martin Scorsese into the Disney fold. But one project that Scorsese brought with him to Disney proved to be both quite controversial and embarrassing to Ovitz. It was a film called *Kundun,* and it dealt with the early life of the Dalai Lama, the Tibetan spiritual leader who was in open conflict with the Chinese government. The project stirred the Chinese to anger, which was hardly what Disney was eager to have happen at the very time it was making a major effort, via Ovitz, to penetrate the vast Chinese market. But Disney was in a real bind. For while it was eager to enter into a commercial relationship with China, it didn't want a foreign government to be able to dictate to it what movies it could make. The Chinese threatened to prevent Disney from conducting business in China if the film was released; but to its credit, Disney decided to stand up for what it believed was right and announced that it planned to proceed with the film. Eisner hoped that Ovitz would be able, in keeping with his mandate to open up China for Disney, to calm the Chinese down about this matter. And indeed, Ovitz was confident that the Chinese would not seek to punish Disney on account of just this one movie. Yet when Disney's efforts in China stalled, Ovitz took the blame, which he believes was unfair: "Joe Roth made the deal and I got blasted, because Roth was my client for ten years." But regardless of who, if anyone, was "to blame," "the *Kundun* affair" certainly became yet another unneeded source of friction between Ovitz and his fellow Disney executives.

Deciding that another good way to make an early impact on Disney would be to hire some highly visible, talented executives, Ovitz undertook a search for the right kind of people. He had been aware for some time of a remarkable young woman, someone he had met at the February 1995 NBA All-Star game in Phoenix, Arizona. She was a former schoolteacher by the name of Geraldine Laybourne. Laybourne took the children's channel Nickelodeon, founded in 1977, and turned it into a huge commercial success. Taking command of the station gradually, first as program manager in 1980, then president in 1986, she sought to add variety to children's television. By the time Ovitz met her nine years later, Nickelodeon was in 66 million homes and was the highest-rated cable network. In 1996, it was worth $4.5 billion. In its June 17, 1996 edition, *Time* listed Laybourne as one of the 25 most influential people in America.

At that All-Star game, Laybourne happened to be sitting two rows in front of Michael Ovitz, who was there with his son Eric and Edgar Bronfman Jr. David Stern, the NBA Commissioner, introduced Ovitz to Laybourne, who immediately struck up a warm conversation with Eric. Soon thereafter Ovitz called Laybourne, and told her that his son thought she was the most interesting person at the game. "I've got to meet you," Ovitz said.

It took a while for them to set a date. Finally Ovitz's assistant tracked Laybourne down at a staff meeting of MTV, where she was vice chairman. Laybourne was seated far from the phone, so someone else answered it. "Mike Ovitz is on the line," he said, looking at Laybourne. "He wants you." All heads popped up from their notebooks. *Michael Ovitz was on the line and wanted Geraldine Laybourne!* Suddenly everyone was staring at her, but having met the man only once, there was no reason to interrupt a staff meeting just to take his call. She would call him back later, she said.

Laybourne heard whispering and snickering, but she couldn't tell what her colleagues were saying to one another. Then it dawned on her that she had refused to take Michael Ovitz's phone call, something that no one *ever* dared to do.

In late May of 1995, Laybourne and Ovitz finally got together for dinner at a small Italian restaurant near CAA. This was during the 10-day period when Ovitz was "secretly" negotiating with MCA. Laybourne had read about the MCA negotiations, and she assumed that Ovitz would cancel their dinner, but he didn't. "He was completely unruffled," she reported later. During the dinner Kevin Costner approached their table and said hello to Ovitz, who introduced him to his dinner partner.

Laybourne assumed that Ovitz wanted to talk to her about taking a job at MCA under his new leadership. But he never asked her if she had any interest in leaving Nickelodeon. All he said was that if he did take a new job, he would want to bring in strong people to work for him. Laybourne, eager to ply Ovitz with questions about both the MCA deal and his career, asked away, but Ovitz deflected all of the questions. She wasn't used to that, "but then again, I wasn't used to talking to Michael Ovitz either." He kept steering the conversation back to her, asking her all about her family and how she developed Nickelodeon. Laybourne was impressed: "It was one of the most amazingly flattering interviews you could have."

Then the MCA–Ovitz talks collapsed and Ovitz went to Disney. But he still remembered his dinner with Geraldine Laybourne. It turned out that Bob Iger, head of ABC, had been trying to lure Laybourne over to his network for some time. Eisner, Ovitz, and Iger all agreed that Laybourne would make a great choice to become president of Disney/ABC Cable Networks. In December 1995, Iger phoned her and made the offer. She was flattered and somewhat enticed, but hesitant nonetheless, for the new job would represent a very major change in her life. Her contract with Viacom, which owned Nickelodeon, would expire the following February.

Laybourne was torn. Nervous about losing her, Viacom made an offer that would keep her on beyond February; in reply, Disney counteroffered. Still, Laybourne was conflicted.

Ovitz stepped up the pressure. Before leaving for Japan on one occasion, Ovitz called Laybourne and asked her if she needed anything, something he could bring her from the Orient. "Bring me back plastic sushi," Laybourne joked with him. The next morning, Ovitz sent her plastic sushi via Federal Express. "Your wish is my command," read the note wrapped in a bow. From Japan, Ovitz called Laybourne three times a day. "Are you still interested?" was how he began each conversation. "He didn't miss a beat," she recalls. "He just hit all the right notes." Geraldine Laybourne became the president of The Walt Disney Company's cable-television operation on December 14, 1995.

Stephen Bollenbach left Disney in February 1996. His dream of succeeding Eisner one day had gone up in smoke on the day it was announced that Michael Ovitz would become Disney's new president.

Ovitz's actual arrival, the previous October, had proved to be very awkward for Bollenbach as well.

Other Disney executives viewed Bollenbach's departure, in the words of one Disney board member, as a "disaster," but Bollenbach himself felt that he had no choice but to leave Disney, and he sensed that he had a brighter future elsewhere. He became chief executive of the Hilton Hotels Corporation, and for a while he appeared to have put the Disney experience behind him. But as it turned out, he wasn't through with Michael Ovitz yet.

BEYOND THAT MEETING with the media on October 1, 1995, his first day on his new job, Ovitz made no public appearances in his first few months at Disney, nor did he grant any on-the-record interviews. Indeed, during his entire tenure at Disney he never granted a single one-on-one, on-the-record interview; he did sit down for one joint television interview, however, with Michael Eisner, on *Larry King Live.*

Ovitz's first public appearance as Disney president came on January 4, 1996, when he spoke to the shareholders in a ballroom at New York's Waldorf-Astoria Hotel. The shareholders had been summoned in order to give their approval of Disney's acquisition of Capital Cities/ABC. Ovitz's speech was well received, and Eisner earned credit for the generous way in which he shared the platform with Ovitz and didn't get upset even when Ovitz interrupted his answers.

BY THE END of 1995, however, Michael Ovitz's problems at The Walt Disney Company were accumulating. First and foremost, he was having trouble being a subordinate, not to mention to a figure like Eisner who currently was considered Hollywood's single most powerful figure. Had Eisner lived up to his part of the bargain, Ovitz almost certainly would have found it easier to function. But the Disney chairman now seemed like "the Bionic Man," moving briskly from meeting to meeting, event to event, always in charge, always treating Ovitz not like a co-chairman or the *real* Disney CEO but like just another junior executive. And Ovitz was furious. "He promised me the world and delivered nothing," Ovitz would say later, his voice growing louder and angrier as he spoke of his relationship with Eisner.

Making matters worse, Ovitz was forced to confront the embarrassment of being isolated and voided of authority in the direct glare of the spotlight. Now that he had left CAA and joined a public company, there was no longer any shield of quasi-anonymity to protect him from the media's withering scrutiny. His critics, long silent and long eager to take Ovitz on, sensed that he was in trouble at Disney, that he was growing weaker by the minute, and moved in for the kill. For years Ovitz had made it oh-so-clear to Hollywood's movers and shakers, especially the studio chiefs and some senior producers, that he knew how to conduct business more expertly than they did. And every time, during the CAA years, that he put together a film package and used his talent-heavy client list as leverage against the studios, he rubbed more salt in their wounds.

For years Michael Ovitz had been able to live down his reputation of being Hollywood's strongman, and all during that time he acquired many friends, but also an assortment of enemies. The friends always were happy to say a kind word about Ovitz, but the enemies laid low, unwilling to alienate a man they knew they might be forced to do business with in the future.

Still, Ovitz knew that his enemies were out there, and he knew why they had become his enemies. He knew that many of them would have preferred a Hollywood without any Michael Ovitz, or at least with only some kinder, gentler version of him. Walking out of the funeral of Frank Wells in April 1994, Ovitz looked around at the other 5000 mourners, and told his wife Judy: "If I died tomorrow, there'd be twenty-five thousand people at my funeral. Why? Because everyone would want to know that I was dead." Ovitz always insists that he never actually threatened anyone, but he does acknowledge that, as his critics had been charging in whispers for so many years, CAA did use strong-arm tactics in order to drum up work for its clients: "I spent twenty years in my business where we dominated it for twelve, thirteen, fourteen years. If someone crossed our clients, we didn't work for them. If someone crossed an agent, we cut them out. We didn't have to threaten anybody."

For anyone to hold and to wield so much power, Ovitz understood, was bound to produce enemies: "When you're sitting with all the cards, you can't win, because someone is going to attribute their failure to you, whatever you do. Twenty offers came in every day for Tom Cruise, fifty offers a week. All the scripts were read, and ultimately we would massage the right projects for him, based on who he wanted to work with, or who was a great director; and all the other people would spin around. And it all got laid at my feet. If you offered ten million dollars for Tom Cruise, and his last price was six and it wasn't what we wanted him to do, if it wasn't *Top Gun*, or working with Paul Newman or Sydney Pollack, we hung on to your offer as long as we could. We'd give you somebody else but it wasn't Cruise. And we would convince you it was good. We would say Val Kilmer is not

Cruise, but he's talented. Then the movie [starring Val Kilmer] comes out, and if it's a hit we're geniuses, and if it's a failure it was our fault."

Ovitz always was shuffling his talent list in such a way as to ensure that the largest possible number of CAA clients found work. Still, the more high-powered the talent, the greater were the problems for CAA and Michael Ovitz. Yet he learned how to meet that challenge as well, by juggling some of Hollywood's best-known actors and making sure they didn't take acting roles away from one another. For instance, the three top actors of the day—Al Pacino, Dustin Hoffman, and Robert De Niro—all played similar "character" roles. Says Ovitz: "All the offers came in to the same place. Imagine the leverage we had. It was very easy to move their prices up. They always held each other's price up. We had enough material for them that they could do different things. If you're a studio and a director says 'I need a De Niro type,' you could only go to one place to get them. You could only go to CAA. *We* made the choice whether a studio got one of them or not. We had enormous power. My relations were good because we had what the studios wanted. The minute I left they bad mouthed me. It came from people we sold to whom we made look stupid."

Ovitz is candid too in describing the methods he employed to keep studios from trying to undermine the agency: "I wouldn't allow a studio to call a CAA client directly. I made everyone go through our agents to get to the clients. If they went around them, we cut their legs off. We ignored them. We didn't threaten, shake, or abuse them. We ignored them. We returned their calls at the end of the day, not at the start of the day. Do you think that made me popular? We were so effective it was frightening."

Nonetheless, the Ovitz enemies list, a relatively long one at times, never caused him trouble while he was at CAA. The studio chief forced to take Val Kilmer instead of Tom Cruise may have been angry at Ovitz for a while, but he never would dare to lash out at him in public, or even in off-the-record remarks to a journalist, for fear that word would get back to Ovitz and the CAA chairman would punish the studio chief by not giving him priority on some future deal. That was how Ovitz worked for years. He knew it, the studio chiefs and producers knew it, and everyone kept quiet about it. It was to everyone's advantage to keep their mouths shut.

Ovitz knew exactly who his main critics were. The names mentioned most often in the media were David Geffen, Jeffrey Katzenberg, and producer Ray Stark. But Lew Wasserman and Sidney Sheinberg were cool toward Ovitz as well. Ovitz knew that for many years he had held these people hostage, and he sensed that they all wanted him to fail now. In fact, they would just love it.

And now that he had gone to Disney, and things weren't going so well, perhaps at last they would get their chance to bring him down. Now he was simply another studio executive—not even a studio *chief*. That alone brought Ovitz's critics some needed satisfaction, but still they weren't prepared to attack him in public. They waited, because they had to. There was still a chance that Ovitz would become as powerful a figure as the president of Disney as he had been as chairman of CAA. Perhaps he would continue to hold his critics hostage, forced to do business with him even when they didn't approve of his tactics. Thus, while they saw it as being too early to take action, the Ovitz enemies definitely were on red-alert. The minute they saw their chance, they would strike.

And joining in that battle, alongside Hollywood powerhouses such as Geffen and Wasserman, would be some new recruits such as NBC's Don Ohlmeyer, that network's senior West Coast executive and, now that Ovitz was in charge of ABC, yet another rival of the new Disney president.

Early in 1996 came news reports that the ABC television network had been trying to lure a highly-regarded program executive, Jamie McDermott, away from rival NBC; McDermott had played a major role in developing such hit shows as *Friends*. According to *The New York Post* and *New York* magazine, McDermott tried to get out of her NBC contract by charging sexual harassment against Ohlmeyer, the network's senior West Coast executive, so that she could go to work for ABC. In an interview with *Time*, Ohlmeyer asserted that he was entirely innocent of the charge of sexual harassment, and he blamed Disney's Michael Ovitz, to whom ABC's executives reported directly, for fomenting "rumors and innuendo that have no basis in fact." Then he added, in words that had to be the strongest ever spoken publicly about the new Disney president: "Michael Ovitz is the Antichrist, and you can quote me on that." Ovitz chose not to comment. McDermott denied that she had threatened Ohlmeyer with charges of sexual harassment. She was eventually appointed President of Entertainment for ABC.

Five or ten years earlier, Don Ohlmeyer, or anyone else for that matter, would never have dared to make such a statement. But the fact was that Ovitz no longer loomed so large. "Ovitz," said Jeff Berg, the chairman and CEO of International Creative Management in March 1996, "has certainly more responsibility and weight on his shoulders now, but in a funny way he had a more defined niche in the agency business, because the only major players were CAA and ICM. Now there's Michael Eisner, Jeffrey Katzenberg, David Geffen, Sumner Redstone, Rupert Murdoch, and Edgar Bronfman. It's a bigger landscape in terms of principal owners and operators. Mike's no longer an owner of CAA. That gave him strength and power."

While it would be absurd to place the media as a whole on the Ovitz enemy list, it certainly was the case at this time, as the *Time* story and other articles showed, that editors had jettisoned their former fawning attitude toward Michael Ovitz. They now were watching to see whether Ovitz would falter. The very fact that he and Eisner, jointly the two most powerful figures in Hollywood, had teamed up to run an entertainment empire, made this one of the great Hollywood dramas, and taking the temperature of their relationship from time to time seemed very much in order.

Tina Brown, now the editor of *The New Yorker*, thought that the media had turned against Ovitz because he took the job at Disney too soon after the MCA talks collapsed: "The move to Disney seemed like a very precipitous one that came out of a sense of beleaguerment. Michael Ovitz would have gotten better press if he had waited. But it's a very sadistic culture. The press smelt weakness and moved in for the kill." Underscoring Ovitz's diminished power, or at least the perception thereof, he fell from number two all the way down to number seven on the *Premiere* Power List that appeared in May of 1996. Michael Eisner topped the list. The magazine scolded Ovitz for leaving a bad taste in the mouths of CAA agents (presumably, by recanting on promises to take certain CAA agents with him to MCA) and for overplaying his hand in the MCA negotiations—only to take a larger job, but for less money, at Disney.

Ovitz seems to assign more blame for his bad image to his personal critics than to the media. He suggests that there was "a small group of people, kind of a mafia, who engaged in spin control."

To be sure, the number of people who were openly on the warpath against Ovitz was tiny. But their numbers didn't matter, for they were among the most powerful figures in town, and what they said to reporters suddenly mattered a good deal. The media was eager to interview this handful of anti-Ovitz partisans, sensing that the story of how Hollywood's most influential power broker had fallen off his pedestal was simply too good to pass up. What these partisans had once refused to say even in off-the-record conversations now became mere grist for the mill. Their public comments, while short on specifics, were all the more deadly in their effect, if only because it had once been so uncommon to hear anything negative about Ovitz in public. All sorts of ways of puncturing the Ovitz balloon were tried out, including the assertion that most of his corporate deal-making, especially the Sony and Matsushita experiences, had gone bad. At the time, Ovitz chose not to respond. But later he would insist that "my job wasn't to operate these companies. They both [Sony and Matsushita] said they wanted to be in the entertainment business. It's not like I called up Sony and said, 'You should be in the entertainment business.' They called me, and said, 'We want to merge software and hardware.' What should I say, 'Don't do that, it's ridiculous, that's not my problem'?"

Had Michael Ovitz cared less about what other Hollywood executives thought of him, or what the media wrote of him, he might have experienced a smoother sail through his days at Disney. But the fact was that he cared deeply about what others thought and wrote about him. "Michael is very thin-skinned," says one acquaintance of long standing. "He's hurt so easily." Adds his friend Arne Glimcher: "He's a very sensitive man. Someone who's involved with the subtleties of art, anyone with that level of sensitivity, is not going to be thick-skinned. He doesn't understand the attacks."

Ovitz may not have understood the attacks, but by the spring of 1996 he and Eisner had both begun to feel that his Disney job might not work out. "We knew this wasn't working in April," Ovitz would say later. But at the time, he still hoped that a way might be found to straighten things out. "In the back of my head I thought there might be a problem, but I didn't want to believe it." Ovitz wrote Eisner a letter, broaching various ways in which they might still manage to salvage his job. Such was the strain upon their relationship that Ovitz felt it would be best to communicate his thoughts on this delicate matter in writing. In June the two men and their wives, along with five other couples, went on a bicycling tour of the Loire Valley in France. Ovitz thought that the conversations they had had then were friendly and constructive, and that things might improve. He looked forward to a quiet and even more productive rest-of-the-summer. But the press just wouldn't let up on him.

Media columnist Ken Auletta was the first to mention in public a strain in the Ovitz–Eisner relationship. Writing in the July 29, 1996 issue of *The New Yorker*, he described a testimonial dinner given at a New York restaurant on May 23 for Thomas S. Murphy, the recently retired chairman and CEO of Capital Cities/ABC. Hosted by Roone Arledge, the president of ABC News, the dinner also was attended by Peter Jennings, Barbara Walters, Ted Koppel, Diane Sawyer, Sam Donaldson, and Bob Iger. Speaking of Eisner and Ovitz, Murphy said: "I hope they can work out their problems." Donaldson, ever the reporter with a nose for a good story, asked: "What are those differences?" Barbara Walters added: "What about Ovitz?" Donaldson then turned to Diane Sawyer, married to CAA client Mike Nichols, and said, "Diane, you probably know Ovitz the best. What do you think?" She began to reply, but Iger, touching her arm to keep her from continuing, said that it wasn't appropriate for him to sit there and listen to a discussion of Michael Ovitz.

As for Eisner, he was seeking to play down the rift. At ABC's annual meeting of affiliates, held at Disney World in Orlando, Florida, from June 4 to 6, he publicly denied accounts of friction by saying, "Despite what may have been written, we're having a good time."

But Auletta reported that Eisner was complaining privately about Ovitz's management style, telling associates that Ovitz often pursued too many deal options and flitted from one subject to another. Auletta quoted an executive as saying that Eisner had told him that, although he had known Michael Ovitz for 25 years, "I didn't know him at all. That's the mistake I made when I brought him in here. He doesn't know how business operates."

Ovitz attempted to quell the rumors of a rift between him and Eisner by asking associates why they thought he and Eisner had vacationed together in June, if the relationship was as bad as the rumor-mongers were suggesting?

When *The London Times* wrote that summer that Eisner planned to fire his company's president, Ovitz "thought it was funny," says Arne Glimcher. "It was just too preposterous." Eisner tried to calm Ovitz by saying, "You can't do anything about it. Just forget about it." Arne Glimcher told Ovitz: "What are you going to do? Call the newspaper and say, 'We're not fighting'?" In July, Ovitz tried to take a philosophical approach to the media attacks, suggesting that he had known even before they started that they would come: "I factored it into my strategic outlook. I knew it would happen. It will last another three or four months." But the question was, could he weather the storm for another three or four months?

19

I Made a Smart Deal

THE SUMMER OF 1996 passed uneventfully for Ovitz, and so he began to feel slightly more hopeful that he would hang on as Disney's president. Perhaps, he thought, he might be able to soothe ruffled spirits by talking directly to some of his critics. His most dramatic attempt at reconciliation came when a friend of David Geffen's suggested to Ovitz that the two men meet and try to settle their differences. Ovitz agreed to the meeting, but wasn't sure what those differences *were*. The session was a disaster, degenerating into a shouting match. Ovitz recalls what happened: "He said terrible things about my family. I made a mistake in going, one of the many errors I made in the last year. Even Geffen's friend admitted it was a mistake for me to see him. I don't have a clue why Geffen is upset with me."

In August, Ovitz still was hopeful that he would be given a chance to prove his worth to Disney. However, he thought it a bad sign that Michael Eisner had planned to take off the entire month of August, but in the end did not. The man seemed invincible.

Then in early September Ovitz attended the Disney conference for senior executives in Aspen, Colorado. Finding Michael Eisner in a buoyant mood, Ovitz felt good about his prospects of remaining at Disney. But one incident at that conference dampened his optimism about surviving at the company. The incident occurred when Ovitz's remarks, urging Disney executives to cease leaking information aimed at undermining his efforts, were divulged to the media the very next day. Ovitz felt that all was lost. "That's when I said this is stupid. I made the biggest mistake of my business career. It was a stupid idea that I could come in and change this culture. The insanity of my thought process overwhelmed me."

Ovitz said nothing about what he was feeling to Eisner. Instead, he wrote him a six-page handwritten letter in which he said that serving as president of Disney wasn't going to work for him, and he felt that the two of them should talk about it. But no opportunity for doing that arose over the next few weeks. Ovitz was often abroad, and all he could do was brood about the untenable position he was in.

Later, in an interview with the author, Ovitz said: "[Eisner] was my best friend for twenty-five years. To this day I don't know why he brought me in there. As [investor] Ron Perelman said to me, 'It was the smartest move in business. I can't understand why it didn't work.' But the guy [Eisner] seemed to increase his activity. He was supposed to be less hands-on. He says I didn't know what I was doing, but he didn't give me the opportunity to do anything. We were going to be partners. We were going to run the company together. He brought me in as his successor. I thought there'd be a two- or three-year learning curve. But it didn't work from the day I started. He hired all the people. When Bollenbach and Litvack wouldn't report to me, that was the beginning of the end. I didn't go there to be number two for the rest of my life. Eisner put me in a position where I had no job. The chief financial officer didn't report to me. The head of operations didn't report to me. Eisner was working harder than he ever had been, and I was floating around looking for something to do."

It was in this crisis-ridden atmosphere that Eisner and Ovitz agreed to do a joint interview on September 30 on *Larry King Live* on CNN. This represented a first for Ovitz, since in all of his career he had never been interviewed on a nationwide TV talk show. There had been plenty of requests from shows such as *60 Minutes*, but until now he had turned them all down. He and Michael Eisner happened to be in Florida celebrating the twenty-fifth anniversary of Disney World, and doing the King show provided the two with a good chance to promote Disney. But otherwise, the timing was terrible. Inevitably, Larry King would ask about their relationship, and the two men would have to put a good face on it. Even if their relationship had been much better than it was, neither man would have dared to speak candidly about it. And yet the mere fact that Eisner had agreed to appear with Ovitz by his side seemed to indicate that the two men really were getting along. Nothing, of course, could have been further from the truth. Still, just before going on, Eisner and Ovitz agreed to be upbeat about their relationship, as that would be best for the company.

It didn't take Larry King long to ask how the two men were getting along.

"Typical, competitive Hollywood gossip," Eisner said with a sneer. Then, defending Ovitz, the Disney chairman added: "I don't know who is spreading stuff. First of all, it's minuscule. Michael was the top agent in the world for twenty years, and if you are representing Tom Cruise and you are angry at Tom Cruise for what you pay him, what you do is you take it out on Michael. . . . As far as we're concerned, it's an irrelevant, gossip-mongering kind of thing, and they wouldn't be interested in us if we weren't doing well, so I guess we should sort of be flattered. . . . There has not been one story where one person is quoted directly about any problems inside our company. It's just all baloney. The fact of the matter is we together have almost as many enemies as Saddam Hussein, and so it's very difficult to not have this kind of gossip."

And yet, what Eisner failed to say was even more important than what he did say. He did not ringingly endorse Ovitz as Disney president. He did not go out of his way to dispute the actual content of the various media stories. He did not declare that Ovitz had been doing a great job, and was certain to be his successor. Yet he did feel compelled to answer in the affirmative, when he was asked by King if he would hire Michael Ovitz all over again. But while it would of course have been jarring for Eisner to speak frankly in that regard, the evidence most certainly does suggest that Eisner had learned one hard lesson: If he had it all to do over again, he would *not* offer Ovitz the job.

When it was his turn to speak, Ovitz felt forced to take much the same line as Eisner: "We have been living with a sensation in the media business that really has little or nothing to do with the results of particular businesses. There seems to be an extraordinarily deep interest in the fascinations of the gossip side of our business." What particularly galled Ovitz—apart from being the chief target of these attacks—was the fact that The Walt Disney Company was having its best year ever. Eisner then tried to suggest that the gossip was entirely an embittered response to Disney's doing so well; but that oversimplified matters, and left out the central fact: Michael Ovitz had plenty of personal enemies out there, and as soon as they realized that Eisner was feeling less than enthusiastic about his choice of Ovitz as president, they used the media to get at Ovitz in every way they could.

Ovitz's appearance on *Larry King Live* bolstered the impression in some minds that his relationship with Eisner was indeed shaky. They pointed to the unease both men seemed to reveal when in the presence of the other, and to the fact that they scarcely looked at one another. Yet Ovitz took a measure of comfort from the show, if only because it perhaps hinted at a brighter future. "What you saw on King," he would say later, "was how the partnership was supposed to work."

But it was not only his relationship with Michael Eisner that was plaguing Michael Ovitz now. For there was a feeling, both inside and outside of Disney, that he wasn't succeeding in defining a role for himself within the company. Disney executives, board members, and Ovitz business acquaintances, when asked to mention the highlights of Ovitz's first year at Disney, had a hard time singling out any notable achievements. As Shelly Hochron observed at the time, "I don't think it's been clear to the community or to the press what his current role is. That is breeding a lot of suspicion and cynicism. He's feeling a bit under pressure and under attack." What an understatement! He was feeling under *great* pressure and under *lethal* attack. On the few occasions when he did say publicly that he still had a lot to learn at Disney before he could come into his own, Ovitz sounded humble. He had admitted to Larry King: "Frankly, when we first talked about this, we talked about a two-year learning curve. So I must say, having been here just about a year now, I probably know about one percent of what I need to know." To Ovitz's critics, that statement was an admission that he really didn't know very much about Disney at all, that he hadn't made a big effort to learn, and that he had a long way to go before he could be called "knowledgeable."

Yet behind the scenes Ovitz was indeed very busy probing, trying to find out what the various Disney managers did and how the company as a whole operated. His goal was to create synergy, but some of the managers were afraid that Ovitz's synergy would come only at the expense of their job independence. "Because he was so interested in getting people to work together, he's gotten into a lot of people's faces," says Susan Lyne. "This is a company which reported in fairly separate entities and reported to Michael Eisner. When someone new comes in and asks people what is it you do and how can we do it better, it has gotten some backs up."

And Eisner did little or nothing to make Disney's size and bureaucracy seem less daunting to Ovitz. Says one executive: "Mike wasn't able to bring people in. Our hands were tied. Disney's divisions are established institutions. I thought Mike would be able to exercise what he wanted to do. It was a miscalculation." Disney's massive size seemed to make Ovitz's task that much harder. "It takes a lot more sophistication managing a large company," says Donald Wilson, co-chairman of Northwest Airlines and a member of the Disney board. "You're dealing with departments, and bureaucrats; you're not dealing with entrepreneurial, as

Michael did at CAA. You don't need a lot of staff at CAA to handle talent."

Ovitz kept looking for ways to remedy the bad situation he found himself in. He met with Disney public relations executives, to put together a statement to be issued to the press that showcased the company's many achievements of the past year. The fact was that Disney had never performed better, and Ovitz felt that that message should be beamed out loud and clear to journalists. John Dreyer, Disney's vice president for corporate communications, wrote the "letter" and sent it to a dozen journalists who were known to be working on Disney stories or were likely to do so in the future. And yet in retrospect, Ovitz says that even the letter didn't improve his standing within the company.

On Saturday evening, October 12, 1996, Ovitz flew from Chicago to Bermuda to give a speech at the American Magazine Publishers conference. While The Walt Disney Company usually isn't thought of as being a magazine publisher, it does in fact own around 100 magazines including *Disney Adventures*, which has one million readers. Ovitz's private jet, a Gulfstream-3, was due to leave O'Hare Airport at 11:00 p.m. A young man named David, who served as both flight mechanic and steward, greeted a guest to the thirteen-seat plane. The two pilots were up front behind closed doors. This was no crowded commuter plane: The 13 seats were of luxurious brown leather, and four of the seats surrounded a beautifully-finished desk with a small box-like device resting upon it. It was a telephone.

Because this was a jet carrying the president of Disney, one automatically looked for signs of Mickey Mouse and the other well-known Disney characters, but none was to be found on the plane's exterior. This could have been the corporate jet of any other American executive. Inside, however, the Disney touch was noticeable. Mickey was on the cocktail napkin served with coffee. Donald and Goofy were on the coffee mug. In the rear, next to the toilet, Mickey graced the bath towel hanging on a rack. The plane came equipped with a television and videotape recorder. David proudly showed the guest the list of movies that were available for viewing on the videotape recorder: *Sabrina*, *Bridges of Madison County*, *The Late Shift*, and the new Julia Roberts movie, *Mary Reilly*.

Ovitz boarded the plane at 11:50 p.m. dressed in a black tuxedo and bowtie, having just come from a charity event and a wedding. He undid his bowtie, and warned a guest that the takeoff would be steep. Then he called home and spoke first to his wife and then to his son Chris. Ovitz told his guest with a twinkle in his eye that something big was going to happen to him in the next two weeks, but he couldn't talk about it yet. "I knew I was leaving," he would say later, "and I was in the process of putting together the deal that I'm doing now. I thought I'd make an announcement while I was there [at Disney]." He planned to announce that he was leaving Disney in two weeks to enter a new business.

Over the next 90 minutes of conversation on the way to Bermuda, Ovitz talked at length about world events, the Middle East, and terrorism in America, but he made only oblique mention of the negative news stories about him. Then food was served: lasagna for the guest and sushi for Ovitz, which he ate deftly with chopsticks.

Ovitz then showed the guest a video, one that he was debating whether to show the magazine editors who would be listening to his presentation that Monday in Bermuda. The video explained the concept of an electronic magazine, an important feature of Ovitz's speech. Ovitz noted that he hoped the editors would ask questions: "The one thing I don't want to be is boring."

In the past year, Ovitz had been to China on several occasions, on Disney business. Now he spoke warmly of the Chinese and their economy. He had suggested to his son Chris that he learn Chinese. Then Ovitz said an odd thing: He wished he could start his life all over again, and live it in China. He had met someone recently to whom he had recommended that he go live in Shanghai, for that was a place, he was sure, that would produce many millionaires over the next decade. Conversation coming to an end, Ovitz walked to the front of the plane, lay down in a bunk, and slept for an hour. The plane landed in Bermuda at 5:00 a.m. local time Sunday. Ovitz spent the rest of the day resting and going over his speech with a number of Disney aides who had flown in from Los Angeles earlier; included in the retinue was a makeup specialist, since Ovitz was concerned that he would look too white and pale during his speech, under all of the hot lights.

When he delivered his speech on Monday morning, Ovitz was anything but boring. He spoke for 35 minutes, the precise amount of time that had been allotted to him. Midway through the speech he pulled out a prototype of a futuristic electronic magazine and said he would be glad to show it to people after his talk. He had just put it back in a bag and begun to speak, when the bag suddenly exploded! Without missing a beat, Ovitz said that it looked like more work needed to be done on the prototype. The audience howled in laughter, both at Ovitz's pyrotechnics and his clever remark.

The speech provided the audience with an overview of the new media age that is now already upon us. Ovitz's message was a bold one: In the electronic age, magazines had better become electronic—or else. But he was upbeat, and none of his questioners demurred from his premise that traditional paper-bound magazines were on their way out. He spoke forcefully, confidently, and quickly, just as he does in private conversation, although his public-speaking voice is more rhythmic. Ovitz went directly to the Bermuda airport right after the speech, taking no time to see the island. On the drive to the airport, he talked continuously. An adept conversationalist, he moved from one subject to another with the greatest of ease, dropping names casually but never gratuitously. Once he was on the plane, Ovitz reached for his sky-phone. Later, upon joining the rest of the group for a light lunch, Ovitz seemed to be enjoying himself. He remembered that Bob the makeup man was in the back of the plane alone, and he joked that he was making too much noise; Ovitz has a definite knack for putting people at ease.

Ovitz moved the conversation easily from art and architecture to magazines; to Hollywood; to computers; to a recent trip he had taken to Germany. He seemed to be unable to get his mind off a *New York Times* article ("A Mouseketeer With an Attitude") that had appeared the week before; it had led off by telling the tale of Ovitz and Geffen's misbegotten attempt at reconciliation. But its main thrust was an indictment of Ovitz's year at Disney: He "has not only made missteps and antagonized executives in and outside of Disney but is also still struggling to carve out his role and define his relations with Michael Eisner, the chairman." The *Times* story further noted that Ovitz had found that the "masterful but imperious management style that created the aura of intimidation at Creative Artists was inappropriate at a corporate culture like that at Disney." Both Dream-Works co-founder David Geffen and veteran producer Ray Stark were quoted in the article saying negative things about Ovitz. "I heard you've been saying bad things about me," Ovitz was quoted as saying to Geffen, at their attempted-reconciliation luncheon on the Universal lot. "It's because I think bad things about you," Geffen reportedly replied. Stark was quoted as saying simply: "Mike isn't certain of the meaning of the word 'friendship.' "

At one point on the plane, Ovitz joked about the article, although it was apparent from his tone that the *Times* piece annoyed him. He talked about how *The New York Times* had been going in for gossip more and more often lately, and here was a good example of that. The press was after him, Ovitz insisted, especially *The New York Times*. He couldn't understand why the *Times* had decided to do a big magazine piece about David Geffen, whose DreamWorks enterprise was, as he understood, spending a good deal of money but not getting its projects out on time.

I<small>N THE LAST</small> two weeks of October 1996, Michael Ovitz was wrestling with a particularly difficult decision. He and Michael Eisner already had concluded that it would be best for him to leave Disney at some point in the near future, preferably right at the beginning of the new year. Ovitz didn't want to leave, but given both Eisner's firmness and the fact that Ovitz was putting together a business proposition that would make him much happier, he was ready to go along with Eisner. Ovitz had at first intended to announce his departure from Disney in late October, while at the same time announcing that he was going to set up a business. But when he realized that such a course of action would cost him a considerable amount of money, he decided to forego making any announcement at that time. In a conversation with the author on October 31, he made no reference to the "something big" that he had planned to announce at this time but said only that he wished that he had not taken the Disney job.

Newspaper stories marking Ovitz's first anniversary at Disney were decidedly downbeat. "A Bumpy First Year at Disney" was the headline of the *Los Angeles Times* anniversary piece. On November 25, the same newspaper reported the rumor that Ovitz was planning to leave Disney in order to run Sony's American entertainment operations, a rumor denied by Sony. But it was in fact the case that for a number of months Sony executives had been urging Ovitz to leave Disney and take over the job once performed by Michael Schulhof, head of the Sony Corporation of America. "I didn't want to take it," Ovitz admits. "To go from the frying pan into the fire? I didn't want a job. I didn't want a job, period. I didn't want a job in a big corporation." But Ovitz asserts that all he had to do was say "Yes," and then negotiate the details.

Even with a secret plan in place for Ovitz to leave after January 1, he had still not made any official announcement about leaving the company. If Ovitz held out even the faintest hope that a miracle might occur that would make it possible for him to stay on at Disney, it was utterly dashed when *Vanity Fair* published a major investigative piece on him in its December 1996 issue. Other articles had appeared that fall in which his critics anonymously charged Ovitz with having under-performed at Disney, but none of the newspapers in which they appeared carried as much weight as the prestigious *Vanity Fair,* read by many of the heavyweights in Hollywood.

It was well known at the studios and talent agencies that *Vanity Fair* reporters Bryan Burroughs and Kim Masters were working on a major exposé of Ovitz's tenure at Disney. Ovitz refused to cooperate with the article, as he did with all articles written about him in that tumultuous year. Yet what gave this particular article its special edge was the fact that the reporters were able to include in it on-the-record quotes from former Disney executive Stephen Bollenbach, speaking of his disgruntlement over the hiring and performance of Ovitz at Disney. And however much one might have wanted to discount Bollenbach's swipes at Ovitz, the magazine's portrait of the deteriorating Eisner–Ovitz relationship, providing as it did a number of telling glimpses into Eisner's irritation with Ovitz, certainly made for compelling reading. Burroughs and Masters also wrote of how Ovitz got into the habit of whispering into Eisner's ear at private meetings and public events, as a way of showing how close he was to the Disney chairman. And Bollenbach was quoted at length about Eisner's dissatisfaction with Ovitz in a variety of regards: Ovitz hadn't relieved Eisner of the burden of running Disney as Eisner had hoped he would; rather, he had added a new burden; Ovitz had employed six or seven secretaries; he had drivers sitting around outside unnecessarily.

The article also managed to get some of the leading figures on the Ovitz enemies list to come forward. David Geffen suggested that Ovitz had lost much of his old clout: "He's not Michael Ovitz anymore. He's a guy who has a job working for Michael Eisner." Bernie Brillstein, the manager and producer, claimed in the article that Ovitz had threatened to use his CAA "foot soldiers" to ruin him. "Foot soldiers!" Brillstein said. "Can you believe it? The guy was out of control. Now the past has come back to haunt him, and all these guys want to kill him." Former MCA president Sid Sheinberg felt that Ovitz had deceived him in the course of their talks about selling MCA. The magazine quoted him as saying: "I was seduced by him. That's all part of his mystical craft. I was basically hurt by it. I'm sure he couldn't give a shit."

By contrast, the more generous quotes cited by the article hardly seemed to matter; whether that meant Howard Stringer, the former CBS president recruited by Ovitz to run Tele-TV, saying that much of the Ovitz criticism was based upon envy; or Barry Diller suggesting that the anti-Ovitz talk was totally predictable; such talk happened, Diller noted, whenever senior executives moved from one side of the business to the other. Eisner was quoted in the *Vanity Fair* piece as insisting that he was satisfied with Michael Ovitz's performance, but he sounded less than ebullient, especially when he tried to describe what Ovitz's specific contributions had been over the past year.

An aide to Michael Ovitz, after reading the *Vanity Fair* piece, told him: "Everything happens for a reason." She was trying to comfort him by saying that things would be all right, but he was not to be comforted. "I wish I could be so philosophical," was Ovitz's response.

The effect of the *Vanity Fair* piece was simply to accelerate Ovitz's departure from Disney. And each new article that appeared seemed to add another new reason why Disney executives were upset at Ovitz. A gray cloud hung over him now, and nearly every step that he took was construed as being taken in search of a new post-Disney occupation. Whenever Michael Ovitz met with a leading business figure, whether it was a Sony executive or Viacom's Sumner Redstone, despite his protestations that he was simply going about Disney business, the media assumed that he was being interviewed for a job. And meanwhile, Michael Eisner was growing increasingly perturbed by the media's increasing coverage of Ovitz's presumed imminent departure from Disney. It was bad for business, he argued, and bad for Disney's image—and he was right. Disney, to Eisner's chagrin, sounded like a company in turmoil. Thus it was that the Disney chairman informed Michael Ovitz that he wanted to move his departure forward.

Sunday, December 8, 1996. Ovitz met with his former CAA spokesperson Stephen Rivers and asked him to assist him in the transition. "It became clear that a growing number of people were aware that something was up," Rivers would say later. "And Michael felt we had to be prepared." That evening Ovitz left for New York, planning to be there all week.

Monday, December 9. Ovitz arrived in New York and began to visit with some of his business friends, including Herb Allen, Jerry Speyer, and Ted Forstmann. Sony was holding a board meeting that day, and when the media got wind that Ovitz was in town, journalists were quick to jump to the mistaken conclusion that he had come to New York to nail down a new job with Sony. At the request of director Penny Marshall, he attended a premiere that evening of *The Preacher's Wife.*

Tuesday, December 10. Rumors were spreading that Ovitz was on his way out at Disney.

Wednesday, December 11. Ovitz was feeling the mounting pressure, as he prepared remarks he was supposed to give that evening before The Council on Foreign Relations. Throughout the day he received phone calls from *Wall Street Journal* and *New York Times* reporters, saying that they were working on stories speculating that he was going to leave Disney. What was he going to do? Ovitz refused to comment. "I decided," Ovitz would say later, "that I wasn't going to spend four weeks being terrorized by this press coverage. This wasn't going to end." Ironically, he and Eisner had made plans to vacation together soon, at which time Ovitz hoped that they might yet again discuss the possibility of his staying on. But instead he called Eisner, and the two of them agreed that it was time to pull the plug. Things had gotten out of hand, and thus it wouldn't be wise to wait until after the new year to announce Ovitz's departure. Eisner told Ovitz that he had been planning to come to New York the next day anyway, and they could meet at his apartment at the Hotel Pierre.

Thursday, December 12. The stories appeared at last. *The Wall Street Journal* headline was: "Ovitz Isn't Finding Magic in Kingdom, But Will He Flee?" That day Ovitz canceled an appearance he was supposed to make at the Plaza Hotel, helping to host a luncheon on behalf of Roone Arledge. That evening Ovitz and Eisner met for an hour at the latter's apartment. Most of the details of Ovitz's departure already had been worked out, and they had little else to say to one another. That, of course, had been the trouble all throughout the past turbulent year. But they remained cordial, and Ovitz even tried to lighten the mood by means of a little humor. "I was relieved, he was relieved," Ovitz says tersely of that final brief encounter with the Disney chairman. "He made a very simple decision," Ovitz continues. "This isn't from me; it's from ten friends of mine: I stood in the way of his mortality. It's not that complicated. He made this decision, his best friend or his life. He didn't want to turn over anything." Ovitz was saying something very poignant: Eisner still was not ready to face the possibility that one day he would have to step down as the head of Disney, and seeing Ovitz's face at all times within the company simply spooked him. In short, by making Ovitz's life at Disney so uncomfortable that he virtually had to leave, Eisner was saying: *I'm not going. Not yet.*

Friday, December 13. Ovitz's departure was formally announced in a five-paragraph news release from The Walt Disney Company, observing that Ovitz would be leaving "by mutual agreement" effective January 31, and would continue to consult for the company. In the statement, Ovitz said that "Michael Eisner has been my good friend for twenty-five years, but it is important to recognize when something is not working. I hope that my decision to leave will eliminate any unnecessary distraction for a great company."

Eisner weighed in with some warm words for Ovitz: "I will miss Michael's energy, creativity, and leadership at Disney. We have been doing business together while being friends for many years, and I know that both our personal and professional relationships will continue."

Then, in a stinging rebuff to Ovitz, the press release went on to note that Disney did not plan to appoint a successor to him, that it would continue to operate organizationally as it had done prior to his arrival. Eisner was quoted as saying that he was proud of the "strong creative and management team that we have developed over the past decade."

Ovitz didn't announce what he intended to do next, and that fueled immediate speculation in the media that he would decide to take one of several senior management positions in the entertainment field. One possibility was the post that Michael Schulhof had held at Sony. Another was that Ovitz would be named to replace Frank Biondi, who had been forced out as chief executive at Viacom in January 1996; but for Ovitz to take the job would have meant serving as number two to Viacom chairman Sumner Redstone—not a likely prospect, after his similar sour experience at Disney. It seemed unlikely that Ovitz would be offered a position at such entertainment giants as Time-Warner and Twentieth Century Fox, simply because there were no senior positions open there.

There was never any doubt in Michael Ovitz's mind that he would go on to something else in business, though he could have afforded to retire on that very day and live out the rest of his days in grand style. His wife Judy actually did think it might be nice if he took a breather for a year or two, stuck close to the family, and enjoyed life. But Ovitz knew that that just wasn't his style. Yes, he had been wounded by the Disney experience, and perhaps even cured of the itch to run a major entertainment enterprise. But he still wanted to be where the action was, and if he couldn't get in through one door, he would try another.

He was seething at himself for having decided to take the Disney job, and just as angry at Michael Eisner for having hired him and then having given him nothing to do. Ovitz admitted that he had made a mistake in taking the Disney job, but he didn't feel entirely to blame for all that had happened afterward. He felt that Eisner had duped him, and that a good deal of the criticism directed against him—that he had been too inactive, too slow to get the hang of his new job, etc.—was an outgrowth of Eisner's unwillingness to turn any real responsibility and power over to him at the outset.

At any rate, Ovitz had no intention of making such a mistake again. He had long wanted to run a major company, but he had never dreamed that when he at last got the chance, the whole enterprise would unravel so quickly and so disastrously. Thus he made a sweeping decision: Not only would he never take a Disney-like job again, he also never would work for someone else again. Whatever he did in the future, whatever business he became involved in, he would own. Then he would have the power and responsibility from the start, for better or worse, and he wouldn't have to ask someone else's permission whenever he wanted to do something. All that talk about how he was "the most powerful figure in Hollywood" had taught him one thing: that he just wasn't cut out to be anyone's number two. He had to be in charge, and in the future he would make sure that he was.

Meanwhile, The Walt Disney Company had survived the uproar surrounding the Ovitz departure quite nicely indeed. That weekend, its Christmas-time movie *101 Dalmatians* was the top box-office attraction, grossing over $13 million; the company's studios led in market share at 35.2 percent; and Disney stock had soared during the year amidst a general upsurge in blue-chip stocks, rising 38 percent from its 1996 low of $53.25 earlier in the year to $71.62 at the time of Ovitz's departure from the company. That meant that the value of Ovitz's stock options, if they had been fully vested, came to $75 million.

Investors were indifferent about Ovitz's departure from Disney; it just wasn't a major event for them. Ovitz always had seemed too much the minister-without-portfolio; it was taken for granted that he had made no impact on the company, so no one expected Disney stock to crash as a result of Wall Street's hearing that Michael Ovitz was leaving the firm. Indeed, some predicted that the stock would climb to the $100 range during the next few years. (During Eisner's decade as the man in charge, Disney stock had returned about 24.7 percent a year, compared with only 15.9 percent a year returned by the Standard & Poor's 500 index.)

On Saturday, December 14, 1996, Michael Ovitz spent a quiet day with his family. It was his fiftieth birthday, and ordinarily he might have been expected to attend some major event in his honor. But this year there would be no big parties. The time certainly wasn't right for festivities.

Deciding to say nothing publicly beyond the few words of his included in the statement released by Disney, Ovitz passed word to acquaintances that he was relieved to be leaving Disney, that he had had many job offers (though he didn't say from whom), and that he had decided not to be precipitous this time, as he had been when he took the Disney job back in the summer of 1995. He was going on vacation for several weeks, then would start to think seriously about his future. "He's going to do something huge," one of his aides said. "It's only a matter of time before he figures out what it's going to be. Now he has to think about what he wants to do for the next fifty years."

Ovitz's friends placed the blame squarely on Eisner, for not creating a true partnership with Ovitz and for misleading him at the outset into thinking that he as Disney chairman would be little more than a figurehead.

Ovitz, his friends insisted, never would have taken the job at Disney had he genuinely believed that he was going to be a mere number two. "The real question," Arne Glimcher says, "is why Michael Eisner can't relegate responsibility to anyone else. Why can't he share power?"

But the media played its part too in prompting Ovitz's quick exit from Disney. "When there's a steady drumbeat of stories," says Stephen Rivers, "that makes it very difficult to do your job, because everybody you deal with is reading them and wondering how long you are for the world. And everyone believes that where there's smoke there's fire. So it becomes much more complicated and harder to do your job."

The guessing among his friends was that Ovitz would open a "Deals 'R Us" kind of business: one that drew heavily upon his talents as a corporate consultant and exploited his innumerable contacts in Hollywood, but still steered very clear of the talent-agency business. "He's in a remarkably positive mood," said Chuck Close, who had talked to Ovitz several times in the week after the departure from Disney. "It doesn't mean that things don't hurt him. Lots of things that he thinks are inaccurate really hurt him a lot. It's an indication of what kind of guy he is that he cut his losses early, realized it was a mistake, and got out, instead of limping along when things weren't working and made him unhappy."

Friends and acquaintances from the past sent Ovitz their best wishes. Michael Rosenfeld Sr., a CAA co-founder, faxed Ovitz: "Sorry I wasn't around to pin a note on your back door, but this is the best move you've made since leaving the William Morris office. Good luck."

At CAA, the institution that Michael Ovitz personally had molded into Hollywood's most formidable temple of power, general shock attended the reception of the news of the departure from Disney. Few could believe that Ovitz had remained on top for so long, only to plummet so precipitously and so embarrassingly. "It's truly bizarre," said one senior agent whom Ovitz had trained and nurtured. "Here he was fourteen months ago, and the agency was at the very top of its game and he was at the top of his game. And now he's unemployed and seemingly on the outside of things, as opposed to being the ultimate insider. It's so shockingly sudden." It was, the agent said, a cautionary tale of how quickly things can change in the entertainment business. Some CAA agents who had counted on moving on with Ovitz to bigger and better jobs still felt that Ovitz had manipulated and cheated them; others, who remembered the bonuses that had kept getting bigger and bigger each year, felt that they still owed him a large debt of gratitude. Few, however, thought it wise to count Michael Ovitz out.

THE DISSOLUTION OF the Eisner-Ovitz "partnership" made headlines everywhere, and once it became known that Michael Ovitz would receive millions of dollars in severance pay, the story took on a life of its own. Newspaper reports put the amount of the severance package as high as $120 million. Columnists attacked Michael Eisner, the Disney board, and of course Ovitz. Writing in *The New York Times* on December 17, columnist A. M. Rosenthal noted that: "If he (Ovitz) and Mr. Eisner had learned how to get along, the stockholders would have that much more money in the company treasury which is supposed to belong to them, not to executives who are paid to work together but don't."

Ovitz's departure from Disney, a major business story to begin with, took on huge proportions when average Americans learned of the size of Ovitz's settlement. That Michael Ovitz had become known to large segments of the American public for the first time through the severance-pay controversy was incredibly ironic, given the fact that he had been the most influential figure in the Hollywood of his day. Adding to the irony was the likelihood that, as matters stood in the winter of 1996, when many people heard the name "Michael Ovitz" mentioned, their next thought automatically would be, "Oh, he's the guy Disney paid all that money just to get rid of."

While hundreds of articles appeared, dealing with Ovitz's departure from Disney and the severance-pay controversy, he made no public comment. It had never been his style to engage his critics through the media, and he remained very much in character during this, the most serious business crisis of his career. In a conversation with the author held toward the end of January 1997, Ovitz offered a staunch defense of the settlement he would be receiving from Disney, and he put the total figure at $128 million, higher than all previous estimates. The settlement, he explained, was divided into two parts.

One part provided him with a lump sum of $38,869,000. This arose from his five-year contract, which called for him to receive his $1 million salary for the next four years ($4 million) along with a $7.5 million bonus for each of the next four years ($30 million), as well as $10 million in the event of his leaving Disney. That added up to $44 million. Since Ovitz wanted the total sum to be paid out immediately, the $44 million figure was discounted down to $38 million.

He also was to receive three million Disney shares, with a strike price of $57 a share. With the stock at $72 a share as of the end of January 1997, the options were worth $45 million. Together with the nearly $38 million, the total came to $83 million. Ovitz was told, however, that his options had a "street value" of $90 million, so the actual worth of the set-tlement—$38 million from the lump-sum payment, and $90 million from the stock options—came to $128 million.

When he was asked for his reaction to the immense controversy swirling around the severance-pay issue, Ovitz reacted emotionally: "I just made a smart deal for myself. I find the whole thing embarrassing. But what am I going to do about it? This is America. This isn't the Soviet Union. It's the supply-and-demand of the marketplace. They [Disney] had a need for me. I made a deal. A part of the deal was that if I left, that's what I would get paid. They took a risk. I took a risk. It's part of life in a free marketplace. They [his critics] should quit whining about it. It's the way it is. If a commodity trader makes a killing in the currency market, when George Soros [the Wall Street investor] made a billion dollars by betting on the pound, is that a crime? No, he was just smarter. If an actor gets $20 million and the movie fails, that's life. They [again, his critics] said I failed, and I got paid for the failure. Great. I don't think I failed, because I never got the chance to get started. It's just the way it is. I never look back. People can say whatever they want. It's been that way my entire life."

As those words of defiance suggest, Michael Ovitz was feeling a heady new sense of freedom. He felt that he had learned one valuable lesson from the Disney experience and that was to steer clear of being someone's number two. Though he was extremely upset with himself for having taken the Disney job, and with Michael Eisner for having made promises that he didn't deliver on, Ovitz didn't seem like an unhappy man. He refused to let himself get angry at the many critics who had lashed out at him over the amount of severance pay he would get. Rather, he chose to combat the attacks by keeping his silence in the belief that the contro-versy would eventually subside. He seemed to be trying to put the whole Disney experience behind him. Even when Michael Eisner stood before Disney's shareholders in Anaheim, California on February 25, 1997 and shrugged off the decision to hire Ovitz as simply a "mistake of judgment," Ovitz refused to talk to the media and thus be drawn into a public tiff with the Disney chairman. He did complain that the media continued to track his whereabouts, but that seemed to be the complaint of someone who wouldn't have had it any other way. If he was still Hollywood's obsession, he didn't seem terribly disturbed about it. Amused, yes, but not disturbed. However much he tried to set his sights on the future, every once in a while something happened to jolt Ovitz back to his Disney demons. That was the case on March 24, 1997 when veteran CAA client Billy Crystal,

emcee at the Academy Awards ceremony that evening, noted in his opening monologue to a television audience in the hundreds of millions that
"This year only one out of 163 major releases (*Jerry Maguire*) is nominated for best picture—164 if you count Mike Ovitz." Apart from that
fleeting moment of notoriety, Ovitz managed to keep a low public profile,
and he relished the mystique that seemed to surround him all over again.
He took great satisfaction when friends told him that some of his old enemies wanted to make peace with him. He took that as a sign that they
were feeling edgy about what he would do next.

Perhaps, just as they had in the old days, they would need him again,
and that thought further brightened his day. Perhaps to keep his old enemies off guard, he told many people that he had retired. Few believed him.
To those closest to him, he made it clear that he would be back in the business arena soon. But he remained deliberately vague about what kind of
work he planned to do. He knew that his friends were saying that the
Disney experience would soon be seen as just a temporary setback, that
Ovitz would soon be back in some way, heading some enterprise, negotiating, maneuvering, orchestrating. He liked that thought too. He was not
about to go quietly into the night, or in his case, quietly to the bank.

Meanwhile, during the early months of 1997, Ovitz led a highly active
life. For one thing, he held a number of meetings with high-flying corporate associates. All the while that he had been faltering at Disney, Ovitz
also had been keeping up his high-powered relationships with business
figures both inside and outside of Hollywood. He knew they had been
crucial to his career in the past, and he sensed that they could now be a
lifeline to his future. He believed that in time they would help him to get
back into the thick of things.

He also traveled extensively, and kept up with his charitable work. In
February 1997, UCLA announced that Ovitz had pledged $25 million to
help rebuild the UCLA medical center, damaged during the 1994 Los
Angeles earthquake. Although Ovitz served as chairman of the UCLA
Medical Sciences Executive Board, he preferred to retain a low public
profile, refusing to take a public bow over the gift. When the *Los Angeles
Times* sought to interview him for their story about the grant, he was
unavailable for comment.

By adopting that low profile, Ovitz seemed to be trying to remake himself into that secretive, mysterious figure who for so long had held sway
over Hollywood. From his earliest days at CAA he had longed to be a
deal-maker in Hollywood, though certainly not its most scrutinized. At
the height of his power, he had indeed been the town's most illustrious

and controversial power broker. And now, in the spring of 1997, as he regrouped after the dismal Disney experience, there seemed to be little doubt that Ovitz would become a power player yet again. His friends couldn't wait for that to happen; his enemies worried that it might. But both his friends and enemies were in agreement about one thing: Michael Ovitz could not be counted out.

Acknowledgments

TRACKING PEOPLE DOWN to interview for this book was not always simple. To talk to the people who were closest to Michael Ovitz often meant reaching into the upper echelons of Hollywood. Not surprisingly, most people who reside in those rarified circles were very busy, to say the least. Sometimes I had to wait several months to see someone.

Such was the case with Rob Reiner, who was filming *Ghosts of Mississippi*, and with Dustin Hoffman, who waited to finish filming *Wag the Dog*, before our interview. Sometimes, as with Tom Cruise and Robin Williams, the person would chat with me during a break from a movie. I had no way of knowing what author Michael Crichton was writing at the time, but I assume now that he took time off from writing his best-selling book, *Airframe*, to see me.

Magic Johnson visited with me at a Los Angeles Athletic Club where he was being honored. Barry Levinson was on a promotion tour for the latest movie he had directed, *Sleepers*, when we spoke. Ivan Reitman took a break from directing *Space Jam* (starring famed basketball star, Michael Jordan) to see me. Jerry Seinfeld chatted with me during a lunch break while filming his weekly sitcom *Seinfeld*. David Letterman had just finished shooting *The Late Show* when we conducted our interview.

David Stern had all the time in the world when I visited him one July morning—the NBA was on its summer break. Along with these people, I also wish to thank many others for allowing me to interview them:

Dan Adler, Herbert Allen, Henry Bamberger, Martin Baum, Warren Beatty, Jeff Berg, Armyan Bernstein, Larry Blaustein, Sandy Bressler, Tina Brown, Josh Bycel, John Calley, Bill Carruthers, Graydon Carter,

Gil Cates, Charles Champlin, Al Checchi, Michael Cieply, Alan Citron, Sandy Climan, Chuck Close, Sam Cohen, Sean Connery, Norman Corwin, Lester Crown, Barry Diller, Christopher Dixon, Lauren Shuler Donner, Richard Donner, John Dreyer, Sally Field, Barbara Guggenheim Fields, Bert Fields, Freddy Fields, Arne Glimcher, Bob Goldman, Marco Greenberg, Amy Grossman, Bruce Hensel, Shelly Hochron, Judy Hofflund, Dustin Hoffman, Doug Ivester, Mort Janklow, Dean Jones, J. J. Jordan, Marvin Josephson, Jerry Katzman, Kathy Kennedy, Phil Knight, Jill Krutick, Ray Kurtzman, Rick Kurtzman, Sherry Lansing, Gerry Laybourne, Norman Lear, David Letterman, Gerald Levey, Roy Lichtenstein, David Londoner, Bryan Lourd, Richard Lovett, Susan Lyne, Bob Markowitz, Andrea Marozas, Frank Marshall, Penny Marshall, Dennis B. McAlpine, Ron Meyer, Jeff Miller, Jay Moloney, S. I. Newhouse, Paul Newman, David Ovitz, Judy Ovitz, Sylvia Ovitz, David O'Connor, Jerry Pam, I. M. Pei, Ron Perelman, Jerry Perenchio, Anna Perez, Rowland Perkins, Laurie Perlman, Sydney Pollack, Gavin Polone, Richard Riordan, Stephen M. Rivers, Lon Rosen, Lee Rosenbaum, Marion Rosenberg, Michael Rosenfeld Sr., Michael Rosenfeld Jr., Steve Sauer, Ivan Seidenberg, Terry Semel, Joel Shapiro, Joe Siegman, Joe Smith, Fred Spektor, Jerry Speyer, Steve Stearns, Jerry Sussman, Tony Thomopoulos, Harold Vogel, Paula Wagner, Phil Weltman, Howard West, Fred Westheimer, Marcia Williams, Gary Wilson, Fred Worstbrook, Robert Wright, Charles Young, and Mort Zuckerman, and others who wished to remain anonymous.

I also want to give special thanks to Judith Resnik and Dennis Curtis whose warm hospitality helped to make my visits to Los Angeles that much easier. I thank them too for the encouragement and advice they offered on this project. I also wish to thank: Jordan Bonfante, Ben Bycel and Laura Geller, Ron Dicker, Murray and Dodi Fromson, Bruce Liebman, Jean Max, Susan Miller, Jill Ornitz, Julie McArthur, Frankie Meppen, Russ Meppen, Roland Flamini, Jeff Ressner, Roslyn and Judd Winick, Jack and Bea Slater, William Tynan, Sheldon Weinig, Michael and Bobbi Winick, Jane and Craig Jacobs, Mel and Anat Laytner, Toby and John Atlas, and Stacy Jacobs.

My colleagues at McGraw-Hill have been enthusiastic and supportive and I truly appreciate all their efforts. First, to my long-time editor Jeffrey Krames, I give special thanks, for his dedication, hard work, and the excitement he has always showed toward this project. A special thanks to Peter Roberts who helped to make this a much better book through his copy-editing skills. I also want to thank Philip Ruppel, Publisher of Business McGraw-Hill; and my other friends at McGraw-Hill: Claudia Riemer

Boutote, Lynda Luppino, Evan Boorstyn, Kathleen Gilligan, Fred Bernardi, and Andrew Seagren.

Finally, a word of thanks to my family, who have made it possible for me to spend hours at the computer, and who have tolerated my visits to Los Angeles and elsewhere with good cheer: to my wife Elinor, and my children: Miriam, Shimi, Adam, and Rachel; and to my grandson Edo.

Author's Chapter Notes

THE FOLLOWING CHAPTER notes indicate the sources used by the author in writing the book, including the people interviewed, the documents examined, and the published sources consulted.

2
King Ovitz

Page

16   "There was real affection . . . ," Sylvia Ovitz, interview, October 31, 1996.

16   "He could do no wrong . . . ," ibid.

17   "If there was something . . . ," ibid.

17   "It was a way of life for us . . . ," ibid.

17   "He liked to be in the game . . . ," David Ovitz, interview, October 31, 1996.

18   "And so he always liked . . . ," Sylvia Ovitz, interview, October 31, 1996.

18   "I've been working since . . . ," Michael Ovitz, interview, May 29, 1996.

18   "He'd do all the talking . . . ," David Ovitz, interview, October 31, 1996.

19   "What he said he would . . . ," Steve Stearns, interview, August 22, 1996.

19   "With stars as Mike Ovitz . . . and a new motto . . . ," from a scrapbook kept by Michael Ovitz, shown to the author October 28, 1996.

20   "I want to buy a piece . . . ," anecdote recounted to author by Sylvia Ovitz, October 31, 1996.

20   "I am not, by far, saying . . . ," from Ovitz scrapbook.

20   "We have only one candidate . . . ," story told to author by David Ovitz, October 31, 1996.

21   "People impute I had certain role . . . ," Michael Ovitz, interview, July 17, 1996.

21   "My dad knew when to slip . . . ," Michael Ovitz, interview, May 29, 1996.

21   "People will hate you . . . ," recounted to author by Michael Ovitz, July 17, 1996.

23   "The year at Universal ruined me . . . ," Michael Ovitz, interview, May 29, 1996.

23   "He could psychoanalyze me . . . ," Sylvia Ovitz, interview, October 31, 1996.

23   "It's the single most frustrating . . . ," Michael Ovitz, January 19, 1996.

23   "I thought she was absolutely gorgeous . . . ," Michael Ovitz, interview, September 1, 1996.

24   "Marshall recalls that Ovitz . . . ," Frank Marshall, interview, July 11, 1996.

25   "I was desperate to move ahead . . . ," Michael Ovitz, May 29, 1996.

3
A Deal a Second

Page

27   "I liked their access . . . ," Michael Ovitz, interview, October 31, 1996.

29   "I didn't know what the others did . . . ," Michael Ovitz, interview, May 29, 1996.

29   "I drove people crazy . . . ," Michael Ovitz, interview, May 29, 1996.

30   "I loved the business . . . ," ibid.

30   "I realized I could be . . . ," ibid.

30   "Re: progress report . . . ," from Ovitz scrapbook.

31   " 'Hey man,' Sly Stone . . . ," anecdote recounted to author by Michael Ovitz, May 29, 1996.

32   "Sixties rock and roll . . . ," Michael Ovitz, interview, May 29, 1996.

32   "had a vision . . . ," Bill Carruthers, interview, August 11, 1996.

33   "It was all so casual . . . ," Barry Levinson, interview, October 22, 1996.

36   "Everything Michael Ovitz did . . . ," Phil Weltman, interview, May 20, 1996.

38   "We were starting to feel this piling . . . ," interview, Michael Rosenfeld Sr., May 25, 1996.

39   "Everyone was healthy . . . ," Ron Meyer, interview, July 22, 1996.

40   "We complemented each other . . . ," ibid.

40   "Mike was smart enough . . . ," ibid.

4
Now, Perkins, This Is Treason!

Page

44   ". . . the knot that . . . ," Ron Meyer, interview, July 22, 1996.

44   "He was a Jewish drill . . . ," Michael Ovitz, interview, May 29, 1996.

45   "You know, you would make . . . ," Michael Rosenfeld Sr., interview, May 25, 1996.

45   "If you're working for someone . . . ," David Ovitz, interview, October 31, 1996.

46   "The Morris office is like heart-attack . . . ," Fred Westheimer, interview, October 16, 1996.

46   "We needed every dollar . . . ," Michael Rosenfeld Sr., interview, May 25, 1996.

47   "How are you going to do . . . ," Frank Marshall, interview, July 11, 1996.

49   ". . . several thousand dollars' . . . ," Michael Rosenfeld Jr., interview, November 2, 1996.

49   "You should be sending . . . ," Michael Rosenfeld Sr., interview, May 25, 1996.

50   "I had a good career going . . . ," Michael Ovitz, interview, January 12, 1997.

50   "He was just totally abusive . . . ," ibid.

51   "We had no money . . . ," Michael Ovitz, interview, May 29, 1996.

52   "It was sort of like . . . ," Ron Meyer, interview, July 22, 1996.

53   "They're all good men . . . ," Sam Weisbord quoted in *Daily Variety,* January 9, 1975.

53   "The Morris office was a place . . . ," Jerry Katzman, interview, May 29, 1996.

53   "The guys really want . . . ," Michael Rosenfeld Sr. quoted in *Daily Variety,* January 9, 1975.

54   "What basically prompted us . . . ," Rowland Perkins, *The Hollywood Reporter,* January 9, 1975.

54   "We would have gone . . . ," Michael Rosenfeld Sr., August 14, 1996.

54   "I will never negotiate . . . ," ibid.

55   "It looks like we're booking . . . ," Michael Rosenfeld Sr., interview, December 24, 1996.

56   "There was . . . ," Michael Rosenfeld Sr., interview, May 25, 1996.

56   "there had been people at Morris . . . ," Ron Meyer, interview, July 22, 1996.

56   "The Morris office is . . . ," Sam Weisbord quoted in *The Hollywood Reporter,* January 22, 1974.

56   "I just automatically took over . . . ," Michael Ovitz, July 17, 1996.

56   "You don't get respect . . . ," ibid.

57   "May God bless . . . ," Dean Jones, interview, May 21, 1996.

57   "Dean, if we can have . . . ," ibid.

57   "Actual chain of command . . . ," *Hollywood Reporter,* January 23, 1975.

58   "Marvin, you've got to stop them . . ." Marvin Josephson, interview, January 31, 1996.

58   "We were just five guys . . . ," Rowland Perkins, April 2, 1996.

60   "I want to come with you . . . ," Rowland Perkins, interview, April 2, 1996.

61   "When Michael mentioned to me . . . ," Sally Struthers in a statement to the author relayed by her publicist, October 18, 1996.

61   "Before, it was Morris or ICM . . . ," Rowland Perkins, interview, April 2, 1996.

61   "He was driven . . . ," Bill Carruthers, interview, August 11, 1996.

61   "I had three models . . . ," ibid.

62   ". . . was too rich . . . ," Michael Ovitz, interview, January 12, 1997.

62   "we can't let him . . . ," Rowland Perkins, interview, April 2, 1996.

62   "I knew we were doing . . . ," ibid.

5

Master Illusionist

Page

67   "You don't know me . . . ," Mort Janklow, interview, July 10, 1996.

67   "His directness was appealing . . . ," ibid.

67   "He was very intense . . . ," ibid.

67   "That was a very astute . . . ," ibid.

68   "You could set your watch . . . ," ibid.

70   "This is for you . . . ," story told to author by Michael Ovitz, July 24, 1996.

70   "Going to La Scala . . . ," Michael Ovitz, interview, July 24, 1996.

70   "We made a strategic . . . ," Michael Ovitz, interview, October 31, 1996.

71   "The dinner was marvelous . . . ," story told to author by Michael Rosenfeld Sr., May 25, 1996.

72   "You might find . . . ," Martin Baum, interview, July 22, 1996.

6

Pretzels, Tennis Balls, and Soapsuds

Page

77   "the horrific caste system . . . ," Amy Grossman, interview, October 30, 1996.

77   "Nazi piranhas . . . ," ibid.

78   "I wasn't that type of girl . . . ," ibid.

78   "Everyone was walking . . . ," ibid.

78   "CAA was so poor they couldn't even afford . . . ," Laurie Perlman, interview, October 22, 1996.

79   "He had a strength . . . ," ibid.

80   "That's the way we do it . . . ," The Sherry Lansing anecdote was recounted to me by Michael Rosenfeld Sr., August 19, 1996, and Sherry Lansing, October 29, 1996.

83   "You don't understand . . . ," Michael Rosenfeld Sr., August 19, 1996.

84	"The combination worked . . . ," Ron Meyer, interview, July 22, 1996.
85	"I elevated their tastes . . . ," Martin Baum, interview, July 15, 1996.
87	"She fell in love . . . ," Michael Ovitz, interview, January 2, 1997.
87	"Everyone thought we were . . . ," ibid.
88	"We couldn't sign big clients . . . ," Michael Ovitz, interview, October 31, 1996.
89	"It's time for you . . . ," Richard Donner, interview, May 23, 1996.
89	"You don't know me . . . ," Michael Crichton, interview, March 19, 1996.
91	"It seemed like that's what . . . ," Ivan Reitman, interview, July 16, 1996.

7

Hollywood's New Rainmakers

Page	
94	"At the time it wasn't that easy . . . ," Sean Connery, interview, July 16, 1996.
95	"He wasn't making any great . . . ," ibid.
95	"Michael was very good . . . ," ibid.
96	"The business was changing . . . ," Paul Newman, interview, June 3, 1996.
96	"If an agent doesn't do anything . . . ," ibid.
96	"A half-Mafia, Italian . . . ," ibid.
97	"He's a cross between . . . ," ibid.
97	"Hendler thought any time . . . ," John Calley, interview, March 22, 1996.
97	"I'd like to pay you a dollar . . . ," Bert Fields, interview, May 31, 1995.
98	". . . sophisticated representation . . . ," Dustin Hoffman, interview, March 11, 1997.
98	"I liked him . . . ," ibid.
98	"We are totally new . . . ," Michael Ovitz, interview, January 12, 1997.
98	"What do you think . . . ?" Dustin Hoffman, interview, March 11, 1997.
99	"Michael was so thoroughly persistent . . . ," Sydney Pollack, interview, May 30, 1996.
99	"He talked about my career . . . ," ibid.
99	"He wasn't effusive . . . ," ibid.
99	"I'm impressed with what . . . ," ibid.
101	"They wanted companionship . . . ," Michael Ovitz, January 19, 1996.
102	"My attitude was that whatever . . . ," Ron Meyer, interview, October 17, 1996.
102	"Who's the best?" Armyan Bernstein, interview, July 12, 1996.
103	"You've come to the right . . . ," ibid.

103   "Mike Rosenfeld was like the . . . ," ibid.

103   "We're going to have an auction . . . ," Armyan Bernstein, interview, July 12, 1996.

105   "It was a great partnership . . . ," Michael Ovitz, January 30, 1997.

106   "He sat down on the couch . . . ," Michael Ovitz, January 19, 1996.

106   "I liked Michael Ovitz immediately . . . ," Tom Cruise, interview, August 19, 1996.

106   "You should work . . . ," ibid.

106   "Paul Newman is like in another . . . ," ibid.

107   "He didn't treat me any differently . . . ," ibid.

107   "The next thing you knew . . . ," ibid.

108   "It's one hundred percent . . . ," Michael Ovitz, January 30, 1997.

108   "Embassy got to say . . . ," Lee Rosenbaum, interview, May 28, 1996.

109   "Most agents like myself . . . ," Marion Rosenberg, interview, April 3, 1996.

8
A Shroud of Secrecy

Page

111   "I hated the disrespect . . . ," Michael Ovitz, interview, July 17, 1996.

111   "I ran the company . . . ," Michael Ovitz, interview, July 24, 1996.

113   "Leaving for ICM . . . ," Josh Bycel, interview, March 25, 1996.

113   "Michael knows who he is . . . ," Arne Glimcher, interview, July 9, 1996.

113   ". . . sort of spectral . . . ," David O'Connor, interview, July 23, 1996.

113   "circumspect, careful, measured . . . ," Norman Lear, interview, May 23, 1996.

113   "This is a private . . . ," Al Checchi, interview, May 28, 1996.

114   "You can only create fires . . . ," Rowland Perkins, interview, April 9, 1996.

114   "There was always a perception . . . ," Marion Rosenberg, interview, April 3, 1996.

114   "Oh, you're in early . . . ," Armyan Bernstein, interview, July 12, 1996.

115   "Mike, how many three-by-five cards . . . ," Dustin Hoffman, interview, March 11, 1997.

115   "The gift I would give him . . . ," Barbara Guggenheim Fields, interview, October 16, 1996.

115   "There were no hours . . . ," Michael Ovitz, interview, May 29, 1996.

115   "He worked harder than . . . ," David O'Connor, interview, July 23, 1996.

116   "He didn't say it . . . ," Michael Rosenfeld Jr., interview, November 2, 1996.

116   "If you got up in the . . . ," Michael Rosenfeld Sr., interview, May 25, 1996.

116   "There was a certain intimidation . . . ," Amy Grossman, interview, October 30, 1996.

116   "This was a guy who didn't want . . . ," Michael Rosenfeld Jr., interview, November 2, 1996.

116   "The product was service . . . ," Michael Ovitz, interview, July 17, 1996.

117   "The only sin that we could . . . ," Amy Grossman, interview, October 30, 1996.

117   "If you sat around . . . ," ibid.

117   "Michael's presence was so strong . . . ," Richard Lovett, interview, July 19, 1996.

119   "I was to service him . . . ," David O'Connor, interview, July 23, 1996.

119   "If I couldn't get something . . . ," ibid.

120   ". . . the opportunity to work for Michael . . . ," Jay Moloney, interview, February 2, 1997.

120   "We all felt . . . ," ibid.

120   "It was one of the first times . . . ," ibid.

120   "The biggest crime I could commit . . . ," ibid.

122   ". . . that agent would husband him . . . ," Ray Kurtzman, interview, July 16, 1996.

122   "Ovitz had enough confidence . . . ," John Calley, interview, March 22, 1996.

123   "Agents were constantly reminded . . . ," Bob Goldman, interview, July 18, 1996.

123   "It was socialistic . . . ," Michael Ovitz, interview, July 17, 1996.

123   "We constantly found ways . . . ," Richard Lovett, interview, July 19, 1996.

124   "We need to speak . . . ," Laurie Perlman, interview, October 22, 1996.

124   "What made CAA different . . . ," Marty Baum, interview, July 16, 1996.

125   "At CAA if you had an opinion . . . ," Bryan Lourd, interview, July 19, 1996.

125   "Ovitz was smart enough . . . ," Gavin Polone, interview, May 21, 1996.

125   "You knew exactly where he shopped . . . ," Laurie Perlman, interview, October 22, 1996.

126   "We were very fortunate . . . ," Bob Goldman, interview, July 18, 1996.

126   "you never got paid . . . ," David O'Connor, interview, July 16, 1996.

9

I *Am* a Control Freak

129   "He would stop at nothing . . . ," Laurie Perlman, interview, October 22, 1996.

130   "I had accepted that one of the . . . ," Michael Crichton, March 19, 1996.

130   "It had the quiet hum of crisp . . . ," Graydon Carter, interview, July 31, 1996.

131   "It was fantastic . . . ," Michael Ovitz, interview, May 29, 1996.

131   "Every day I get transported . . . ," Michael Ovitz, interview, July 17, 1996.

131   "I was free . . . ," Michael Ovitz, ibid.

131   "I enjoyed the organizational . . . ," Michael Ovitz, interview, May 29, 1996.

132   "CAA ran like a Swiss watch . . . ," Michael Ovitz, May 29, 1996.

132   "The place had something going . . . ," Richard Lovett, interview, July 19, 1996.

132   ". . . has a need to control . . . ," Bob Goldman, interview, July 18, 1996.

132   "It was one of the less stellar . . . ," Rick Kurtzman, interview, November 3, 1996.

133   "We were careful . . . ," Rowland Perkins, interview, April 9, 1996.

134   "Michael takes these very tough . . . ," Rob Reiner, interview, August 23, 1996.

134   "I didn't utilize Ovitz . . . ," ibid.

134   "Ovitz wasn't really my agent . . . ," ibid.

135   "I had a nice agent . . . ," Penny Marshall, interview, October 30, 1996.

135   "I told him . . . ," ibid.

135   "I didn't need any . . . ," ibid.

135   "He was scared . . . ," ibid.

136   "He spread the rumor that . . . ," ibid.

136   "I'll never do that again . . . ," ibid.

136   "still perhaps the most . . . ," *The Art of War,* Sun Tzu, paperback version translated by Thomas Cleary, Shambala, Boston & London, 1988, back jacket.

137   "It is never beneficial . . . ," ibid., p. 58.

137   "One who is good at martial . . . ," ibid., p. 72.

137   "Those who are good at knighthood . . . ," ibid., p. 5.

137   "Best of all . . . ," ibid., p. 68.

137   "Ninety-nine percent . . . ," Michael Ovitz, interview, July 24, 1996.

137   "You must create the impression . . . ," Michael Ovitz, interview, July 24, 1996.

138   "Those skilled in defense . . . ," *The Art of War,* p. 87.

138 ". . . not that complicated . . . ," Michael Ovitz, interview, July 17, 1996.

138 "People say you're a control . . . ," quoted in *Time* magazine, "The Ultimate Mogul," April 19, 1993.

139 "If he said he would do something . . . ," Jerry Perenchio, interview, May 23, 1996.

139 "We felt that the critical . . . ," Michael Ovitz, interview, July 24, 1996.

139 "If Mike had a technique . . . ," Kathy Kennedy, interview, July 11, 1996.

139 ". . . unusually smart and disciplined . . . ," Michael Crichton, March 19, 1996.

139 "People signed on with . . . ," Mort Janklow, interview, July 10, 1996.

139 "The word *agent* wasn't a . . . ," Dustin Hoffman, interview, March 11, 1997.

140 "It's a one-joke picture . . . ," Sydney Pollack, interview, May 30, 1996.

142 "I was worried . . . ," ibid.

142 " 'Persuasive' with Mike . . . ," ibid.

143 ". . . the intensity and persistence . . . ," ibid.

143 "Michael Ovitz built a great . . . ," Herb Allen, interview, June 4, 1996.

143 "I need to give you some advice . . . ," Frank Marshall provided this anecdote, July 11, 1996.

144 " 'Do it,' Ovitz said . . . ," Armyan Bernstein provided this anecdote, July 12, 1996.

145 "Do me a favor, read it . . . ," Richard Donner provided this anecdote, May 23, 1996.

10
Renaissance Man

Page

147 "Michael was talking . . . ," Al Checchi, interview, May 28, 1996.

147 "Very few people . . . ," Michael Ovitz, interview, July 17, 1996.

148 "He reads magazines on every subject . . . ," Arne Glimcher, interview, July 9, 1996.

149 "He has a way of generating . . . ," Bert Fields, interview, May 31, 1996.

149 "One of the things I really . . . ," Michael Crichton, interview, March 19, 1996.

149 "I got a call once from his secretary . . . ," Mort Zuckerman, interview, June 5, 1996.

149 ". . . is like a bumper on the road to him . . . ," Robert Wright, interview, January 22, 1996.

150 "So much of success . . . ," Norman Lear, interview, May 23, 1996.

150 "Most people . . . ," Ron Perelman, interview, August 21, 1996.

150 "I'm a Rolodex friend . . . ," Herb Allen, interview, June 4, 1996.

150   "Sometimes, I didn't take his . . . ," Sydney Pollack, interview, May 30, 1996.

150   "He gets other people to call . . . ," Michael Crichton, interview, March 19, 1996.

150   "We'd send gifts out like . . . ," David O'Connor, interview, July 16, 1996.

151   "business is common sense . . . ," Al Checchi, interview, May 28, 1996.

151   "I wanted to be the guy . . . ," Michael Ovitz, interview, October 3, 1996.

152   "Michael is probably the most . . . ," Al Checchi, interview, May 28, 1996.

153   "He asked me to assist . . . ," ibid.

153   "Even the slightest little reference . . . ," Roy Lichtenstein, interview, June 3, 1996.

154   "You don't have to find a health club . . . ," Al Checchi, interview, May 28, 1996.

155   "How could you do this? . . . ," Joe Smith, interview, October 30, 1996.

155   "Listen pal, if I can help . . . ," Bert Fields, interview, May 31, 1996.

156   "It's easy to say Ovitz behaved . . . ," ibid.

156   "He talked me into getting . . ." Richard Donner, interview, May 23, 1996.

156   "I know it's early for you," Barbara Guggenheim Fields, interview, October 16, 1996.

157   "He's got to be an innovator . . . ," Laurie Perlman, interview, October 22, 1996.

157   "My nightmare was to wind . . . ," Michael Ovitz, interview, October 31, 1996.

158   "The single most important priority . . . ," Michael Ovitz, interview, March 13, 1996.

158   "He was utterly riveted . . . ," Norman Lear, interview, May 29, 1996.

159   "It didn't come from us . . . ," Sylvia Ovitz, interview, October 31, 1996.

159   "Nine hundred thousand dollars . . . ," This anecdote was provided by Arne Glimcher, July 9, 1996.

161   ". . . wasn't a self-aggrandizing move . . . ," Arne Glimcher, interview, July 9, 1996.

161   ". . . director Richard Donner looked . . . ," This anecdote was provided by Richard Donner, May 23, 1996.

162   "When he gets involved in . . . ," Chuck Close, interview, August 1, 1996.

162   "When you get a painting of mine . . . ," ibid.

162   "It stops being my . . . ," ibid.

162   "You can tell that he's . . . ," ibid.

162   "I would be working . . . ," ibid.

163   ". . . couldn't stand that someone . . . ," ibid.

163   "Anyone with money can be . . . ," ibid.

163   "We talk about everything . . . ," Roy Lichtenstein, interview, June 3, 1996.

163   "The grown-ups were fascinated . . . ," ibid.

163   "They sent this embarrassingly large . . . ," ibid.

164   "But of course I would never . . . ," Joel Shapiro, interview, August 9, 1996.

164   "I'm really upset . . . ," anecdote told by Sylvia Ovitz, October 31, 1996.

11
Stepping Out of the Shadows

Page

166   "It's all over . . . ," The Dian Fossey anecdote was told to me by Arne Glimcher, July 9, 1996.

168   "If you said there was a . . . ," Terry Semel, interview, July 24, 1996.

168   "We saw Stan's death . . . ," ibid.

170   "I didn't know if they'd . . . ," Sally Field, interview, July 24, 1996.

174   "Can I call you?" Alan Cieply told of his pursuit of the December 19, 1986 *Wall Street Journal* story in an interview, October 30, 1996.

177   "Just how much power did Michael . . . ," The *Rain Man* anecdote was based on interviews with Michael Ovitz, Barry Levinson, Tony Thomopoulos, Tom Cruise, Paula Wagner, and Sydney Pollack.

178   "Each time a director fell out . . . ," Tony Thomopoulos, interview, July 12, 1996.

179   "Michael begged me . . . ," Sydney Pollack, interview, May 30, 1996.

179   "We had been working . . . ," Tom Cruise, interview, August 19, 1996.

179   "He believed strongly . . . ," Barry Levinson, interview, October 22, 1996.

179   "Ovitz wanted this to . . . ," Tony Thomopoulos, interview, July 12, 1996.

180   "I absolutely loved the script . . . ," Michael Ovitz, interview, January 19, 1996.

180   "We struggled in our . . . ," ibid.

180   "the film would have been shelved . . . ," Dustin Hoffman, interview, March 11, 1997.

183   "I wanted to be the Hollywood gateway . . . ," Michael Ovitz, interview, January 30, 1997.

183   "I tried to tie him up . . . ," ibid.

12
No Photos, Please

Page

185   "mythical place . . . ," Bryan Lourd, interview, July 19, 1996.

185   "This guy knew . . . ," ibid.

186   "The sessions were . . . ," ibid.

186   "He was slightly put off . . . ," ibid.

187   "There's part of him . . . ," Jay Moloney, interview, February 2, 1997.

187   "Michael reacted ninety percent . . . ," David O'Connor, interview, July 23, 1996.

187   "Michael was always very mindful . . . ," ibid.

188   "Ovitz was always looking . . . ," Robin Williams, interview, July 23, 1996.

188   "Michael made sure . . . ," Marcia Williams, interview, July 16, 1996.

188   "There's a great power there . . . ," Robin Williams, interview, July 23, 1996.

188   "If Michael Ovitz was anything . . . ," The Magic Johnson anecdote was based on interviews with Michael Ovitz, Magic Johnson, Lon Rosen, David Stern, and Joe Smith.

191   "That was when we . . . ," Lon Rosen, interview, August 15, 1996.

191   "When we started meeting . . . ," Magic Johnson, interview, October 17, 1996.

191   "I was intimidated more . . . ," ibid.

192   "He makes your mind work . . . ," ibid.

193   "He was direct, grasped . . . ," David Stern, interview, July 8, 1996.

194   "Just having Ovitz . . . ," Lon Rosen, interview, August 16, 1996.

194   "Michael taught me more . . . ," Magic Johnson, interview, October 17, 1996.

195   "He taught me how to make . . . ," ibid.

195   "We agents were not supposed . . . ," Ron Meyer, interview, July 22, 1996.

197   "I was stupid. I didn't understand . . . ," Michael Ovitz, interview, October 31, 1996.

198   "We had the cheeky idea," Susan Lyne, interview, August 5, 1996.

198   "He hated the press . . . ," ibid.

199   "After *The Wall Street Journal* article . . . ," Michael Ovitz, interview, October 31, 1996.

199   "I figured that if they didn't . . . ," ibid.

199   "Taking a photo of him . . . ," Anna Perez, interview, October 16, 1996.

200   ". . . when the heads of two film studios . . . ," *Time* magazine, April 19, 1993.

200   "The relationship won't be . . . ," *Los Angeles Times*, October 19, 1988.

201   "I think it was a mixed bag . . . ," Richard Lovett, interview, July 19, 1996.

202   "This is not a comfortable experience . . . ," Michael Ovitz quoted in *Los Angeles Times*, July 2, 1989.

203   "CAA has become one of the most . . . ," ibid.

203   "CAA is stronger than . . . ," ibid.

203   "We have been accused . . . ," Michael Ovitz quoted, ibid.

13
Foot Soldiers

Page

205   "Mike drove me crazy to find . . . ," Bob Goldman, interview, July 18, 1996.

206   "He wanted nothing less . . . ," ibid.

206   "I'm from the East Coast . . . ," I. M. Pei, interview, July 25, 1996.

206   "He never said, 'Guess who I am?' . . . ," ibid.

206   "I. M. Pei is the most impressive . . . ," Bob Goldman, interview, July 18, 1996.

206   "Everybody came up to him . . . ," I. M. Pei, interview, July 25, 1996.

206   "I had never done anything . . . ," ibid.

207   "I wanted to do something . . . ," Michael Ovitz, interview, January 19, 1996.

207   "spirituality . . . ," Michael Ovitz, interview, May 29, 1996.

208   ". . . this New York sense . . . ," Michael Ovitz, interview, May 29, 1996.

208   "We didn't want to have . . . ," Bob Goldman, interview, July 18, 1996.

208   "We didn't want to fall into that trap . . . ," ibid.

208   "It established us as more . . . ," ibid.

209   "Everyone felt that the momentum . . . ," Michael Rosenfeld Jr., interview, November 2, 1996.

211   "but I was unprepared for the crudity . . . ," The Eszterhas letter appeared in the *L.A. Weekly*, November 3–9, 1989, p. 33; *Spy* magazine, "There's no business like show business," June 1990, pp. 1–7.

212   "When I received your letter . . . ," The Ovitz letter appeared in *Harper's* magazine, "Bidding Mr. Ovitz Adieu," January 1995.

213   "It hurts me that people . . . ," Bill Carruthers, interview, August 11, 1996.

213   "They wanted to nail . . . ," Sydney Pollack, interview, May 30, 1996.

214   "I had no idea how to handle . . . ," Ray Kurtzman, interview, July 16, 1996.

216   "He was an important client . . . ," Michael Ovitz, interview, July 24, 1996.

216   "Yes, said Ovitz, it was . . . ," ibid.

14
The Über-Agent

Page

217 "How long are you going to do this?" Dustin Hoffman, interview, March 11, 1997.

218 "I didn't want to die having . . . ," Michael Ovitz, interview, October 31, 1996.

218 "I wanted CAA not to be . . . ," Michael Ovitz, interview, October 31, 1996.

219 "It wasn't that they liked . . . ," ibid.

222 "I never wanted anyone to know . . . ," Michael Ovitz, interview, January 30, 1997.

225 "We can't talk about this . . . ," Stephen Rivers, interview, July 19, 1996.

225 "we probably had a more conservative . . . ," Herb Allen, interview, June 4, 1996.

227 "The complicated part that Mike . . . ," ibid.

227 "He was very effective . . . ," ibid.

228 "I don't see it as a culmination. I see it as a plateau." *New Yorker,* "The World of Business," September 9, 1991.

228 "I loved his work . . . ," Michael Ovitz, interview, January 19, 1996.

228 "None of it happened . . . ," Jerry Katzman, interview, May 29, 1996.

228 "I had high hopes . . . ," Michael Ovitz, interview, January 19, 1996.

229 "We were not only looking . . . ," ibid.

230 "This is at most a technical . . . ," Stephen Rivers quoted in *The Hollywood Reporter,* September 3, 1991.

232 "It was very impressive . . . ," Shelly Hochron, interview, May 28, 1996.

233 "He always had three . . . ," ibid.

234 "No matter what, I felt Michael . . . ," ibid.

234 ". . . should be a partner . . . ," the letter was read to the author by Shelly Hochron, May 28, 1996.

15
I've Been to See the Godfather!

Page

237 "There was a time . . . ," Alan Citron, interview, July 23, 1996.

238 ". . . the mythic, highly-charged . . . ," Tina Brown, interview, October 15, 1996.

238 "I always found . . . ," ibid.

239 "Thus Connery got on the phone . . . ," the editor in question requested anonymity.

239 "It could be a tiring experience . . . ," Alan Citron, interview, July 23, 1996.

239 "From that point on . . . ," ibid.

239 "... so many that I didn't ...," ibid.

242 "We're dead ...," John Bergin quoted in *AdWeek*, "The Real Story," February 8, 1993, pp. 28–36.

242 "... so goddamn charming ...," ibid.

242 "... one of the power plays ...," ibid.

243 "He is brilliant ...," Sherry Lansing, interview, October 29, 1996.

244 "... evoke everything ...," *Los Angeles Times*, February 11, 1993.

245 "Enormously creative ...," S. I. Newhouse, interview, June 5, 1996.

245 "The whole idea that ...," Robert Wright, interview, January 22, 1996.

246 "That kind of intrigues me ...," David Letterman, interview, August 21, 1996.

246 "... young, bright-faced ...," ibid.

247 "I've been to see the godfather ...," ibid.

247 "... a lot of what Ovitz ...," ibid.

247 "I couldn't wait to begin ...," ibid.

248 "That was an amazing ...," ibid.

249 "It was a lovely piece of work ...," ibid.

251 "Either we retired the ...," Susan Lyne, interview, August 5, 1996.

252 "Mr. Ovitz was leapfrogging ...," *The New York Times*, April 5, 1993.

253 "I am not dealing with MGM ...," ibid.

253 "The question is, 'What ...," Jeff Berg quoted in *Newsweek* magazine, "Taking on 'Big O'," April 19, 1993.

254 "I'm not advising MGM ...," *Time* magazine, "The Ultimate Mogul," April 19, 1993.

254 "Look, this industry ...," ibid.

254 "There was no love lost ...," Jerry Katzman, interview, May 29, 1996.

255 "How's your life? ...," anecdote told to author by John Calley, March 22, 1996.

256 "I've talked to Frank ...," John Calley, interview, March 22, 1996.

256 "I wanted to change my life ...," ibid.

16
I Have a '95 Ovitz

Page

259 "He makes a terrific ...," Phil Knight, interview, August 21, 1996.

260 "I know this audience ...," Charles Young, interview, April 8, 1996.

260 "It was one of the few unsuccessful ...," ibid.

261 "Those kind of projects ...," Phil Knight, interview, August 21, 1996.

262 "I was the techie ...," Ivan Seidenberg, interview, June 4, 1996.

263 "If we could ...," ibid.

264 "It was the only place ...," Michael Crichton, interview, March 19, 1996.

264 "With an agency so large ...," ibid.

265 "It was pretty much ...," ibid.

265   "We don't make stars . . . ," Jerry Seinfeld, interview, October 18, 1996.

265   "Lots of joking . . . ," Howard West, interview, May 22, 1996.

265   ". . . too strong, too powerful . . . ," ibid.

266   "In agenting as in all . . . ," Jerry Seinfeld, interview, October 18, 1996.

266   "I thought the guys . . . ," ibid.

266   ". . . is very much about . . . ," ibid.

266   "Very aikido . . . ," ibid.

266   "His understanding of the . . . ," ibid.

267   "He's got so much experience . . . ," ibid.

267   "I like to brag . . . ," ibid.

268   "We'll bring technology . . . ," Ivan Seidenberg, interview, June 4, 1996.

268   The report of Ovitz's $50-million fee for the telephone companies appeared in *The Wall Street Journal,* August 15, 1995.

268   "Michael Ovitz is sort of the corporate . . . ," David Stern, interview, July 8, 1996.

268   "After a time it became clear and assumed . . . ," Richard Lovett, interview, July 19, 1996.

268   "It was important to hold . . . ," Ron Meyer, interview, July 22, 1996.

269   "The publicity was very helpful . . . ," Bob Goldman, interview, July 18, 1996.

269   ". . . a lot of people on Wall Street . . . ," Harold Vogel, interview, January 17, 1996.

269   ". . . for refining the talent-agency business . . . ," Jerry Katzman, interview, May 29, 1996.

269   "We didn't try to emulate . . . ," Jeff Berg, interview, March 29, 1996.

269   ". . . Ovitz had broadened the concept . . . ," Marvin Josephson, interview, January 31, 1996.

269   "Every time we get involved . . . ," *The New York Times,* April 12, 1993.

270   "If Michael picked up the phone . . . ," Dustin Hoffman, interview, March 11, 1997.

270   "If you wanted to do business . . . ," Graydon Carter, interview, July 31, 1996.

271   "Everyone said all I wanted . . . ," Michael Ovitz, interview, July 17, 1996.

272   "In a town . . . ," Sydney Pollack, interview, May 30, 1996.

272   "Because if he wasn't . . . ," David Letterman, interview, August 21, 1996.

17

Hollywood Obsession

Page

273   "I wanted to do . . . ," Michael Ovitz, interview, October 31, 1996.

274   "Michael had reached the point . . . ," Ron Perelman, interview, August 21, 1996.

274 "... the business figure ...," Susan Lyne, interview, August 8, 1996.

274 "... planning a major life-change ...," Ivan Seidenberg, interview, June 4, 1996.

275 "... it's all going to change ...," Peter Bart, *GQ*, "Grumpy, Happy, Mikey," December 1995.

276 "Bronfman was considering asking ...," *The New York Times*, April 11, 1995.

276 "We were extremely nervous ...," Bryan Lourd, interview, July 19, 1996.

276 "... mainly because we were dealing ...," Jay Moloney, interview, February 2, 1997.

276 "It was more information ...," ibid.

277 "Hollywood's most closely-watched deal ...," *The New York Times*, June 6, 1995.

277 "Mike would never betray ...," *Vanity Fair*, "Edgar Bets the House," July 1995.

277 "I enjoyed speculating ...," Michael Crichton, interview, March 19, 1996.

278 "I can't predict the future ...," *Newsweek* magazine, "King of the Deal," June 12, 1995, pp. 44–51.

278 "Somehow Michael didn't have ...," Mort Zuckerman, interview, June 5, 1996.

278 "I carried the negotiations on too long ...," Michael Ovitz, January 30, 1996.

278 "It destroyed the fabric ...," ibid.

279 "I didn't want to leave ...," ibid.

279 "Not to be able to consummate ...," Sam Cohen, interview, January 26, 1996.

279 "What no one understands is that it was really fun ...," Michael Ovitz, interview, October 31, 1996.

280 "And the reality is ...," *The Hollywood Reporter*, June 6, 1995.

280 "He was really heartened ...," Shelly Hochron, interview, May 28, 1996.

280 "My heart isn't really ...," Arne Glimcher, interview, July 31, 1996.

281 "... it didn't mean ...," ibid.

281 "Tomorrow we're going to ...," Shelly Hochron, interview, July 21, 1996.

282 "They wanted the whole ...," David O'Connor, interview, July 23, 1996.

282 "It was clear that if ...," ibid.

283 "Once I had left ...," Ron Meyer, interview, July 22, 1996.

284 "Frank selflessly would say to me ...," Michael Eisner, quoted on *Larry King Live*, CNN, September 30, 1996.

285   "We are going to be partners . . . ," Michael Ovitz, interview, January 29, 1997.

285   "He brought me in . . . ," ibid.

286   "He's telling us what . . . ," David O'Connor, interview, July 23, 1996.

286   "I'm going to be making an announcement . . . ," Shelly Hochron, interview, May 28, 1996.

288   "At that moment we went . . . ," Richard Lovett, interview, July 19, 1996.

288   "The next couple of years . . . ," David O'Connor, interview, July 23, 1996.

288   ". . . because I knew . . . ," Bryan Lourd, interview, July 19, 1996.

289   "If I had known *how* enormous . . . ," David O'Connor, interview, July 23, 1996.

290   "Before they believed . . . ," Richard Lovett, interview, July 19, 1996.

290   "I'm burned out . . . ," Michael Rosenfeld Sr., interview, August 14, 1996.

290   "The first thing we had . . . ," Richard Lovett, interview, July 19, 1996.

291   "Redford had a very complicated . . . ," David O'Connor, July 23, 1996.

291   "There's no question that a number of clients . . . ," Jerry Katzman, interview, May 29, 1996.

292   "You can have everything but three things . . . ," Michael Ovitz, interview, October 14, 1996.

292   "We have an interesting . . . ," Bryan Lourd, interview, July 19, 1996.

292   "People at CAA were really removed . . . ," ibid.

292   "Oh my God, it's the end . . . ," David Letterman, *Time* magazine, August 28, 1995.

294   "Disney is a wonderful . . . ," Bert Fields, interview, May 31, 1996.

294   "This place is thriving . . . ," Bob Goldman, interview, July 18, 1996.

18
Disney Demons

Page

296   "Looking toward the future . . . ," Michael Ovitz quoted in *USA Today*, August 15, 1995.

297   "I think it will be a better company . . . ," Herb Allen, interview, June 4, 1996.

300   "It's going to require . . . ," *Weekly Variety*, December 16, 1996.

301   "Eisner wanted me to . . . ," Michael Ovitz, interview, January 29, 1997.

301   ". . . much more buoyant, less anxious . . . ," Joel Shapiro, interview, August 9, 1996.

301   "He's learning much more . . . ," Sean Connery, interview, July 16, 1996.

302 "I was trying to learn . . . ," Michael Ovitz, interview, January 29, 1997.

302 "Michael could do . . . ," ibid.

302 "Joe Roth made . . . ," ibid.

304 "He was completely unruffled . . . ," Gerry Laybourne, interview, July 25, 1996.

304 ". . . but then again . . . ," ibid.

304 "It was one of the most . . . ," ibid.

304 "He didn't miss a beat . . . ," ibid.

305 ". . . disaster . . . ," Gary Wilson, interview, July 22, 1996.

305 "He promised me the world . . . ," Michael Ovitz, interview, January 29, 1997.

306 "If I died tomorrow . . . ," Michael Ovitz, interview, January 30, 1997.

306 "I spent twenty years . . . ," ibid.

307 "All the offers . . . ," ibid.

307 "I wouldn't allow . . . ," ibid.

308 ". . . rumors and innuendo that have no . . . ," *Time* magazine, April 15, 1996.

308 "Michael Ovitz is the Antichrist . . . ," ibid.

308 "Ovitz has certainly . . . ," Jeff Berg, interview, March 29, 1996.

309 "The move to Disney . . . ," Tina Brown, interview, October 15, 1996.

309 ". . . a small group . . . ," Michael Ovitz, interview, March 13, 1996.

309 "my job wasn't . . . ," Michael Ovitz, interview, January 30, 1997.

310 "He's a very sensitive man . . . ," Arne Glimcher, interview, July 9, 1996.

310 "We knew this wasn't . . . ," Michael Ovitz, interview, January 29, 1997.

310 "In the back of my . . . ," ibid.

310 Media columnist Ken Auletta was the first . . . ," *New Yorker* magazine, "Marriages, No Honeymoon," July 29, 1996, pp. 26–31.

311 "Despite what may have been written . . . ," ibid.

311 "I didn't know him at all . . . ," ibid.

311 ". . . thought it was funny . . . ," Arne Glimcher, interview, July 9, 1996.

311 "I factored it into my strategic . . . ," Michael Ovitz, interview, July 24, 1996.

19

Page

I Made a Smart Deal

313 "He said terrible things . . . ," Michael Ovitz, interview, January 30, 1997.

313 "That's when I said . . . ," Michael Ovitz, interview, January 29, 1997.

314 "[Eisner] was my best friend . . . ," ibid.

314 "Typical, competitive Hollywood gossip," Eisner said, *Larry King Live*, CNN, September 30, 1996.

315   "We have been living . . . ," Michael Ovitz quoted on *Larry King Live*.

315   "What you saw . . . ," Michael Ovitz, interview, January 29, 1997.

316   "I don't think it's been clear . . . ," Shelly Hochron, interview, May 28, 1996.

316   "Frankly, when we first . . . ," Michael Ovitz quoted on *Larry King Live*.

316   "It takes a lot more . . . ," Donald Wilson, interview, July 22, 1996.

317   "I knew I was leaving . . . ," Michael Ovitz, interview, January 29, 1997.

318   "The one thing I don't want to be is boring . . . ," Michael Ovitz, interview, October 13, 1996.

319   ". . . has not only made missteps . . . ," *The New York Times*, October 7, 1996.

319   "masterful but imperious . . . ," ibid.

319   "I heard you've been saying . . . ," ibid.

319   "Mike isn't certain of the . . . ," ibid.

320   "I didn't want to take it . . . ," Michael Ovitz, interview, January 29, 1997.

321   "He's not Michael Ovitz . . . ," David Geffen quoted in *Vanity Fair,* "The Mouse Trap," December 1996, pp. 142–197.

321   "Foot soldiers! Can you believe . . . ," Bernie Brillstein quoted, ibid.

321   "I was seduced by . . . ," Sidney Sheinberg quoted, ibid.

321   ". . . he sounded less than ebullient . . . ," Michael Eisner quoted, ibid.

322   "It became clear that a growing . . . ," Stephen Rivers, interview, July 19, 1996.

322   "I decided that I wasn't going . . . ," Michael Ovitz, interview, January 29, 1997.

323   "I was relieved . . . ," ibid.

323   "He made a very simple . . . ," ibid.

325   "The real question . . . is why . . . ," Arne Glimcher, interview, January 6, 1997.

326   "When there's a steady drumbeat . . . ," Stephen Rivers, interview, January 6, 1997.

326   "He's in a remarkably positive . . . ," Chuck Close, interview, December 18, 1996.

328   "I just made . . . ," Michael Ovitz, interview, January 29, 1997.

Index